Supporting Leaders for School Improvement Through Self-Care and Well-Being

A Volume in Leadership for School Improvement

Series Editor

Sonya D. Hayes
The University of Tennessee

Leadership for School Improvement

Sonya D. Hayes, Series Editor

*Supporting Leaders for School Improvement
Through Self-Care and Well-Being* (2024)
edited by Bradley W. Carpenter, Julia Mahfouz, and Kerry Robinson

Maximizing the Policy Relevance of Research for School Improvement (2021)
edited by Angela Urick, David DeMatthews, and Timothy G. Ford

Leadership for School Improvement: Reflection and Renewal (2019)
edited by Cherie B. Gaines

Supporting Leaders for School Improvement Through Self-Care and Well-Being

Editors

Bradley W. Carpenter
Sul Ross State University

Julia Mahfouz
University of Colorado Denver

Kerry Robinson
University of North Carolina Wilmington

INFORMATION AGE PUBLISHING, INC.
Charlotte, NC • www.infoagepub.com

Library of Congress Cataloging-in-Publication Data

CIP record for this book is available from the Library of Congress
http://www.loc.gov

ISBNs: 979-8-88730-277-5 (Paperback)

979-8-88730-278-2 (Hardcover)

979-8-88730-279-9 (ebook)

Copyright © 2024 Information Age Publishing Inc.

All rights reserved. No part of this publication may be reproduced, stored in a retrieval system, or transmitted, in any form or by any means, electronic, mechanical, photocopying, microfilming, recording or otherwise, without written permission from the publisher.

Printed in the United States of America

CONTENTS

Overview and Introduction to the Project
   Bradley W. Carpenter, Julia Mahfouz, and Kerry Robinson ix

SECTION I: PROMISES AND PROBLEMS—
OVERVIEW OF THE FIELD

1. Exploring the Landscape of Educational Leader Wellness
   Kathleen B. King, April Harris, and Angel Vales 3

2. School Leadership in the United States: An In-Depth Analysis of the Increasing Principal Turnover Crisis in America
   Denver J. Fowler and Sarah M. Jouganatos 21

3. Considering How Professional Norms and Practices Influence Leaders' Well-Being
   Kara Lasater, John C. Pijanowski, and Joshua Ray 35

4. Building a School Leader's Personal Well-Being Plan
   Vicki Bautista and Gretchen Oltman 53

5. Flourishing as School Leaders: Perspectives of Canada's Outstanding Principals
   Benjamin Kutsyuruba, Terry Kharyati, and Nadia Arghash 71

6. The Future of Higher Education Is Human: A Call for Contemplative Leadership Preparation
   Maryann Krikorian 93

7. Leading From the Center: Leadership Well-Being and Team
   Effectiveness in Education Agencies
   Irma Eloff and Ruth "Molly" McGee Hewitt *111*

SECTION II: EMPIRICAL REASONING

8. Promoting Well-Being in School Principals and Vice
   Principals Requires Structural Change, Not Just Self-Care
   Cameron Hauseman, Katrina Pollock, and Fei Wang *131*

9. Student Adversity and Leader Stress: A Critical Race
   Contextualization and Analysis of New York State Social
   Emotional Learning Policy
   Melinda Lemke and Anthony L. White II... *151*

SECTION III: MODELS FOR WELL-BEING

10. THRIVE: A Guiding Model for Facilitating School Leader
    Well-Being
    *Connor M. Moriarty, Kimberly Joy Rushing, and
    Lisa A. W. Kensler*... *177*

11. School Administrators' Well-Being and Mindfulness as
    Critical Components of Leadership and Building Healthy Teams
    Nancy Norman, Adrienne Castellon, and David D. Stinson *201*

12. Positive Leadership for Flourishing Learning Communities
    Sabre Cherkowski, Benjamin Kutsyuruba, and Keith Walker *221*

13. Educational Leadership as Emotional Labor: A Framework for
    the Values-Driven Emotion Work of School Leaders
    *Kristina N. LaVenia, Christy Galletta Horner, and
    Judy Jackson May* *239*

14. An Urban District's Approach to Scaling Up Social-Emotional
    Learning Competencies Through a Leadership Lens
    Delia Estrada, Marco A. Nava, and Susan Ward-Roncalli................. *257*

15. An Urban District's Approach to Scaling Up Social-Emotional
    Learning Competencies Through a Leadership Lens
    Jonathan Eckert *277*

SECTION IV: WELL-BEING PRACTICES AND FRAMEWORKS FOR PRACTITIONERS TO USE

16. Applying Brain Research and Positive Psychology to Promote the Well-Being of Principals
    Kent Divoll and Angelica Ribeiro 297

17. Cultivating Awareness and Resilience in Education: Caring for Yourself So You Have the Resources to Care for Others
    Sebrina L. Doyle Fosco... 317

18. Respecting Communication Skills: The Missing Link for the Well-Being of Educators and Their Schools
    Deborah L. Schussler and Jennifer L. Frank 337

19. Caring for the Caretaker: Using Mentoring as Support for School Principals in Self-Care and Mindfulness
    Sonya D. Hayes and Jerry Burkett 355

20. Soul of Leadership: Sustaining Principals Through Courage, Presence, and Integrity
    Rick Rogers and Mary Watkins 375

About the Authors.. 383

OVERVIEW AND INTRODUCTION TO THE PROJECT

Bradley W. Carpenter, Julia Mahfouz, and Kerry Robinson

School leadership instability is particularly problematic for scholars and practitioners concerned with PK–12 school improvement, as second only to teachers, campus leadership has been identified as a primary factor in students' academic success (Young et al., 2007). Yet, while principals play an indispensable role in students' academic success, the job has become considerably more stressful as the role of a school leader continues to evolve. Specifically, added responsibilities, increased work intensity, and the ever-present menace of high stakes accountability have intensified the stress levels encountered by today's school leaders (Carpenter & Brewer, 2012; Chaplain, 2001; Darmody & Smyth, 2016; Wang et al., 2018). This intensification negatively impacts a school's teaching staff and its students, as the overall quality of the school experience can deteriorate if principals are unable to meet their potential due to the burnout and fatigue associated with chronic stress (Darmody & Smyth, 2016; Devos et al., 2007).

For principals to fully realize their ability to serve as catalysts for school improvement, they should be allowed to prioritize physical, mental, cognitive, and emotional health. Desired levels of well-being occur in the absence of chronic physical, social, psychological, emotional, economic, and cognitive distress (La Placa et al., 2013). As authors in this volume demonstrate, many school leaders have commenced specific practices

Supporting Leaders for School Improvement Through Self-Care and Well-Being, pp. ix–xvii
Copyright © 2024 by Information Age Publishing
www.infoagepub.com
All rights of reproduction in any form reserved.

targeting cognitive, emotional, and behavioral well-being to cope with occupational stress and flourishing—or, at the very least, surviving- in such a challenging environment. Among coping strategies leaders have adopted include mindfulness and other well-being interventions/strategies intended to facilitate healthier lifestyles, relieve stress, and improve personal resilience (Aviles & Dent, 2015; Mahfouz, 2018; Wells, 2015).

Recently, there has been a call to consider educational leadership through a positive human flourishing lens. Research in this area focuses on integrating well-being practices in professional development programs for teachers and school administrators to highlight the positive effects of personal and collective well-being in schools (Cherkowski & Walker, 2014). For example, empirical studies have examined how incorporating mindfulness practice promotes positive adaptive skills, stress resilience, and social and emotional skills needed in a school environment (Abenavoli et al., 2013; Benn et al., 2012; Dvořáková et al., 2017; Jennings, 2015; Mahfouz, 2018; Meiklejohn et al., 2012). New understandings about the relationship between school administrators' well-being and school improvement efforts should ignite interest within the field. As such, this book's chapters are organized into four distinct sections that provide: (a) an overview of the field (Section I), (b) an empirical argument for why such research is essential (Section II), (c) well-being models to be considered for use in the PK–12 setting (Section III), and, (d) specific well-being practices and frameworks currently being in PK–12 (Section IV).

Review of Section I

Section I, titled "Promises and Problems: Overview of the Field," provides context regarding the condition of educational leaders. This section focuses not only on the challenges that exist for a variety of leadership positions but on plans and practices for addressing leader well-being. It is worth noting that the idea behind this edited book existed prior to the COVID-19 pandemic. The issues discussed throughout this section and throughout the book were present for educational leaders before the pandemic. If nothing else, leading schools and districts during COVID has only intensified the current struggles.

"Exploring the Landscape of Educational Leader Wellness," authored by King, Harris, and Vales reviews challenges for superintendents, principals, and assistant principals in isolation before addressing the broader issues of stress, burnout, turnover, and attrition, as well as how these issues affect these have on overall school performance. The authors do not solely focus on the problems. They identify promising practices that have become more prevalent when addressing leader well-being, including focusing on overall wellness, including stress management, practicing self-care, integrating mindfulness practices, and improving social-emotional learning.

The crisis of leadership turnover is more deeply explored in the Fowler and Jouganatos contribution, "School Leadership in the United States: An In-Depth Analysis of the Increasing Epidemic of Principal Turnover in America." While this chapter highlights the significant research on issues about principal turnover, what makes it especially important is its implications for schools and its overall effect on students. As a volume in the *Leadership for School Improvement Series*, we must not forget these topics should "ensure that policies and procedures are in place to help retain our nation's school leaders" where they can be most effective (p. 35, this volume).

One way to support leaders' effectiveness is to closely inspect the written and unwritten demands identified with a school leader's position. The Lasater, Pijanowski, and Ray chapter, "Considering How Professional Norms and Practices Influence Leaders' Well-Being," unpacks the unrealistic expectations put on school leaders and suggests an opportunity to reframe the purpose of leader well-being. Instead of continuing the practice where "self-care strategies are sometimes framed as a mechanism for leadership preservation and not as strategies intended to promote leaders' overall well-being" (p. 41, this volume), the authors recommend a shift in norms and practices to better serve leaders as well as the larger educational community.

Shifting to the needs of the leader requires a deliberate focus and a plan of action. The Bautista and Oltman chapter, "Building a School Leader's Personal Well-Being Plan," provides a rationale behind the importance of such a plan and tools and strategies to put these processes in place to address stressors and other symptoms of burnout. The authors provide the reader with additional resources to help leaders consider how they might construct their own well-being plan.

Review of Section II

Section II, titled "Empirical Reasoning," as to why this is important, provides evidence-based studies examining the significance of leader well-being. A substantial body of research indicates that self-care is positively related to positive school outcomes and effective leadership. In this section, the authors discuss the results of influential publications that have brought principal self-care and well-being into prominence and summarize their findings, calling for ways to address various issues related to the promotion of leader well-being.

In their chapter "Promoting Well-Being in School Principals and Vice Principals Requires Structural Change, Not Just Self-Care," Hauseman,

Pollock, and Wang report on a survey of 1,400 principals and 862 vice-principals exploring perceptions of work-life balance and the coping strategies they use. The findings highlight how Ontario school leaders' well-being is influenced by what they define as "work intensification." The authors argue that structural changes are required to promote school leaders' well-being and suggest the problem cannot be solved by increasing self-care practices alone.

In the chapter, "The Future of Higher Education is Human: A Call for Contemplative Leadership Preparation," Krikorian brings forth a new understanding of value-belief systems deconstructing the American conception of work. Krikorian examines the literature on how leadership preparation programs might support leader well-being while honoring the innate human condition. It invites faculty to prioritize contemplation and facilitate human growth needs for greater well-being.

From the emergent concept of "leading from the middle," in the chapter, "Leading from the Center: Leadership Well-Being and Team Effectiveness in Education Agencies," Eloff and Hewitt focus on how a collaborative and collegial leadership style could promote the development of team culture that fosters accountability and group responsibility—and inherently the well-being of all team members.

The chapter, "Student Adversity and Leader Stress: A Critical Race Contextualization and Analysis of New York State Social Emotional Learning Policy," Lemke and White II examine the extent to which New York State Education Department (NYDE) guidelines, titled *Social Emotional Learning Guide to Systematic Whole School Implementation*, a state education policy reform to increase student SEL, can also achieve the goal of well-being for educational leaders and systems.

In their chapter, "Positive Leadership for Flourishing Learning Communities," Cherkowski, Kutsyuruba, and Walker synthesize their research and present a conceptual model of positive leadership. The model is grounded within the values of purpose, passion, play, and presence—all of which emphasize the potential for these concepts to aid in the flourishing of the school cultures and principal well-being.

Review of Section III

In Section III, titled "Models for Well-Being," the authors provide an in-depth examination of theoretical and conceptual well-being models that should interest PK–12 practitioners and scholars. Authors Moriarity, Rushing, and Kensler present "THRIVE: A Guiding Model." The THRIVE model (Thoughts, Health, Resilience, Interdependence, Vitality, and Empathy) provides practitioners with a conceptual framework embedded with activities and reflective tools intended to "enable principals to improve their physical, emotional, and mental states" amid complex working conditions.

In their chapter, "School Administrators' Well-Being and Mindfulness as Critical Components of Leadership and Building Healthy Teams," Norman, Castellon, and Stinson examine the "intersectionality of administrators' and educators' well-being" (p. 203, this volume) in the real-world context, of a PK–12 school community setting. Specifically, the authors offer readers a personal and organizational wellness model—Stinson Wellness Model—which school communities can "leverage for greater effectiveness and human flourishing" (p. 203, this volume). This chapter stipulates that administrators must realize their responsibilities in creating an environment that allows others to navigate the complex and often chaotic world in which they operate.

In the following chapter, "Positive Leadership for Flourishing Learning Communities," Cherkowski, Kutsyuruba, and Walker extend the thinking on traditional stress-management approaches to provide readers with a "complimentary and organizational" perspective and analysis on numerous issues surrounding the well-being of our school leaders. While not in denial of the stressors leading to administrator burnout, the authors seek to expand the well-being continuum by focusing on the ideal of personal and professional flourishing. Detailing the findings from a multiday Positive Leadership for Flourishing Schools Forum in Kingston, Ontario, the authors present readers with a more nuanced understanding of how school leaders might "foster and sustain" well-being for themselves and other school and community stakeholders.

Next, the chapter "Educational Leadership as Emotional Labor: A Framework for the Values-Driven Emotion Work of School Leaders," authored by LaVenia, Horner, and May, presents readers with a conceptual framework that embeds key constructs relating to leadership theory within the emotional demands faced by today's school leaders. The authors ignite a fresh and "novel" set of discussions around understanding how leadership in schools is, in fact, emotional labor. Stating that the field of educational leadership pays little notice to how school leaders must navigate the emotional complexities associated with schooling, the authors attempt to convince readers of the need to include the connection between emotional labor and leadership into our research agendas, practice, and leadership preparation curriculum.

Estrada, Nava, and Ward-Roncalli present the final chapter in Section III, "An Urban District's Approach to Scaling Up Social-Emotional Learning Competencies through a Leadership Lens." The contents of this chapter are based upon a mixed-methods study examining the Los Angeles Unified School District's (LUSD) effort to "elevate SEL [social-emotional learning] as a part of daily practice in schools." The authors make the case that school districts must "invest in building leadership capacity" by ensuring school leaders are competent in the areas of SEL and can recognize the importance of self-care. This mixed-methods study suggests that school leaders are aware of and support alternative student success and flourishing measures. They understand that the limited focus on academic measures prohibits efforts for a climate of flourishing students and adults.

Review of Section IV

Section IV, titled "Well-Being Practices and Frameworks for Practitioners to Use," provides several opportunities for putting plans into action. These chapters approach the work from both individual and collective practices. The programs and supports presented provide models not only focusing on the individual leader's development but also in the broader school community.

The Divoll and Ribeiro chapter "Applying Brain Research and Positive Psychology to Promote the Well-Being of Principals" recognizes the continued lack of research on well-being and the principalship. While new studies and proposed interventions are beginning to increase, the authors highlight the importance of understanding the interconnected nature of the brain, emotions, stress, and challenging situations by utilizing components based on positive psychology. The chapter concludes with protocols, activities, and further readings to assist leaders as they meet the ongoing challenges of their positions.

Educational leaders experience significant stress as they serve various groups, with their primary focus being on the support of others. Doyle's contribution, "Caring for Yourself So You Have the Resources to Care for Others," reminds leaders of the importance of focusing on yourself first, not only for your own social and emotional well-being but also challenges leaders to model these practices for others in their care. The author highlights the power of the Cultivating Awareness and Resilience in Educators (CARE) (Jennings et al., 2016) in professional development programs focusing on educational leaders. The program helps address stressful situations a leader encounters and improves social-emotional competence and well-being.

If an educational leader understands the importance of self-care, it does not always mean they will put these ideas into practice. Having a support system that understands the issues is one way to better ensure such practices are adopted. The Hayes and Burkett chapter, "Caring for the Caretaker: Using Mentoring as Support for School Principals in Self-Care and Mindfulness," identifies the complexity of work-related stressors and provides systems of support and recommended practices that encourage connected professional learning and provide opportunities to feel less isolated as they address the ongoing challenges associated with their position.

How can leaders move from their individual reflective practices to develop and support the social-emotional growth of the adults they support? The chapter "Soul of Leadership: Sustaining Principals Through Courage, Presence, and Integrity" authored by Rogers and Watkins emphasizes the power of contemplative practices as a component of a leader's daily work. By sharing the program's features and embedded protocols, participants speak of their transformational growth and strengthened collaborative relationships with others by focusing on a collective approach to social-emotional growth.

The connection between leaders' social-emotional competency (SEC) and the teachers and students they serve can influence classrooms and the larger school environment. The Schussler and Frank chapter "Respecting Communication Skills: The Missing Link for the Well-Being of Educators and Their Schools" highlights the critical role communication plays in the development of educators and the prosocial process in both classrooms and the wider school environment. This chapter focuses on results from Project RESPECT (Responding in Emotionally Supportive and Positive Ways in Education Communication Skills Training), a professional development program focused on all educators serving in secondary schools, including paraprofessionals, teachers, and administrators, with project outcomes that benefit only participants and the students with whom they work.

While the focus on leader well-being and self-care has often been explored as an individual pursuit throughout this book, the support of others truly makes a difference for both the leader and the larger group. "Collective Leadership for Well-Being and Sustainable School Improvement," authored by Eckert, highlights the power of collaborative relationships when the seven conditions for collective leadership are enacted within a school. The chapter highlights this model and its effective use in urban, rural, and suburban settings through mini case examples.

Conclusions/Questions

So, where do we go from here? We hope this book provides readers with valuable insights into the important, yet often neglected, connection between leadership well-being and the sundry knowledge, skills, attitudes, and understandings needed for school improvement efforts. Our intention is to provide a rationale, definitions, conceptual frameworks, and practices to drive the field forward. We are well aware this is an overview; however, we expect this to ignite an ongoing conversation that must be discussed and integrated more widely into research, practice, and policy spaces.

There are still many questions that must be answered: What are the explicit ingredients of leader well-being we are missing and thus still need attention? How do we deconstruct and reconstruct norms and systems so leader well-being is an integral aspect of schooling? What programs and professional development do we need to prepare educational leaders to lead school improvement efforts without enduring burnout? What critical and unresolved issues affecting leader well-being related to theory and research, assessment, evaluation, professional development, implementation, finding, and policy must the field address?

At this moment in history, we must refocus schools on the holistic social and emotional development of all stakeholders, including school leaders. Attending to the well-being of school leaders is as much a part of quality education as ensuring students have their social-emotional needs met. We believe this book will help launch a series of continuous conversations on how we might transform our perceptions of current systems to bring forth a holistic approach to well-being at schools that include leader well-being.

REFERENCES

Abenavoli, R. M., Jennings, P. A., Greenberg, M. T., Harris, A. R., & Katz, D. A. (2013). The protective effects of mindfulness against burnout among educators. *Psychology of Education Review*, *37*(2), 57–69.

Aviles, P. R., & Dent, E. (2015). The role of mindfulness in leading organizational transformation: a systematic review. *The Journal of Applied Management and Entrepreneurship*, *20*(3), 31–55.

Benn, R., Akiva, T., Arel, S., & Roeser, R. W. (2012). Mindfulness training effects for parents and educators of children with special needs. *Developmental Psychology*, *48*(5), 1476.

Carpenter, B. W., & Brewer, C. (2014). The implicated advocate: The discursive construction of the democratic practices of school principals in the USA. *Discourse: Studies in the Cultural Politics of Education*, *35*(2), 294–306.

Chaplain, R. P. (2001). Stress and job satisfaction among primary headteachers: A question of balance? *Educational Management & Administration*, *29*(2), 197–215.

Cherkowski, S., & Walker, K. (2014). Flourishing communities: Re-storying educational leadership using a positive research lens. *International Journal of Leadership in Education*, *17*(2), 200–216.

Darmody, M., & Smyth, E. (2016). Primary school principals' job satisfaction and occupational stress. *International Journal of Educational Management*, *30*(1), 115–128.

Devos, G., Bouckenooghe, D., Engels, N., Hotton, G., & Aelterman, A. (2007). An assessment of well-being of principals in Flemish primary schools. *Journal of Educational Administration*, *45*(1), 33–61.

Dvořáková, K., Kishida, M., Li, J., Elavsky, S., Broderick, P. C., Agrusti, M. R., & Greenberg, M. T. (2017). Promoting healthy transition to college through mindfulness training with first-year college students: Pilot randomized controlled trial. *Journal of American College Health*, *65*(4), 259–267.

Jennings, P. A. (2015). Early childhood teachers' well-being, mindfulness, and self-compassion in relation to classroom quality and attitudes towards challenging students. *Mindfulness*, *6*(4), 732–743.

La Placa, V., McNaught, A., & Knight, A. (2013). Discourse on wellbeing in research and practice. *International Journal of Wellbeing*, *3*(1).

Mahfouz, J. (2018). Mindfulness training for school administrators: Effects on well-being and leadership. *Journal of Educational Administration*, *56*(6), 602–619.

Meiklejohn, J., Phillips, C., Freedman, M. L., Griffin, M. L., Biegel, G., Roach, A., Frank, J., Burke, C., Pinger, L., Soloway, G., Isberg, R., Sibinga, E., Grossman, L., & Saltzman, A. (2012). Integrating mindfulness training into K–12 education: Fostering the resilience of teachers and students. *Mindfulness*, *3*(4), 291–307.

Wang, F., Pollock, K. E., & Hauseman, C. (2018). School principals' job satisfaction: The effects of work intensification. *Canadian Journal of Educational Administration and Policy*, *185*, 73.

Wells, C. M. (2015). Conceptualizing mindful leadership in schools: how the practice of mindfulness informs the practice of leading. *Education Leadership Review of Doctoral Research*, *2*(1), 1–23.

Young, M. D., Fuller, E., Brewer, C., Carpenter, B., & Mansfield, K. C. (2007). *Quality leadership matters quality leadership matters*. https://files.eric.ed.gov/fulltext/ED520580.pdf

SECTION I

PROMISES AND PROBLEMS: OVERVIEW OF THE FIELD

CHAPTER 1

EXPLORING THE LANDSCAPE OF EDUCATIONAL LEADER WELLNESS

Kathleen B. King, April Harris, and Angel Vales

The role of school administrators has undergone a remarkable evolution over the last several decades, resulting in a shift in responsibilities and burdens. The increasing demands on educational leaders have had an indisputable impact on the leaders themselves, but also on schools, teachers, and students. Increased work hours, district demands, school violence, decreased resources, and expectations related to school accountability from the Every Student Succeeds Act (ESSA) have led school leaders to emotional and mental exhaustion; more and more is expected of leaders, and the unreasonable workload takes a toll—not just on leaders, but on those they are trying to lead (Oskolkoff, 2019). Superintendents, principals, and assistant principals have seen their roles expand exponentially, resulting in rising rates of stress, burnout, and attrition. The well-being of educational leaders has emerged as a critical issue, essential to the personal and professional efficacy of leaders as well as the school communities they serve. The resulting costs to their lives and to the productivity of the school environments need to be explored. Even more important, opportunities for improving school leader well-being need to be investigated, an investment with far-reaching dividends. Wellness programs, coping techniques, self-care, and mindfulness are just some examples of the rich tools available to develop school leader well-being so they are better equipped to foster flourishing school communities.

Supporting Leaders for School Improvement Through Self-Care and Well-Being, pp. 3–20
Copyright © 2024 by Information Age Publishing
www.infoagepub.com
All rights of reproduction in any form reserved.

SUPERINTENDENTS

The role of a superintendent has shifted over the past decades. Superintendents who may have been seen as a teacher of teachers must now navigate the political landscape of varied stakeholders (Bredeson & Kose, 2007). School finances, federal and state mandates, shifting school standards, and conflicting interests at the local, state, and national levels have reshaped the superintendent's role (Bjork et al., 2014; Farkas et al., 2001; Hall & McHenry-Sorber, 2017; Lecker, 2002; Sherman & Crogan, 2003). While balancing the role's many external pressures, superintendents are still expected to weigh in on internal factors such as the instruction, curriculum, and assessment practices of district schools (Rallis et al., 2006).

Superintendents have acknowledged that they are handling too much (Bjork et al., 2014; Glass et al., 2000; Hall & McHenry-Sorber, 2017). Despite this awareness, superintendents continue to face achievement gaps, school board conflicts, and shifting sociocultural and political contexts while dealing with a lack of professional training and authority (Bredeson & Kose, 2007). These challenges are further exacerbated by the misalignment of their use of time to manage priorities, as superintendent calendars are disproportionately dominated by governance issues and politics (Bredeson, 1996). The result is rising stress levels and educational leaders buckled by fatigue, frustration, and limited resources (Solomon, 2012). One district leader explained how they were trying to "bring that balance and assurance into leadership ... bringing them back to life, restoring their spirits" (Mahfouz et al., 2021, p. 6). Not surprisingly, rising stress and demands impacts a decreased pool of qualified superintendents, a high resignation rate, and rising contract nonrenewals. This tempest of overwhelming demands on a decreasing pool of leaders is alarming, yet such a perfect storm is not limited to superintendents.

PRINCIPALS

Principals face similar challenges and effects. The role of the school principal has continued to evolve from being primarily teachers who handled administrative work in the mid-20th century to bureaucratic managers working somewhat separately from teachers in the 1990s, and eventually to leaders as facilitators of school improvement, held accountable for student performance (Fullan, 2009; Hattie, 2015; Malone, 2013; Organisation for Economic Co-operation and Development, 2014; Sahlberg & Sahlberg, 2010). Today, principals are expected to be collaborative leaders, working with a variety of competing stakeholder interests and demands. This workload has led to increased levels of stress, time management concerns, and employee relational demands (Oskolkoff, 2019). More than 96%

of principals identified work-related stress as negatively affecting their work efficacy and health, including such causes as people conflicts, time constraints, school crises, policy demands, budget limitations, fear of failure, and negative publicity (Sogunro, 2012). The cost of these stressors is not limited to the principals.

Research clearly indicates that the principal role directly affects school improvement (Leithwood et al., 2004) and that teaching and learning outcomes have a dependent relationship to school leader competencies (G. Branch et al., 2013; R. Branch, 2013; Di Liberto et al., 2015; Harris & Hopkins, 2006; Leithwood et al., 2004; Leithwood & Louis, 2011; Mahfouz et al., 2019). Yet increased stressors continue to challenge principal efficacy. Until principals are able to get support to remediate their own burdens, their positive impact on others will be hindered. One elementary principal, who was involved in the mindfulness training Cultivating Awareness and Resilience in Education (CARE), described this need for self-care:

> CARE has taught me to put my own oxygen mask on first by teaching me the skills to set intentions, pause to breathe, check my emotional elevator, listen mindfully, and show compassion for myself and others (elementary principal). (Mahfouz et al., 2019, p. 8)

This nurturing of school leaders is necessary to develop the bandwidth necessary for effectively serving school communities. Teachers, staff, and students are impacted by principal well-being.

ASSISTANT PRINCIPALS

Meanwhile, assistant principals suffer from the ambiguousness of their role. Though the number of assistant principals has continued to increase over the last 25 years, consensus still does not exist on what their role should involve or how they should be prepared or supported (Goldring et al., 2021). Though critical to schools, assistant principals have varied responsibilities based on their particular school, a recipe rich in the potential for competing demands and frustration. Often the full potential of the assistant principal role is not realized or is underutilized. Ambiguity causes individual frustration on the job because it is not clear what is expected, what the outcomes are, how individuals should interact in the social and work environment, and how their role performance should be evaluated (Katz & Kahn, 2003). Role conflict, along with other job strains and lack of support, further increases stress and frustrations for assistant principals. No school leader in the 21st century should feel unsupported in the face of growing job complexity, increased public scrutiny and accountability, and the decreased control over how the accountability targets are met

(Riley & Langan-Fox, 2013). If, as some researchers argue, school leaders are the second most significant influence on student outcomes behind the teacher (Day et al., 2008; Leithwood & Day, 2008), when the leader is not functioning well, arguably the whole school suffers. Certainly, the unique stressors and challenges of the assistant principal role is in need of additional research (Shoho et al., 2012). As an assistant principal notes: "I gained 25 pounds over the first two years on this job. I am managing my health better, but often prioritize work over working out" (Delgado, 2016, p. 86).

STRESS

Educational leaders deal with a multitude of demands as well as mental and social strains that are core to the definition of stress (Levi, 1984). Stress involves a perceived threat that taxes or exhausts one's resources (LePine et al., 2004) and the resulting emotions are likely to compromise an individual's performance (Farmer, 2020; Kersaint et al., 2007; Williams & Dikes, 2015). Studies indicate that work-related stress across professions is often due to a lack of work-life balance, weak workplace support, a demanding workload, deadlines, and inconsistent expectations from supervisors (Mathis & Jackson, 2004). Certainly, school leaders are experiencing unprecedented stressors. Assistant principals, principals, and superintendents continue to juggle enormous responsibilities, competing priorities, and multifaceted relationships while also trying to foster a safe, effective, yet challenging learning environment. The stress of their jobs can be attributed to its many competing demands.

Principals and assistant principals have noted great difficulty dealing with student discipline, but have also identified disgruntled parents as a particularly challenging cause of stress (Barnett et al., 2012). Another alarming indicator of tensions can be found in the rising number of leaders experiencing threats of violence or reporting occurrences of violence—as did more than a third of participants in a 2018 Australian study (Horwood et al., 2019). Other research has indicated the causes of leadership burnout involve poor time management, a heavy workload, unrealistic expectations, decreased autonomy, organizational policies, poor recognition of achievements, long hours, and lack of support (Friedman, 1995; Peeters & Rutte, 2005; Sari, 2004; Tomic & Tomic, 2008; Whitaker, 1995; Whitehead et al., 2000). In short, the sources of stress for educational leaders are plentiful but with very little attention given to supporting these leaders in managing these stressors.

PERSONAL COST

It should be no surprise that all this stress on educational leaders comes at a cost. "The great personal cost from inadequately addressing the stressors of educational leaders includes depression and impaired occupational functioning" (Plastidou & Agaliotis, 2008, p. 61). Associated health issues from stress can be damaging to a leader's physical and mental health while also leading to decreased productivity, absenteeism, and higher job dissatisfaction (Plastidou & Agaliotis, 2008; Sarafis et al., 2016; Sorenson, 2007). A study by Robinson and Shakeshaft (2016) noted that superintendents identified such material physical effects as high cholesterol, high blood pressure, obesity, gastrointestinal problems, insomnia, anxiety, sleep apnea, and chronic headaches. Mental health also deteriorated, worsening immune-related diseases, chronic conditions, and life-threatening illnesses (Robinson & Shakeshaft, 2015). To combat these negative effects, recommendations spoke to healthy habits and perspectives, including a healthy diet, exercise, and a balanced perspective for both one's personal well-being and for improved efficacy as an educator (Delgado, 2016).

Beyond the physical and mental costs to health, leaders overwhelmed by job stressors also experienced a negative impact on their marriage, family relations, and lifestyle choices (Lefdal & De Jong, 2019). Stress spillover occurs when leaders are unable to manage the stress of their jobs, incurring mental and emotional needs that prove a detriment to their personal lives (Staines, 1980). Such stress spillover is all too often a job hazard of educational leaders. Research indicates educational leadership is among the busiest of professions, causing its practitioners to neglect their own well-being as well as that of their families (Gupton, 2010). Work-life balance issues can destroy home support systems that help bolster success in the work environment, leading to less achievements at work and an ongoing cycle of increasing work demands. This negative cycle generates additional stress both personally and professionally, a hamster wheel without forward progression toward wellness.

More generally, the American Institute of Stress has identified that stress is a significant factor in 80% of work-related injuries and 40% of workplace turnovers (Atkinson, 2004). In a four-year period, absenteeism related to stress tripled (Richardson & Rothstein, 2008), and a quarter of U.S. employees surveyed reported overwhelming levels of stress (American Institute of Stress, 2016). This has resulted in an additional financial cost of $300 billion a year nationally from absenteeism (American Institute of Stress, 2016). Such a figure is a high price to pay economically, personally, and professionally, and educational institutions are not immune to the problem. The high stress on educational leaders does not serve the purpose of educational institutions nor advance the cause of students. Until educational leaders can nurture wellness while meeting job demands, the achievement of goals for our schools continues to be jeopardized. If this stress is sustained over long periods of time, it can lead to job burnout and turnover (Darmody & Smyth, 2014; Maslach & Leiter, 2016; Maslach et al., 2001).

BURNOUT AND ATTRITION

Educational leaders who have experienced long-term exposure to debilitating levels of stress are, not surprisingly, more prone to job burnout; job burnout itself carries burdensome physical, intellectual, social, emotional, and spiritual symptoms (Brock & Grady, 2002). Decreased motivation and a loss of work-related passion are additional characteristics (Darmody & Smyth, 2014). Leaders experiencing burnout are more likely to feel emotional exhaustion, negative self-evaluation, a lack of accomplishment, and depersonalization, impairing relationships with others (Maslach et al., 2001; Ozkan & Özdevecioğlu, 2013; Ross et al., 2012). Deprioritizing the well-being of educators perpetuates job burnout, which is marked by decreases in work performance and productivity as well as increases in absences and job turnover (Schaufeli & Buunk, 2003). The need to identify and reduce stressors and prevent job burnout is compellingly clear. In fact, research from the Collaborative for Academic, Social, and Emotional Learning (2019) indicates that principals' social-emotional competencies can positively enhance their well-being, lessen stress, and reduce job burnout. Unfortunately, little attention has been given to the promotion of these competencies as a support for superintendents, principals, and assistant principals. Instead, the leadership ranks in education continue to suffer from an exodus of talent.

Unacknowledged stress and job burnout leads to educational leaders ill equipped to foster positive decision-making and quality relationships as well as rising attrition rates (Tickle, 1999). Losing good leaders has an impact beyond the individual position lost. If leaders were supported in developing practices to endure difficult conditions despite the demands and stressors of their work environment, the positive impact would be significant. A mindful leader's mental endurance has great promise to aid their organization's focus on goals; their good influence on an organization includes employee welfare, employee job performance, and leadership (Burmansah et al., 2019). Thus, the impact of a mindful leader is not just on the efficacy of the leader's performance but also on the school community. Rather than losing leaders to the ravages of stress and burnout, schools could stem the tide of attrition through proactive professional development that is prepared and willing to face the challenges.

It would be good for reducing costs as well. Replacing teachers who have left the field runs up the tab an average of $2.2 billion a year nationwide, according to Castro and his colleagues (2018), and administrator salaries are traditionally higher. Transferring educator costs soar to over $4.9 billion (Castro et al., 2018), including the costs of investing in initial professional learning and training (Farley-Ripple et al., 2012). Onboarding a new administrator was estimated to cost $75,000 when accounting for preparing, hiring, and placing the person in the role (Superville, 2014). According to a 2014 study on principal turnover, nationally the average yearly principal turnover rate is 22% with high-poverty districts spending $36 million on hiring costs alone, and that doesn't include the additional costs of onboarding and training (Cone, 2014). These financial costs compound the negative impact of turnover.

SCHOOL PERFORMANCE

The financial costs may not be the most alarming concern, however, as the costs to school efficacy are just as disconcerting. The stressful demands of educational leadership have ramifications of great importance to the success of schools, teachers, and students. A correlation exists between principal burnout and a decrease in student achievement and morale (Wells, 2013). A high turnover in education leadership can lead to declines in student achievement, challenges to program growth, negative trends in teacher morale, and calcified school cultures (Beteille et al., 2011; Fink & Brayman, 2006; Hargreaves & Fink, 2006; MacMillan et al., 2011; Louis et al., 2010). In fact, numerous researchers have indicated educator stress is high and negatively affecting student achievement and readiness (Aritzeta et al., 2015; Boyatzis & McKee, 2005; Dicke et al., 2020; Fikuree et al., 2021; Klocko & Wells, 2015; Pierce, 2014; Taliadorou & Pashiardis, 2015; Wells, 2016).

The wellness requirements of educational leaders must be met to assure successful school learning environments. Several studies support the positive impact that a caring, stable, and compassionate school leader can have on fostering a positive educational climate and the decrease in attrition (Berson & Oreg, 2016; Fuller et al., 2007; Louis & Murphy, 2017; Pijanowski et al., 2009; Tschannen-Moran & Gareis, 2004). Research indicates that individual well-being has a positive correlation to student success (Arens & Morin, 2016; Briner & Dewberry, 2007; Kidger et al., 2016; Liu et al., 2018; Oberle, 2018; Spilt et al., 2011). Individual well-being encompasses educator autonomy and motivation (Liu et al., 2018) and is influenced by working conditions, relationships at schools, available resources, school infrastructure, individual health, professional competence, and opportunities for professional development (Saaranen et al., 2007). Collective well-being involves school collaboration and is also shaped by individual well-being (Liu et al., 2018). School cultures plagued by overwhelming stress, burnout, and attrition are demoralizing and damaging. Unfortunately, research indicates that school leaders lack the tools and strategies to balance their overwhelming professional responsibilities with unencumbered personal time and healthful wellness practices (Beisser et al., 2014).

WELLNESS FOCUS

Wellness programs are emerging in response to the known stress of school leaders (Lefdal & De Jong, 2019). These moves are backed by studies indicating a need for health and wellness programs for current and aspiring superintendents (Robinson & Shakeshaft, 2016). Investigating avenues for reducing the stress on superintendents' well-being has been a significant aspect of the work-life movement (Mahfouz, 2018; Plastidou & Agaliotis, 2008; Wells & Klocko, 2018). Lefdal and De Jong (2019) indicate that the importance of understanding stress's impact on the educational workplace and noting steps to alleviate its negative effects were essential to superintendent retention and their fostering of healthy relationships with their families. As leaders learn to stay active, eat a healthy diet, incorporate accountability partners, utilize a professional network, adopt professional learning communities, and practice mindfulness, they will experience the benefits of wellness and more effective stress management (Beisser et al., 2014). Employee wellness programs help school leaders develop a work-life balance that increases productivity and a positive outlook while modeling healthy behaviors for both staff and students (Sanders et al., 2016).

COPING SKILLS AND SELF-CARE

In addition to wellness programs, some coping skills have been indicated as particularly helpful in managing the stress of school leaders. These coping skills include the support of school board members, getting away from all work responsibilities, professional development, and mentoring (Hawk & Martin, 2011). The data in this same study indicate that half of participants experienced high levels of stress from board of education failure to provide support and from inadequate coping strategies and stress management skills (Hawk & Martin, 2011); a strong need for stress management skills at the district level, in fact, has emerged as well as a need for reform.

Self-care is another approach to proactively developing leader well-being in mind, body, and emotions (Crane & Ward, 2016). The adoption of self-care behavior strategies reduces stress and allows the leader to screen professional problems from a considered sense of self (Bressi & Vaden, 2017). Attention to sleep, nutrition, exercise, relaxation, and one's support network promotes body and mind regulation (Lee & Miller, 2013). The Centers for Disease Control and Prevention (2013) provides evidence about the benefits of exercise to promote the release of endorphins in the brain, which relieves pain and stress, while Crane and Ward (2016) assert the benefit of spirituality to promote the physical and emotional calm that positively enhances mental capacity. Rivera-McCutchen (2020) takes the notion of self-care a step further by calling for radical responses—radical hope, antiracism, authentic relationships, a belief in growth and excellence, and sociopolitical navigation—to confront the ongoing stressors of racism that educational leaders can experience. According to Rivera-McCutchen, this conception of making a radical stance calls for principals and other school leaders to challenge inequitable systems while embracing a spirit of radical hope.

MINDFULNESS

Mindfulness, a term derived from the Sanskrit word "Sati," is another potential practice for reducing workplace stress (Passmore, 2019). Mindfulness-based interventions (MBIs) have been practiced primarily in clinical settings, but emerged at the turn of the 21st century as a promising practice for the law, business, and education fields (Baer, 2003; Bishop, 2002; Brown & Ryan, 2003; Kabat-Zinn, 2003). Research indicates that mindfulness supports effective leadership through the development of perspective, being present in the moment, and increased resiliency for effective problem solving (Boyce, 2011). Despite the clear need for mindfulness and the benefits of having mindful school leaders, state standards, university courses, licensing, and professional development still fall short in the incorporation of such practices (Mahfouz, 2018).

Mindfulness integrates awareness, attention, nonjudgment, acceptance, and kindness (Passmore, 2019)—qualities that could help educational leaders avoid impulsive, hurtful behaviors and detachment (Siegel, 2010). Some simple practices, like mindful breathing, could easily be integrated as a feasible practice incorporated into the school day (Schussler et al., 2021a; specifically, mindfulness could help educational leaders regulate their emotions and manage their thoughts (Siegel, 2010). As a promising approach to improve educator well-being, it is associated with improvements in efficacy, burnout/time pressure, and stress (Mahfouz, 2018).

Educational leaders who demonstrate empathy, compassion, self-control, and self-awareness are better equipped to foster positive decision-making and quality relationships (Tickle, 1999). Though studies of educational leaders and mindfulness practices remain an area in need of additional research (Mahfouz, 2018), mindfulness studies of K–12 students and teachers (Becker et al., 2017; Garner et al., 2018; Wigelsworth & Quinn, 2020) show great promise for application to leadership—specifically, there is a need to explore the impact of mindfulness on not just the individual as a leader but also on the leader's relationship to followers and on the leader's efficacy (Good et al., 2016). Mindful leaders have been described as authentic, genuine, creative, aware of their impact and of their realities, and good decision-makers (Wongkom et al., 2019). Their impact on an organization includes responsive leadership and improved employee welfare and job performance. The mindful leader's mental endurance has great promise to aid their organizations in focusing on goals (Burmansah et al., 2019).

CONCLUSION

In the wake of a global pandemic that wielded unprecedented school stressors, when both the burden and the importance of educational leadership has been pronounced, there has never been a more important time to acknowledge the importance of well-being to creating thriving school communities. Educational leaders must have the competencies to manage job stressors and foster their own physical, mental, cognitive, and emotional well-being in order to serve their school communities. The impact of educational leaders on teachers, students, and the wider school community is profound and the positive ramifications of developing leader well-being is critical to their flourishing. Amid compelling evidence of a growing crisis in leadership, it is imperative that mindfulness and other tools for developing well-being become a priority for school environments. The rich potential of well-being initiatives for identifying and grooming sustainable leaders is a compelling cause for ongoing investment and investigation.

REFERENCES

American Institute of Stress. (2016). *Workplace stress.* https://www.stress.org/workplace-stress

Arens, A. K., & Morin, A. J. S. (2016). Teachers' emotional exhaustion and students' educational outcomes. *Journal of Educational Psychology, 108*(6), 800–813. https://doi.org/10.1037/edu0000105

Aritzeta, A., Balluerkaa, N., Gorostiaga, A., Alonso-Arbiol, I., Haranburua, M., & Gartzia, L. (2015). Classroom emotional intelligence and its relationship with school performance. *The European Journal of Education and Psychology, 9*(1), 1–8. https://www.sciencedirect.com/science/article/pii/S1888899215000343

Atkinson, W. (2004). Stress: Risk management's most serious challenge? *Risk Management, 51*(6), 1–5.

Baer, R. A. (2003). Mindfulness training as a clinical intervention: A conceptual and empirical review. *Clinical Psychology: Science and Practice, 10*(2), 125–143.

Barnett, B. G., Shoho, A. R., & Oleszewski, A. M. (2012). The job realities of beginning and experienced assistant principals. *Leadership and Policy in Schools, 11*(1), 92–128. https://doi.org/10.1080/15700763.2011.611924

Becker, B. D., Gallagher, K. C., & Whitaker, R. C. (2017). Teachers' dispositional mindfulness and the quality of their relationships with children in Head Start classrooms. *Journal of School Psychology, 65*, 40–53. https://doi.org/10.1016/j.jsp.2017.06.004

Beisser, S. R., Peters, R. E., & Thacker, V. M. (2014). Balancing passion and priorities: an investigation of health and wellness practices of secondary school principals. *NASSP Bulletin, 98*(3), 237–255.

Berson, Y., & Oreg, S. (2016). The role of school principals in shaping children's values. *Psychological Science, 27*(12), 1539–1549.

Beteille, T., Kalogrides, D., Loeb, S., & National Bureau of Economic Research (2011). *Stepping stones: Principal career paths and school outcomes.* NBER Working Paper No. 17243. National Bureau of Economic Research. (ERIC Document Reproduction Service No. ED522078).

Bishop, S. R. (2002). What do we really know about mindfulness-based stress reduction?. *Psychosomatic medicine, 64*(1), 71–83.

Bjork, L. G., Browne-Ferrigno, T., & Kowalski, T. J. (2014). The superintendent and educational reform in the United States of America. *Leadership and Policy in Schools, 13,* 444–465. doi:10.1080/15700763.2014.945656

Boyatzis, R., & McKee, A. (2005). *Resonant leadership: Renewing yourself and connecting with others through mindfulness, hope and compassion.* Harvard University Press.

Boyce, B. C. (Ed.). (2011). *The mindfulness revolution: Leading psychologists, scientists, artists, and meditation teachers on the power of mindfulness in daily life.* Shambhala.

Branch, R. (2013). *Leadership practices of a principal in a high school with a high teacher retention rate* [Doctoral dissertation, West Virginia University]. ProQuest Dissertations Publishing.

Branch, G., Hanushek, E., & Rivkin, S. (2013). School leaders matter: Measuring the impact of effective principals. *Education Next, 13*(1), 62–69.

Bredeson, P. V. (1996). Superintendents' roles in curriculum development and instructional leadership: Instructional visionaries, collaborators, supporters, and delegators. *Journal of School Leadership, 6*(3), 243–264.

Bredeson, P. V., & Kose, B. W. (2007). Responding to the education reform agenda: A study of school superintendents' instructional leadership. *Education Policy Analysis Archives, 15*(5), 1–26.

Bressi, S. K., & Vaden, E. R. (2017). Reconsidering self-care. *Clinical Social Work Journal, 45*(1), 33–38. https://doi.org/10.1007/s10615-016-0575-4

Briner, R., & Dewberry, C. (2007). *Staff well-being is key to school success.* Worklife Support/Hamilton House.

Brock, B. L., & Grady, M. L. (2002). *Avoiding burnout: A principal's guide to keeping the fire alive.* Corwin Press.

Brown K. W., & Bryan, R. M. (2003) The benefits of being present: The role of mindfulness in psychological well-being. *Journal of Personality and Social Psychology, 84*, 822–848. https://doi.org/10.1037/0022-3514.84.4.822

Burmansah, B., Rugaiyah, R., Mukhtar, M., Nabilah, S., Ripki, A. J. H., & Fatayan, A. (2019). Mindful leadership: The ability of the leader to develop compassion and attention without judgement: A case study of the leader of the Buddhist Higher Education Institute. *European Journal of Educational Research, 9*(1), 51–65.

Castro, A., Quinn, D. J., Fuller, E., & Barnes, M. (2018). *Policy Brief 2018-1: Addressing the importance and scale of the U.S. teacher shortage.* http://www.ucea.org/wp-content/uploads/2018/01/Addressing-the-Importance-and-Scale-of-the-US-Teacher-Shortage.pdf

Centers for Disease Control and Prevention (CDC). (2020). *Physical activity.* https://www.cdc.gov/physicalactivity/index.html

Collaborative for Academic, Social, and Emotional Learning (CASEL). (2019). *Federal policy: Every Child Succeeds act (ESSA)* [Organization]. https://casel.org/federal-policy-and-legislation/

Cone, M. (2014). *Churn: The high cost of principal turnover.* School Leaders Network. https://www.academia.edu/9813024/Churn_The_High_Cost_of_Principal_Turnover

Crane, P. J., & Ward, S. F. (2016). Self-healing and self-care for nurses. *AORN Journal, 104*(5), 386–400.

Darmody, M., & Smyth, E. (2014). Primary school principal's job satisfaction and occupational stress. *International Journal of Educational Management, 30*(1), 115–128.

Day, C., Sammons, P., Hopkins, D. Leithwood, K., & Kington A. (2008). Research into the impact of school leadership on pupil outcomes: policy and research contexts. *School Leadership and Management, 28*(1), 5–25.

Delgado, C. J. (2016). *The impact of occupational stress on high school assistant principals* [Doctoral dissertation, Oakland University]. Oakland, Michigan. http://search.proquest.com/pqdtglobal/docview/1826917468/abstract/610469E8E8E541C6PQ/3

Dicke, T., Marsh, H. W., Parker, P. D., Guo, J., Riley, P., & Waldeyer, J. (2020). Job satisfaction of teachers and their principals in relation to climate and student achievement. *Journal of Educational Psychology, 112*(5), 1061.

Di Liberto, A., Schivardi, F., & Sulis, G. (2015). Managerial practices and student performance. *Economic Policy, 30*(84), 683–728. https://doi.org/10.1093/epolic/eiv015

Farkas, S., Johnson, J., Duffett, A., & Foleno, T. (2001). *Trying to stay ahead of the game: Superintendents and principals talk about school leadership.* Public Agenda.

Farley-Ripple, E. N., Solano, P. L., & McDuffie, M. J. (2012). Conceptual and methodological issues in research on school administrator career behavior. *Educational Researcher, 41*(6), 220–229. https://doi.org/10.3102/0013189X12451774

Farmer, D. (2020). Teacher attrition: The impacts of stress. *The Delta Kappa Gamma Bulletin: International Journal for Professional Educators, 87*(1), 41–50.

Fikuree, W., Meyer, F., Le Fevre, D., & Alansari, M. (2021). Linking principal task effectiveness to student achievement in secondary schools in the Maldives. *International Journal of Leadership in Education*, 1–18.

Fink, D., & Brayman, C. (2006). School leadership succession and the challenges of change. *Educational Administration Quarterly*, 42, 62–89. https://doi.org/10.1177/0013161X05278186

Friedman, I. A. (1995). Measuring school principal-experienced burnout. *Educational and Psychological Measurement*, 55(4), 641–651. https://doi.org/10.1177/0013164495055004012

Fullan, M. (2009). Leadership development: The larger context. *Educational Leadership*, 67(2), 45–49.

Fuller, E. Baker, B. & Young, M. (2007). *The relationship between principal characteristic, school-level teacher quality and turnover, and student achievement*. University Council for Educational Administration, The University of Texas.

Garner, P. W., Bender, S. L., & Fedor, M. (2018). Mindfulness-based SEL programming to increase preservice teachers' mindfulness and emotional competence. *Psychology in the Schools*, 55(4), 377–390. https://doi.org/10.1002/pits.22114

Glass, T., Bjork, L., & Brunner, C. (2000). *The study of the American school superintendency: A look at the superintendent of education in the new millennium*. American Association of School Administrators.

Goldring, E., Rubin, M., & Herrmann, M. (2021). *The role of assistant principals: Evidence and insights for advancing school leadership*. (Study highlights). The Wallace Foundation. https://www.wallacefoundation.org/knowledge-center/pages/the-role-of-assistant-principals-evidence-insights-for-advancing-school-leadership.aspx

Good, D., Lyddy, C. J., Glomb, T. M., Bono, J. E., Brown, K. W., Duffy, M. K., Baer, R. A., Brewer, J. A., & Lazar, S. W. (2016). Contemplating mindfulness at work: An integrative review. *Journal of Management*, 42(1), 114–142. https://doi.org/10.1177/0149206315617003

Gupton, S. L. (2010). *The instructional leadership toolbox: A handbook for improving practice*. Corwin.

Hall, D., & McHenry-Sorber, E. (2017). Politics first: Examining the practice of the multi-district superintendent. *Education Policy Analysis Archives*, 25(82), 1–29.

Harris, A., & Hopkins, D. (2006). *Seven strong claims about successful school leadership*. National College for School Leadership.

Hargreaves, A., & Fink, D. (2006). Redistributed leadership for sustainable professional learning communities. *Journal of School Leadership*, 16(5), 550–565. https://doi.org/10.1177/105268460601600507

Hattie, J. (2015). Teacher-ready research review: The applicability of visible learning to higher education. *The Scholarship of Teaching and Learning in Psychology*, 1(1), 79–91. http://dx.doi.org/10.1037/stl0000021

Hawk, N., & Martin, B. (2011). Understanding and reducing stress in the superintendency. *Educational Management Administration & Leadership*, 39(3), 364–390.

Horwood, M., Parker, P. D., & Riley, P. (2019). *One in three principals are seriously stressed, here's what we need to do about it.* The Conversation. http://theconversation.com/one-in-three-principals-are-seriously-stressed-heres-what-we-need-to-do-about-it-110774

Kabat-Zinn, J. (2003). Mindfulness-based interventions in context: past, present, and future. *Clinical Psychology: Science and Practice, 10*(2), 144–156.

Katz, D., & Kahn, R. (2003). *The social psychology of organizations* (2nd ed.). John Wiley and Sons.

Kersaint, G., Lewis, J., Potter, R., & Meisels, G. (2007). Why teachers leave: Factors that influence retention and resignation. *Teaching and Teacher Education, 23*, 775–794. https://doi.org/10.1016/j.tate.2005.12.004

Kidger, J., Brockman, R., Tilling, K., Campbell, R., Ford, T., Araya, R., King, A., & Gunnell, D. (2016). Teachers' wellbeing and depressive symptoms, and associated risk factors: A large cross sectional study in English secondary schools. *Journal of Affective Disorders, 192,* 76–82. https://doi.org/10.1016/j.jad.2015.11.054.

Klocko, B. A., & Wells, C. M. (2015). Workload pressures of principals: A focus on renewal, support, and mindfulness. *NASSP Bulletin, 99*(4), 332–355. https://doi.org/10.1177/0192636515619727

Lecker, A. (2002). Listening to leaders: The obstacle course. *American School Board Journal, 189*(2), 32–35.

Lee, J. J., & Miller, S. E. (2013). A self-care framework for social workers: Building a strong foundation for practice. *Families in Society: The Journal of Contemporary Social Services, 94*(2), 96–103.

Lefdal, J., & De Jong, D. (2019). Superintendent stress: Identifying the causes and learning to cope. *AASA Journal of Scholarship and Practice, 16*(3), 56–74.

Leithwood, K., & Day, C. (2008). The impact of school leadership on pupil outcomes. *School Leadership and Management, 28*(1), 1–4.

Leithwood, K., Louis, K. S., Anderson, S., & Wahlstrom, K. (2004). *Executive summary: How leadership influences student learning*. Wallace Foundation. https://www.wallacefoundation.org/knowledge-center/documents/how-leadership-influences-student-learning.pdf

Leithwood, K., & Louis, K. S. (2011). *Linking leadership to student learning*. Jossey Bass.

LePine, J. A., LePine, M. A., & Jackson, C. L. (2004). Challenge and hindrance stress: Relationships with exhaustion, motivation to learn, and learning performance. *Journal of Applied Psychology, 89,* 883–891.

Levi, L. (1984). Stress in industry: Causes, effects, and prevention. *Occupational Safety and Health Series No 51.* International Labour Organisation.

Liu, L. B., Song, H., & Miao, P. (2018). Navigating individual and collective notions of teacher wellbeing as a complex phenomenon shaped by national context. *Compare: A Journal of Comparative and International Education, 48*(1), 128–146. https://doi.org/10.1080/03057925.2017.1283979

Louis, K., Leithwood, K., Anderson, S. E., Wahlstrom, K. L. & Educational Research Service. (2010). *Learning from leadership: Investigating the links to improved student learning. The Informed Educator Series.* Educational Research Service. ERIC Document Reproduction Service No. ED519152

Louis, K. S., & Murphy, J. (2017). Trust, caring and organizational learning: the leader's role. *Journal of Educational Administration*, *55*(1), 103–126.

Macmillan, R. B., Meyer M. J., Northfield S., & Foley, M. (2011). The school district and the development of trust in new principals: Policies and actions that influence succession. In R. E. White & K. Cooper (Eds.), *Principals in succession: Transfer and rotation in educational administration* (pp. 27–40). Springer.

Mahfouz, J. (2018). Mindfulness training for school administrators: Effects on well-being and leadership. *Journal of Educational Administration*, *56*(6), 602–619. https://doi.org/10.1108/JEA-12-2017-0171

Mahfouz, J., Greenberg, M., & Rodriguez, A. (2019). *Principals' social and emotional competence: A key factor for creating caring schools* (Issue Brief No. 1). Pennsylvania State University. https://www.prevention.psu.edu/uploads/files/PSU-Principals-Brief-103119.pdf

Mahfouz, J., King, K., & James, L. (2021). Lessons from the storm: Emotions, meaning-making & leadership during transition. *The Asia-Pacific Education Researcher*, *30*(1), 1–9. https://doi.org/10.1007/s40299-021-00574-w

Malone, M. (2013). *The relationship of the principal's soft skills to school climate* [Doctoral dissertation, University of Texas]. Austin, Texas. ProQuest Dissertations Publishing.

Maslach, C., & Leiter, M. P. (2016). Understanding the burnout experience: Recent research and its implications for psychiatry. *World Psychiatry*, *152*, 103–111.

Maslach, C., Schaufeli, W. B., & Leiter, M. P. (2001). Job burnout. *Annual Review of Psychology*, *52*, 397–422.

Mathis, R. L., & Jackson, H. J. (2004). *Human resource management*. Thomson/SouthWestern.

Oberle, E. (2018). Early adolescents' emotional well-being in the classroom: The role of personal and contextual assets. *Journal of School Health*, *88*(2), 101–111.

Organisation for Economic Co-operation and Development (OECD). (2014). *Education at a Glance 2014: OECD Indicators*. https://doi.org/10.1787/eag-2014-en

Oskolkoff, N. (2019). *Explicit self-care for principals and their teachers: A qualitative transcendental phenomenological study on administrator stress levels* [Unpublished doctoral dissertation, Concordia University], San Antonio, Texas. https://digitalcommons.csp.edu/cup_commons_grad_edd/378.

Ozkan, A., & Özdevecioğlu, M. (2013). The effects of occupational stress on burnout and life satisfaction: A study in accountants. *Quality & Quantity*, *47*, 2785–2798. https://doi.org/10.1007/s11135-012-9688-1

Passmore, J. (2019). Mindfulness in organizations (Part 1): A critical literature review. *Industrial and Commercial Training*, *51*(2), 104–113.

Peeters, M., & Rutte, C. G. (2005). Time management behavior as a moderator for the job demand-control. *Interaction Journal of Occupational Health Psychology*, *10*, 64–75. https://doi.org/10.1037/1076-8998.10.1.64

Pierce, S. S. (2014). Examining the relationship between collective teacher efficacy and the emotional intelligence of elementary school principals. *Journal of School Leadership*, *24*(2), 311–333.

Pijanowski, J. C., Hewitt, P. M., & Brady, K. P. (2009). Superintendents' perceptions of the principal shortage. *NASSP*, *93*(2), 85–95.

Plastidou, M., & Agaliotis, I. (2008). Burnout, job satisfaction and instructional assignment-related sources of stress in Greek special education teachers. *International Journal of Disability, Development and Education, 55*(1), 61–76.

Rallis, S., Tedder, J., Lachman, A., & Elmore, R. (2006). Superintendents in classrooms: From collegial conversations to collaborative action. *Phi Delta Kappan, 87*(7), 537–545.

Richardson, K. M., & Rothstein, H. R. (2008). Effects of occupational stress management intervention programs: A meta-analysis. *Journal of Occupational Health Psychology, 13*(1), 69–93. https://doi.org/10.1037/1076-8998.13.1.69

Riley, P., & Langan-Fox, J. (2013). Bullying, stress and health in school principals and medical professionals: Experiences at the 'Front-line'. In R. Burke, C. L. Cooper, & S. Fox (Eds.), *Human frailties: Wrong turns on the road to success* (pp. 181–200). Gower.

Rivera-McCutchen, R. L. (2020). We don't got time for grumbling: Toward an ethic of radical care in urban school leadership. *Educational Administration Quarterly*, 1–33. https://doi.org/10.1177/0013161X20925892

Robinson, K. K., & Shakeshaft, C. (2015). Women superintendents who leave: Stress and health factors. *Planning and Changing, 46*(3), 440–458.

Robinson, K., & Shakeshaft, C. (2016). Superintendent stress and superintendent health: A national study. *Journal of Education and Human Development, 5*(1), 120–133.

Ross, S. W., Romer, N., & Horner, R. H. (2012). Teacher well-being and the implementation of school-wide positive behavior interventions and supports. *Journal of Positive Behavior Interventions, 14*(2), 118–128. https://doi.org/10.1177/1098300711413820

Saaranen, T., Tossavainen, K., Turunen, H., Kiviniemi, V., & Vertio, H. (2007). Occupational well-being of school staff members: a structural equation model. *Health Education Research, 22*(2), 248–260. https://doi.org/10.1093/her/cy1073

Sanders, J. P., Loveday, A., Pearson, N., Edwardson, C., Yates, T., Biddle, S. J., & Esliger, D. W. (2016). Devices for self-monitoring sedentary time or physical activity: a scoping review. *Journal of Medical Internet Research, 18*(5), e90.

Sahlberg, P., & Sahlberg, P. (2010). Rethinking accountability in a knowledge society. *Journal of Educational Change, 11*(1), 45–61. https://doi.org/10.1007/s10833-008-9098-2

Sarafis, P., Rousaki, E., Tsounis, A., Malliarou, M., Lahana, L., Bamidis, P., Niakas, D., & Papastavrou, E. (2016). The impact of occupational stress on nurses' caring behaviors and their health-related quality of life. *BMC Nursing, 15*(56), 1–9. https://doi.org/10.1186/s12912-016-0178-y

Sari, H. (2004). An analysis of burnout and job satisfaction among Turkish special school headteachers and teacher, and the factors affecting their burnout and job satisfaction. *Educational Studies, 30*(3), 291–306. https://doi.org/10.1080/0305569042000224233

Schaufeli, W. B., & Bunnk, B. P. (2003). Burnout: An overview of 25 years of research and theorizing. In M. J. Schabracq, J. Winnubst, A. M. Cooper, & L. Cary (Eds.), *The handbook of work and health psychology* (pp. 383–425). John Wiley.

Schussler, D., Oh, Y., Mahfouz, J., Levitan, J., Frank, J. L., Broderick, P. C., Mitral, J. L., Berrenal, E., Kohler, K., & Greenberg, M. T. (2021a). Stress and well-being: A systematic case study of adolescents' experiences in a mindfulness-based program. *Journal of Child and Family Studies, 30*, 431–446. https://doi.org/10.1007/s10826-020-01864-5

Schussler, D., Oh, Y., Mahfouz, J., Levitan, J., Frank, J., Broderick, P., Mitra, J., & Greenberg, M. (2021b). Learning to manage stress: Combining qualitative and quantitative data to understand adolescents' experiences in a mindfulness-based intervention. *Journal of Child and Family Studies, 30*(2), 431–446. https://doi.org/10.1007/s10826-020-01864-5

Sherman, W. H., & Crogan, M. (2003). Superintendents' responses to the achievement gap: An ethical critique. *International Journal of Educational Research, 6*(3), 223–237.

Shoho, A., Oleszewski, A., & Barnett, B. (2012). The development of assistant principals: A literature review. *Journal of Educational Administration, 50*(3), 264–286. https://doi.org/10.1108/09578231211223301

Siegel, D. J. (2010). *Mindsight: The new science of personal transformation*, Bantam Dell.

Sogunro, O. A. (2012). Stress in school administration: Coping tips for principals. *Journal of School Leadership, 22*, 664–700.

Solomon, D. J. (2012). Superintendent's frustration grows, but intangible rewards remain high. *District Administration, 48*(9), 63–64.

Sorenson, R. D. (2007). Stress management in education: Warning signs and coping mechanisms. *Management in Education, 21*(3), 10–13.

Spilt, J., Koomen, H., & Thijs, J. (2011). Teacher wellbeing: The importance of teacher-student relationships. *Educational Psychology Review, 23*(4), 457–477. https://doi.org/10.1007/s10648-011- 9170-y

Staines, G. L. (1980). Spillover versus compensation: A review of the literature on the relationship between work and nonwork. *Human Relations, 33*(2), 111–129.

Superville, D. R. (2014). Study finds principal mobility takes toll on budgets, learning; "Churn: The high cost of principal turnover." *Editorial Projects in Education, Inc., 34*(12), 5. https://go-gale-com.ezproxy.baylor.edu/ps/i.do?id=GALE%7CA391277542&v=2.1&u=txshracd2488&it=r&p=AONE&sw=w

Taliadorou, N., & Pashiardis, P. (2015). Examining the role of emotional intelligence and political skill to educational leadership and their effects to teachers' job satisfaction. *Journal of Educational Administration, 53*(5), 642–666. http://cupdx.idm.oclc.org/login?url=https://search-proquest- com.cupdx.idm.oclc.org/docview/1694933693?accountid=10248

Tickle, L. (1999). Teacher self-appraisal and appraisal of self. In R. P. Lipka, & T. M. Brinthaupt (Eds.), *The role of self in teacher development* (pp. 121–141). State University of New York Press.

Tomic, W., & Tomic, E. (2008). Existential fulfillment and burnout among principals and teachers. *Journal of Beliefs & Values, 29*(1), 11–27. https://doi.org/10.1080/13617670801928191

Tschannen-Moran, M. & Gareis, C. R. (2004). Principals' sense of efficacy: assessing a promising construct. *Journal of Educational Administration, 42*(5), 573–585.

Wells, C. (2013). Principals responding to constant pressure: Finding a source of stress management. *NASSP Bulletin.* https://doi.org/10.1177101926365135044453

Wells, C. (2016). *Mindfulness: How school leaders can reduce stress and thrive on the job.* Rowman and Littlefield.

Wells, C. M., & Klocko, B. A. (2018). Principal well-being and resilience: Mindfulness as a means to that end. *NASSP Bulletin, 102*(2), 161–173. https://doi.org/10.1177/0192636518777813

Whitaker, K. S. (1995). Principal burnout: Implications for professional development. *Journal of Personnel Evaluation in Education, 9*(3), 287–296. https://doi.org/10.1007/BF00972643.

Whitehead, A., Ryba, K., & O'Driscoll, M. (2000). Burnout among New Zealand primary school teachers. *New Zealand Journal of Psychology, 29*(2), 52–60.

Wigelsworth, M., & Quinn, A. (2020). Mindfulness in schools: An exploration of teachers' perceptions of mindfulness-based interventions. *Pastoral Care in Education, 38*(4), 293–310. https://doi.org/10.1080/02643944.2020.1725908

Williams, J., & Dikes, C. (2015). The implications of demographic variables as related to burnout among a sample of special education teachers. *Education, 135*(3), 337–345.

Wongkom, S., Sanrattana, W., & Chusorn, P. (2019). The structural relationship model of indicators of mindful leadership for primary school principals. *International Journal of Higher Education, 8*(5), 134–142. https://doi.org/10.5430/ijhe.v8n5p134

CHAPTER 2

SCHOOL LEADERSHIP IN THE UNITED STATES

An In-Depth Analysis of the Increasing Principal Turnover Crisis in America

Denver J. Fowler and Sarah M. Jouganatos

Introduction

As one might imagine, in any setting, be it within the PreK–12 educational setting or any given organizational setting, there are negative effects associated with a high rate of employee turnover. Furthermore, we might imagine those negative effects to be amplified if it is the organization's leadership that is experiencing the high rate of turnover. In the United States, we find an alarming rate of school leadership turnover within the PreK–12 educational setting. That is, we continue to see an increase in both superintendent and principal turnover across the nation. In fact, in a study[1] conducted by Kowalski et al. (2010), a decennial study for the American Association of School Administrators (AASA [The School Superintendents association]), it was reported that the national average tenure of a superintendent in the United States was five to six years. However, and perhaps worth noting here, depending on district locale, turnover rates can certainly vary. For example, Falk (2020) found that this superintendent turnover average is less than five years for urban school superintendents. We continue to see similar rates with building level leadership. That is, we continue to see increasing turnover rates of school principals in the United

Supporting Leaders for School Improvement Through Self-Care and Well-Being, pp. 21–34
Copyright © 2024 by Information Age Publishing
www.infoagepub.com
All rights of reproduction in any form reserved.

States. In a study conducted by Levin et al. (2020), for the National Association of Secondary School Principals (NASSP), it was determined that the national turnover rate of school principals was under four years. This same study found that "nearly one in five principals, approximately 18 percent, turnover annually" (p. 3). In a report released by *Education Week*, Superville (2019) found that the national principal turnover rate may in fact be somewhat higher. In this report, it was determined that nearly half of all principals leave around the three-year mark with an alarming 20% leaving annually (Superville, 2019). Although both superintendent and principal turnover are currently at alarming rates in the United States, this chapter will focus on the latter. That is, the authors of this chapter will focus the content on principal turnover in the United States. Furthermore, the authors will share possible causes for this increased turnover rate and offer potential evidence-based solutions to combat the principal turnover crisis. The authors will also highlight how principal turnover can negatively affect other school constructs, namely, student achievement. Finally, the authors hope this in-depth analysis will shed much needed light on this growing epidemic in the United States, while offering possible solutions for the dilemma.

Principal Turnover in the United States

The principal turnover rate continues to increase in the United States. In fact, today, many argue that the principal turnover rate in the United States has reached epidemic levels. As previously mentioned, the national turnover rate for school principals in the United States is currently somewhere between three and four years (Levin et al., 2020; Superville, 2019). In addition, as previously reported, somewhere between 18 and 20% of principals turnover annually (Levin et al., 2020; Superville, 2019). FutureEd (2019) reported this rate is now higher than the (turnover) rate for teachers. However, even these alarming rates tend to mask variation easily found within the data. For example, Levin and Bradley (2019) found that if we focus on principals in the United States who leave after two years on the job, the turnover rate jumps to 35%. Additionally, if we look at the other end of the spectrum, only 11% of principals are at their respective school buildings 10 years or more (Levin & Bradley, 2019). In a study analyzing principal turnover from the 2008–2009 academic school year compared to the 2012–2013 academic school year, it was determined that principal turnover has increased across all school types as well as within charter and traditional public schools (Goldring & Taie, 2014). In fact, the only school type that did not see an increase in principal turnover was private schools (Goldring & Taie, 2014). See Figure 2.1.

Figure 2.1

Principal Turnover

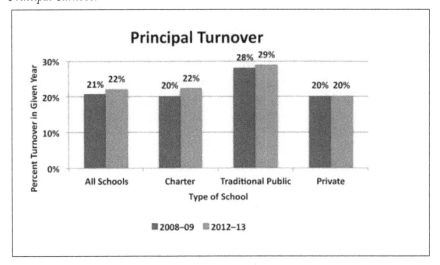

Note. ©The Wing Institute (2020). The Wing Institute utilized data from Goldring and Taie (2014) study to create Figure 2.1.

If we move to analyzing similar data points at the state level, we tend to find similar patterns. For example, if we look at one U.S. state from 2008–2011, we find that of 1,100 principals, more than 30% of the principals were no longer at the same school building, with another 10% leaving the state's PreK-12 educational system altogether (Davis & Anderson, 2021). Sadly, although these numbers are certainly alarming at both the national and state levels, they only get worse when we begin to analyze the turnover rates of principals serving our nation's poorest and lowest performing schools. In fact, Marzano et al. (2005) found that low-income students are much more likely to experience the negative effects of higher rates of principal turnover. In 2012, the National Education Policy Center (NEPC) released a report focused solely on examining principal turnover in the United States. In this report, the NEPC (2012) described that the state of Texas closed a school building for low academic performance, and later determined that the school had 13 principals in the 11 years leading up to the closure. Levin and Bradley (2019) found similar outcomes in their study as they determined that higher rates of principal turnover are more prevalent in high-poverty low-achieving schools. There is little to no doubt that we have a turnover crisis as it applies to the principalship in the United States, and the implications of such a turnover rate have devastating consequences for the students in those schools, especially, as it applies to our nation's low-income students.

Implications of Principal Turnover

Marzano et al. (2005), reported that that principals are second only to teachers in the classroom as it applies to overall influence on student achievement. In fact, they determined that principals account for around one quarter of total school effects on student achievement (Marzano et al., 2005). In the United States, and perhaps elsewhere, we tend to almost solely determine a school's success (or failure) based on student achievement. Thus, as one might imagine, it has long ago been determined that principals influence the academic achievement of students in a given. However, nailing down the effects of principal turnover can be all encompassing. That is, what can sometimes be harder to see, unless we look more closely, is that principal turnover negatively effects numerous other constructs in the educational setting, namely, teaching effectiveness and teacher retention, which in turn, ultimately negatively affect student achievement (Béteille et al., 2012; Burkhauser, et al., 2012; Robinson et al., 2008; Seashore et al., 2010). Nevertheless, the extant literature and research continues to show a statistically significant correlation between principal turnover and namely two constructs: (1) student achievement; and (2) teacher turnover.

As previously reported, principals account for about 25% of total influence on student achievement (Marzano et al., 2005). Other studies have found similar results. In a study by Harbatkin and Henry (2019), it was determined that principal turnover accounted for lower test scores and lower overall school proficiency rates. In yet another study (Bartanen et al., 2019), it was determined that principal turnover lowers school achievement. Study by study on principal turnover reports similar findings. In addition to negatively affecting student achievement, principal turnover negatively affects teacher retention. In a study by Bartanen et al. (2019), it was determined that principal turnover also accounted for increases in teacher turnover. Likewise, Harbatkin and Henry (2019) found similar results. Study after study reports an increase in teacher turnover in conjunction with principal turnover. Although other school constructs are most certainly negatively affected by principal turnover (i.e., climate and culture, the climate and culture of a given school, teacher self-efficacy, stakeholder engagement and satisfaction, recruitment, hiring, and onboarding of teachers, teacher evaluation outcomes, school safety, district finances, etc.), little to no research has linked such constructs directly to principal turnover. However, in more recent years, researchers have pivoted and begun to identify the possible causes for principal turnover in an effort to help combat this national crisis.

Possible Causes for Principal Turnover

In 2020, Levin et al. completed perhaps the most recent large-scale study focused on principal turnover to date. The study, consisting of 26 U.S. states and numerous focus groups found numerous factors that were contributing to principal turnover. Levin et al. (2020) reported the following factors as contributing to principal turnover:

- Heavy workload.
- Less than adequate student services personnel to support students' emotional well-being.
- Lack of district office support for their needs.
- Inequitable compensation.
- Student loan debt from principal preparation.
- State accountability measures that include:
    o *Principal evaluations.*
    o *State report cards.*
- Decision-making authority on:
    o *School's curriculum.*
    o *Poorly performing staff.*
- Lack of professional development and lack of support for professional development.

Additionally, and perhaps worth noting here, 42% of all respondents indicated they were considering leaving their principal position (Levin et al., 2020). This percentage was higher for principals who:

- Led a school that is considered to be high poverty.
- Led a school in a rural locale.

Interestingly, when we look at factors that lead to high employee turnover in other organizational settings, we see similar factors emerging. For example, in a report by Muniz (2017), it was found that low compensation, poor work/life balance, overscheduling, favoritism, and lax enforcement of labor rules were factors leading to high rates of employee turnover. As one can see, some of these same factors can easily seem transferable to the factors contributing to principal turnover. It begs the question, does principal turnover differ from other employee turnover? Nevertheless, as one might imagine, there are certainly other causes that may be considered outliers in addition to the aforementioned factors causing principal turnover (and employee turnover for that matter); however, by aiming to determine the causes of principal turnover, we might be able to more accurately and effectively determine solutions to this ongoing (and increasing) crisis.

Possible Solutions for Principal Turnover

As iterated in the previous section, only by beginning to determine the causes of principal turnover, can we better understand possible approaches to creating solutions to reduce the rates of principal turnover on a national scale. As previously reported, Levin et al. (2020) have conducted what is believed to be the most recent large-scale study on principal turnover. In doing so, Levin et al. shared numerous suggestions on how we might as a nation better retain our school principals. A summary of that list is included below followed by additional suggestions made by the authors of this chapter:

- Improve working conditions.
- Address school needs.
- Ensure equitable compensation.
- Improve principal evaluations policies, procedures, and processes as a whole:
    - *Feedback*
    - *Mentoring*
    - *Evaluations*
- Allow for autonomy and decision-making authority.
- Remove barriers to principal professional development.
- Support local efforts to support students.
- Help advocate for affordable high-quality principal preparation programs.

In addition to the possible solutions shared above, the authors also suggest other potential solutions that include (but are not limited to):

- Identify options for accelerated student loan forgiveness for practicing school leaders:
    - *Work with federal loan servicers to identify possible policy to be adopted and implemented.*

- Identify how districts can utilize funds to help pay for principal preparation.
- Identify external funding opportunities to help support professional development experiences for aspiring and practicing principals:
  - *Example: National Education Association's Learning and Leadership Grant for aspiring school leaders.*
- Provide meaningful in district professional development opportunities for principals.
- Identify and advocate for changes to local, state, and federal policy that contributes to the factors determined to cause principal turnover.
- Identify and implement low-cost initiatives and strategies to improve working conditions (including climate and culture).
  - *Example: Encourage, recognize, and celebrate principals often ... via social media outlets, and the like.*
- Ensure principal evaluation processes are meaningful, positive, and not seen as a punitive experience/process versus a process to improve and obtain timely and meaningful feedback.
  - *Work with state departments of education to ensure the required evaluation process supports the statements and characteristics above.*
- Implement district-wide mentoring programs for principals.
- Clearly define all decisions that are made at district office versus at the building level in an effort to avoid confusion as it applies to decision-making authority:
  - *Look at this through the lens of role theory.*
- Identify other school related characteristics (versus just state mandated achievement accountability results) to celebrate year-to-year.
- Ensure an equity audit data collection and analysis is conducted each academic school year (for the district as a whole and for each school building) and that SMART goals with timelines are created from the data collected and analyzed as part of this audit.

In addition to the strategies shared above, the authors would be remiss not to share the growing and effective trend of in-district principal pipelines.[2] Gates et al. (2019) reported that school districts who implemented in-district principal pipelines did a better job of retaining their principals. More specifically, when compared to other principal retention percentages in comparison schools, the study determined that principals were 5.8% more likely to remain in their school for at least two years and 7.8% more likely to remain in their school for at least three years if part of the principal pipeline initiative (Gates et al., 2019). The authors contend that amongst the strategies listed above as it applies to lowering principal turnover in the United States, in-district principal pipelines may be the most effective, affordable, and feasible strategy to combat this increasing pandemic. See Figure 2.2.

Nevertheless, the authors do not contend that the list above is all inclusive; however, it is certainly a start (and based on the most recent extant research and literature on causes to principal turnover) in sharing possible strategies to combat principal turnover in a given school district, across the United States. Finally, the authors of this chapter are both former practitioners in the field, and currently prepare our nation's aspiring principals, superintendents, and future professors who will prepare our nation's aspiring principals and superintendents. With that said, the authors agree that above all else, principals are more likely to be retained by districts and schools who have a positive climate and culture. All other school characteristics and student demographics aside, the authors contend that principals are more likely to stay in schools where they experience a positive work climate and culture. Many of the factors identified that seem to be contributing to our nation's principal turnover crisis can be linked back to school climate and culture. Thus, again, we contend that we start by examining what factors (causes) are more directly linked to a school's climate and culture, and begin our work there, to tackle this dilemma. Afterall, when

Figure 2.2

Principal Pipelines

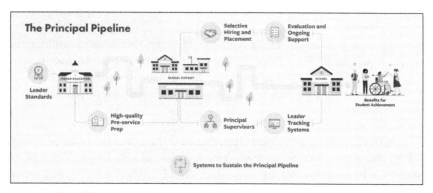

Note. © The Wallace Foundation (2020).

we look at the aforementioned Muniz (2017) article, we find similar factors for turnover for all employees across any given organizational setting. Similarly, when we look at *What makes people happy at work?* (Lattice Team, 2017), we can easily make connections to the very causes determined to cause principal turnover. Lattice Team (2017) reports that making enough money, having a good boss, having autonomy, variety, and healthy work-life balance, as the top five key contributing factors to happiness at work. Finally, in the same article, Lattice Team cites an article by Revesencio (2015) that reported that happy employees are 12% more productive than their unhappy counterparts. Thus, it does ultimately pay to foster a positive climate and culture in schools.

Discussion

Teachers enter the field enthusiastic to educate our youth and quickly recognize that being a teacher is far more than enlightening minds. Teachers carry the responsibility of caring for the whole child, their social, emotional, and educational needs, in addition to many other needs that arise for individual students. When moving into principalships, these responsibilities do not change, rather principals take on this responsibility for all the students in their schools. At the same time, taking on duties such as, to name a few, supervision, evaluation, training, and support for all teachers, relationships building with the community, parents, the district office and other stakeholders, data collection and analysis, implementing and sustaining policies, creating schedules, discipline, monitoring halls, assessments and improving the learning of all students (Dhuey & Smith, 2018; Tekleselassie & Choi, 2019). This is by no means an exhaustive list of principal responsibilities, but it does begin to paint the picture of why burnout happens. Again, principal turnover is high, as previously reported, nearly 20% of principal leave the field annually (Goldring & Taie, 2018) and 42% consider leaving at some point in their career (Levin et al., 2020). As discussed throughout this chapter, student achievement and teacher retention are statistically significantly correlated to principal turnover, therefore mitigating the attrition of high-quality principals is vital to our students and teachers' success. Worth noting here is that principal turnover impacts all schools, but even more so, our nation's low-performing schools, high poverty schools, rural schools, and schools serving diverse student bodies (Gates et al., 2006; Levin et al., 2020; Papa, 2007; Tekleselassie & Choi, 2019). Therefore, finding ways to strengthen our principals' well-being so they do not burnout, leave tough schools, or exit the field entirely must be a focus of both policy and practice.

The more experience principals have, the less likely they are to leave the field (Gates et al., 2006), similarly principals get better at managing the responsibilities of the position the longer they are in the position (Tekleselassie & Choi, 2019). This shows us that keeping our principals in the position is vital to student success. Principals that have left the field have explained that they would have liked more autonomy to make decisions and even more individualized feedback (Tekleselassie & Choi, 2019). The authors suggest that district leaders purposely and strategically support principals with meaningful professional development and guidance, instead of micromanaging their work and in effect taking away their autonomy to lead schools. This can certainly look different in each school/district, based on resources available. For example, some schools may have coprincipals, others may use lead teachers to help take on some administrative responsibilities. Not only could another administrative person help cover the duties required to run a school effectively but they can also offer emotional support to one another in a very tough and autonomous role.

Continuous education is another key to supporting our principals in the field. Beginning with quality principal preparation (Gates et al., 2019). Preparation programs must grow equity focused and ethically practiced school leaders that are knowledgeable of policy and skills but also aware of where to go for support when entering leadership roles. Likewise, professional development should be offered to all principals, both novice and experienced. Principals should be knowledgeable of the professional development of their teachers and staff experience but should also get professional development of their own, based on their needs and interests. Engaging in professional development can support principals beyond just learning new information, it can help them connect with like minds and gain support from their colleagues in the field. These supports and connections could in fact help principals feel less fatigued and result in less burnout.

When looking at how to positively impact student achievement, supporting principal retention should be among the discussions. However, it is important to note that not all principals are high quality principals, it is essential to support and help develop those principals that can become high quality as well as to weed out those that may be a better fit in other positions. One such way to be sure we are drawing in and developing high quality leaders is to monitor and get to know our school leaders. By building relationships with district level leadership and collaborating with other school leaders, principals begin to develop a leadership community and will be more apt to feel supported in their role. Additionally, finding ways to diversify the outreach for future principals and finding the "best-fit" (Dhuey & Smith, 2018) for the school and the leader could be very beneficial to the success and longevity of a principalship. That said, the school systems throughout the nation needs more principals from diverse backgrounds and experiences to serve our student population, therefore it would also behoove the education system to make recruitment of diverse candidates a focus starting in principal preparation programs. Lastly, supporting all of our principals through mentorships with experienced principals that are serving similar schools would be beneficial to their retention and overall well-being.

Recommendations and Resources for Practitioners in the Field

Principals serve a vital role in our schools, one that impacts the greater community, the teachers and most importantly the students. Finding innovative ways to support our school leaders is vital to their retention and well-being. We recognize the difficult position and extreme amount of responsibility with too little compensation. Therefore, we offer some practices and resources that might be of value to our practices and future principals. More so, do know you are not in this predicament alone and we recognize you and the work you do for our present and our future.

- Give yourself time for self-care, whatever that might look like (running, yoga, exercise, playing with your kids/grandkids, friends, quiet time, etc.). This is important to your own mental health and growth as a leader.
- Let yourself get away from your work. Have a separation, do not respond to all emails, all weekend and night. You have to allow yourself and your loved ones a healthy separation of life and work.
- Reach out to other principals, get into a principal networking group (perhaps through social media or state and local leadership associations). Surrounding yourself with colleagues in the field will both empower you and provide the understanding that you are not alone.
- Advocate for teacher retention through supporting teachers (i.e., professional development, self-care, mentorship), if your teachers are supported and happy the school culture and climate will show this, and the leadership role will be much less strenuous.
- Build a team at your school site that can help with decision making on things such as but not limited to budget development, data analysis, and schedules.

- Know that being a principal is a difficult position and that every day may not be perfect, but each day you can impact a student's life in a positive way.

Although this list is not extensive, the authors see it as a place in avoiding burnout and ensuring a healthy work-life balance, which we hope will lead to less principal turnover.

Conclusions and Recommendations for Future Considerations

As previously noted and discussed, there continues to be little to no extant literature or research on how principal turnover affects other school constructs that we know are tied to student achievement and teacher turnover. Such constructs include an array of identifiers the authors recommend that need further investigation. These constructs could be (but are certainly not limited to), the climate and culture of a given school, teacher self-efficacy, stakeholder engagement and satisfaction, recruitment, hiring, and onboarding of teachers, teacher evaluation outcomes, school safety, district finances, and more. Furthermore, when we start to categorize principal turnover into types (i.e., transfers, exits, promotions, and demotions) as some studies have achieved in the past, we begin to see how the type of principal turnover can affect other school constructs more or less negatively than others. For example, in a study by Bartanen et al. (2019), it found variations in the level of negative effects on student achievement based on turnover (or transition) types. In this study, they found the negative effect on student achievement to be more profound if the principal when a principal transfers to a different school or are promoted to district office (Bartanen et al., 2019). This is just one example; however, the authors recommend future research that not only collects and includes turnover type in the study, but also examines and investigates how principal turnover is tied to other school constructs that we know have long been tied to student achievement in a given school building. By doing so, the authors contend that such research will not only further highlight the continued principal turnover crisis in the United States, but do so in a way that allows us to more accurately determine the negative effects associated with the increasing crisis. Finally, the authors contend that by including the aforementioned additional constructs more consistently in future studies (i.e., the climate and culture of a given school, teacher self-efficacy, stakeholder engagement and satisfaction, recruitment, hiring, and onboarding of teachers, teacher evaluation outcomes, school safety, district finances), we can aim to determine the effect principal turnover has on other school constructs in addition to negative effects on student achievement and teacher retention. In doing so, we can further garner support in an effort to ensure policies and procedures are in place to better retain our nation's school leaders, which at the very least, will immediately and positively affect student achievement and teacher retention.

REFERENCES

Bartanen B., Grissom J. A., & Rogers L. K. (2019). The impacts of principal turnover. *Educational Evaluation and Policy Analysis, 41*(3), 350–374. https://doi.org/10.3102/0162373719855044

Béteille, T., Kalogrides, D., & Loeb, S. (2012). Stepping stones: Principal career paths and school outcomes. *Social Science Research, 41*(4), 904–919.

Burkhauser, S., Gates, S. M., Hamilton, L. S., & Ikemoto, G. S. (2012). *First-year principals in urban school districts: How actions and working conditions relate to outcomes.* Rand Corporation.

Davis, B. & Anderson, E. (2021). Visualizing differential principal turnover. *Journal of Educational Administration, 59*(2), 177–198. https://doi.org/10.1108/JEA-03-2020-0054

Dhuey, E., & Smith, J. (2018). How school principals influence student learning. *Empirical Economics, 54*, 851–882.

Falk, T. (2020, June 15). *High rate of turnover for school superintendents.* Urban Milwaukee. https://urbanmilwaukee.com/2020/06/15/high-rate-of-turnover-for-school-superintendents/

FutureEd. (2019). *The impacts of principal turnover.* https://www.future-ed.org/the-impact-of-principal-turnover/

Gates, S. M., Ringel, J. S., Santibanez, L., Guarino, C., Ghosh-Dastidar, B., & Brown, A. (2006). Mobility and turnover among school principals. *Economics of Education Review, 25*, 289–302.

Gates, S. M., Baird, M. D., Master, B. K., & Chavez-Herrerias, E. R. (2019). *Report—Principal pipelines: A feasible, affordable, and effective way for districts to improve schools.* https://www.wallacefoundation.org/knowledge-center/pages/principal-pipelines-a-feasible,-affordable,-and-effective-way-for-districts-to-improve-schools.aspx

Goldring, R., & Taie, S. (2018). *Principal attrition and mobility: Results from the 2016–17 principal follow-up survey* (NCES 2018-066) (Technical report). National Center for Education Statistics.

Harbatkin, E. & Henry, G. (2019). *The cascading effects of principal turnover on students and schools.* Brookings. https://www.brookings.edu/blog/brown-center-chalkboard/2019/10/21/the-cascading-effects-of-principal-turnover-on-students-and-schools/

Kowalski, T., McCord, R., Petersen, G., Young, I. P., & Ellerson, N. (2010). *The American school superintendent: 2010 decennial study.* Pearson.

Lattice Team. (2017). *What makes people happy at work?* https://lattice.com/library/what-makes-people-happy-at-work

Levin, S., Scott, C., Yang, M., Leung, M., & Bradley, K. (2020). *Supporting a strong, stable principal workforce: What matters and what can be done*. National Association of Secondary School Principals & Learning Policy Institute.

Levin, S., & Bradley, K. (2019). *Understanding and addressing principal turnover: A review of the research*. National Association of Secondary School Principals & Learning Policy Institute.

Marzano, R. J., Waters, T., & McNulty, B. A. (2005). *School leadership that works: From research to results*. Association for Supervision and Curriculum Development.

Muniz, K. (2017). *5 factors that lead to high employee turnover*. Finger Check. https://fingercheck.com/5-factors-that-lead-to-high-employee-turnover/

National Education Policy Center. (2012). *Examining principal turnover*. https://nepc.colorado.edu/blog/examining-principal-turnover

Papa, F. C. (2007). Why do principals change schools? A multivariate analysis of principal retention. *Leadership and Policy in Schools, 6*, 267–290.

Revesencio, J. (2015). *Why employees are 12% more productive*. The Future of Work. https://www.fastcompany.com/3048751/happy-employees-are-12-more-productive-at-work

Robinson, V. M. J., Lloyd, C. A., & Rowe, K. J. (2008). The impact of leadership on student outcomes: An analysis of the differential effects of leadership types. *Educational Administration Quarterly, 44*(5), 635–674.

Seashore, L., K., Leithwood, K., Wahlstrom, K. L., & Anderson, S. E. (2010). *Investigating the links to improved student learning: Final report of research findings*. The Wallace Foundation.

Superville, D. R. (2019). *Principal turnover is a problem: New data could help districts combat it*. Education Week. https://www.edweek.org/leadership/principal-turnover-is-a-problem-new-data-could-help-districts-combat-it/2019/12

Tekleselassie, A. A., & Choi, J. (2019). Understanding school attrition and mobility through hierarchical generalized linear modeling. *Educational Policy, 0*, 1–47.

The Wallace Foundation (2020). *The principal pipeline*. https://www.wallacefoundation.org/knowledge-center/PublishingImages/190405_WallaceFoundation_PrincipalPipeline_7_domains_w_title.jp

The Wing Institute (2020). *What is the turnover rate for school principals?* https://www.winginstitute.org/what-is-turnover-rate

NOTES

1. The study was replicated in 2019–2020 and the 2020 AASA Decennial Study is currently in review, to be published in late 2020.
2. "The term principal pipeline is shorthand for the range of talent management activities that fall within a school district's scope of responsibility when it comes to school leaders, including leader standards, preservice preparation opportunities for assistant principals and principals, selective hiring and placement, and on-the-job induction, evaluation, and support" (Gates et al., 2019).

CHAPTER 3

CONSIDERING HOW PROFESSIONAL NORMS AND PRACTICES INFLUENCE LEADERS' WELL-BEING

Kara Lasater, John C. Pijanowski, and Joshua Ray

School leaders are less healthy, more stressed, work longer hours, and less likely than the general population to engage in basic self-care practices (Ray et al., 2020). This is largely due to the complex demands of the job—a job that has grown more difficult, time-consuming, and stressful over the past two decades. In response to these demands, there are increasing calls from the field to better support leaders in developing the social and emotional competencies necessary to cope with extreme stress (Mahfouz & Richardson, 2020). We echo these calls; however, we also suggest that the time is ripe for systemic, cultural changes in the way school systems, university preparation programs, and governing bodies value and protect leaders' well-being.

The COVID-19 pandemic and social justice events of 2020 placed unprecedented pressure on school leaders to navigate through historic, catastrophic moments. COVID-19 created a sense of collective grief, stress, and uncertainty for communities worldwide, and it necessitated that leaders quickly develop supports to meet students and families' evolving needs. The events of 2020 also prompted deep, wide-ranging conversations about what we value as a society, and these conversations will likely spur lasting changes in *how* and *why* schools function. For many leaders, the struggle to preserve their physical, mental, and emotional health will be tested in ways heretofore unknown (Urick et al., 2021).

The multitude and magnitude of challenges currently facing school leaders necessitate a deeper awareness of, and commitment to, leaders' well-being. In this chapter, we explore professional norms that interfere with leaders' well-being. We begin by discussing the pressures leaders experience that make it difficult for them to attend to their own well-being and then describe the state of leaders' well-being given current professional norms; we conclude with a discussion of how present frameworks could be leveraged to intentionally shift professional norms and practices to protect and nurture leaders' well-being.

PROFESSIONAL NORMS THAT INTERFERE WITH WELL-BEING

Norms refer to the "implicit standards and values that evolve in working groups" (Schein, 2017, p. 4). They represent the consolidation of a group's beliefs, values, and assumptions and act as a blueprint to guide group members' expected behaviors (Deal & Peterson, 2009). Within the educational leadership field, multiple professional norms perpetuate unhealthy behaviors among school leaders. Not only do these professional norms make it difficult for leaders to practice effective self-care, they also stand in direct opposition to leaders' well-being.

External Demands

Perhaps the most dominant professional norm working against leaders' well-being is the expectation of universal availability. Examples of this include unannounced parent visits to school, the immediacy of student office referrals, and the number of stakeholders associated with a single leader. Email and other technologies have also contributed to the expectation of anytime, anywhere availability, making it difficult for principals to effectively manage their time. In a recent survey, 71% of principals identified spending time with family and friends as the most important aspect of their lives. Despite this belief, 87.5% of these leaders reported spending at least 30 extra minutes each day electronically communicating for work, and over 42.4% reported spending more than an additional hour each day (Ray et al., 2020). Though leaders valued time with family and friends, they sacrificed their personal time to remain electronically connected to the job. When asked about this, many leaders cited their need to be available to families and staff, while others indicated they struggle to keep up if they neglect email or text messages during personal time; a related reaction is that leaders face pressure to *immediately respond* to others' concerns and demands. The common trope of principals spending their days "putting out fires" has strengthened over time, and working to meet the external demands of others leaves leaders with little time to engage in the aspects of the work they value most (Ray et al., 2020; Theoharis, 2009).

The "always on" and "immediately responsive" norms of the profession contradict the purposeful nature of well-being by externalizing the locus of control for administrators. Rather than controlling the pace and structure of their professional day, leaders feel controlled by the impossible task of solving every problem as it arises. This reactionary approach extends beyond the school day through digital communication, eroding already limited personal time. While leaders may justify this as a means of "not falling behind," they unintentionally set professional precedents that give others license to expect their continued connection and immediate responsiveness. The result: school leaders perpetuate professional norms in which they are *expected* to sacrifice their own well-being to meet the ever-increasing demands of the job.

Internal Pressure

The sacrificial norms of educational leadership are further propelled by leaders' internal reactions to external demands, and these reactions serve to foster a martyrdom mentality within the profession. Caregiving professions, such as teaching, are built on a foundation of glorifying the importance of work to people and society. Long, hard hours of work and personal sacrifice are not only justified by how meaningful the work is, but they also become a mechanism for determining professional success. When professional success is defined by the amount, difficulty, and degree of personal sacrifice involved in the work, then a focus on wellness (either implicitly or explicitly) can symbolize a lack of professional competence and effort. For example, though leaders have the power to manage the times and places for responding to work emails, they fear what their delayed response might signal to others about their commitment and competence as a leader. Thus, they perceive decisions related to their own time management as beyond their control, and they react by throwing themselves even deeper into the work—because at least the work generates feelings of value and meaning. In essence, many leaders respond to external pressures by serving as martyrs for their schools and communities—so much so that martyrdom is a part of many leaders' professional identity. Once "living the job" becomes embedded in a principal's identity, rearranging priorities can feel impossible.

Unfortunately, the martyr mentality is perpetuated by the discourse of the field. This discourse acknowledges the intractable challenges facing school leaders and the costly emotional, mental, and physical toll these challenges take on leaders' well-being; yet, the discourse simultaneously implies that this toll is simply a sacrifice leaders must make to serve the greater good. Leaders in Theoharis (2009) described the sacrifices they made in the following ways: "I'm exhausted, my body aches, my soul feels wilted"; "I had no idea I would be tormented this way"; "[the work is] endangering my health and my family"; "I am gaining weight and losing sleep and drinking more": "there were periods of months when I vomited every morning": "every day I would cry alone in my office because I could see the pain that was being inflicted on kids ... I was ultimately responsible for that pain" (pp. 109–110). Similarly, leaders in Ray et al. (2020) reported sacrificing significant time with loved ones to meet professional demands, and principals in Pepper et al. (2010) described how they made personal sacrifices that placed them in acute physical danger while they led their schools through crises.

Leader martyrdom brings with it an inherent isolation that comes from a sense of "ultimate responsibility" for school success (Spillane & Lee, 2014, p. 442), and this sense competes with leaders' ability to delegate and collaborate. Because this mindset elevates the work ethic and inexhaustible nature of the leader, it feels counterproductive to share the load, as sharing the load might suggest personal failure and inadequacy. This creates a self-perpetuating cycle in which leaders find value in their ability to fix every problem, and under that assumption every problem is brought to them to fix. As these tasks overwhelm, leaders feed the expectation of self-neglect on behalf of the whole. Leaders in Ray (2019) illustrated this when stating, "Days that I don't have work, I can't have a hobby because I've already taken enough time from my family" and "After school I want to spend time with my own kids. I forfeit time for myself—exercise, hobbies, etc.—for more time with my family" (p. 104). Leaders who adopt this persona place unrealistic expectations on themselves and unwittingly solidify a professional norm that suggests self-preservation and well-being are incompatible with effective school leadership. As one principal described:

> I felt I always wanted to get more done. I tried to outwork the job. I would do more and more things, work harder, work longer.... My best tools coming into this position were that I could outwork and outthink just about anyone or any problem. (Theoharis, 2009, p. 126)

When leaders' value is enmeshed with their unique ability to outwork every problem, eventually their energy fades, fatigue sets in, and burnout soon follows.

Self-Care in Response to Demands and Pressure

In response to these challenges, the discourse of the field suggests that school leaders should practice effective self-care (Pepper et al., 2010). This has led to a new professional norm, at least in rhetoric, in which self-care is recognized as an important aspect of leadership sustainability; increased activity from scholars and practitioners recognizes the difficulties school leaders face in managing their own wellness and identifies ways they can better sustain their physical and mental health. While well-intentioned, however, attempts to create new professional norms of self-care can be problematic. Counter to its purpose, the rhetoric of self-care can place additional stress and responsibility on leaders' shoulders. Amid 60- to 80-hour work weeks, leaders often struggle to find time to exercise, meditate, meal plan, spend time with family, pursue a hobby, and sleep seven to eight hours each night. The promotion of self-care seemingly overlooks the fact that there are only 24 hours in each day, and encouraging leaders to add self-care to their already demanding schedules risks setting yet another professional expectation that is impossible for them to meet.

It is also troubling that self-care strategies are sometimes framed as a mechanism for leadership preservation and not as strategies intended to promote leaders' overall well-being. As Theoharis (2009) states:

> Without mechanisms of self-care, leaders capable of creating more just and equitable schools can burn out. This can lead to the principal's either leaving the position that so desperately needs him or her or slowly but steadily accepting a compromised vision of equity. Both these options are equally bleak. (p. 128)

This message implies that the only reason self-care matters is to prevent leaders from leaving the field or becoming less effective at their jobs—pushing aside the primary goal of leader well-being. There is danger in suggesting that the *only* reason leaders' well-being matters is because of its broader impact on the organization and field. This discourse serves to perpetuate the martyr mentality and contributes to the downward spiral of leaders' well-being, because in response to incredible demands, leaders cope by working even harder—sacrificing more of themselves to fulfill the unrelenting demands of the profession (Theoharis, 2009).

CURRENT STATE OF LEADERS' WELL-BEING

Meeting Impossible Expectations

In pursuit of unrealistic expectations, school leaders often push themselves beyond healthy limits to pursue success for their schools. Research from New Zealand suggests that principals experience significantly higher rates of burnout, stress, and sleeplessness than other professions (Nicoll, 2018). In the United States, one survey showed that 67% of administrators intended to leave their positions within five years (Moore, 2018), and another survey indicated that school leaders spent 16.55 more hours working each week than the average American (Ray et al., 2020).

While many school leaders quietly carry the burden of the job, for many others it is too much to bear. In a 2020 survey, 42% of principals in the United States indicated that they considered leaving the principalship (Levin et al., 2020). The top three reasons prompting their potential exodus: an untenable workload, lack of support, and inadequate time and resources to meet compliance requirements. As one principal described, the job can be all-consuming:

> When you go into the principalship ... you know that it's not a 7 to 3 or whatever job. It's all the time, really. And there are a lot of commitments that are on the weekends or in the evening and things like that. And that is the job. Those aren't extras ... if you don't understand that, then it's probably not the right job for you. (Levin et al., 2020, p. 14)

Sadly, many educators fully understand the demands of the job and are choosing *not* to enter the principalship as a result (Davis et al., 2017; DiPaola & Tschannen-Moran, 2003). Ultimately, the complex challenges leaders face amid unrelenting pressure "reflect a reality that the position of principal continues to move in the direction of impossibility" (Theoharis, 2009, p. 112).

Rising Job Pressures

The impossibility of the job is more obvious today than ever before. The COVID-19 pandemic magnified the demands placed on schools to care for students and families, and the mechanisms traditionally available to meet those needs were challenged. Schools were forced to quickly develop new systems for delivering school-based services that complied with public health protocols (e.g., stay-at-home orders, social distancing)—making an already stressful job immeasurably more stressful.

The summer of 2020 also galvanized the nation around issues of social justice. Educational institutions faced increased scrutiny for their role in perpetuating systemic injustices, and the need for school leaders to actively confront social injustices moved to the forefront of educational conversations. While the events of 2020 created unique challenges for school leaders, they also represent the types of complex, unforeseen, and uncontainable circumstances that schools are particularly vulnerable to and will experience far beyond the pandemic (Pepper et al., 2010).

HOPE FOR THE FIELD: SHIFTING PROFESSIONAL NORMS AND PRACTICES

Despite the barriers, there is hope moving forward. The field is changing, and leaders have the power to actively shape these changes (Stone-Johnson & Weiner, 2020)—*if* they are ready and willing to leverage the moment. In the rest of this chapter, we describe ways in which the field could collectively establish healthy, productive professional norms and practices that are truly supportive of leaders' well-being.

From Self-Care to Well-Being

Recently, the language of the field has started to shift from "self-care" to "well-being." This represents a subtle shift, but it has important implications for the field. Self-care refers to individualistic attendance to one's physical or psychological health. It is the process by which one seeks to achieve well-being. Well-being, on the other hand, represents the condition of being healthy.

Three key points relate to the shift from self-care to well-being. First, self-care is a means to an end, with the intended goal of personal well-being. Unfortunately, however, in educational leadership, this desired end has been distorted so that it no longer reflects an interest in well-being but a relentless dedication to the field. Shifting the focus from self-care to well-being reorients the field toward the desired outcome of healthy, thriving individuals.

Second, self-care refers to activities (e.g., exercising and meditating) that help an individual cope with the stresses of life. Self-care practices, however, do *not* uncover the underlying sources of stress; in effect, they work to ameliorate the symptoms of stress but do nothing to change its root cause. For example, Theoharis (2009) described principals using multiple strategies to cope with the challenges of their positions; yet, not all of these strategies (e.g., working harder and drinking more alcohol) were advantageous to the leaders' well-being, and many leaders reported experiencing tremendous amounts of stress and anxiety despite their respective self-care practices. Thus, while self-care may help reduce occasional feelings of stress, it is possible for leaders to engage in multiple self-care practices and still experience stress at debilitating levels and duration.

Finally, self-care places the onus for action exclusively on the individual (i.e., the school leader). This not only drops yet another responsibility on the shoulders of overburdened individuals, but it also misrepresents or totally obscures the root cause of the problem. The problem, then, is not school leaders' poor self-care. The problem is the overwhelming amount of stress associated with the work, coupled with increasingly unrealistic expectations about how leaders should respond to this stress.

Shifting toward well-being represents an important movement for school leaders. Because self-care practices do not look for root causes of stress, they can only provide leaders with temporary respite from stress and anxiety. School leaders may experience short-term rest and rejuvenation after engaging in self-care but find themselves quickly returning to previous levels of stress once back at work. Conversely, well-being necessitates a focus on persistent health outcomes, and as such necessitates attending to the underlying sources of leaders' stress. In this way, focusing on well-being shifts the conversation from *enduring* stress to actively *decreasing* it. Finally, unlike self-care, well-being constitutes collective work. It represents a shared commitment to and responsibility for others' health outcomes. Thus, one way the field can leverage the current moment is to refrain from mantras of leader self-care and instead advocate for a heightened focus on leaders' well-being.

Sense of agency. Sense of agency is a leader's belief that they can exert control over professional decisions and that their professional decisions can meaningfully shape practice. This is an ability that the field can support leaders in developing. The demands of the profession are undoubtedly stressful, but it is leaders' lack of agency amid these demands that can cause additional stress and frustration. District-level bureaucracy, institutional-level regulations, and state and federal mandates can limit leaders' sense of agency, and this constraint can lead educators to feel distrusted, deprofessionalized, powerless, and immobilized (Connolly et al., 2018; Daly, 2009; Tschannen-Moran, 2004).

Even within these limitations, however, leaders can develop a sense of agency related to their professional decision-making and personal well-being. In fact, the COVID-19 pandemic and social justice events of 2020 uniquely set the stage for leaders to exercise agency and advocate on behalf of their own and others' well-being:

> Decoupled from many state-level accountability measures, principals can emphasize what matters: community, relationships, health and safety. While it may have taken a devastating disease to shine the light on what is important, the opportunity to ensure that the message continues can and should be led by principals. The public nature of school leadership work supporting students, families and their communities necessitates our deeper exploration of principal professionalism, as the current context of COVID-19 both bounds and broadens it. Principals may not have much of a voice in whether or how schools should reopen, but they can be loud and clear about what matters in the process. Such work may not only help their school communities; it might ultimately be the cornerstone of building a

true profession—valuing expertise, promoting autonomy, developing an ethic of service and rewarding the work of principals. (Stone-Johnson & Weiner, 2020, p. 6)

There are multiple ways educational leaders can develop a sense of agency in their work. First, they must seize opportunities to exercise their voice in systems-based decision making. District leaders can assist in this process by creating opportunities for school leaders to share input and establishing district policies and procedures that provide school leaders with autonomy *and* support in their work, which is central to personal well-being and positive workplace attitudes, engagement, and behaviors (Slemp et al., 2018). School leaders must also create opportunities for others to authentically engage in site-based decisions. When leaders create opportunities for others to share their perspectives and actively participate in building-level decision making, they can establish a culture in which professional agency is valued and fostered.

Leaders must also develop a sense of self-efficacy related to their work. This can be challenging in a complex, ever-changing profession with few available measures of performance; however, leaders who "have a firm belief in their efficacy, through ingenuity and perseverance, figure out ways of exercising some control, even in environments containing limited opportunities and many constraints" (Bandura, 1993, p. 125). One way leaders can develop self-efficacy is to "disentangle" from their stress, anxiety, and upsetting emotions (Murphy, 2016, p. 111). As Bandura (1982) explains:

> People rely partly on information from their physiological state in judging their capabilities. They read their visceral arousal in stressful and taxing situations as an ominous sign of vulnerability to dysfunction. Because high arousal usually debilitates performance, people are more inclined to expect success when they are not beset by aversive arousal than if they are tense and viscerally agitated. In activities involving strength and stamina, people read their fatigue, aches, and pains as indicants of physical inefficacy. (p. 127)

In other words, leaders interpret their own stress and anxiety as signs of ineptitude and are unlikely to develop a sense of agency in their work while simultaneously feeling ineffective at it. Thus, it is important that leaders learn to experience their negative emotions without *being* their negative emotions. Mindful practices can help leaders develop the mental acuity necessary to acknowledge upsets without being "totally entangled, defined, or consumed by them" (Murphy, 2016, p. 111). Mindfulness not only helps leaders develop self-efficacy in controlling negative thoughts, it can also help reduce leaders' stress and depression and subsequently improve leaders' overall sense of self-efficacy (Bandura, 1993, p. 133).

Leading with mindfulness. Perhaps one of the most powerful tools to support leaders' well-being is mindfulness. School leaders spend considerable time ruminating on past events and future decisions, and this rumination can have a detrimental impact on their overall well-being (Murphy, 2016). Mindfulness can help leaders overcome this stress and perhaps obsessive rumination by reinforcing the ability to remain fully engaged in the present moment (Mahfouz, 2020).

Murphy (2016) offers several exercises that can assist leaders in developing mindfulness and enhancing their well-being. These exercises are designed to assist leaders in identifying their core values, developing awareness in the present, disengaging from their emotional upsets, recognizing their personal needs, exhibiting self-compassion, and expressing their emotions. Mindfulness exercises that encourage leaders to slow down, recognize their senses, and remain attentive within the present moment—such as, "Mindful Breathing," "Sounds Galore," "Soulful Standing," "Five-Sense Pause," and "Six-Shooter Retort" (Murphy, 2016, pp. 89–98)—may be particularly valuable for leaders during times of extreme stress and uncertainty. Not only do these mindful strategies help reduce leaders' stress, but they also can help leaders "evaluate and improve their leadership skills, especially when dealing with difficult situations" (Mahfouz, 2018, p. 610).

Finally, mindfulness can help leaders harness their sense of power. Leaders, like most people, are prone to living through their reflection on past mistakes or misfortunes and anticipating (often worrying about) future outcomes, yet the only time leaders have any power to act or react is when something actually happens—that is, in the present moment (Murphy, 2016). Learning to live in the moment can help leaders avoid unhealthy distractions of a past they cannot change or a future that has not happened yet and develop a sense of agency in their work by engaging with others in more authentic and compassionate ways.

Shared leadership and collective responsibility. Practically, one of the simplest defenses against the martyr mentality is the collective responsibility of shared leadership and promoting renewal by reflecting with others (Drago-Severson, 2012). Many schools are adopting collaborative processes of decision making that empower staff, enhance professional agency, and ease the isolation of school leaders. While shared leadership requires true vulnerability and transparency by the leader, it also allows for collective intelligence and problem solving that exceeds what is possible from any individual; in addition, it fosters trust within the organization (Tschannen-Moran, 2004). Any division between a leader and staff naturally shrinks as school-wide representation is used in active decision making. Schools that share the load lend themselves to a collaborative process that values the collective while protecting the individual. Such a school culture is primed for the systemic promotion of well-being.

Establishing Professional Norms of Well-Being

Ways exist in which school leaders, leadership preparation programs, and professional organizations can collaboratively work to reshape the norms of the profession to support well-being. Leaders can shift professional norms by intentionally demonstrating openness and vulnerability in their work. Current professional norms, however, perpetuate the image of leaders as consummate professionals. Embedded in this image is the expectation that leaders are "always available" and "always on"—an expectation that stands in direct opposition to leaders' well-being. Thus, rather than working to *protect* the image of consummate professional, leaders can work to dispel it by communicating authentically and transparently about their limitations, mistakes, challenges, need for assistance, and interests and concerns outside the school context. When leaders demonstrate humility, openness, and vulnerability, it allows others to recognize their humanity, and in doing so creates opportunities for leaders to establish trusting, compassionate relationships that are supportive of well-being (Ray et al., 2020; Tschannen-Moran, 2004). It may be difficult for leaders to demonstrate this level of vulnerability, particularly if they feel compelled to project the image of a strong leader who is capable of independently handling difficult tasks. Thus, preparation programs and professional organizations must also support leaders in re-norming the profession toward well-being.

Leadership preparation programs can assist in re-norming the profession by moving well-being to the center of leader development. The National Educational Leadership Preparation (NELP) Program Recognition Standards can support this shift (National Policy Board for Educational Administration [NPBEA], 2018). The NELP standards emphasize the need for educational leaders to promote the success and well-being of all students and adults within the school community. In fact, seven out of eight standards specifically include language related to student and adult well-being (NPBEA, 2018). Leadership preparation programs can respond to this call by ensuring that well-being is central in all programmatic decisions. Specifically, preparation programs could ensure that course readings, assignments, and internship experiences are designed to emphasize and promote well-being. For example, faculty in the Educational Leadership program at the University of Arkansas host an annual doctoral seminar focused on well-being, and they center well-being in student mentorship activities (Lasater et al., 2021).

Additionally, educational leaders, leadership preparation programs, and professional organizations can reconceptualize how leadership success is defined and measured. Currently, the Professional Standards for Educational Leaders (PSEL) reflect a "holistic view of leadership" (NPBEA, 2015, p. 3). For example, educational leaders are expected to "safeguard and promote the values of democracy, individual freedom and responsibility, equity, social justice, community, and diversity" (p. 10). They are also called to "confront and alter institutional biases of student marginalization, deficit-based schooling, and low expectations associated with race, class, culture and language, gender and sexual orientation, and disability or special status" (p. 11). Despite this holistic view, the most notable, publicly recognized *measure* of leader success is school performance on standardized assessments—a measure that provides limited insight into the leader's ability to "confront and alter institutional biases" or "promote the values of democracy." Within the field, there is an apparent disconnect between leader expectations and measures of leader success. This disconnect can result in leaders feeling vulnerable in the face of high-stakes accountability and eager to demonstrate their proficiency in other tangible ways. The seemingly most concrete, quantifiable way leaders can demonstrate their worth is time spent on the job. In this sense, the martyr mentality can be self-serving as leaders use time and personal sacrifices as mechanisms to validate their own self-worth.

The field must develop new measures of leader proficiency and school effectiveness that more closely align with the PSEL and appropriately reflect the time needed to engage in the complex work of school leadership. Because "traditional policy definitions of success such as standardized test scores may be momentarily 'out the door,' it will be up to those on the ground to temporarily define success on their own terms" (Stone-Johnson & Weiner, 2020, p. 4). Reconceptualizing how leadership success is defined and measured could support leaders' well-being, increase their sense of self-efficacy, and subsequently improve their overall performance (Bandura, 1993).

Engaging in Compassionate Leadership

Finally, the field can promote well-being by engaging in compassionate leadership and establishing organizational compassion within schools. Compassionate leadership is based on the principles of compassionate care. Compassionate care involves noticing, feeling, and responding to others' vulnerability or suffering (Dewar et al., 2013). It is the willingness to recognize others' experiences, engage in those experiences with them, and respond in ways that are uniquely meaningful to them. As part of their daily practice, compassionate leaders engage in the interpersonal aspects (e.g., open listening) of compassionate care. They also value and prioritize compassion as a central component of organizational functioning (de Zulueta, 2016). Leaders foster school cultures of compassion by developing systems, routines, practices, and policies that legitimate, propagate, and coordinate compassion at the organizational level (Frost et al., 2006; Kanov et al., 2004).

There are multiple ways compassionate care can enhance well-being. First, compassionate care is "inherently reciprocal—it happens within and between people" (de Zulueta, 2016, p. 2). Thus, as leaders demonstrate compassion for others, they simultaneously increase the likelihood of being on the receiving end of others' compassion. Second, compassionate organizations legitimate the expression of feelings and vulnerability (Frost et al., 2006). This open expression of such emotions is not only psychologically healthy, it also prompts coordinated, compassionate responding at the organizational level to educators' distress and suffering (Frost et al., 2006; Kanov et al., 2004). Third, collective compassion strengthens feelings of connection (Kanov et al., 2004), and this connectedness stands in direct opposition to the isolation and sense of personal liability that impede leaders' well-being. Finally, when supported at the organizational level, compassionate care does not burden, cause fatigue in, or burn out care providers; rather, it rejuvenates, energizes, and nurtures their well-being and provides them with a sense of resilience, solidarity, and fulfillment within the work (see Dewar et al., 2013; de Zulueta, 2016; Kanov et al., 2004). Ultimately, by establishing collective compassion within schools, leaders could shift the experiences of educators from merely *surviving* challenges to *thriving* in the midst of them.

CONCLUSION

Dismantling deeply reinforced professional norms and practices that interfere with well-being is no easy undertaking; nevertheless, it is imperative for the field to recognize well-being, compassion, and the care of others as "central to and expressive of the very essence of being human" (Frost et al., 2006, p. 859). Never has more been asked, expected, or needed from school leaders, and many leaders will undoubtedly respond to the challenging events of 2020 by making tremendous personal sacrifices (see Pepper et al., 2010). In return, the field must work to shift professional norms and practices to support leaders' holistic well-being. In doing so, we create opportunities for healing, restoration, and rejuvenation—not just for school leaders, but also for the students, families, schools, and communities that wholeheartedly need them.

RECOMMENDED PRACTICES FOR LEADERS

- Promote a culture of well-being in your school by routinely engaging students, staff, district administration, and community members in dialogue around health and well-being and actively celebrating behaviors aligned with well-being.
- Share your personal stories related to the individual pursuit of well-being. This could inform the establishment of professional norms specifically targeting protection of well-being, such as an intentional moratorium on digital, professional communication at a certain point in the evening as part of an organizational commitment to protecting individual work-life balance.
- Align school resources to reflect the pursuit of organizational well-being. This could include a water bottle filling station for staff, purchasing (and collectively studying) literature specific to well-being, or a dedicated quiet place in the building for mindfulness practices.

ADDITIONAL RESOURCES FOR PRACTITIONERS

Compassionate Leadership

- Compassionate Schools Project, developed in partnership with the University of Virginia and Jefferson County Public Schools. https://www.compassionschools.org/
- Compassion Resilience, developed in partnership with WISE, Rogers InHealth, and the Wisconsin Department of Public Instruction. https://compassionresiliencetoolkit.org/schools/

Mental Health

- *Beyond worry: How psychologists help with anxiety disorders*. American Psychological Association. https://www.apa.org/topics/anxiety-disorders
- *Overcoming depression: How psychologists help with depressive disorders.* American Psychological Association. https://www.apa.org/topics/overcoming-depression
- *Strategies for controlling your anger.* American Psychological Association. https://www.apa.org/topics/strategies-controlling-anger

Mindfulness

- *Guided meditations.* Healthy Minds Innovations. https://www.youtube.com/channel/UC6e0PDxWZRET6QdSMmPSyQQ
- Jha, A. (2018) *How to tame your wandering mind.* [Ted Talk]. https://www.ted.com/talks/amishi_jha_how_to_tame_your_wandering_mind
- Murphy, J. T. (2016). *Dancing in the rain: Leading with compassion, vitality, and mindfulness in education.* Harvard Education Press.

Physical Health

- Walker, M. (2019). *Sleep is your super power.* [TedTalk]. https://www.ted.com/talks/matt_walker_sleep_is_your_superpower?language=en
- *Improving physical activity in your community.* U.S Department of Health and Human Services. https://www.hhs.gov/fitness/resource-center/physical-activity-resources/index.html

REFERENCES

Bandura, A. (1982). Self-efficacy mechanism in human agency. *American Psychologist, 37*(2), 122–147.

Bandura, A. (1993). Perceived self-efficacy in cognitive development and functioning. *Educational Psychologist, 28*(2), 117–148.

Connolly, M., Hadfield, M., Barnes, Y., & Snook, J. (2018). The accommodation of contested identities: The impact of participation in a practice-based masters programme on beginning teachers' professional identity and sense of agency. *Teaching and Teacher Education, 71,* 241–250. https://doi.org/10.1016/j.tate.2018.01.010

Daly, A. J. (2009). Rigid response in an age of accountability: The potential of leadership and trust. *Educational Administration Quarterly, 45*(2), 168–216. https://doi.org/10.1177/0013161X08330499

Davis, B. W., Gooden, M. A., & Bowers, A. J. (2017). Pathways to the principalship: An event history analysis of the careers of teachers with principal certification. *American Educational Research Journal, 54*(2), 207–240. https://doi.org/10.3102/0002831216687530

Deal, T. E., & Peterson, K. D. (2009). *Shaping school culture: Pitfalls, paradoxes, & promises* (2nd ed.). Jossey-Bass.

Dewar, B., Adamson, E., Smith, S., Surfleet, J., & King, L. (2013). Clarifying misconceptions about compassionate care. *Journal of Advanced Nursing, 70*(8), 1738–1747. http://dx.doi.org/10.1111/jan.12322

de Zulueta, P. C. (2016). Developing compassionate leadership in health care: An integrative review. *Journal of Healthcare Leadership, 8*, 1–10. http://dx.doi.org/10.2147/JHL.S93724

DiPaola, M., & Tschannen-Moran, M. (2003). The principalship at a crossroads: A study of the conditions and concerns of principals. *NASSP Bulletin, 87*(634), 43–65. https://doi.org/10.1177/019263650308763404

Drago-Severson, E. (2012). The need for principal renewal: The promise of sustaining principals through principal-to-principal reflective practice. *Teachers College Record, 114*(12), 1–56.

Frost, P. J., Dutton, J. E., Maitlis, S., Lilius, J. M., Kanov, J. M., & Worline, M. C. (2006). Seeing organizations differently: Three lenses on compassion. In C. Hardy, S. Clegg, T. Lawrence, & W. Nord (Eds.), *Handbook of organizational studies* (2nd ed., pp. 843–866). SAGE.

Kanov, J. M., Maitlis, S., Worline, M., Dutton, J. E., Frost, P. J., & Lilius, J. M. (2004). Compassion in organizational life. *American Behavioral Scientist, 47*(6), 808–827. https://doi.org/10.1177/0002764203260211

Lasater, K., Smith, C., Pijanowski, J., & Brady, K. P. (2021). Redefining mentorship in an era of crisis: responding to COVID-19 through compassionate relationships. *International Journal of Mentoring and Coaching in Education, 10*(2), 158-172. https://doi.org/10.1108/IJMCE-11-2020-0078

Levin, S., Scott, C., Yang, M., Leung, M., & Bradley, K. (2020). *Supporting a strong, stable principal workforce: What matters and what can be done*. Learning Policy Institute. https://learningpolicyinstitute.org/sites/default/files/product-files/NASSP_LPI_Supporting_Strong_Stable_Principal_Workforce_REPORT.pdf

Mahfouz, J. (2018). Mindfulness training for school administrators: Effects on well-being and leadership. *Journal of Educational Administration, 56*(6), 602–619. https://doi.org/10.1108/JEA-12-2017-0171

Mahfouz, J. (2020). Principals and stress: Few coping strategies for abundant stressors. *Educational Management Administration & Leadership, 48*(3), 440–458. https://doi.org/10.1177/1741143218817562

Mahfouz, J., & Richardson, J. (2020). At the crossroads: Wellbeing and principalship preparation. *Journal of Research on Leadership Education*. Advance online publication. https://doi.org/10.1177/1942775120933914

Moore, J. (2018, September 4). [Broadcast]. *Stressed out: two-thirds of DC principals say they may leave job within 5 years, survey finds*. WTOP News. https://wtop.com/dc/2018/09/stressed-out-two-thirds-of-dc-principals-say-they-may-leave-job-within-5-years-survey-finds/

Murphy, J. T. (2016). *Dancing in the rain: Leading with compassion, vitality, and mindfulness in education*. Harvard Education Press.

Nicoll, J. (2018, March 1). *Survey reveals primary school principals are overworked and struggling to sleep*. Stuff. https://www.stuff.co.nz/national/education/101884413/survey-reveals-primary-schoolprincipals-are-overworked-and-struggling-to-sleep

National Policy Board for Educational Administration. (2015). *Professional Standards for Educational Leaders 2015*. http://www.npbea.org/wp-content/uploads/2017/06/Professional-Standards-for-Educational-Leaders_2015.pdf

National Policy Board for Educational Administration. (2018). *National Educational Leadership Preparation (NELP) Program Standards—Building Level*. http://www.npbea.org/wp-content/uploads/2018/11/NELP-Building-Standards.pdf

Pepper, M. J., London, T. D., Dishman, M. L., & Lewis, J. L. (2010). *Leading schools during crisis: What school administrators must know*. Rowman & Littlefield Education.

Ray, J. (2019). *Crumbling foundations: The case for prioritizing self-care among educational leaders* (Publication No. 13881652) [Doctoral dissertation, University of Arkansas]. ProQuest Dissertations and Theses.

Ray, J., Pijanowski, J., & Lasater, K. (2020). The self-care practices of school principals. *Journal of Educational Administration*, *58*(4), 435–451. https://doi.org/10.1108/JEA-04-2019-0073

Schein, E. H. (2017). *Organizational culture and leadership* (5th ed.). Wiley.

Slemp, G. R., Kern, M. L., Patrick, K. J., & Ryan, R. M. (2018). Leader autonomy support in the workplace: A meta-analytic review. *Motivation and Emotion*, *42*(5), 706–724. https://doi.org/10.1007/s11031-018-9698-y

Spillane, J., & Lee, L. (2014). Novice school principals' sense of ultimate responsibility: Problems of practice in transitioning to the principal's office. *Educational Administration Quarterly*, *50*(3), 431–465. https://doi.org/10.1177/0013161X13505290

Stone-Johnson, C., & Weiner, J. M. (2020). Principal professionalism in the time of COVID-19. *Journal of Professional Capital and Community*. Advance online publication. https://doi.org/10.1108/JPCC-05-2020-0020

Theoharis, G. (2009). *The school leaders our children deserve: Seven keys to equity, social justice, and school reform*. Teachers College Press.

Tschannen-Moran, M. (2004). *Trust matters: Leadership for successful schools*. Jossey-Bass.

Urick, A., Carpenter, B. W., & Eckert, J. (2021). Confronting COVID: Crisis leadership, turbulence, and self-care. *Frontiers in Education*, *6*, Article 642861. https://doi.org/ 10.3389/feduc.2021.642861

CHAPTER 4

BUILDING A SCHOOL LEADER'S PERSONAL WELL-BEING PLAN

Vicki Bautista and Gretchen Oltman

WELL-BEING AND THE SCHOOL LEADER

Today's school leaders face an unprecedented level of job-related stressors. While many professionals have adapted a balanced work-life approach, at times it seems the school leader is left behind on wellness and well-being efforts that just do not seem to fit the daily life of a school leader. Demands on school leaders to perform at exemplary levels while ensuring that every student meets highly ambitious academic goals comes from multiple layers—the federal and state government, the school district, the local school board, the community, parents, and of course, and most important, the students themselves. Growing pressures facing school leaders are well documented in the literature and identify that in most school leadership settings, chronic pressure and high expectations generate long-lasting stress, much of which leads to burnout and high turnover rates. As such, school leaders, who spend much of their time serving others, often place their own health, wellness, and emotional well-being as secondary to the more immediate demands of the school day. This in turn leads to personal and professional burnout, emotional instability, and physical manifestations of unhealthy habits. The role of school leader, as rewarding and fulfilling as it can be, must be carefully managed in order to ensure longevity in the position.

The average tenure of a superintendent, according to the School Superintendents Association (AASA), is five to six years, with an annual turnover rate of 14 to 16% (AASA, 2006). A national survey conducted by Robinson and Shakeshaft (2016) found that an analysis to better understand the link between a superintendent's level of stress, health, and well-being status produced alarming results. The top stressors included dealing with changing state and federal regulations, hours required daily by the job, inadequate school finances, poor work-life balance, and challenges of student testing and performance accountability. Of the superintendents sampled, the researchers found health conditions developed while in the superintendency were insomnia, high blood pressure, obesity, high cholesterol, gastrointestinal problems, anxiety, and chronic headaches. Furthermore, school principals average just five years of service in the position. Principals identify insufficient time to get the job done, diminished revenues, constant interruptions, volumes of paperwork, keeping up with email communication, work-life balance, loss of personal self-care time, ever-increasing job expectations, more demanding teacher evaluations, and feelings of being overwhelmed with job demands in general as the main stressors of the position (Wells & Klocko, 2018).

Complex school administrator roles can challenge school leaders to separate their professional and administrative responsibilities from their personal well-being—in essence, pretending that one does not impact the other. As a result, a conflict arises wherein a dual identity with a separation of personal and professional concerns causes dissention in priorities and where the school leader places priority. In managing numerous roles ranging from administrator, visionary, colleague, mentor, and teacher, it is imperative that school leaders consider their own role in promoting well-being and self-care for those they lead as well as for themselves. These two roles are not exclusive and do not live in isolation from each other. The fact remains, though, that school leaders are often driven to do more with less and to keep moving forward in an effort to provide a successful learning environment for students, even at their own personal expense.

It remains, however, readily within the school leader's responsibility to protect their own well-being; that is, school leaders need to work to create both coping mechanisms and health and wellness programs for themselves rather than relying on fate or employer-sponsored wellness programs to substitute for a personalized well-being plan.

KEY TERMS

As we discuss well-being in the field of school leadership, it is important to draw attention to certain key terms and their meanings. The following list provides context for the key terms used throughout this chapter.

This term was first used in a clinical sense by Herbert Freudenberger, an American psychoanalyst (Maslach & Leiter, 2006). In his 1981 book *Burnout: The High Cost of High Achievement*, Freudenberger described burnout as the loss of motivation or incentive, especially where one's devotion to a cause or relationship fails to produce the desired results. In more modern terms, according to the World Health Organization, burnout is known as a syndrome resulting from chronic workplace stress that has not been successfully managed (World Health Organization, 2019).

The harmful physical and emotional responses that can occur when the requirements of a job do not match the capabilities, resources, or needs of the worker. Job stress can lead to poor health, including psychological and physiological symptoms and even injury (National Institute for Occupational Safety and Health, 2014).

The process of actively working toward the goal of supporting holistic well-being. A basic set of six components must be considered to positively support self-care: physical, psychological, emotional, spiritual, relationship, and professional factors (Cox & Steiner, 2013; National Wellness Institute, 2021). These components are discussed more fully in the section on creating your own action plan later in this chapter.

A growing field of research, yet the definition remains unclear (Dodge et al., 2012; Schulte & Vainio, 2010). The meaning of wellness and well-being are not the same, even though the terms are often used interchangeably. Merriam-Webster (n.d.) online dictionary states wellness is being in a state of good health, particularly when it is a goal that is actively sought out to achieve. While well-being builds upon this definition to include the presence of positive emotions and moods, the absence of negative emotions, satisfaction with life, and feeling healthy and full of energy (Centers for Disease Control and Prevention, 2018).

JOB-RELATED STRESS IN SCHOOL LEADERS

Studies support the assumption that the demands of school leaders' jobs are stressful, demanding, and exhausting. As recent as 2020, the year a worldwide pandemic shuttered the doors of many school buildings, a resurgence in the public conversation about the well-being of teachers and school leaders occurred. A survey from the National Association of Secondary School Principals (NASSP) found the pandemic prompted nearly 45% of principals to leave their jobs earlier than they had previously planned (Maxwell & Superville, 2020). One of the main reasons principals were revisiting plans to leave school leadership focused on the changing dynamics of health presented by the pandemic, not only for the school leader and their immediate family, but also for the impact of potential liability and constantly changing conditions required to keep schools open and safe.

The impact of constant change can cause disorientation, disillusionment, and eventual mental and physical demise. One of the most interesting facets to consider in light of the common challenges to school leaders (stress, long hours, conflict on the job) is the emotional toll that they often face in managing the multiple challenges that arise at one time. Mahfouz (2020) identified three stressors noted by principals in today's schools: work-related stressors, relationship-related stressors, and time-related stressors. In all these thematically arranged responses from practicing principals, Mahfouz noted that these stressors then lead to certain emotional responses—feelings of guilt, fear, disrespect, or being undervalued. Some school leaders even attested to feeling guilty for taking time to tend to their personal well-being or needs of their families because it felt like time was being taken away from the job (Mahfouz identified this as compassion fatigue or "sacrifice syndrome" (Mahfouz, 2020, p. 453). Thus, it is not simply the fact that the job has inherent stress in and of itself, but that the residual effects can be long-lasting and deeply rooted in emotional well-being.

The causes of job-related stress are often difficult to capture precisely or with much consistency. Because the role of school leader is often a public job—one that has a certain amount of public recognition and community awareness built into it—school leaders face challenges from multiple sources. Demands from students, parents and family members, community members, and teachers can range from polite exchanges to heated conflicts. Challenges may arise in person, during a meeting, in the school parking lot, or on social media—basically in any area of life. There is simply no identified place for a school leader to escape the job. In addition, not all problems are solved quickly or cleanly, leaving the administrator what Mahfouz terms as "socially or emotionally unprepared" for the ongoing nature of leadership (Mahfouz, 2020, p. 452).

In sum, both physical and emotional stress are inherent in the job of school leadership. With that comes both a physical and emotional toll that can cause increasing numbers of school leaders to devise plans to leave the profession early. This, in turn, causes frequent turnover in schools and leaves leadership in a constant state of flux. As an observable pattern, this lack of consistency can impact teacher and student performance and community support, and present a looming dearth of leadership candidates to take over.

A RATIONALE FOR A SCHOOL LEADERS' WELL-BEING PLAN

All hope is not lost because of the known workload and stress load experienced by today's school leaders. One way to better address these challenges, rather than demanding sudden change or an overhaul of the system, is to focus instead on what a school leader can do to become more mindful of their workload and the impact of stress on their overall well-being. As a school leader, it is important to understand not only what well-being means to you on a personal basis so you can better understand how to support those you lead, but also what it means when you demonstrate and lead with well-being as a leadership priority. When you understand how to successfully manage your own well-being, it shows in the way you approach relationships with teachers, interactions with students, and how you balance the time you invest in work-related duties. Teachers and school staff take cues from their leaders—a leader who promotes well-being will often find a staff willing to prioritize this as well. Research suggests that employees are more likely to take ownership of their own well-being when their leaders demonstrate a life well lived; those in leadership positions set the mood and tone of work environments and have the ability to create or dismantle a culture of well-being (Wood & Nelson, 2017). For this reason, school leaders, in particular, should role model well-being as way to encourage teachers and staff to invest in their own well-being practices—and in fact should lead the conversation on how this can be done.

Inspiring and motivating employees is the most important driver of effective leadership (Caver et al., 2015). In schools, engagement and well-being have the ability to work together and synergize the beneficial effects of the other (Mann & Wood, 2015). For example, engaged employees are three to four times more likely to be aware and receptive to workplace wellness and well-being programs (Caver et al., 2015), in addition to giving heightened attention to their employer's wellness efforts and take actions to live healthier lifestyles. On the other hand, low employee well-being is related to reduced engagement and morale, increased overtime, overstaffing, increased turnover, and increased number of accidents (Grant et al., 2007; Lister, 2014; McLellan, 2017).

Considering the impact school leaders can have on well-being, culture, and employee engagement, it is vital for every school leader to have working knowledge of their stress levels, the sources of stressors, and the emotional result of these stressors. Self-awareness, then, can develop habits of uncovering unnoticed signs of burnout, seeking a community of support, and building a school-wide conversation about well-being and wellness. In addition, a school leader's willingness to admit the difficulties of the job and seek ways to remediate job-related stress can in turn promote better work-life balance and improved personal relationships at home and at work, helping school leaders deal with both the physical and emotional toll of work-related stress. Once these factors are known, school leaders can then devise a purposeful plan to not only manage but also predict responses that promote physical and emotional well-being as opposed to those that cause reactionary stress.

CREATING YOUR WELL-BEING BASELINE

Rather than overlook or dismiss the overwhelming stressors and burnout rate that faces school leaders today, we suggest a proactive approach to examining, understanding, and planning for one's own well-being while in the role of school leader. Doing so not only provides self-awareness, but also provides time for purposeful reflection in order to build actionable steps to manage job-related stress and the emotional toll it creates. Thus, to create a plan for well-being, you first need to establish a baseline of your current state of well-being. The self-assessment listings found here that accompany Tables 4.1–4.4 at the end of this chapter will guide you in discovering your current rate of burnout and in assessing how well you are managing a work-life balance, your current level of stress, and self-care practices.

BURNOUT ASSESSMENT

The first step in creating your well-being plan is to determine your current level of professional burnout; see the Burnout Assessment, Table 4.1, found at the end of this chapter. This list of statements requires you to indicate whether the statement is true or false in your professional life. Once you have tallied your burnout score you can you use the following descriptions for interpretation.

Level Green: 1–5 True Responses: You feel the stressors of your profession, but you are probably managing well. You are satisfied with your job and maintain passion and enthusiasm towards your work. Be cautious about how you spend your energy as burnout can creep up on you anytime.

Level Yellow: Score 6–10 True Responses: You are tired and may try to hide some of your burnout through coping mechanisms. You may be starting to feel the physical effects of burnout like being overly tired, emotionally drained, and agitated. You may feel like you are losing passion for your work—you still enjoy your job but are less motivated to go above and beyond the basic requirements of it. Burnout is real in your life and finding a work-life balance may help prevent burnout from taking over.

Level Red: Score 11–15 True Responses: You are suffering—it might be physically, emotionally, or relationally (or all of these). Problems at work are significant and your passion for your profession is fading. You struggle to make it through each workday. You feel lost and hopeless.

At this point, you have reached burnout and must acknowledge it and take action to mitigate its effects.

With burnout, the best option is to take regular steps to prevent it from happening, not to attempt to deal with it after it emerges. It will be important to consider your Burnout Assessment Score when you create your Self-Care Action Plan, discussed later in this chapter.

WORK-LIFE BALANCE ASSESSMENT: STRESS DIARY

Now that you have some general idea of your level of job burnout, let us focus on the people, events, things, and processes that can cause the stress leading to burnout for today's school leader. We all experience stress in some form every day, whether it is caused by rush-hour traffic, ongoing teacher evaluations, student conflicts, demands from parents, a never-ending to-do list, or new state or federal student achievement guidelines. If stress goes unmanaged, it can affect your productivity, and, even worse, your physical health. To better understand your personal relationship with stress, keep a Stress Diary—see Table 4.2 at the end of this chapter—for one week to document your stress triggers and how you respond to them. The purpose of a Stress Diary is to help you record information about the stressors you are experiencing. Keep track of your stressors each day, noting time of day, stressor trigger, cause, physical symptoms of stress, and how you handled the stress trigger (either negatively or positively).

Once you have kept your Stress Diary for a week, you will need to analyze the results. Use these steps to review and make sense of your Stress Diary.

- Review the different stressors that you experienced throughout the week. Circle the most common, frequently experienced stressors. Using this list as a reference, note which category the most common stressors in your life fall into. You may even find that some of your stressors fall into more than one of these categories.
    - Include feelings of tension, irritability, restlessness, guilt, concern, worry, and the inability to relax.
    - Include feelings related to your relationship with your significant other, parents, children, and other family members.
    - Interactions with both your professional and personal community, including those caused by social media.
    - Feelings of stress related to any instance of change in our lives.

- o Caused by pressures of the workplace.
- o Involve the stress caused by having to make critical decisions either professionally or personally.
- o Situations that overtax your body, such as working long hours without sleep, depriving yourself of healthy food, or standing on your feet all day.
- o Including noise, pollution, lack of space, too much heat or cold.
- o Consider the cause of your stressors. Do these identify or connect with any ongoing problems or challenges that need to be tackled? If so, list how you plan to approach each.
- o Next, look at the symptoms you experience under stress. Are there any that you need to visit a health-care provider about?
- o Last, review how you handled the stress trigger. Did you have more positive or negative reactions? List ways in which you can change these reactions for the better.

After you have analyzed your diary, you should have a better understanding of what sources of stress are present in your life and which causes you the most stress.

SELF-CARE CHECKLIST

The Self-Care Behavior Assessment, Table 4.3 at the end of this chapter, is designed to identify your current self-care practices and your potential willingness to invest in future self-care behaviors. This assessment was adapted by combining a variety of sources from Saakvitne et al. (1996), Kanter and Sherman (2016), and the National Wellness Institute (2021) to personalize the assessment for school leaders. Keep in mind that the list of self-care behaviors is not exhaustive, but suggestions to help you determine your self-care baseline. Because the set of six components listed above—physical, psychological, emotional, spiritual, social, and professional—must be considered to positively support self-care (Cox & Steiner, 2013), the Self-Care Behavior Assessment asks you to consider self-care behaviors associated with each component. Physical self-care focuses on activities that help you stay fit and healthy, with enough energy to complete both your professional and personal responsibilities and commitments. Psychological self-care are activities that help you feel clear-headed and able to intellectually engage with challenges that are found in your professional and personal life. Emotional self-care brings attention to activities that allow you to safely experience and cope effectively with your full range of emotions. Spiritual self-care activities can provide a sense of perspective beyond the day to day of life. Social self-care focuses on building, supporting, and maintaining supportive relationships in both your professional and personal life. Last but certainly not least, professional self-care are activities that help you work toward the professional level you desire (National Wellness Institute, 2021).

CREATING YOUR SELF-CARE ACTION PLAN

Once you have identified key areas of concern related to burnout, stress, and self-care, a more precise view of the design of your own self-care action plan can take flight. A self-care action plan identifies the self-care goals or behaviors you want to include and maintain in your daily life to enhance your health and well-being. Notice the name of the plan has the term "action" in the title. This term is intentionally added to remind you that this plan is designed to be put into action rather than created and forgotten. It is also always a work in progress. So, as you create your self-care action plan, make sure to include goals and behaviors that are both important to you and that excite you. Most important, always keep in mind that when your self-care action plan is tailored to goals and behaviors that are realistic, you will be more likely to put the plan into action. For each of the self-care categories discussed in this chapter—physical, psychological, emotional, spiritual, relationship, and professional—select at least one behavior or activity that is doable for you to incorporate into your lifestyle. The key here is being realistic—choose something you don't have to invest a lot of time, money, or personnel in order to accomplish, but things or activities you can reasonably fit into the life you lead. You might notice there are areas of overlap between the self-care categories. That is normal and perfectly fine; these concepts tend to blend into one another, and what is good for one's emotional well-being is often good for one's physical well-being—and vice versa.

It is also important to develop a self-care action plan that is tailored to your current burnout level, stressors, and self-care practices as an interacting group of negative elements working simultaneously rather than independently. Be sure to review, reflect, and use the assessments you complete in this chapter to help create your individualized plan. A written self-care action plan does not need to be a long or detailed list. It is better to start simple and add or reorder self-care practices once you have success with your initial plan. When creating your self-care action plan, make sure to include specific details such as how often you will complete the self-care activity, when you will complete it, and who you might complete it with. In Table 4.4, at the end of this chapter, there is an example of a self-care action plan for you to study. Note that none of these action items should cause an upheaval in one's life or a disruption in dedication to work commitments—it is simply presented as a purposeful prioritizing of time.

Once you create your self-care action plan, it is important that you share it with those around you who will encourage and support you as you work toward your goals—for example, a family member, friend, or colleague (Kanter & Sherman, 2016). It is also important to have your self-care action plan visible to keep you motivated. Some find it helpful to print their self-care action plan and place it in locations they see often, like the refrigerator door, laptop screen, or office door. Other strategies might include setting alarms or reminders on your phone (like a reminder every hour to drink water or to take a stroll), utilizing a self-care calendar that is color-coded with each of the areas to provide quick access to viewing the balance of each of the areas, or within a personal journal.

DISCUSSIONS AND IMPLICATIONS OF CREATING A SELF-CARE PLAN

As discussed earlier, the toll of burnout is not only emotional and physical, but also is the cause of frequent turnover and a resulting shortage of qualified school leader candidates. It is essential that schools begin to promote self-care for their administrators and to provide actionable steps that school leaders can take to help ensure longevity in their role. A few suggestions include:

   a. Identifying trusted colleagues. Find a few trusted colleagues you feel comfortable being vulnerable with whom you can confide in on a regular basis. That way, if you are going through a challenging situation, you have someone to talk with about it; chances are they have been in the same or similar situation or known someone who has. Given this shared experience, they would be a good resource for helping you figure out a plan for moving forward.
   b. Prioritizing time management. Have you ever found yourself in a situation in which you expected to spend 10 minutes on a task, and then before you realize it an hour goes by? If this happens frequently, identify time management techniques for daily tasks. While you want to be an effective educational administrator and respond appropriately, it is also important to have a healthy plan to complete tasks. Begin to identify timelines of need, urgency, and priority when tasks and demands are placed on you.

c. Recognizing emotional consequences. Your job as a school leader will not change simply because you have a self-care plan in place, but the emotional weight you carry from your job might just become more manageable. In addition, recognizing the fallout of job-created stress and putting a name with the feeling can also provide legitimacy to feelings we sometimes have a hard time capturing or explaining to someone else. Thus, the worry you feel when a student does not show up to school for weeks or the guilt you feel when a teacher evaluation does not go as well as expected will be something you can identify, accept, and begin to purposefully evaluate rather than let simmer in your mind without being able to form any positive remedies.
d. Challenges of self-care. Recognizing that "life happens" is the key to self-care. There may be occasional days that demand your time and energy, causing you to skip the self-care activity you had planned; this is understandable. When "life happens" all the time, however, you need to ask yourself if you really do not have enough time or if you are using time as an excuse for freezing up. The answer—to include self-care into your routine—may lie in changing your mindset from "I don't have time" to "It is important to make time."

In sum, when you start feeling the symptoms of burnout, start by revising your self-care plan. What have you been neglecting? What needs more attention? Who can you turn to as a trusted colleague? Burnout can have serious consequences for your overall health and well-being. If you are struggling, reevaluate and identify your areas of struggle. The duties of your job should not dictate whether you are well or not, but you can certainly create the conditions of physical and emotional awareness that keep you in tune with cultivating self-care that promotes longevity rather than forces a quick exit.

ADDITIONAL WELL-BEING AND SELF-CARE RESOURCES

- American Heart Association. Tips, ideas, and strategies for living a heart healthy lifestyle. https://www.heart.org/en/healthy-living
- American Psychological Association. Leading scientific and professional organization representing psychology in the United States. https://www.apa.org/topics
- MyPlate. Dietary guidance. https://www.choosemyplate.gov/

- MedlinePlus. Symptoms, causes, treatment and prevention for over 1,000 diseases, illnesses, health conditions, and wellness issues. https://medlineplus.gov/healthtopics.html
- Maslach Burnout Inventory. Copies can be purchased at https://www.mindgarden.com/117-maslach-burnout-inventory-mbi
- The Teacher Self-Care Conference. Conference supporting self-care for teachers. https://teacherselfcare.org/home/
- Toolkit: Mental wellness resources for educators. https://content.acsa.org/mental-wellness-task-force/toolkit-mental-wellness-resources-for-educators
- The Sleep Foundation. Topics related to sleep and health. https://www.sleepfoundation.org/
- Your Healthiest Self. Wellness toolkits. https://www.nih.gov/health-information/your-healthiest-self-wellness-toolkits

REFERENCES

Caver, K., Davenport, T. O., & Nyce, S. (2015). Capturing the value of health and productivity programs. *People and Strategy, 38*(1), 30–354.

Centers for Disease Control and Prevention. (2018, October 31). *Well-being concepts*. https://www.cdc.gov/hrqol/wellbeing.htm

Cox, K., & Steiner, S. (2013). *Self-care in social work. A guide for practitioners, supervisors, and administrators*. NASW Press.

Dodge, R., Daly, A., Huyton, J., & Sanders, L. (2012). The challenge of defining wellbeing. *International Journal of Wellbeing, 2*(3), 222–235. https://doi.org/10.5502/ijw.v2i3

Freudenberger, H. (1981). *Burnout: The high cost of high achievement*. Bantam.

Grant, A. M., Christianson, M. K., & Price, R. H. (2007). Happiness, health, or relationships? Managerial practices and employee well-being tradeoffs. *The Academy of Management Perspectives, 21*(3), 51–63.

Kanter, B., & Sherman, A. (2016). *The happy, healthy nonprofit: Strategies for impact without burnout*. John Wiley & Sons.

Lister, K. (2014). *What's good for people? Moving from wellness to well-being*. https://www.knoll.com/document/1353003180652/Well_Being_wp.pdf

Mahfouz, J. (2020). Principals and stress: Few coping strategies for abundant stressors. *Educational Management, Administration, and Leadership, 48*, 440–458.

Mann, A., & Wood, J. (2015). *Managers with high well-being twice as likely to be engaged*. http://news.gallup.com/businessjournal/182861/managers-high-twice-likely-engaged.aspx

Maslach, C., & Leiter, M. P. (2006). Burnout. *Stress and Quality of Working Life: Current Perspectives in Occupational Health, 37*, 42–49.

Maxwell, L. A., & Superville, D. R. (2020). COVID-19 may drive principals to quit. *Education Week, 40*(3), 6.

McLellan, R. K. (2017). Work, health, and worker well-being: Roles and opportunities for employers. *Health Affairs, 36*(2), 206–213.

Merriam-Webster (n.d.). Wellness. *In Merriam-Webster* dictionary. Retrieved December 20, 2020, from https://www.merriam-webster.com/dictionary/wellness

National Institute for Occupational Safety and Health. (2014, June 6). *What is job stress?* https://www.cdc.gov/niosh/docs/99-101/default.html#What%20Is%20Job%20Stress?

National Wellness Institute. (2021). *The six dimensions of wellness.* https://nationalwellness.org/resources/six-dimensions-of-wellness/

Robinson, K., & Shakeshaft, C. (2016). Superintendent stress and superintendent health: A national study. *Journal of Education and Human Development, 5*(1), 120–133.

Saakvitne, K., & Pearlman, L. A. (1996). *Transforming the pain: A workbook on vicarious traumatization.* Norton.

School Superintendents Association. (2006). *Superintendent and district data.* https://www.aasa.org/content.aspx?id=740

Schulte, P., & Vainio, H. (2010). Well-being at work–overview and perspective. *Scandinavian Journal of Work, Environment & Health,* 422–429.

Wells, C. M., & Klocko, B. A. (2018). Principal well-being and resilience: Mindfulness as a means to that end. *NASSP Bulletin, 102*(2), 161–173. https://doi.org/10.1177/0192636518777813

Wood, J. & Nelson, B. (2017). *The manager's role in employee well-being.* https://www.gallup.com/workplace/236249/manager-role-employee.aspx

World Health Organization. (2019). *Burn-out an "occupational phenomenon": International classification of diseases.* https://www.who.int/news/item/28-05-2019-burn-out-an-occupational-phenomenon-international-classification-of-diseases

Table 4.1

Burnout Assessment

For each statement circle if the response is true or false. Then tally how many true statements you

I am frustrated at work.	True	False
I am not as motivated at work as I used to be.	True	False
Work related stress impacts me more now than before.	True	False
I avoid interacting with others.	True	False
I am tired more than usual.	True	False
I feel job related pressure even when I am not at work.	True	False
I am agitated and irritated.	True	False
My physical health or emotional health has declined recently.	True	False
I feel sick when I think about my job.	True	False
I feel that I may have chosen the wrong profession.	True	False
I get frustrated more often than I used to.	True	False
I feel like I am not treated fairly at work.	True	False
I don't have enough time to do my work.	True	False
I feel hopeless.	True	False
My work quality has diminished.	True	False
TOTAL		

Use the circled guide within the chapter to interpret your results.

Table 4.2

Stress Diary

Date: August 1, 2020				
Time	Stressor (events or conditions that cause stress)	Cause (what was the reason that the stressor happened?)	Symptoms (headache, sweaty palms, raised pulse, and so on)	How did you handle the stress trigger? + or –
7:30 A.M.	Traffic	Woke up late and hit rush-hour traffic	Raised pulse, sweaty hands	–Was irritated with office staff
7:45 A.M.	Phone call from parent	Teacher-student conflict	Exasperated, tired	–Got off the phone angry

(Table continued on next page)

Table 4.2 (Continued)

Stress Diary

Date: August 1, 2020				
Time	Stressor (events or conditions that cause stress)	Cause (what was the reason that the stressor happened?)	Symptoms (headache, sweaty palms, raised pulse, and so on)	How did you handle the stress trigger? + or –
8:30 A.M.	Teacher evaluation	Visit to the ninth-grade band room	Instruments need repair—haven't seen a request for this	+Provided necessary paperwork to help inventory for repairs; good conversation with teacher
9:15 A.M.	Chronic student absences	Call to student's home	Concern for student's well-being; worry	+Positive conversation with parent; shared my concern for the student; encouraged by interaction

Table 4.3

Self-Care Behavior Assessment

Directions:	Engagement
In this self-assessment, select the types of self-care behaviors in which you currently participate by circling the exclamation point (!).	!: I do this now +: I hope to do this in the future
If you do not currently participate in the self-care behavior, but hope to in the future, circle the plus (+) sign.	

Physical Self-Care		
Ensure you get 6-8 hours of sleep each night	!	+
Disconnect from electronics prior to bedtime	!	+
Allow yourself 30 min to wake up before engaging with electronics	!	+
Eat well-balanced meals at least 3 times a day	!	+
Keep a supply of healthy snacks available nearby	!	+
Limit caffeine consumption	!	+
Drink 6-8 cups of water per day	!	+
Exercise regularly	!	+
Participate in a variety of types of movement (strength-training, cardio, stretching)	!	+
Get regular checkups with your medical team	!	+

(Table continued on next page)

Table 4.3 (Continued)

Self-Care Behavior Assessment

Directions: In this self-assessment, select the types of self-care behaviors in which you currently participate by circling the exclamation point (!). If you do not currently participate in the self-care behavior, but hope to in the future, circle the plus (+) sign.	Engagement !: I do this now +: I hope to do this in the future
Psychological Self Care	! +
Purposefully step away from electronics	! +
Gather a group of non-work friends for a social outing	! +
Check in with a loved one	! +
Read a book you've always wanted to read	! +
Build stress-reducing habits	! +
Take a class and learn a skill you've always wanted to learn	! +
Go to a movie/concert/event	! +
Visit a tourist attraction in your city/state (museum, baseball game, etc.)	! +
Get regular checkup with your psychological care team	! +
Sit outside and enjoy nature	! +
Emotional Self-Care	! +
Connect with a friend	! +
Send an encouraging email to someone	
Listen for complainers and limit your time with them	! +
Be honest	! +
Rehearse positive self-talk	! +
Visit a favorite place	! +
Allow yourself to be angry, mad, sad when appropriate	! +
Spend time in reflection, prayer, or meditation	! +
Prioritize your own emotional needs	! +
Eliminate toxic people from your social media feed	! +
Spiritual Self-Care	! +
Write a list of things you are grateful for	! +
Spend time alone	! +
Read an inspirational book or listen to an encouraging speaker	! +
Explore local churches, communities of faith, or other organizations	! +

(Table continued on next page)

Building a School Leader's Personal Well-Being Plan   69

Table 4.3 (Continued)

Self-Care Behavior Assessment

Directions:	Engagement
In this self-assessment, select the types of self-care behaviors in which you currently participate by circling the exclamation point (!). If you do not currently participate in the self-care behavior, but hope to in the future, circle the plus (+) sign.	!: I do this now +: I hope to do this in the future

Volunteer for an organization that serves others	!	+
Perform a random act of kindness	!	+
Engage in prayer/meditation/reflection	!	+
Take a hike and get outside	!	+
Get coffee with a close friend	!	+
Allow yourself to explore ideas bigger than yourself	!	+
Social Self-Care	!	+
Reach out to a friend or family member you haven't talked to in a while	!	+
Spend time chatting with colleagues about non-work topics	!	+
Be the instigator of a social gathering after work or on the weekend	!	+
Attend social events for local organizations to which you belong or participate	!	+
Be one of the first to arrive or last to leave a social event	!	+
Take a weekend trip with friends/family	!	+
Devote regular, undistracted work time to your family	!	+
Plan an adventure with family or friends and visit someplace new	!	+
Take a class/join a club with friends	!	+
Strike up a conversation with someone you do not know well	!	+
Professional Self-Care	!	+
Learn to delegate	!	+
Build a network of others in similar professional roles	!	+
Attend professional development sessions	!	+
Practice saying no to unnecessary additional work	!	+
Seek out the advice of a coach/mentor	!	+
Block out time on your schedule to complete integral tasks	!	+
Communicate your boundaries		
Celebrate achievements	!	+
Ask for help	!	+
Design a motivating workspace for yourself	!	+

Table 4.4

Example of Self-Care Action Plan

1.	Physical self-care	Drink enough water each day.
2.	Psychological self-care	Write in gratitude journal most days of the week before bed.
3.	Emotional self-care	Write in gratitude journal most days of the week before bed.
4.	Spiritual self-care	Spend time in nature at least once a week; hike with family.
5.	Relationship self-care	Make time to see friends at least once a month in social activity.
6.	Professional self-care	Take lunch break at work; will block time on my calendar.

CHAPTER 5

FLOURISHING AS SCHOOL LEADERS

Perspectives of Canada's Outstanding Principals

Benjamin Kutsyuruba, Terry Kharyati, and Nadia Arghash

INTRODUCTION

The role of a school administrator has undergone significant changes over the last several decades, with societal, economic, and political factors transforming the role's expectations and duties and making it extremely multi-layered and complex (Beck & Murphy, 1993; Renihan et al., 2006; The Wallace Foundation, 2013). From the daily obligations of answering the, at times, endless strings of emails to dealing with a global pandemic and everything in between, school leadership requires tremendous efforts of a capable, decisive, and compassionate administrator. Some of the prevalent challenges faced by principals today include punishing working hours, imposed government/union requirements, lack of support, and navigating funding and staffing issues. As a result, the alarming decline in school principals' mental health and well-being has been described as a "growing global crisis" (Ontario Principals' Council, 2017, p. 19). Studies around the world have documented the significant pressures experienced by school leaders related to stress, declining mental health, increased workload, and lack of work-life balance (Australian Primary Principals Association, 2017; Bland et al., 2011; Bristow et al., 2007; Mahfouz, 2018; Riley, 2014; Wylie, 2016). Evidence of work intensification, stress and burnout, and declining well-being among school administrators has also been documented in Canada (Alberta Teachers' Association, 2014; Canadian Association of Principals, 2014; Markin & Wang, 2020; Ontario Principals' Council, 2017; Pollock, 2014; Pollock et al., 2017). Principals tend to experience much higher job stress than other professionals as a result of ever-increasing tasks that crowd their role (Mahfouz, 2018; Wells & Klocko, 2015) and "work demands and pressures that are not matched to their knowledge and abilities and which challenge their ability to cope" (World Health Organization, 2020, para. 1). Consequently, principals feel less inclined to reach out for the help they require to decrease the potentially debilitating effects of their everyday responsibilities. To shed light on the half-hearted help-seeking behaviors among principals—such attempts were judged to be a reaction to worry about incurring the perceived stigmatization associated with any search for help—many of the above studies identified a need to provide meaningful resources to aid principals as they maneuver the inherent challenges of their profession.

It is interesting to note, however, that despite the increase in work intensification and stress, principals across different locales continue to report high job satisfaction rates (e.g., Alberta Teachers Association, 2014; Goldring & Taie, 2018; Pollock, 2014; Riley, 2014; Tennessee Education Research Alliance, 2019), as well as motivation (Australian Lutheran Institute for Theology and Ethics, 2013) and work enjoyment (Wylie, 2016). Many principals have indicated time and again that they are mostly fulfilled with their chosen profession and, if taken back in time, they would still choose to be school principals. Nevertheless, the fact remains that "while the principalship is rewarding with high levels of job satisfaction, growing complexities and expectations make this an increasingly challenging career" (Alberta Teachers Association, 2014, p. 4). Some principals, especially in their early career stages—despite reporting high levels of general satisfaction with their roles—also reported that their jobs are simply not sustainable and left them (Ontario Principals Council, 2017). Others, despite recognizing the sheer volume of their daily tasks, continue to be satisfied with their chosen profession, excel in their new roles, and even go on to receive national and international awards for their exceptional work. One wonders if learning from those principals, who have been successful in fulfilling their professional obligations despite the tremendous challenges they faced on a daily basis, may offer a greater understanding of coping strategies and resilience-building approaches for school leadership. In addition, principals who have been recognized for their outstanding contributions may help us better understand what efforts they make to maintain their well-being and what more can be done to arm them with the tools they need to continue their great work while also remaining well and even growing in balance and skills.

This exploratory study focused on national award-winning principals in Canada's Outstanding Principals (COP) program, which recognizes the unique and vital contributions of principals in publicly funded schools who "demonstrate innovation and entrepreneurial spirit, and who have done something truly remarkable in public education" (The Learning Partnership, 2021, para. 5). We examined the perceptions of flourishing in COP work lives through two research questions: (a) How do outstanding principals experience the sense of flourishing? and (b) What factors contribute to school lworking environments where flourishing is possible and sustainable? In this chapter, we detail findings from one of the research phases: the qualitative interviews with COP ($N = 20$). Following a brief review of relevant literature and research methodology, we describe and quote from the participants' perceptions regarding what flourishing meant to them, what they felt when they experienced flourishing, and the supports they perceived to be influential in their overall sense of flourishing. We conclude by discussing the findings of this study in relation to the literature.

LITERATURE REVIEW: FLOURISHING IN SCHOOL LEADERSHIP

In recent years, school leaders' role in Canada has transcended its administerial component and is now regarded as spearheading innovation and transforming teaching and learning (Canadian Association of Principals, 2014). Shaping the future generation is among the most important commitments we have, one requiring dedicated and delicate undertakings. School leaders are key players in the educational system, whose actions and decisions can have enormous impact on many generations to come. Therefore, they hold the key to a positive school environment where students, teachers, and staff can experience well-being and flourish (Roffey, 2008). Such principals focus on relational values and practices as a central platform of their vision for their schools and model positive relationships among school members. School leaders have the ability and responsibility to lead in such a way that allows individuals to have a meaningful learning and working experience. However, we must first consider how school leaders are capable of achieving such experiences—for, after all, how can they truly foster positivity if they do not experience flourishing themselves? Understanding how this is possible is at the core of positive psychology and positive organizational scholarship (Dutton et al., 2005; Joseph, 2015).

Florishing: What It Is

Human flourishing is a state whereby humans "live within an optimal range of human functioning, one that connotes goodness, generativity, growth, and resilience" (Fredrickson & Losada, 2005, p. 678). In a broad sense, flourishing can be defined as the "optimal functioning of humans, groups, and institutions" (Gable & Haidt, 2005, p. 103). More specifically, Keyes (2016) defined flourishing as "the achievement of a balanced life in which individuals feel good about lives in which they are functioning well" (p. 101). Flourishing, therefore, extends beyond the parameters of inner happiness to what is referred to as psychological and social well-being. In other words, flourishing concerns "self-acceptance, positive relations with others, personal growth, purpose in life, environmental mastery, and autonomy," or *positive psychological functioning*, and "social coherence, social actualization, social integration, social acceptance, and social contribution," or *social well-being* (Keyes, 2002, pp. 108–109). Many studies show that flourishing may be a strong precursor to other positive attributes such as resilience, self-fulfillment, contentment, happiness, and general health and well-being (Haybron, 2008; Martin & Marsh, 2006; Shellman & Hill, 2017; Yildirim & Belen, 2019). In sum, flourishing is an all-encompassing and holistic concept that takes into consideration all the positive attributes that allow individuals to live well.

Positive Organizational Scholarship

The notion of flourishing is grounded in Positive Organizational Scholarship (POS) literature (Cameron & Spreitzer, 2012; Carr, 2004; Roberts & Dutton, 2009). Studies show that prioritizing positive behaviors may have far more benefits than focusing on the negatives and can improve performance across the organization (Cameron, 2017). For example, having a positive attitude may correlate with increased resilience, vitality, and happiness and dismissively with stress, anxiety, and depression, and can result in general well-being (Sin & Lyubomirsky, 2009). Focus on well-being has additionally been profoundly associated with good health and positive relationships (Diener et al., 2017) as well as with success (Lyubomirsky et al., 2005). Such may be the reason behind the recent surge in strength-based studies of mental health and well-being (Diener et al., 2018). In the leadership context, studies have shown that positive leadership may have a transformative impact on the workplace culture (Cameron, 2012; Dutton & Spreitzer, 2014; Quinn & Quinn, 2015). Moreover, recent studies showed that incorporating activities derived from the positive psychology theories, such as mindfulness, may have a significant positive impact on stress reduction among school principals (Molineux et al., 2020). This strength-based approach allows researchers to hone on the inner workings of the conditions in which these behaviors can be nurtured, thus creating a framework for organizations to foster environments where forming positive and sustainable relationships are possible (Cameron et al., 2003)

Putting Flourishing to Use

Taking a positive approach to understanding leadership, combined with the notion of human flourishing as the pinnacle of positive living, has led to the emerging concept of flourishing leadership. However, positive organizational research in the K–12 educational leadership context is scarce (Hoy & Tartar, 2011). Recently, scholars have begun to investigate flourishing in the school environment; specifically, fostering flourishing school climates and its underpinnings has sparked some interest among scholars (e.g., Cherkowski et al., 2018; Cherkowski & Walker, 2013, 2014). Flourishing in the school has been described as a complex phenomenon, consisting of "creating conditions for teachers, students and others in the school to work together towards shared goals in climates of care, connection, trust, innovation and improvement, fun and laughter" (Cherkowski & Walker, 2016, p. 385). Yet, there is a lack of consistency regarding decriptions of flourishing in the school context, and a clear understanding of flourishing among school leaders remains absent from the literature (Cherkowski & Walker, 2016). Scholars propose that school leaders can only foster flourishing schools and promote flourishing for teachers and students when they are first able to experience it themselves (Cherkowski et al., 2020). In our study, we sought to unpack flourishing among award-winning school principals of Canada and factors that help them flourish.

METHODOLOGY

Our multi-phase research study used a mixed-methods design to allow for elaboration on themes and triangulation of data (Johnson & Onwuegbuzie, 2004). The first phase of the study entailed an online survey constructed by the researchers based on the prior-completed systematic review of the literature and adaptations of similar survey instruments (Bakker, 2008; Duckworth et al., 2007; Patterson et al., 2009; Spreitzer et al., 2005). After being piloted among school principals, the final version of the survey included 62 closed questions and 12 open-ended questions which were then thematically organized into the following categories: flow, flourishing and thriving, resilience, grit, and wellbeing. In collaboration with The Learning Partnership, an organization that administers the COP program, the invitation to participate in the online survey was distributed to individuals who have received the award in the past. The survey yielded participants' responses ($N = 73$) within the following categories: flow, flourishing and thriving, resilience, grit, and well-being (for more information on survey findings (see Kutsyuruba et al., 2021). As a follow-up to the survey, respondents were invited to participate in telephone interviews. In total, 20 COP awardees agreed to be interviewed (see Table 5.1). This chapter draws solely on the data from the interview research phase.

Table 5.1

Demographics of Interview Participants

No.	Pseudonym	Gender	Age	Teaching Experience	Principal Experience	Province
1	Connor	M	54	21 – 30	6 – 10	Ontario
2	Samuel	M	56	31 +	16 +	Ontario
3	Monique	F	68	31 +	6 – 10	Ontario
4	Ryan	M	41	21 – 30	11 – 15	Ontario
5	Rosa	F	56	31 +	11 – 15	Manitoba
6	Anna	F	68	21 – 30	6 – 10	Alberta
7	Chad	M	48	21 – 30	11 – 15	Ontario
8	Courtney	F	60	21 – 30	11 – 15	Alberta
9	Christa	F	69	31 +	16 +	Ontario
10	Delores	F	67	31 +	16 +	Quebec
11	Patrick	M	65	31 +	16 +	Northwest Territories
12	Morris	M	48	21 – 30	11 – 15	Ontario
13	Daisy	F	62	31 +	11 – 15	Saskatchewan
14	Amelie	F	53	21 – 30	6 – 10	Ontario
15	Michelle	F	55	21 – 30	11 – 15	British Columbia
16	Selena	F	51	21 –v 30	6 – 10	Ontario
17	Wilson	M	60	31 +	16 +	Alberta
18	Arnold	M	55	21 – 30	16 +	Northwest Territories
19	Ann-Mary (retired)	F	61	21– 30	11 – 15	BC
20	Matt	M	47	11– 20	11 – 15	New Brunswick

Interviews were conducted in a semi-structured manner (Hays & Singh, 2012) in the summer and fall of 2019, lasting on average for 30 minutes and providing rich descriptive data. After participants' responses were compiled and transcribed by the researchers, they were analyzed both deductively and inductively following standard coding processes for etic and emic approaches to data analysis (MacMillan & Schumacher, 2006). First, we used the inductive method for themes to emerge from the data (Jebb et al., 2017). Once general themes were established, the remaining data were analyzed in both an inductive and deductive manner to draw on previous themes and allow for new themes to emerge (Fereday & Muir-Cochrane, 2006). Both etic and emic codes were then combined into categories, and categories into patterns or concepts (Lichtman, 2010). This chapter draws on selected data from the interview questions that inquired into the participants' experiences of flourishing and work-life balance, as well as the factors that supported and hindered their flourishing and that of the school's teachers, students, and staff.

RESEARCH FINDINGS

The research findings have been categorized according to two broad themes: (a) the outstanding principals' experiences of sense of flourishing; and (b) the supports that helped the outstanding principals to flourish.

How Do the Outstanding Principals Experience a Sense of Flourishing?

The participating outstanding principals identified various ways in which they experienced, and continue to experience, flourishing throughout their careers as school leaders. They noted distinct periods where they particularly felt they were flourishing, as well as techniques, mindsets, and attitudes that curated such experiences for them. Four subthemes have emerged from their responses, indicating that outstanding principals experienced a sense of flourishing when they were able to mirror such sense in students and teachers, prioritize their own well-being, fulfill their capacity, and achieve synergy. Unattributed quotes are from the principals.

Mirroring the sense of flourishing. We asked the outstanding principals to describe what flourishing meant to them and how they experienced it on a daily basis. The majority of the principals tied their experiences of flourishing with that of the teachers and students. In other words, flourishing appeared to encapsulate the success, health, and general happiness of the students, as well as the professional development and wellness of the teachers. The interconnectedness of the principals' sense of flourishing with the flourishing of the students and teachers was evident in most of their accounts and anecdotes.

Moreover, for many of the outstanding principals, a sense of flourishing appeared to feed on their ability to maintain a positive influence as school leaders. The principals felt that their ability to help students to grow and succeed, teachers to inspire and lead, and the school to meet and exceed goals and expectations were all testaments to their own flourishing and that of the school as a whole. Influenced by the "climate and culture in the school" and nurtured through the example set by the school leaders, all signs of flourishing can be evident "right on the [students'] faces," as some principals described. Principals agreed that they can only truly feel like they are flourishing when those they work with are flourishing as well. As Christa, a principal from Ontario with over fifteen years of experience in school leadership, said: "If I see those around me flourish, then I feel like I am too."

Prioritizing well-being. The overall state of health, both physical and psychological, was integral to the principals' sense of flourishing. Such a state required from the principals a conscious decision to prioritize personal well-being, or the act of self-care—especially at physically and emotionally demanding junctures of their careers. Maintaining personal well-being appeared to reflect an ongoing effort to have a flow in their sense of wellness—the ability to maintain wellness over a prolonged period of time. Integral to their chosen profession, principals recognized that constant hardships and challenges pose a serious threat to their well-being and therefore might not always allow them to flourish. However, many stressed that putting an effort into getting sufficient sleep, keeping work out of personal life, exercising, accessing mental health resources, and establishing a satisfactory work-life balance could aid them in maintaining their wellness.

Principals prioritized well-being on various levels; for some, taking their health and wellness into consideration in every aspect of their lives was crucial to their flourishing. For many others, incorporating self-care practices into daily routines when possible was more sustainable. That said, a general consensus among all participating principals showed that maintaining a total sense of wellness may be unattainable. Prioritizing well-being appeared to help participants to better "meet the challenges of the day" and to feel that they were "on top of things" and that they "don't have anything hanging over [them]."

Fulfilling capacity. To many of the principals, the notion of performing to the best of their ability appeared to be another strong indicator of their sense of flourishing. Fulfilling the ethical obligations pertaining to their job, having the opportunity to engage in meaningful activities such as mentoring, and feeling a sense of continuous progress were examples of fulfilling their capacity as leaders. This capacity extended beyond meeting the responsibilities intrinsic to their role as school leader, or "getting things done and moving the agenda forward." To these principals, fulfilling capacity was also about the inner sense of resolve and satisfaction that they "haven't left any options untried," and the extent to which they were able to "inspire others to adopt the core values that made [them] flourish" and spend time with the teachers and students "observing and then afterwards giving feedback."

Achieving synergy. A collective, deep, and unwavering commitment to achieving goals shared by all members of the school community—leaders, stakeholders, teachers, and students alike—appeared to have helped the principals flourish. Having a common ideology and sense of urgency to guide their actions and decisions has allowed the principals to experience synergy, which they further described as an antecedent to their flourishing. This idea also aligns with the consensus that the flourishing of all members of the school can be the indicator of a flourishing school leader. To the participating principals, a notion of synergy encapsulated what they described as "teachers approaching their work with that extra zest," "students in tune with what they are doing," and stakeholders engaged and offering "positive feedback." That, in turn, could amount to "everyone [being] actively involved in addressing key priorities of the school community," which made the principals "feel good about what [they are] doing and want to do more."

Most importantly, the outstanding principals perceived encouraging and motivating student and teacher initiatives as a fundamental part of their role as school leaders and as an integral aspect of achieving synergy. The notion that everyone involved in the school climate could "take on responsibilities or start taking initiative and working together instead of in isolation," one principal conceded, was a strong indicative of collective contribution and "pride." To many principals, flourishing was more about allowing teachers and students to take the metaphorical "driver's seat"; Morris, a principal in Ontario, described his experience as "the less I'm in charge and the more [the teachers and student] are, the more they flourish, which means to me that I'm doing my job and my students are flourishing, my staff is flourishing, my school is flourishing."

What Are the Supports Necessary to Help the Principals Flourish?

A system of supports the outstanding principals perceived necessary for their own and others' flourishing included a variety of resources that together could assist them in leading their schools effectively. Several principals expressed that their sense of flourishing was contingent on both external and internal resources. Although participants highlighted different supports based on their unique experiences, there was a great deal of similarities in their responses regarding factors that helped them flourish in their role. Four themes emerged from the data: (a) relationships, (b) internal supports and personal characteristics, (c) external supports, and (d) professional development and training. Each principal referred to at least three of the four themes.

Relationships. The concept of building strong relationships was a prominent theme in relation to achieving success in school leadership and the leaders' sense of flourishing. As a multifaceted concept, building relationships on various levels of the organizations entailed recognition that such was the nature of the principals' work, which demanded constant interactions with a variety of people. Multidirectional interactions allowed them to foster meaningful relationships, which the principals described as one of the most important factors that supported their flourishing. Several principals described the importance of fostering the development of strong connections with individuals in the school, as well as the school board and the wider community, as antecedents to general school flourishing.

Additionally, as some of the principals explained, building relationships helped make the role feel less isolating; a strong relational network with other principals appeared to be of great significance in that regard. Sharing experiences and having the ability to "reach out and talk with others and solve problems," along with trusting the school staff and their ability to solve issues as they come up, allowed several principals to flourish. As Patrick, a principal from the Northwest Territories with more than 30 years' experience, summarized, "[The] school is much more fun, if you got people all working together, going in the same direction, realizing projects, realizing successes, academic, performing, music, dance, you name it." Showing appreciation was another way to build relationships, as Rosa, a principal from Alberta, noted:

> We have made little postcards that have either got pictures of student artwork or pictures of different things around our school that we will write a little note to staff when we see something that we're thankful for, or if we [see] someone is languishing a bit and they need a little note of encouragement. So, that's one way that I think we help others flourish. Just to make them feel appreciated and to know that their efforts are recognized and valued.

Internal resources and personal characteristics. While external factors may be the most obvious sources of support for administrators, most of the principals in our sample instead emphasized drawing from internal (personal, inner) resources to excel at their job and flourish. The concept of personal characteristics and inner strengths was the second major theme related to the resources that principals found necessary in helping them flourish in their role as school leader. The principals talked about developing trust, such as honesty and openness in communication, as a necessary effort towards maintaining a sense of flourishing. For example, Arnold, a principal based in the Northwest Territories, described openness and honesty as crucial factors that supported his flourishing, saying: "it's key that you have someone that you can talk to confidentially, someone that you have a trustful relationship and that you can be open and honest. If you can't do that, then you're not going to be doing well." Perseverance was another internal resource that helped several principals withstand challenges and overcome obstacles. For example, Delores, a Quebec-based principal, described perseverance to be what helped her in times of adversity: "If there were small little hiccups along the way, we just picked [ourselves up] as a team and we moved on, you know, we tried something else. It wasn't a huge deal." The Ontario principal Christa, on the other hand, spoke of a combination of perseverance and confidence that allowed her to "jump in and just do in spite of the rest of the system." Finally, a strong moral compass and personal ethics were rooted in the principals' deep and unwavering passion for their job and the spirit of helpfulness. Expressions such as "doing the right thing" and "making a difference" have seemingly enveloped principals' experiences of flourishing.

External resources. Many principals expressed the belief that their ability to flourish in their role as school leaders was in part contingent upon external resources that they had at their disposal. Aside from financial resources, many of the principals spoke about how they were able to flourish when they were allocated more forms of external supports. Some principals discussed these resources in terms of community supports and teaching resources in addition to government funding that their schools received, while others explained the direct positive outcomes of having extended health benefits or the ability to take time off.

Systemic supports available for all members of the school community also supported the principals. Several participants noted that when teachers were properly and adequately supported, they felt valued and performed better, which then helped the principals attend to their responsibilities in a more efficient way. Ann-Mary, a retired principal from British Columbia with a wealth of experience, explained the positive cycle of support that starts with the teachers: "If the supports are in place for teachers, teachers will then support the work, and that's [the] lovely loop that begins to happen." Schools further needed to be supported by the communities in which they are housed, some principals believed. Viewing schools as "visible" structures within the communities means that schools need the support of the larger community as Chad, an Ontario-based principal, explained: "[Schools are] doing things for the community; [they are] maintaining those connections in positive ways. [They are] bringing outside people in to talk with the kids. It's not just a factory where we put the kids through."

Professional development and training. Finally, an important way for outstanding principals to remain current and knowledgeable appeared to be related to the ability to continually participate in professional development and training opportunities. Continuous growth, participants agreed, contributed greatly to their development as strong and effective leaders, and achieving a sense of flourishing. That may be of particular importance for novice leaders, as many of the principals agreed that professional development opportunities can potentially help flatten the (at times) sharp learning curve of becoming an effective leader. The commitment to train principals properly can reduce the pressure that school leaders must "learn on the job"; it helps novice school leaders, many principals agreed, gain experience and confidence and maximize how they flourish in their school. Even the more experienced leaders, those with decades of leadership experience, expressed the need for continuous growth and receiving meaningful training that helps them stay relevant and keep up with the continuous demands of this job. For instance, Samuel, an Ontario principal, strived to pursue personal growth in school and beyond. Being a principal and a university professor, he viewed balance as the ability to feel engaged and pursue interests: "the balance is [when] I pursue my own teaching." Having a mentor, many principals noted, was a great way to receive support as they learned the ins and outs of school leadership and "being able to have an ear of somebody to talk about it with." Anna, from Alberta, felt rewarded by imparting her knowledge for the benefit of teachers and students:

> My work this morning was coaching my acting principal on how to coach the teacher who was being asked to work with these students who challenge. The work that I do with the teachers is supporting their professional growth through coaching and mentoring.

DISCUSSION

The results of our exploratory study allowed us to begin to understand the factors that shape flourishing for Canada's outstanding principals. We pursued to better understand what shape's school leaders' flourishing because "it is believed that the flourishing of school leaders is a vital antecedent and a catalyzer for a flourishing school climate, that in which students, teachers, and staff are flourishing as well" (Leithwood & McAdie, 2007, p. 44). Findings from the survey phase of our study (Kutsyuruba et al., 2021) indicated that outstanding principals, who have managed to flourish in challenging conditions, also experienced a sense of vitality, excelled in relationship building, learned from adversities, sustained a sense of learning, led mindfully, and maintained a positive work-life balance. Overall, their thriving and well-being were connected to vitality, energy, and spirit and a positive outlook on personal growth, learning, and improvement as leaders. Deeper examination of these findings through interviews (as discussed in this chapter), allowed us to offer nuances and details of their flourishing experiences.

Altruism

Grounded in the concepts of positive psychology and human flourishing, our research findings from the interview corroborate the view that flourishing is experienced through a combination of intrapersonal and interpersonal factors (Keyes, 2010). While concepts of "self-acceptance, positive relations with others, personal growth, purpose in life, environmental mastery, and autonomy" signify positive psychological functioning, "social coherence, social actualization, social integration, social acceptance, and social contribution" represent aspects of positive social functioning (Keyes, 2002, pp. 108–109). The outstanding principals' responses highlight a mixture of positive psychological and social functioning, thus supporting the growing body of literature in that regard. Interesting to note, however, is the effect of supporting the flourishing of others on the principals' own flourishing. Many studies suggested that altruism, whether in the context of helping people or changing the world for the better, can be a major source of support for those who carry out this behavior and may thus improve their own well-being (e.g., Nelson et al., 2015; Sheldon et al., 2012; Weinstein & Ryan, 2010). Compared to the intrapersonal aspects of flourishing, behaviors that benefit other people (prosocial behaviors), may have greater positive influence on flourishing than behaviors that prioritize one's own well-being over others (self-focused behaviors) (Nelson et al., 2016, p. 856). Thus, achieving a state of flourishing may have more to do with other people than it does with the individual, or in this case the school principal. Similar to previous studies, the results of this study indicate that, for this group of principals, other people's flourishing was a major, if not the most important, indicator of their own flourishing. A recent study demonstrates that fostering flourishing in the school community requires leaders who can exemplify flourishing—that is, those who are themselves flourishing (Cherkowski et al., 2020). Furthermore, for principals to be able to support others in experiencing and developing these capacities, they themselves need to experience and develop them first (Dutton et al., 2005).

Principals in our study relied on their inner strengths and characteristics, as well as external supports, to develop their flourishing capacity.

Distributed Leadership

Positive relationships play a key role in flourishing in the workplace (Colbert et al., 2016) and in life in general (VanderWeele, 2017). Another key finding of this study points to the deep entanglement of the principals' flourishing with that of others through the relational aspects of their work lives. Specifically, notions of community and working together toward a common goal (i.e., synergy) were of particular importance. A synergetic community is one where the mindset of working together and empowering one another as a team for the betterment of the school community is prevalent. Many participants identified encouraging others to lead and inspire—the hallmark of distributed leadership—to be an important part of their flourishing experience. Deeper than the idea of multiple people taking responsibility in schools—or the "leader plus" mentality—distributed leadership is a "leadership practice that results from interactions among leaders, followers, and their situations" (Spillane, 2005, pp. 144–145). Therefore, it is not simply that school leaders divide their responsibilities with teachers and students, but also that they encourage others to work together and grow as leaders within their own spheres. Similar to the findings of this study, research suggests that the practice of distributed leadership has been positively associated with teachers' job satisfaction (Torres, 2019) and facilitating trust and mutual respect (Bellibas & Liu, 2018). In that sense, distributed leadership is "an all-inclusive phenomenon that encompasses the practice of delegation, sharing, collaboration, dispersion and democratizing leadership in schools" (Gronn, 2002, p. 656). Furthermore, we contend that shared leadership practices of our participants demonstrate features of appreciative leadership (Stocker et al., 2014). For leaders, displaying elementary appreciative behavior is a simple but important tool for enhancing employees, and in turn, their own health and well-being. Taking into consideration that flourishing encompasses a myriad of positive notions, the sharing in leadership practice may have positive results on the leaders' sense of flourishing and the school's collective sense of flourishing.

Research Cautions

We are cognizant that any research study carries assumptions and limitations due to the research design (Creswell & Creswell, 2017). Perspectives cited in this chapter are limited to a specific group of individuals—that is, past recipients of Canada's Outstanding Principals award, shared during the interview phase. Therefore, we complemented the interview data with survey findings for a more comprehensive understanding of these principals' experiences. Due to the fact that our study involved successful, award-winning school administrators, one assumption might be that they flourish all the time. However, as results showed, this conclusion is flawed, as outstanding principals managed to flourish when certain negative factors were present in their work as well. We suggest that contextual nuances be taken into consideration when applying the findings of this study to the school principalship community as a whole. We encourage further research into the factors and antecedents that are necessary for principals, whether struggling or successful, to flourish themselves and create conditions where others can flourish in their schools.

CONCLUSIONS, IMPLICATIONS, AND REFLECTIONS

Our study has highlighted a few of the conditions, behaviors, mindsets, and characteristics that may shape flourishing for Canada's outstanding principals and, by extension and contextual application, school leaders in general. Based on the findings, we offer a summary of the factors that were found to contribute to flourishing. Flourishing in school leadership occurs:

- When principals prioritize well-being, work-life balance, and health.
- When principals draw on internal (personal, inner) resources to excel at their job and flourish.
- When relationships in a school are conducive to collaboration, support, and collective flourishing.
- When leadership is distributed in a synergistic, appreciative manner.
- When professional development opportunities are supported by the system, both financially and pedagogically.

A key implication of these findings is that implementing policies that directly acknowledge the principals' well-being, attend to their needs, support their development, and encourage collaboration in schools, may allow leaders to better manage their work-life balance and thus remain well.

Furthermore, we invite the reader to consider the following reflective questions that might help better understand on a practical level how best to support flourishing among principals.

- In what tangible ways can the system (school board/central office) better respect the *voice* of principals?
- What types of *distractions* and/or *obstacles* (perceived or real) are put in place by the school board/central office?
- How can the system (school board/central office) better support principals in dealing with challenging parents, staff, and students?
- Can systems offer customized, structured mentoring and coaching for both new and experienced principals?
- In what ways does the workload of principals need to be respected to minimize distractions from the focus of leading and managing the school?

Finally, we posit that if the principal is a central figure in the success of a school, then finding the appropriate ways to effectively support the principal should be a priority. In this regard, school systems should consider what leadership and pedagogical price should be paid when the principals are not flourishing.

REFERENCES

Alberta Teachers' Association. (2014). *The future of the principalship in Canada: A national study*.

Australian Lutheran Institute for Theology and Ethics (ALITE). (2013). *Principal health and wellbeing in Australian Lutheran schools*. Lutheran Education Australia. https://www.lutheran.edu.au/download/principal-health-and-wellbeing-in-australian-lutheran-schools/?wpdmdl=6902&ind=1619741411906

Australian Primary Principals Association (APPA). (2017). *Back to balance: How policy and practice can make primary principals highly effective*. https://appa.asn.au/wp-content/uploads/2020/05/Back-To-Balance_v3-publication-1.pdf

Bakker, A. B. (2008). The work-related flow inventory: Construction and initial validation of the WOLF. *Journal of Vocational Behavior, 72*(3), 400–414.

Beck, L., & Murphy, J. (1993). *Understanding the principalship: Metaphorical themes 1920s–1980s*. Teachers College Press.

Bellibas, M. S., & Liu, Y. (2018). The effects of principals' perceived instructional and distributed leadership practices on their perceptions of school climate. *International Journal of Leadership in Education, 21*(2), 226–244.

Bland, J., Sherer, D., Guha, R., Woodworth, K., Shields, P., Tiffany-Morales, J., & Campbell, A. (2011). *The status of the teaching profession 2011*. The Center for the Future of Teaching and Learning at WestEd. https://files.eric.ed.gov/fulltext/ED527741.pdf

Bristow, M., Ireson, G., & Coleman, A. (2007). *A day in the life of a headteacher: A study of practice and well-being*. National College for School Leadership. http://dera.ioe.ac.uk/7066/2/download%3Fid%3D17101%26filename%3Da-life-in-the-day-of-a-headteacher.pdf

Cameron, K. (2012). *Positive leadership: Strategies for extraordinary performance*. Berrett-Koehler.

Cameron, K. (2017). Cross-cultural research and positive organizational scholarship. *Cross Cultural & Strategic Management, 24*(1), 13–32.

Cameron, K. S., Dutton, J. E., & Quinn, R. E. (2003). Foundations of positive organizational scholarship. In Cameron, K. S., Dutton, J. E., & Quinn R. E. (Eds.), *Positive organizational scholarship: Foundations of a new discipline* (pp. 3–14). Berrett-Koehler.

Cameron, K. S., & Spreitzer, G. M. (2012). Introduction: What is positive about positive organizational scholarship? In K. S. Cameron & G. M. Spreitzer (Eds.), *The Oxford handbook of Positive Organizational Scholarship* (pp. 1–16). Oxford University Press.

Canadian Association of Principals. (2014). *The future of the principalship in Canada: A national research study*. Alberta Teachers' Association. https://www.teachers.ab.ca/SiteCollectionDocuments/ATA/Publications/Research/The%20Future%20of%20the%20Principalship%20in%20Canada.pdf

Carr, A. (2004). *Positive psychology: The science of happiness and humans strengths*. Routledge.

Cherkowski, S., Hanson, K., & Walker, K. (2018). Flourishing in adaptive community: Balancing structures and flexibilities. *Journal of Professional Capital and Community, 3*(2), 123–136.

Cherkowski, S., Kutsyuruba, B., & Walker, K. (2020). Positive leadership: Animating purpose, presence, passion and play for flourishing in schools. *Journal of Educational Administration, 58*(4), 401–415.

Cherkowski, S., & Walker, K. (2013). Schools as sites of human flourishing: Musings on efforts to foster sustainable learning communities. *Journal of Educational Administration and Foundations, 23*(2), 139–154.

Cherkowski, S., & Walker, K. (2014). Flourishing communities: Re-storying educational leadership using a positive research lens. *International Journal of Leadership in Education, 17*(2), 200–216.

Cherkowski, S., & Walker, K. (2016). Purpose, passion and play: Exploring the construct of flourishing from the perspective of school principals. *Journal of Educational Administration, 54*(4), 378–392.

Colbert, A. E., Bono, J. E., & Purvanova, R. K. (2016). Flourishing via workplace relationships: Moving beyond instrumental support. *Academy of Management Journal, 59*(4), 1199–1223.

Creswell, J. W., & Creswell, J. D. (2017). *Research design: Qualitative, quantitative, and mixed methods approaches*. SAGE.

Diener, E., Heintzelman, S. J., Kushlev, K., Tay, L., Wirtz, D., Lutes, L. D., & Oishi, S. (2017). Findings all psychologists should know from the new science on subjective well-being. *Canadian Psychology/Psychologie Canadienne, 58*(2), 87–104.

Diener, E., Oishi, S., & Tay, L. (2018). Advances in subjective well-being research. *Nature Human Behaviour, 2*, 253–260.

Duckworth, A. L., Peterson, C., Mathews, M. D., & Kelly, D. R. (2007). Grit: Perseverance and passion for long term goals. *Journal of Personality and Social Psychology, 92*(6), 1087–1101.

Dutton, J. E., Glynn, M. A., & Spreitzer, G. (2005). *Positive organizational scholarship. Encyclopedia of positive psychology*. Blackwell.

Dutton, J. E., & Spreitzer, G. M. (2014). *How to be a positive leader: Insights from the leading thinkers on positive organizations*. Berrett-Koehler.

Fereday, J., & Muir-Cochrane, E. (2006). Demonstrating rigor using thematic analysis: A hybrid approach of inductive and deductive coding and theme development. *International Journal of Qualitative Methods, 5*(1), 80–92.

Fredrickson, B. L., & Losada, M. F. (2005). Positive affect and the complex dynamics of human flourishing. *American Psychologist, 60*(7), 678–686.

Gable, S. L., & Haidt, J. (2005). What (and why) is positive psychology? *Review of General Psychology, 9*(2), 103–110.

Goldring, R., & Taie, S. (2018). *Principal attrition and mobility: Results from the 2016–17 principal follow-up survey First Look* (NCES 2018-066). National Center for Education Statistics, U.S. Department of Education. https://nces.ed.gov/pubs2018/2018066.pdf

Gronn, P. (2002). Distributed Leadership. In K. Leithwood, P. Hallinger, G. C. Furman, K. Riley, J. MacBeath, P. Gronn, & B. Mulford (Eds.), *Second international handbook of educational leadership and administration* (pp. 653–696). Springer. https://doi.org/10.1007/978-94-010-0375-9_23

Haybron, D. M. (2008). Happiness, the self and human flourishing. *Utilitas, 20*(1), 21–49.

Hays, D. G., & Singh, A. A. (2012). *Qualitative inquiry in clinical and educational settings*. Guilford Press.

Hoy, W. K., & Tarter, C. J. (2011). Power principles for educational leaders: Research into practice. *International Journal of Educational Management, 25*(2), 124–133.

Jebb, A. T., Parrigon, S., & Woo, S. E. (2017). Exploratory data analysis as a foundation of inductive research. *Human Resource Management Review, 27*(2), 265–276.

Johnson, R. B., & Onwuegbuzie, A. J. (2004). Mixed methods research: A research paradigm whose time has come. *Educational Researcher, 33*(7), 14–26.

Joseph, S. (Ed.). (2015). *Positive psychology in practice: Promoting human flourishing in work, health, education, and everyday life*. Wiley.

Keyes, C. L. (2002). The mental health continuum: From languishing to flourishing in life. *Journal of Health and Social Behavior, 43*(2), 207–222.

Keyes, C., L. (2010). The next steps in the promotion and protection of positive mental health. *Canadian Journal of Nursing Research, 42*(3), 17–28.

Keyes, C. L. (2016). Why flourishing? In D. W. Harward (Ed.), *Well-being and higher education* (pp. 99–107). Bringing Theory to Practice.

Kutsyuruba, B., Kharyati, T., & Arghash, N. (2021). Exploring the sense of flourishing among Canada's outstanding principals. In K. D. Walker, B. Kutsyuruba, & S. Cherkowski (Eds.), *Positive leadership for flourishing schools* (pp. 231–252). Information Age Publishing.

Learning Partnership. (2021). *Canada's outstanding principals*. https://www.thelearningpartnership.ca/programs/canadas-outstanding-principals/faq

Leithwood, K., & McAdie, P. (2007). Teacher working conditions that matter. *Education Canada, 47*(2), 42–45.

Lichtman, M. (2010). *Qualitative research in education: A user's guide*. SAGE.

Lyubomirsky, S., King, L., & Diener, E. (2005). The benefits of frequent positive affect: Does happiness lead to success? *Psychological Bulletin, 131*, 803–855.

MacMillan, J. H., & Schumacher, S. (2006). *Research in education: Evidence-based inquiry*. Pearson.

Mahfouz, J. (2018). Principals and stress: Few coping strategies for abundant stressors. *Educational Management Administration & Leadership, 48*(3), 440–458.

Markin, G., & Wang, F. (2020). *Stress and burnout are on the rise among Canadian principals and vice-principals*. https://www.edcan.ca/articles/burnout-principals-and-vice-principals/

Martin, A. J., & Marsh, H. W. (2006). Academic resilience and its psychological and educational correlates: A construct validity approach. *Psychology in Schools, 43*(3), 267–281.

Molineux, J., Billsberry, J., & Fraser, A. (2020). The flourishing of school principals: An intervention study. *Academy of Management Proceedings, 2020*(1), [Abstract]. https://doi.org/10.5465/AMBPP.2020.18370abstract

Nelson, S. K., Della Porta, M. D., Jacobs Bao, K., Lee, H. C., Choi, I., & Lyubomirsky, S. (2015). "It's up to you": Experimentally manipulated autonomy support for prosocial behavior improves well-being in two cultures over six weeks. *The Journal of Positive Psychology, 10*(5), 463–476.

Nelson, S. K., Layous, K., Cole, S. W., & Lyubomirsky, S. (2016). Do unto others or treat yourself? The effects of prosocial and self-focused behavior on psychological flourishing. *Emotion, 16*(6), 850–861.

Ontario Principals' Council. (2017). *International symposium white paper: Principal work–life balance and well-being matters*. https://www.principals.ca/en/professional-learning/resources/Documents/OPC-White-Paper-2017---Principal-Work-Life-Balance-and-Well-Being---2017.pdf

Patterson, J. L., Goens, G. A., & Reed, D. E. (2009). *Resilient leadership for turbulent times: A guide to thriving in the face of adversity*. Rowman & Littlefield.

Pollock, K. (2014). *The changing nature of principals' work. Final report*. Ontario Principals' Council. https://www.principals.ca/en/professional-learning/resources/Documents/Changing-Nature-of-Principals-Work---Summary.pdf

Pollock, K., Wang, F., & Hauseman, C. (2017). *The changing nature of vice principals' work. Final report*. Ontario Principals' Council. https://www.principals.ca/en/professionallearning/resources/Documents/Changing-Nature-of-Vice-Principals-Work---K-Pollock---2017.pdf

Quinn, R. W., & Quinn, R. E. (2015). *Lift: The fundamental state of leadership*. Berrett-Koehler Publishers.

Renihan, P., Phillips, S., & Raham, H. (2006). *The role of the school principal: Present status and future challenges in managing effective schools*. Society for the Advancement of Excellence in Education.

Riley, P. (2014, December). *Australian principal occupational health, safety and wellbeing survey: 2011–2014 data*. https://www.principalhealth.org/reports/2015_Final_Report.pdf

Roberts, L., & Dutton, J. (2009). *Exploring positive identities and organizations: Building a theoretical and research foundation*. Routledge.

Roffey, S. (2008). Emotional literacy and the ecology of school wellbeing. *Educational & Child Psychology, 25*(2), 29–39.

Sheldon, K. M., Boehm, J. K., & Lyubomirsky, S. (2012). Variety is the spice of happiness: The hedonic adaptation prevention (HAP) model. In I. Boniwell & S. David (Eds.), *Oxford handbook of happiness* (pp. 901–914). Oxford University Press.

Shellman, A., & Hill, E. (2017). Flourishing through resilience: The impact of a college outdoor education program. *Journal of Park and Recreation Administration, 35*(4), 59–68. https://doi.org/10.18666/jpra-2017-v35-i4-7779

Sin, N. L., & Lyubomirsky, S. (2009). Enhancing well-being and alleviating depressive symptoms with positive psychology interventions: A practice-friendly meta-analysis. *Journal of Clinical Psychology, 65*(5), 467–487.

Spillane, J. P. (2005). Distributed leadership. *The Educational Forum, 69*(2), 143–150. Taylor & Francis Group.

Spreitzer, G., Sutcliffe, K., Dutton, J., Sonenshein, S., & Grant, A. M. (2005). A socially embedded model of thriving at work. *Organization Science, 16*(5), 537–549.

Stocker, D., Jacobshagen, N., Krings, R., Pfister, I. B., & Semmer, N. K. (2014). Appreciative leadership and employee well-being in everyday working life. *German Journal of Human Resource Management, 28*(1–2), 73–95. https://doi.org/10.1177/239700221402800105

Tennessee Education Research Alliance. (2019). *Trends in principal job satisfaction*. https://peabody.vanderbilt.edu/TERA/files/Survey_Snapshot_Principal_Satisfaction_FINAL.pdf

Torres, D. G. (2019). Distributed leadership, professional collaboration, and teachers' job satisfaction in US schools. *Teaching and Teacher Education, 79*, 111–123.

VanderWeele, T. J. (2017). On the promotion of human flourishing. *Proceedings of the National Academy of Sciences, 114*(31), 8148–8156.

The Wallace Foundation. (2013). *The school principal as leader: Guiding schools to better teaching and learning*. https://www.wallacefoundation.org/knowledge-center/Documents/The-School-Principal-as-Leader-Guiding-Schools-to-Better-Teaching-and-Learning-2nd-Ed.pdf

Weinstein, N., & Ryan, R. M. (2010). When helping helps: Autonomous motivation for prosocial behavior and its influence on well-being for the helper and recipient. *Journal of Personality and Social Psychology, 98*(2), 222–244.

Wells, C. M., & Klocko, B. A. (2015). Can teacher leadership reduce principal stress? *Journal of School Leadership, 25*(2), 313–344.

World Health Organization. (2020). *Occupational health: Stress at the workplace*. https://www.who.int/news-room/q-a-detail/ccupational-health-stress-at-the-workplace

Wylie, C. (2016). *Principals and their work*. New Zealand Council for Educational Research. https://www.nzcer.org.nz/system/files/National%20Survey_Principals_Nov17.pdf

Yildirim, M., & Belen, H. (2019). The role of resilience in the relationships between externality of happiness and subjective well-being and flourishing: A structural equation model approach. *Journal of Positive School Psychology*, *3*(1), 62–67.

CHAPTER 6

THE FUTURE OF HIGHER EDUCATION IS HUMAN

A Call for Contemplative Leadership Preparation

Maryann Krikorian

INTRODUCTION

Human beings are meant to love, connect, and find meaning in life. However, when emotional needs are not realized, humanity is not able to function at its fullest potential (Brown, 2010). According to lifespan theory, humans have an innate need for self-actualization—mental and emotional health—to experience the fullest in human potential (Sternberg & Williams, 2010). Maslow (1954) theorized actualization to be influenced by the basic needs of human survival: food, rest, and security. Thereafter, growth needs of love, belonging, and esteem are essential to the progression of human development. Maslow argued, however, that full actualization cannot be realized without initially satisfying psychological needs. For this reason, it is important to engage in critical reflection about value-belief systems undergirding cultural contexts. Value-belief systems are defined as "values [that] influence every aspect of life: moral judgements, responses to others, commitments to personal and organizational goals. Values set the parameters for the hundreds of decisions [made] every day, consciously or subconsciously" (Kouzes & Posner, 2012, p. 49). It is valuable to question how the American work ethic supports or hinders growth needs of human survival, as well-being depends less on objective events and more on how events are perceived (Brackett, 2019). The aims of this chapter are to: (a) examine the value-belief systems that undergird the American conception of work, (b) consider practical and conceptual limitations of the American work ethic, (c) pursue further conversations in the field for contemplative leadership in educator preparation, and (d) share practices that are counterculture to the American conception of work in support of future educational leader well-being. Along with this intention comes the potential to counterbalance the American work ethic with a moral stance honoring the innate human condition (Palmer et al., 2010). This chapter invites faculty in institutions of higher education to prioritize contemplation as one way to facilitate human growth needs for greater well-being in the next generation of educational leaders.

THE AMERICAN CONCEPTION OF WORK

During human development, formative learning is largely influenced by socialization and schooling within a particular culture. Mezirow (1991) explains how the nature of reality is understood by interpretations of events, which depend heavily on the cultural context of past experiences. Mezirow explains how such interpretations are formulated by a given ideology that constitutes a mental code in the human mind, regulating patterns of thought, emotion, and behavior in everyday life. Interpretations then become interdependent with cultural standards, guiding the way adult learners experience, comprehend, and assess information. Ultimately, interpretations determine adult learners' scope of attention and attribute causality within a given value-belief system, aiding in the perception of future experiences. Yet, when experiences of adult learners appear incompatible with existing mental codes, recollection may likely become distorted in the human mind. Mezirow depicts learning distortions as "perspectives of adults that have not been fully developed ... [or subjected to] critical judgment" (p. 119).

Adult learners who passively and uncritically accept a social reality based on cultural standards may experience cognitive incongruence, where interpretations conflict with personal viewpoints. In this case, adult learners may do or think things contradictory to personal value-belief systems, prompting feelings of incompatibility, dissonance, and isolation (Festinger, 1957). The refinement of existing mental codes may limit such feelings of incongruence to create positive leadership capacities and more satisfying lives (Brackett, 2019). The cognitive science behind human development and learning calls faculty to work with adult learners to examine, understand, and deconstruct cultural contexts to rework, recategorize, and regeneralize information in new ways, expanding consciousness to choose human growth needs over cultural standards for greater congruence in regulating thought, emotion, and behavior in American life.

In the United States, the economic evolution has been credited to a market-centric ideology. An era of free-market capitalism informs the American conception of work, supporting privatization and for-profit interests as a means to acquire material advantages and rewards (Porter, 2010). As Thompson (2019) explains, "[T]he American dream—that hoary mythology that hard work always guarantees upward mobility—has for more than a century made the United States obsessed with material success and the exhaustive striving required to earn it" (para. 6). Thompson goes on, "[T]he American conception of work has shifted from … *necessity* to *status* to *meaning*" (para. 15 [emphasis added]). When work establishes meaning, interpretative elements are formulated by a market-centric ideology. In this way, levels of achievement are falsely perceived as interconnected with human growth needs.

Adult learners depend on causation to explain their experiences and observations in the world. For this reason, a market-driven ideology may revert awareness to a focus on status, capital, scarcity, and competition. As a result, human capital value for national economic interests emerges as a force for human learning, causing undue stress and moral injury by "funnel[ing] … dreams of self-actualization into salaried jobs" and stunting human growth, as it never is able to move past psychological needs for survival (Thompson, 2019, para. 14). In the past decade, news articles continue to report on the collective anxiety, mass disappointment, and inevitable burnout in the workforce (Thompson, 2019). Petersen (2019) writes, "[B]urnout [is] not a temporary affliction: It's the [American] condition" (para. 10). Burnout itself is a newly adopted medical diagnosis, generally accepted in the literature as emotional exhaustion, depersonalization, and reduced professional efficacy (Prior, 2019). The concept of burnout was first introduced as a psychological diagnosis in 1974, referring to "physical or mental collapse caused by overwork or stress" (Petersen, 2019, para. 47). Petersen (2019), however, described the term in a more modern sense: "reaching [the point of exhaustion] and pushing yourself to keep going; whether for days or weeks or years" (para. 47). Consequently, the World Health Organization (WHO) now recognizes a state of burnout, working under conditions of unmanageable chronic stress that elicits medical attention (Capritto, 2019). What's more, a 2018 American Psychiatric Association poll reported that 39% of respondents experienced greater levels of anxiety when compared to feelings from the previous year (Petersen, 2019). This occupational phenomenon, if not properly managed, may limit the extent to which knowledge and skills are successfully applied in leadership and the workplace (Capritto, 2019). For this reason, organizations are now responding to rising mental health concerns, creating new leadership positions to reduce the mental health epidemic, such as appointing a chief wellness officer (Reilly, 2020).

Institutions of higher education, like any other organization, are subject to external socio-cultural-political pressures that affect and shape institutional culture (Frey, 2018). Petersen (2019) asserts that cultural contexts reinforce a market-driven system during the educational experience, conditioning adult learners to win, even at a cost to human welfare. At present, adult learners are reporting increasing rates of mental health concerns during the higher education experience. To illustrate, 2,279 students reported anxiety on clinically validated scales six times as likely as the general graduate student population (Evans et al., 2018), and 790 respondents showed 47% of PhD and 37% of master's students experienced depression in two separate studies (UC Berkeley Graduate Assembly, 2014). Moreover, a University of Arizona report found that a majority of doctoral students experienced "tremendous" stress and recognized school and education-related issues as the most influential factors (Smith & Brooks, 2015, para. 6). The emerging understanding about mental health demonstrates how higher education reflects the cultural context of the larger society.

To date, researchers associate the concept of well-being with factors such as satisfaction, acceptance, authenticity, and purpose that may lead to enhanced work performance and creativity across multidisciplinary fields (Brackett, 2019). Therefore, it is important that adult learners reflect upon their own mental codes to better understand how market driven values influence growth needs of human survival. Faculty have an educational opportunity to help adult learners refine their existing mental codes to act in more congruent ways, specifically in honoring innate human value. Critical reflection about cultural contexts urges adult learners to question how the American conception of work reinforces psychological patterns that may impede well-being. Because emotional well-being is rationalized in many theories of predicted human survival and emerging research (e.g., Erikson, 1950, 1968; Fowler, 1981; Kohlberg, 1963, 1983, 1984; Maslow, 1954; Rogers, 1961), faculty are called to consider critical reflection of cultural contexts during leadership preparation in higher education, prompting future educational leaders to renegotiate the American work ethic in favor of human growth needs, including but not limited to esteem, affiliation, and fulfillment.

Esteem. The American conception of work insists on external markers of success to rationalize intangible concepts like that of esteem—the confidence that emerges from the perception of value or worth (Sternberg & Williams, 2010). In a meritocratic culture, growth needs in developing esteem are perceived as conditional upon material success, establishing an endless pursuit to earn worthiness; defense mechanisms such as perfectionism thrive in a culture where growth needs are materialized (Brown, 2010).

Study participants responded to free-market governance structures by adopting perfectionism, "a combination of excessively high personal standards and overly critical self-evaluations" (Curran & Hill, 2019, p. 410). The authors also found that recent generations perceived an increase in social demands in the following ways: (a) social demands imposed by others, (b) social demands insisted on by others, and (c) social demands that were self-inflicted. The researchers associate perfectionism with extreme standards to achieve and the mental burden to perform, perpetuating a desire to earn approval and acceptance. To date, many researchers have also found perfectionism to be correlated with depressive symptoms and "life-paralysis," defined as inaction due to fear of failure (Brown, 2010, p. 56; Smith et al., 2020). In education, school culture emphasizes external markers of success through rewards and punishments (Purpel, 1989). The educational experience may feel like a win-or-lose atmosphere where learners demonstrate worthiness by way of grades, awards, and acknowledgments. Neff (2011) counts human value, arguing that human beings have no pre-qualifying factors to self-worth—worthiness is an automatic attribute of being. For that reason, faculty may consider integrating self-compassion practices in leadership preparation, facilitating human growth needs of esteem for greater acceptance.

Affiliation. In for-profit sociopolitical systems, education is strongly correlated with the economy's supply and demand, using scarcity as a motive for human learning (Giroux, 2012); in a scarcity culture, perceptions of high threat reinforce a work ethic of isolation to outperform the other (Brown, 2015). Defense mechanisms like self-promotion thrive in a culture where growth needs of affiliation are recognized as competition. For example, Bellezza et al. (2016) found that those who perceived an increase in levels of busyness understood it as an indication of higher status. The researchers created a term to capture this new phenomenon, called the *busy-brag*—busyness as a means to market status for recognition and positionality. The busy-brag shifts the emphasis from a scarcity of goods to a scarcity of humans, increasing competition to justify status with human capital value. As a result, loneliness may emerge from too much competition, focusing attention on status symbols over human connection. Recently, researchers found greater feelings of loneliness in American life. According to a national survey of 20,000 respondents, 46% express feeling alone, 43% feel their relationships are not meaningful, and 43% report isolation from others—nearly half of the population reported experiences with loneliness (Cigna, 2018). In education, school culture emphasizes individualism through scarcity and global competition. Some learners may perceive the educational experience to necessitate isolation as a means to justify human capital value in a competitive environment (Purpel, 1989). Brown (2015) counterbalances a culture of scarcity by drawing attention to the shared human experience, contending that an ethic of care, outreach, and connection with others may disrupt the need to compete for status. With that in mind, faculty may consider the facilitation of authentic relationships and listening skills to nurture human growth needs of affiliation in leadership preparation.

Fulfillment. Capitalism reshaped the meaning of American life, prioritizing work as life purpose (Cass, 2018). As a result, a culture of productivity creates a spirit of overdoing, contributing to performance burnout when a natural human limit is met (Dever & Justice, 2019). Defense mechanisms like overworking thrive in a capitalistic culture where growth needs of fulfillment are based on the production of capital. Thompson (2019) describes this phenomenon as workism, an expression of life's purpose and meaning via the workplace. Here, focused attention on capital creates habits of overworking to fit the American narrative: work as existential purpose (Harris, 2017). As an illustration, purpose and meaning at work are now a top priority in American life. Recent findings from a Pew Research report indicated that 95% of participants ranked a job or career above marital goals or social-support systems (Horowitz & Graf, 2019). Another study showed that of 5,641 participants, 43% of stressed American employees avoid taking time off as a way to prove their commitment (Valencia, 2020). Critics counter the idea of workism with an existential-humanistic tradition, arguing that human beings have a unique and intrinsic calling for life purpose. Viktor Frankl (1959), a Holocaust survivor and psychotherapist, theorized that even under the most extreme cases of duress, many prisoners chose to cope by meaning-making. His positive view of the most inhumane conditions allowed focused attention away from the situation toward something meaningful, enabling intrinsic purpose and a will to survive. Many researchers are discovering how intrinsic life purpose may "lead to numerous benefits including improved health, longevity, sleep, mental health, cognitive function, [and] resilience" (Reilly, 2020, para. 9). By way of example, a Gallup research study found that employees who reported a clear understanding of their purpose in the workplace also made positive contributions to the advancement of the organization (CliftonStrengths, 2020). In education, school culture emphasizes workism through the significance placed on productivity; schooling itself may feel like a fragmented experience where learners compartmentalize their full range of personal interests to increase levels of academic achievement (Purpel, 1989). Because of this, faculty may consider introducing mindfulness strategies in leadership as preparation to reinforce growth needs of personal fulfillment, establishing work as less central to purpose.

According to theories of predicted human survival, growth is only possible if psychological needs are met. Critical consciousness educates for the advancement of human growth needs, rehumanizing work for the next generation of educational leaders. Once there is language, awareness, and understanding, future educational leaders are more likely to renegotiate the way they lead and live (Brown, 2015). To that end, it is important that faculty in higher education consider how adult learners vary in the way they reconcile growth needs based on socio-cultural-political contexts, as well as available resources, during leadership preparation. For example, adult learners similar in age range may experience comparable developmental phases but still maintain different demographic variables, influencing phases at different levels. Growth needs may influence the extent to which future educational leaders are able to create the conditions for positive school impact. The concept of transformative learning, and practices like that of contemplation, are lacking serious consideration in the current narrative of the American work ethic. The time has come to reimagine the American conception of work by reprioritizing human growth needs to support human welfare. The next section introduces the value of contemplation in such reimagining.

Contemplative Leadership Preparation

There is nothing in life that proceeds without paradox, creating dissonance that either prompts mental roadblocks or generates transformative learning. Jack Mezirow's transformative learning theory describes a shift in perspective, a "learning that transforms problematic frames of reference to make them more inclusive, discriminating, reflective, open, and emotionally able to change" (Mezirow, 2009, p. 22). This conceptual shift engages unconscious aspects of everyday life, developing awareness of value-belief systems undergirding cultural contexts for greater agency and social change (Taylor, 2009). With critical consciousness, adult learners may act against oppressive methods of cultural practice to transform, lead, and shape communities for the common good (Mezirow, 2000). Transformative learning theory provides a conceptual framework that contextualizes contemplative practice as one way to facilitate human growth needs for greater well-being in the next generation of educational leaders.

Contemplation is gaining attention in mainstream education (Kroll, 2010). Despite recent developments in education, Zajonc (2016) reminds us that contemplative practice has been used during the course of human history, dating back thousands of years in areas of Asia and the West with a rich background in religious and spiritual practices. In particular, he describes the Western tradition of contemplation as the facilitation of human growth through education and training. The stages of contemplation are as follows and may be adapted for leadership preparation: (a) basic comprehension of content, (b) critical rationalization and dialogue, and (c) action and repetition to internalize material (p. 20). Contemplation, Zajonc observes, is a practical approach that "has the possibility of ... dispelling the false views of self and world that lead to unnecessary suffering" (p. 21). It is both a process and an outcome, aiding in the ability to sustain critical reflection to settle dissonance for more congruent states of mind and leadership capacity building.

In recent years, scholars have argued for a secular approach to contemplation. For this reason, continuing discourse to decontextualize contemplation in higher education is common, serving a wide-ranging population diverse in demographics (Zajonc, 2016). In attempts to provide a secular understanding, Barbezat and Bush (2014) offer five elements of contemplative practice: emotional intelligence, compassion/self-compassion, listening competency, mindfulness, and reflection. Krikorian and Busse (2019) explain emotional intelligence and reflection as interdependent elements with the outstanding constructs. On this premise, the following working definition is used for contemplation: compassion/self-compassion, listening competency, and mindfulness. Together, authentic relationships are nurtured as a result.

A contemplative perspective on leadership suggests that all people have the human potential to hold leadership capacities (Zajonc, 2011). Those willing to accept this important role assume:

> an approach to leadership that evolves as one seeks to live in right relationships with self, others, [and] nature ... and strives toward meaning, purpose, ethics and trust in a world of action. It results in a conscious use of power and presence to influence the work of a group or organization, realize human potential, and improve the human condition. (Drey, 2011, p. 9)

Contemplative leadership accepts life paradoxes as invitations for critical reflection to continuously learn, grow, and work toward greater resolve *with* others. In leadership preparation, a critical consciousness of the American work ethic, in addition to the practice of contemplation, may better equip future educational leaders with the knowledge and skills to facilitate greater well-being, creating the conditions necessary for positive school impact. Contemplative practice may be used to support the process and exploration of the self in relation to the world for greater congruence. Krikorian (2022) offers strategies for a more contemplative approach to leadeship preparation that may include, but are not limited to compassion, authentic relationships, listening competency, and mindfulness.

Compassion. Compassion is enacted when care is displayed toward the self and others. Neff (2011) describes compassion as the acknowledgement of, and desire to alleviate, suffering in others. The act of compassion may reduce competition and social distancing, allowing for a sense of affiliation to emerge. In practice, Keltner (2017) and Seligman (as cited by Ben-Shahar, 2009) suggest expressions of gratitude, including: (a) thank-you notes as part of specific interactions with others, (b) public acknowledgements for team contributions, and (c) gratitude office visits to express appreciation for a specific work-related experience. The practice of compassion in the workplace may be included as part of course lectures in leadership preparation. Future educational leaders are likely to acknowledge the shared human condition when compassion is realized, prioritizing an understanding of others over competition with others to put into perspective narratives of scarcity and status in the American conception of work.

Neff (2011) goes on to explain self-compassion as "health and well-being … [that] leads to proactive behavior to better one's situation" (p. 12). Self-compassion has the power to reduce protective measures of perfectionism, allowing for lasting satisfaction and esteem. Robertson (as cited in Corwin, 2020) recommends the development of a self-care plan to implement self-compassion. First, Robertson differentiates self-care from stress relief, where stress relief is an indulgence and/or aspiration that does not change responses to stress (e.g., Netflix/vacation). Second, Robertson points out that though self-compassion means different things to different people, it must always include actions that can be put into use even on the toughest of days. Here, basic needs such as sleep, healthy eating, boundaries, asking for help, and supportive relationships are suggested. And finally, Robertson recommends excluding stress-relief acts from the self-care plan to avoid developing additional forms of self-judgment for failing to meet aspirational goals.

An additional aspect of a self-care plan may include Borges's (2020) use of calendared time off and Sexton's The Three Good Things exercise (MidMichigan Health, 2014). Borges (2020) advocates for regular relaxation because so much time is spent processing information every day. At a minimum, current research recommends that employees take time off once every six weeks, avoiding as well the urge to do something functional (Elsworthy, 2020). A self-care plan that values rest, much in the same way that physical or dental appointments are prioritized, may reduce busyness and overcrowding of time to help avoid burnout. Moreover, Sexton's activity is another great addition to a self-care plan. During high-stress situations, Sexton suggests responding to the following question: "What are three things that went well today and what was my role in making them happen?" (MidMichigan Health, 2014). As discussed in Seligman et al. (2005), Sexton recommends using this practice before sleeping each night for a two-week period, promoting lasting effects on well-being. The creation of a self-care plan may be assigned as part of course requirements in leadership preparation. Future educational leaders are likely to be kind— that is, exhibiting self-compassion—in challenging moments, accepting failure as part of the shared human experience to counter narratives of perfectionism and external rewards in the American conception of work.

Authentic relationships. Authentic relationships allow for space to reflect and explore. Rogers (1961) conceived authentic relationships as open, nonjudgmental, and supportive, constructing a safe environment for productive interactions to take place. In authentic relationships, unconditional positive regard has the power to advance human growth that otherwise may not have occurred. To facilitate this type of relationship, Brown (2010) encourages open communication, while Blankson (as cited in Achor & Gielan, 2017) suggests technology-free spaces. Brown (2010) recommends asking for help, setting boundaries, and holding people accountable, and explains how help-seeking behavior may reduce experiences of loneliness to improve social connections. In addition, boundary setting establishes expectations early on for more transparent and trusting work relationships. When boundaries are not honored, Brown stresses focusing on the act or behavior in the given situation to avoid a perceived personal attack by the individual. Furthermore, Blankson (as cited in Achor & Gielan, 2017) suggests downloading the Offtime or Unplugged phone applications, contending that technology is meant to serve as a tool for communication and not as a substitute for human connection. During personal time off, the applications may schedule automatic airplane-mode periods to minimize work distractions, and implementing work boundaries to prioritize meaningful connections with others. Authentic relationships in the workplace may be discussed as part of course lectures in leadership preparation. Future educational leaders are likely to create spaces for community in the workplace when authentic relationships are nurtured, sustaining affiliation and countering narratives of scarcity and individualism in the American conception of work.

Listening competency. In the literature, listening competency is conceptualized as a way of processing information and an outcome of its function (Fontana et al., 2015). During the listening process, Martin (2010) emphasizes the importance of a perception of listening—an understanding of the speaker characterized through responsive behaviors from the listener that are essential to an effective listening experience. To accomplish this, Martin brings attention to the practice of articulate and reflective responses, silent pauses, and nonverbal cues. Articulate and reflective responses support a deeper understanding of the topic at hand, creating a space for problem-solving in complex situations. The incorporation of silent pauses allows for greater acceptance of emerging emotions, whereas nonverbal cues aid in the ability to infer emotions in understanding the intended message more accurately. As an exercise, Brown (2015) urges honest, constructive, and engaged feedback as one way to practice listening, and highly recommends that feedback be shared within a strengths-based lens, contextualizing it for competencies, capacities, and talents. First, Brown suggests the presentation of three observable strengths as they relate to the task at hand. Then, she proposes that the strengths be used to formulate a recommendation on how to improve the opportunity area. The practice of giving and receiving feedback may be integrated as part of a course requirement for classroom presentations in leadership preparation. Researchers associate feedback from a strength-based lens with greater self-efficacy and work performance over time.

Listening may also be implemented within interactive groupwork. In practice, two members of a group agree to engage with listening techniques while the other members observe for notetaking and feedback. During this time, one partner listens as the other shares a story about a challenging project, work, or school, providing both sides of the issue as well as their own viewpoint and assumptions (Mezirow, 2009). Upon conclusion, those observing offer real-time feedback about listening competencies; the interaction may prompt others to reflect on experiences and examine assumptions. This exercise may also be accomplished virtually using video recordings or virtual-reality simulation.

Listening for understanding supports diverse perspectives in the workplace. Interactive groupwork may be used as part of a course activity in leadership preparation. Future educational leaders are likely to guide challenging situations in real time with the art of listening, calling for pause and reflection to more appropriately respond to the needs of a given situation with greater acceptance and a clearer purpose aligned with personal values, which may counter narratives of workism in the American conception of work (Lippincott, 2018).

Mindfulness. Tolle (2004) describes mindfulness as nonjudgmental awareness of the present moment, and explains how focused attention frees people from fear of failure as it discounts past worries. It also desensitizes people from the concept of success, keeping away from future anxieties of the unknown. Thought patterns primarily derived from experiences of past and/or future emotion may lead to rumination—that is, overthinking about life events; researchers have found an association between rumination and depression and/or anxiety (Ben-Shahar, 2009). Tolle (2004) emphasizes the ability of a present mind to combat undesirable feelings. In practice, researchers recommend steering clear of email in the morning and perceiving weekends like a vacation. Hougaard and Carter (2017) explain how the human body releases the most stress hormones in the brain upon waking. This physiological state may trigger pleasurable hormones that draw people to low-priority email tasks, causing a false perception of productivity first thing in the morning. As a result of this misperception, people may be left feeling stressed about work and distracted for the rest of the day. Instead, Hougaard and Carter suggest building a mindful morning routine, including deep breathing, making breakfast, sipping coffee or tea, and connecting with family or pets. A new morning routine starts the day with little to no outside distractions, releasing cognitive space once occupied by stress to more appropriately order work priorities. Furthermore, Holmes (2019) points out that too many Americans ruminate about work during personal time off, staying engaged in little ways such as checking email and work-based phone applications (e.g., Slack). During the average work week, Holmes urges people to experience weekends like a vacation, positing that the concept of vacation is a state of mind, boosting emotional health and job satisfaction by maximizing rest and relaxation. As part of leadership preparation, mindfulness and its benefits may be considered. Future educational leaders are likely to avoid automatic and reactive responses with the practice of mindfulness to downplay narratives of productivity and overdoing in the American conception of work, sustaining focused and nonjudgmental attention in high-pressure work environments to build equanimity.

CALM

Given the contemplative literature, this chapter presents a working definition informed by four principles, or constructs, summed up in the acronym CALM: (a) compassion, (b) authentic relationships, (c) listening competency, and (d) mindfulness (see Table 6.1). CALM is one way to prepare future educational leaders to combat the American conception of work by attention to human growth needs. As meaning-making species, human beings tell stories to understand their reality. CALM may help future educational leaders refine stories, acting in ways that are more congruent with human growth needs for greater well-being. Educational leader well-being may inspire a more conscious life, reprioritizing the self over cultural standards in the workplace. In general, CALM approaches to educational leadership reinforce holistic human growth, supporting capacities for positive school impact as a result. The sources for the creation of Table 6.1 are given on the next page.

Contemplative leadership preparation may prompt a revised or new consciousness, questioning how the American conception of work supports or hinders human growth needs (Reis, 2020). Contemplation offers a narrative of innate human value and shared human condition, renegotiating cultural standards to learn, grow, and work *with* others, reinforcing agency and capacity for intentional action in context. Given the shifting school landscape and continuous improvement toward public results, professional development is vital but not sufficient to support leadership capacities for optimal school impact. Critical examination of cultural contexts may rehumanize the workplace, functioning at the intersection of personal-

Table 6.1

A CALM Approach to Leadership Preparation

	Construct	Practice Examples	Intended Outcomes
C	Compassion/ Self-Compassion	*Gratitude Practices*: Write thank-you notes; offer public acknowledgements; practice high fives and fist bumps (Keltner, 2017). Self-Care Plan: Stress-relief versus self-care (Robertson, as cited by Corwin, 2020); mental health days (Borges, 2020); Sexton's Three Good Things (MidMichigan Health, 2014).	**Acceptance (Neff, 2011)**
A	Authentic Relationships	*Boundary Setting*: Ask for help; set boundaries; hold people accountable (Brown, 2010). *Technology Free Spaces*: Personal time off (Blankson, as cited in Achor & Gielan, 2017).	**Authenticity (Rogers, 1961)**
L	Listening Skills	*Strength-Based Feedback*: Offer strengths; use strengths to recommend growth areas (Brown, 2015). *Interactive Groupwork*: Identify two individuals in the group to practice listening; instruct others to observe for feedback (Mezirow, 2009).	**Purpose and Meaning-Making (Martin, 2010)**
M	Mindfulness	*Mindful Email*: Avoid email in the morning; develop new morning routine (e.g., sipping coffee/tea (Hougaard & Carter, 2017). *Mindful Weekends*: Perceive weekends like a vacation; refrain from staying connected (Holmes, 2019).	**Equanimity (Tolle, 2004)**

professional life for greater educational leader well-being; in particular, contemplative practice may assist faculty in course design, incorporating critical reflection about the American conception of work. Faculty cannot teach about leadership without identifying cultural contexts, analyzing value-belief systems and the purpose they serve. Contemplative practice is intended to support leadership content and not replace it. Moreover, it is not meant to replace professional mental health consultation if undesirable feelings become unmanageable. In general, contemplative leadership is driven by acceptance of humanity, concern over authenticity, good purpose, and equanimity.

REFLECTIONS

The human mind is hard wired to formulate interpretations based on existing mental codes, operating by the scope of attention attributed to a given value-belief system. Educational leaders have the power to redirect their scope of attention, reframing cultural standards for more congruent states of mind. A path of consciousness and choice is necessary to actualize human growth needs. That said, the journey to wellness starts with critical reflection for consciousness, examining the American conception of work that conditions preceding thought patterns and then governing human behavior. Mezirow (1991) states: "[I]t is not so much what happens to people but how they interpret and explain what happens to them that determines their ... emotional well-being, and their performance" (p. xiii). Moving forward, educational leader well-being depends heavily on more conscious choices to create new experiences of reality. Here, the most integral resource for leadership is the self. Therefore, recreating mental codes in the human mind establishes greater congruence for emotional well-being. Contemplative leadership may serve as one way to facilitate human growth needs to create the conditions necessary for maintaining a positive school environment in ever-changing school contexts.

REFERENCES

Achor, S., & Gielan, M. (2017). Resilience is about how you recharge, not how you endure. In D. Goleman, J. A. Sonnenfeld, & S. Achor (Eds.), *Resilience: Emotional intelligence series* (pp. 109–122). Harvard Business Review.

Bellezza, S., Paharia, N., & Keinan, A. (2017). Conspicuous consumption of time: When busyness and lack of leisure time become a status symbol. *Journal of Consumer Research, 44*(1), 118–138.

Barbezat, D., & Bush, M. (2014). *Contemplative practices in higher education*. Jossey-Bass.

Ben-Shahar, T. (2009). *The pursuit of perfect: Stop chasing perfection and find your path to lasting happiness!* McGraw-Hill.

Borges, A. (2020, February 18). *9 smart tips for taking a mental health day that actually work*. Self. https://www.self.com/story/mental-health-day-tips

Brackett, M. (2019). *Permission to feel*. Celadon Books.

Brown, B. (2010). *The gifts of imperfection: Let go of who you think you are supposed to be and embrace who you are*. Hazeldon.

Brown, B. (2015). *Daring greatly: How the courage to be vulnerable transforms the way we live, love, parent, and lead*. Penguin.

Capritto, A. (2019, May 29). *Burnout is now an official medical diagnosis, says the World Health Organization*. [C|net]. https://www.cnet.com/news/burnout-is-now-an-official-medical-diagnosis-says-the-world-health-organization/

Cass, O. (2018). *The once and future worker: A vision for the renewal of work in America*. Encounter Books.

Cigna. (2018, July 25). *2018 U.S. Loneliness Index*. https://www.cigna.com/assets/docs/newsroom/loneliness-survey-2018-fact-sheet.pdf

CliftonStrengths. (2020, June 27). *Create a culture that inspires: Purpose* [YouTube]. https://www.youtube.com/watch?v=vShSFIzQRWQ&feature=youtu.be&t=

Corwin. (2020, April 27). *Ricky Robertson: Supporting Educator resilience during shelter in place* [YouTube]. https://www.youtube.com/watch?v=OdrUcu592H4&feature=youtu.be

Curran, T., & Hill, A. P. (2019). Perfectionism is increasing over time: A meta-analysis of birth cohort differences from 1989 to 2016. *American Psychological Association Psychological Bulletin, 145*(4), 410–429.

Dever, C., & Justice, G. (2019). *Needed: A real conversation about academic hours worked.* Inside Higher Ed. https://tinyurl.com/w5tnbwn7

Drey, J. (2010, September 13). *Contemplative leadership in organizations.* http://www.contemplative-leadership.com/wp-content/uploads/2011/07/Contemplative-Leadership-Paper.pdf

Elsworthy, E. (2020, July 22). *Office workers need time off every 43 days to avoid burnout, new study shows.* Independent. https://www.independent.co.uk/news/uk/home-news/burnout-office-workplace-time-off-annual-leave-new-study-a9632556.html

Erikson, E. H. (1950). *Childhood and society.* Norton.

Erikson, E. H. (1968). *Identity, youth, and crisis.* Norton.

Evans, T. M., Bira, L., Gastelum, J. B., Weiss, L. T., & Vanderford, N. L. (2018). Evidence for a mental health crisis in graduate education. *Nature Biotechnology, 36*(3), 282–284. https://doi.org/10.1038/nbt.4089

Festinger, L. (1957). *A theory of cognitive dissonance.* Stanford University Press.

Fontana, P. C., Cohen, S. D., & Wolvin, A. D. (2015). Understanding listening competency: A systematic review of research scales. *International Journal of Listening, 29*(3), 148–176. https://doi.org/10.1080/10904018.2015.1015226

Fowler, J. W. (1981). *Stages of faith: The psychology of human development and the quest for meaning.* HarperCollins.

Frankl, V. E. (1959). *Man's search for meaning.* Beacon.

Frey, L. L. (2018). When it hurts to work: Organizational violations and betrayals. *New Directions for Teaching and Learning, 153,* 87–98. https://doi.org/10.1002/tl.20284

Giroux, H. (2012). *Education and the crisis of public values: Challenging the assault on teachers, students, and public education.* Peter Lang.

Harris, M. (2017). *Kids these days: Human capital and the making of millennials.* Hachette Book Group.

Holmes, C. M. (2019). *Treat your weekend like a vacation.* Harvard Business Review. https://hbr.org/2019/01/treat-your-weekend-like-a-vacation

Horowitz, J. M., & Graf, N. (2019, February 20). *Most U.S. teens see anxiety and depression as a major problem among their peers.* Pew Research Center: Social & Demographic Trends. https://www.pewsocialtrends.org/2019/02/20/most-u-s-teens-see-anxiety-and-depression-as-a-major-problem-among-their-peers/

Hougaard, R., & Carter, J. (2017). How to practice mindfulness throughout your work day. In D. Goleman, E. Langer, S. David, & C. Congleton (Eds.), *Mindfulness: Emotional intelligence series* (pp. 37–46). Harvard Business Review.

Keltner, D. (2017). Don't let power corrupt you. In D. Goleman, E. Langer, S. David, & C. Congleton (Eds.), *Mindfulness: Emotional intelligence series* (pp. 71–88). Harvard Business Review.
Kohlberg, L. (1963). The development of moral thought. *Vita Humana, 6*, 11–33.
Kohlberg, L. (1983). *The psychology of moral development*. Harper and Row.
Kohlberg, L. (1984). The psychology of moral development: The nature and validity of moral stages. In *Essays on moral development* (Vol. 2). Harper and Row.
Kouzes, J., & Posner, B. (2012). *The leadership challenge* (5th ed.). Jossey-Bass.
Krikorian, M. (2022). *Higher educaiton for the people*. Information Age Publishing.
Krikorian, M., & Busse, B. T. (2019). Construction of a scale of contemplative practice in higher education: An exploratory study. *Journal of Contemplative Inquiry, 6*(1), 145–174. https://doi.org/10.36837/chapman.000014
Kroll, K. (2010). Contemplative practice in the classroom. *New Directions for Community Colleges, 2010*(151), 111–113.
Lippincott, J. M. (2018, February 9). *Our brains are to blame: The neuroscience of feedback*. Training Industry. https://trainingindustry.com/articles/performancemanagement/our-brains-are-to-blametheneuroscience-of-feedback
Martin, D. G. (2010). *Counseling & therapy skills* (3rd ed.). Waveland.
Maslow, A. H. (1954). *Motivation and personality*. Harper & Row.
Mezirow, J. (1991). *Transformative dimensions of adult learning*. Jossey-Bass.
Mezirow, J. (2000). Learning to think like an adult: Core concepts of transformation theory. In J. Mezirow & Associates (Eds.), *Learning as transformation: Critical perspectives on a theory in progress* (pp. 3–34). Jossey-Bass.
Mezirow, J. (2009). Transformative learning in practice: Insights from community, workplace, and higher education. In J. Mezirow & Associates & E. W. Taylor (Eds.), *Transformative learning theory* (pp. 18–31). Wiley.
MidMichigan Health. (2014). *The 3 good things exercise explained by Bryan Sexton, Ph.D* [PowerPoint presentation]. https://www.midmichigan.org/quality-safety/3-good-things/
Neff, K. (2011). *Self-compassion: The proven power of being kind to yourself*. HarperCollins.
Palmer, P. J., Zajonc, A., & Scribner, M. (2010). *The heart of higher education: A call to renewal*. Jossey-Bass.
Petersen, A. H. (2019, January 5). *How millennials became the burnout generation*. BuzzFeed News. https://www.buzzfeednews.com/article/annehelenpetersen/millennials-burnout-generation-debt-work
Porter, G. (2010). Work ethic and ethical work: Distortions in the American dream. *Journal of Business Ethics, 96*, 535–550. https://doi.org/10.1007/s10551-010-0481-6
Prior, R. (2019, May 27). *Burnout is an official medical diagnosis, World Health Organization says*. [CNN: Health]. https://www.cnn.com/2019/05/27/health/who-burnout-disease-trnd/index.html
Purpel, D. (1989). *The moral & spiritual crisis in education: A curriculum for justice and compassion in education*. Bergin & Garvey.
Reilly, C. (2020, July 7). *The rise of the chief wellbeing officer*. Forbes. https://tinyurl.com/2frv6fda

Reis, R. (2020). *Educational leadership: Motivation*. Tomorrow's Professor Postings. https://tomprof.stanford.edu/posting/1767

Rogers, C. R. (1961). *On becoming a person: A therapist's view of psychotherapy*. Houghton Mifflin.

Seligman, M. E., Steen, T. A., Park, N., & Peterson, C. (2005). Positive psychology progress: Empirical validation of interventions. *American Psychologist, 60*(5), 410.

Smith, E., & Brooks, Z. (2015, August). *Graduate Student Mental Health 2015*. National Association of Graduate-Professional Students (NAGPS) Institute. http://nagps.org/wordpress/wpcontent/uploads/2015/06/NAGPS_Institute_mental_health_survey_report_2015.pdf

Smith, M. M., Sherry, S. B., Vidovic, V., Hewitt, P. L., & Flett, G. L. (2020). Why does perfectionism confer risk for depressive symptoms? A meta-analytic test of the mediating role of stress and social disconnection. *Journal of Research in Personality, 86*, 1–14. https://doi.org/10.1016/j.jrp.2020.103954

Sternberg, R. J., & Williams, W. M. (2010). *Educational psychology* (2nd ed.). Pearson Education.

Taylor, E. W. (2009). Transformative learning in practice: Insights from community, workplace, and higher education. In J. Mezirow & Associates & E. W. Taylor (Eds.), *Fostering transformative learning* (pp. 3–17). Wiley.

Thompson, D. (2019, February 24). *Workism is making Americans miserable*. The Atlantic. https://www.theatlantic.com/ideas/archive/2019/02/religion-workmsm-making-americans-miserable/583441/

Tolle, E. (2004). *The power of now: A guide to spiritual enlightenment*. New World Library.

UC Berkeley Graduate Assembly. (2015, April 22). *Graduate student happiness and well-being report*. The Graduate Assembly. http://ga.berkeley.edu/wellbeingreport

Valencia, J. (2020, June 2). *How to convince your boss you need time off*. Harvard Business Review. https://hbr.org/2020/06/how-to-convince-your-boss-you-need-time-off

Zajonc, A. (2011). *Contemplative practices in leadership education*. The Center for Contemplative Mind in Society. https://www.contemplativemind.org/archives/leadership

Zajonc, A. (2016). Contemplation in education. In Schonert-Reichl, K. A., & Roeser, R. W. (Eds.), *The handbook of mindfulness in education: Emerging theory, research, and programs* (pp. 17–28). Springer. https://doi.org/oi 10.1007/978-1-4939-3506-2_2

CHAPTER 7

LEADING FROM THE CENTER

Leadership Well-Being and Team Effectiveness in Education Agencies

Irma Eloff and Ruth "Molly" McGee Hewitt

The job requirements and responsibilities of educational administrators continue to evolve as organizational challenges, demands, and expectations increase. Job descriptions for today's school leaders often fail to acknowledge the complexities and demands of leadership and the management of schools and school systems. With duties that include site and district management, leading a diverse workforce, providing instructional leadership, ensuring staff accountability, improving student achievement, promoting diversity, managing public and community expectations, negotiating union issues, and administering school sites and educational programs that must be delivered both virtually and in person, those in leadership could easily be overwhelmed by the prospects of the duties before them. As a result, personal well-being may easily be ignored in order to serve students and staff. Long hours, lack of attention to personal needs and health, stress and anxiety, and family challenges may subsequently hamper effective leadership.

In this chapter, the notion of "leading from the center" is explored. The concept emanates from the emergent concept of "leading from the middle" in various fields (DeRusso et al., 2020; Kauffman, 2016; Knies, 2017; Nickerson, 2014), advocating a collaborative and collegial leadership style that challenges traditional leadership by encouraging and promoting the development of a team culture and fostering accountability and group responsibility—and inherently the well-being of all team members. While a senior executive leader still maintains authority, the leadership team develops a culture of trust, honesty, accountability, and responsibility about the organization and the team's efforts. The leadership group cultivates and supports individual and group efforts, and promotes well-being by developing a culture of strong personal and interpersonal relationships and understanding. The well-being of both the individual and the group is paramount to their long-term success. As such, well-being in a center-led organization becomes an expected standard.

This chapter explores the concept of senior executive leadership teams and senior leaders in education administration organizations working collaboratively to ensure high-quality education. An embedded, multiple-case-study methodology of four educational agencies in California were used to explore leadership well-being and team effectiveness in education agencies. The case studies comprised a school district, a government educational agency, and two for-profit educational organizations in which 25 senior leaders and team members participated for over two years. Focus groups, in-depth interviews, and personal observations were used as data collection strategies. The study builds on the literature on the emergent concept of leading from the center, which pivots on a strong team culture, high levels of trust and honesty among leadership team members, and explicit shared core values. The chapter argues that by deliberately designing teams that are led from the center, pathways to organizational excellence and leadership well-being can be created.

BACKGROUND

This chapter explores leadership well-being in senior executive teams and senior educational leaders who are working collaboratively to ensure high-quality education in schools. While substantive research has focused on teacher well-being (Abenavoli et al., 2013; Cherkowski, 2018; Simmons et al., 2019), limited research to date has considered the issues affecting educational agencies with responsibilities for comprehensive school systems. This chapter and the related research will explore, study, and identify the leadership, the well-being, and the characteristics of effective leadership teams in business and educational organizations. The chapter also provides key constructs for education leaders to develop the capacity to replicate these characteristics in their own organizations.

METHODOLOGY

Using a mixed-methods approach that included a multiple case study methodology of four educational agencies in California, we explored the factors that contribute to the universality of leadership and team effectiveness and leadership well-being. There is a significant amount of research focused on classroom or school-site leadership as well as corporate leadership (Al-Safran et al., 2014; Anderson, 2012; DuFour & Fullan, 2013; Dumay et al., 2013; Fullan & Quinn, 2016; Laloux & Wilber, 2014; Lambert, 2003). Much of this research is focused on the development of effective and productive teams (Groysberg & Slind, 2012; Laloux & Wilber, 2014; Lee & Edmondson, 2017; Törnblom, 2018). LaFasto and Larson's (2002) study of over 6,000 team members and leaders identified the connection between leadership behaviors and how it contributes to team effectiveness. In school systems, school-site teams have become interested in the team approach as pioneered in the movement for professional learning communities (Tan & Caleon, 2015; DuFour & Eaker, 2009; DuFour & Fullan, 2013; Voelkel & Chrispeels, 2017). While the research is extensive for the corporate environment and school settings, there is little study of the universality of leadership and team effectiveness in relation to educational organizations and school systems, with a specific focus on educational administration.

For the purposes of this study, the identification of effective schools has been determined by student achievement, parent satisfaction, employee satisfaction, standardized test scores, and fiscal solvency within the various school districts (Hawley, 2007; McInerney et al., 2006). Effective educational organizations incorporate multiple divisions and units designed to support the classroom and the student. In a large urban school district, the organization employs a central administrative team of executives and managers that handle a complete range of services, from instruction, transportation, child nutrition and food services, facilities and maintenance, finance and accounting, technology, human resources, purchasing and procurement, and student health and safety to assessment and governance. If the school district is to be successful in supporting the classroom and school sites, these services should operate with efficiency and effectiveness. If individuals or divisions operate as independent silos, they are independent and do not create an interdependent team that works cooperatively and cohesively to meet the needs of the students.

School systems around the globe need to examine their leadership practices and central administration functions in order to ensure efficiencies and optimal learning environments. Our study endeavored to identify key performance indications and core principles that can be replicated in school districts to build strong executive and leadership teams that will support student achievement and efficiencies in management. Well-being is acknowledged in our study by including longevity of leaders, consistency in leadership, and the value of culture and collegiality.

RATIONALE FOR THE STUDY

The rationale for this study is based on the concept that by creating and sustaining effective teams and investing in leadership well-being, organizations will be better able to manage their operations and continue to focus their priorities on students and student achievement. While the cost of system inefficiencies has not been characterized, in California, the Fiscal Crisis and Management Assistance Team (FCMAT) considers these issues in its process of Extraordinary Audits. Over 50 Extraordinary Audits have been conducted on California schools, and the reports indicate that financial and human resources were expended on litigation and issues related to school district management (Fiscal Crisis and Management Assistance Team, 2019). If we can improve the leadership and team practices of schools, it can be argued that these resources could be used to further student achievement and progress. It could also be argued that it would enhance the well-being and job satisfaction of key executives by promoting strong leadership and working to eliminate stress and conflict.

LEADERSHIP, WELL-BEING, AND TEAM EFFECTIVENESS IN EDUCATION ORGANIZATIONS

To stay relevant and current, organizations must continually evolve (Anderson, 2012; LaLoux & Wilbur, 2014). In the education world, this evolution includes creating effective schools and learning environments for students, and investing in well-being (Eloff, 2013). In this new atmosphere, while talented administrators and leaders may help to identify gaps in organizational process, only skilled and knowledgeable teams are equipped to fill these gaps (Sperber & Linder, 2018). The shift from a single leader to a team of leaders is a fairly new phenomenon in schools and the education field.

We note the growing interest in developing effective teams in the public and private sectors that are interested in conducting research into the development of key performance indicators/characteristics and in identifying best practices that support effective team development in education administration. We relied on a combination of literature that discusses not only the role of the superintendent or senior leader, but also the role of effective teams (Hackman, 2011; Sperber & Linder, 2016). Effective teams exist, but they often exist in a vacuum and are also often considered the exception rather than the rule in educational governance. The success of district administrative teams is normally attributed to the leadership of the superintendent rather than to the leadership of the management team. Because most superintendents in school systems rise to their positions from the instructional arena, many have limited knowledge or expertise in organizing or directing complex organizations with multiple units, divisions, or school sites. They may have been recognized for their instructional or curriculum expertise or political acumen, but with little regard for their management or executive leadership skills. With such a leader inexperienced in team leadership. The result is often a dysfunctional organization with silos or groups working in opposition or isolation from each other. In the worst-case scenarios, the central administration can be viewed as being indifferent or in opposition, leaving the school sites to operate as individual organizations with little regard or respect for the efforts of others. This can cause organizational inefficiency and disappointment as well as costly problems in serving the business needs of school systems.

To better understand how effective team leadership can enhance the educational administration of schools, research is needed to identify specific characteristics and key performance indicators that are essential in the development of a productive and cohesive administrative team in education. Once identified, these characteristics and best practices could be used to assist school systems in improving leadership and governance. The purpose of this study is to investigate how leadership team effectiveness can be created and sustained in educational organizations.

In the four case studies, each organization has shown the ability to maintain a successful organization. The outcomes of the study identify what those case studies have in common or what sustainable practices they use to provide ongoing leadership and to avoid issues that waste time, resources, and focus. This study provides insights into the ways that some of these factors may be mediated at the leadership level.

Teams are a basic structure of human organizations. An organizational team is often designed to meet and lead an organization's plan for innovative performance (Sperber & Linder, 2016). This study reflects on how these teams are used in a variety of organizations, including public education, private business, medical, and military organizations, among others. In this chapter, we examine four specific senior executive teams and their senior leaders. The literature supports the concept that teamwork is a definitive and powerful advantage in today's competitive markets, and it is argued that effective teaming is also necessary for education organizations to thrive (Garmston & Wellman, 2009; Jones & Bearley, 2001; LaFasto & Larson, 2002).

The terms "teams" and "groups" are often used interchangeably. For this study, we defined a "team" as a group of people united by a common purpose (Block, n.d.). Another definition is that teams are groups of two or more people who interact and influence each other. They may be mutually accountable for achieving goals and find their work associated with and aligned to organizational objectives; they also perceive themselves as a social entity within an organization (McShane & Von Glinow, 2018). For this study, the focus was on the senior executive team. These individuals include the senior leader and top senior executive management personnel in each case study organization.

METHODOLOGY AND CASE STUDY DESIGN

The study used an embedded, multiple-case design study (Yin, 2009) that included focus groups, in-depth interviews, and personal observations as data collection strategies, which were applied during multiple onsite visits, Skype meetings, and conference calls. Each senior leader and case study participant was involved in group focus meetings as well as individual and personal interviews. The focus group meetings were used to explain the study and to gain group insight into leadership well-being and team effectiveness in education agencies. Individual meetings and telephone calls were used to conduct structured and semi-structured interviews (McGee Hewitt, 2019).

In the design of the research methodology for this study, the perception that multiple methods could be used to explore a research problem was a significant factor (McMillan & Schumacher, 2010; Patton, 2015). The study explores four very different organizations, and the options available in this approach were a positive fit. Case studies could be used to explain and interpret, to explore phenomena, to develop or to test new instruments, and to pose a relevant question at different levels (Denzin & Lincoln, 2011, 2018; Johnson et al., 2007).

CASE STUDIES

The study, which comprised the senior executive team of a large urban California school system and three other educational agencies, used multiple levels of analysis to explore a unique variety of questions, focusing on: How can leadership team effectiveness and well-being be created and sustained in educational organizations? The supporting questions included: How do organizational factors or leadership methods contribute to creating and sustaining effective teams? How does the senior/executive leader affect team success?

The main unit of analysis was the senior executive teams and their roles, actions, and influence in creating and sustaining a successful team; a secondary level of analysis was developed for analyzing the styles, skills, and leadership profiles of the senior/executive team. The goal was to use the senior executive leadership teams' group to understand how the team creates, motivates, and sustains the effectiveness of a leadership team.

Case Study One—Clovis Unified School District

The Clovis Unified School District is a K–12 school district serving a suburban community located in central California. The district was formed in 1960; serves 43,000 students; and has 33 elementary schools, five intermediate schools, five high schools, four alternative schools, one adult school, one online school (the Center for Advanced Research and Technology [CART]), and one outdoor and environmental education school. It is a growing community, with over 6,400 full- and part-time employees serving the student population.

In an era where there is great turnover in executive leadership in public education, Clovis remains a stable district with a low rate of leadership change; the most notable of these have occurred in their governance board with the election of two new members. Throughout these additions to their organization, the district and its leadership team continues to provide stable and award-winning leadership.

Research into this group revealed a strong and cohesive leadership team that placed a high degree of importance on team membership, culture, and mutual accountability. The consistency of their leadership, the longevity of their senior executive leader, and their passion for their work identified an environment that valued workers as individuals and promoted a culture of health and well-being.

Case Study Two—American Fidelity Life Assurance Company

American Fidelity is a large, for-profit corporation that provides services nationally to school systems with a variety of financial and administrative products. They are an international corporation whose subsidiaries include a variety of banks, businesses, and divisions. This study centered on their educational division.

Research for this organization identified the value of individual and group accountability and of the organization's culture and team culture on individual and group success. The longevity of team members and senior executive leaders was also highlighted. This longevity was tied to a commitment to the organization and their personal and professional satisfaction.

Case Study Three—Fiscal Crisis Management Assistance Team

The Fiscal Crisis Management Assistance Team (FCMAT) is a tax-supported agency of the State of California that was created to assist school districts in economic distress. Its mission, leadership, and focus has remained the same since the start of this study. While some may consider FCMAT an unusual case study subject, for us it served as a lighthouse example of a well-run, successful, well-respected organization with a reputation for reliability, honesty, and results.

The findings in this study, while mirroring those of our other case studies in some respects, highlighted the value of passion and dedication to agency purpose and the interpersonal relationships of the leadership team members and their senior executive leader.

Case Study Four—School Services of California

School Services of California (SSC) is a for-profit service and consulting company headquartered in Sacramento. As the providers of fiscal and management consulting services to over 90% of the school districts, offices of education, and community colleges in the state, they are perhaps the most recognized and respected firm in the educational industry.

Our findings on this organization, while again consistent with our other case studies, revealed the positive impact of the senior executive and the team leadership on the long-term growth and well-being of their organization. Attention to the team and their direct reports, and concerns about their work, lives, and future, were brought to light. As in our other studies, the team members wanted to be a part of the organization and felt valued and appreciated. They believed that the senior leader cared about their individual and group well-being.

FINDINGS

Within the unique themes that emerged within each case study, three broad themes arose from the study when all the case studies were considered collectively:

- Team culture.
- Trust and honesty.
- Focus and shared core values.

The initial theme analysis in our study was conducted by the lead researcher and then subsequently refined within the research team. It was evident that each case study organization presented similar key concepts, which emerged as dominant themes in this study.

A primary factor that contributed to team effectiveness in these case studies may be the concept that successful and effective teams happen by design and execution—not by accident. As we explored how they created and developed their teams and how they defined the concept of effectiveness and success, these concepts were consistent: a strong team culture; trust and honesty among leadership; and clear focus and shared core values that manifested in distinct team expectations and agreements. Each of these concepts was regarded as a foundational piece for the creation and sustainability of the senior executive leadership team in all of the case studies. In addition, each of the concepts also connect with key well-being concepts such as relationships, engagement, positive emotions, meaning, and achievement (Seligman, 2018).

Team Culture

While each case study organization had a unique culture, strong leadership and the value of team culture were vital to their success. Each organization could define its culture and identify their leadership styles and expectations and expressed accountability as a top priority.

In individual interviews with senior leadership in all four organizations, the culture of the organization and the team was emphasized over and over as a theme shared universally by all team members. Members of each senior executive team shared their commitment to their organization and their pride in employment.

In the Clovis Unified School District, for instance, the recurring theme was that they were part of the best school district in California. They saw themselves as a winning organization and they wanted to be a part of it. They also used this as a marketing tool and a core value, mentioning that not everyone could work there and that they hired only those who they considered to be the best candidates for positions.

Accountability was also a continuing theme within the descriptions of team culture of each group. Methods to ensure accountability included regular reporting, clear expectations, clear chains of command, group knowledge, involvement in decision-making, problem-solving, and maintaining high standards. Not only did they hold their teams accountable, but they also shared a high level of personal accountability. Each person wanted to make sure that they were adding value to their team.

The value of their reputation in the educational industry was a significant positive for each organization. They valued their reputations and agreed that the continuation of this legacy was a part of their organizational culture. Reputation was also a strong factor in what attracted the participants to their organizations initially; they viewed the organization's reputation as an indicator of the professional trust inherent to the organization. In sum, each organization named trust, commitment, accountability, and results as integral to their reputation.

Closely aligned with the issue of reputation was integrity. While each group cited this issue as a core value, they also identified some challenges that come with the organizations' reputations and viewed integrity as an essential value for building brand influence in the marketplace.

Trust and Honesty

Trust was an important factor for each team. To be a successful team, each group saw this as a foundational aspect of their work and of their relationships. They had trust in the organization and its values and priorities. They had trust in the intention and leadership of their senior leader. They also had high levels of trust with each other. Trust was an expectation for each team.

In the American Fidelity Life Assurance Company, for instance, participants shared that from their initial interviews and orientations to their current professional development, the values of trust and honesty are promoted and expected. In doing so, team members indicated an appreciation for the support this had on their work because it allowed them to request assistance or share concerns without fear.

Individual members of each team in all the organizations shared during interviews that the ability to be candid, open, and honest about their challenges and successes was key to their personal and team well-being. Trust, honesty, and openness were cited in each focus group and in the individual interviews of all the organizations.

In this regard, the concept of "educated trust" was often discussed. Each senior executive team believed that they did not have blind trust, but rather trust that was based on past experiences, histories, and relationships, and thus informed, or "educated." The trust they placed in their senior leader and in each other was paramount to their success.

Focus and Shared Core Values

The case study participants frequently commented on focus, core values, character traits, and morals, and their value to the senior executive team and the organization. Focus allows the senior executive team to keep aligned on their priorities and to structure work to accomplish goals. In leadership, it is easy to lose focus when challenges or crises hit. In this study, it seemed that each senior executive team regularly discusses and agrees upon focus and priorities.

Together, core values, character traits, and morals were noted in the hiring values as the chief component of team culture, reported to be the No. 1 and No. 2 consideration of all new hires, who were added for fitness to the core values first. A team with an established and practiced set of values was a constant in this study. Teams do not develop core values by accident; like team building, it is done with intention. The groups recommended that senior executive teams take the time to identify their core values.

In the Fiscal Crisis Management Assistance Team, for instance, participants shared that due to the nature and importance of their work, focus was vital to their success. Their focus enabled them to concentrate on accuracy and to deliver services that were relevant and timely. They also shared that they believe their work provides a vital and necessary service to public schools that enables the schools to use their resources to adequately support student students and student achievement.

At School Services of California, for instance, participants expressed that shared core values were a major benefit to their employment. The history, reputation, and commitment to their employees and clients, along with clearly articulated values and beliefs, were valued by the employees. Every senior leadership team member indicated that these shared core values were fundamental to their success as an organization and as a team.

During the research, there was consensus within each group when asked to identify the core values of their organization, their personal values, and that of their senior leaders. In the individual interviews, every participant was able to readily identify the core values of the group and explain how these values mirrored their own values. This was evident from the word choices and examples used repeatedly and consistently.

The participants in the case study commented on the topic of focus and core values and their value to the senior executive team and the organization. Focus allows keeping sight on priorities and structuring work to accomplish goals. It is easy to lose focus when challenges or crises hit. Most senior executive team members in this study regularly discuss and agree upon focus and priorities and recommend this activity to others. In these meetings, they not only worked on organizational issues, but also used the time to build strong interpersonal relationships and collegial friendships. They cared about the organization and each other's success and well-being.

This observation was supported by the amount of time the groups spend both formally and informally establishing relationships and participating together in activities. They also recommended that spending time formally reviewing items such as strategic plans and mission or vision statements, and understanding the culture and values of their organization, contributed to this process.

DISCUSSION AND IMPLICATIONS

The findings from this study affirm much of the research that has been done broadly in the realm of leadership, team effectiveness, and well-being (Du et al., 2014; Goodwin et al., 2006; Hackman, 2011; Katzenbach & Smith, 2015; Kerns, 2019). In this case, however, the findings illuminate and explore how the key constructs that emerge within the context of education agencies' leadership team effectiveness and well-being can be created and sustained.

Leadership research during the last five decades has proliferated (Fullan & Hargreaves, 2012; Kotter, 1996). In the last five years, the emphasis in leadership is turning to anything that is team based—that is, top management teams, global virtual teams, and transformational leadership teams:

> In part, the prevalence of teams within organizations is due to the complex problems that the organizations often face and the synergistic benefits that the use of teams can provide to the organizations—that is, teams offer the capability to achieve what cannot be accomplished by one individual acting alone. (Hackman, 2011, p. 1)

The complexity of the world and of the education world is indeed expanding and this may be the harbinger of a renewed interest in leadership teams.

LEADING FROM THE CENTER

Our study supports the notion of leading from the center as a potential pivot to ensure leadership well-being in agencies working in the education sector (Nickerson, 2014). We maintain that by deliberately designing teams that are led from the center, pathways to organizational excellence and leadership well-being may be created by purposefully building team culture, trust and honesty, focus, and shared core values. In this regard, the role of the senior leader in the organization is critical.

Role of the Senior Leader

The role and value of the senior leader is important to the success of the team. The senior leader's emotional intelligence and self-knowledge includes:

- Trustworthiness.
- Ability to interpret and understand personal priorities and proclivities.
- Focused attention to the members of the team—needs, talents, challenges.
- Steadfast leadership.
- Ability to be fair and impartial in dealing with people and issues.

The senior leader consistently:

- Provides constant presence and access.
- Exhibits demonstrated commitment to team members and the organization.
- Gives and receives absolute trust.
- Understands and uses the specific expertise and talent of the team members and the group (team).
- Understands the nature of conflict and engages with issues regularly.
- Shows commitment to the individuals; team members are valued individually by the senior leader, both personally and professionally.
- Is committed to the organization; the longer the tenure and involvement, the more this commitment is demonstrated.
- Clearly identifies expectations.
- Values accountability.
- Communicates that results matter; has a clear ability to review and access the outcomes and results of the team and organization.

Practices

- Continued and consistent attention to the development and ongoing success of the team.
- Team members acknowledge that personal well-being and group well-being are essential for success.
- Investing in the cohesiveness of the team.
- Each member of the team is important to its their success.
- The senior leader's effectiveness and success is inextricably tied to the team.

- Group accountability, responsibility, problem-solving, and support are encouraged.
- Group success is valued over individual success.
- Communication practices that promote honesty, openness, and clarity are evident.
- Social connections exist between team members.
- Identification of organization priorities versus division or individual unit priorities are clearly defined.
- Health and well-being practices that promote individual and group success are encouraged.
- Time commitments and professional expectations are realistic.
- Support of the team members for personal, family, and individual responsibilities of team members.
- Compassion and support for team members experiencing health, family, or personal challenges.
- Development of communication strategies that include, but are not limited to, regular meetings or communications.
- Time dedicated to celebrating success and accomplishments.
- Thoughtful and informed selection and orientation of new team members.
- Continual review of values, goals, and priorities.
- The ability to continually encourage and develop new leaders in senior team leaders is apparent.
- Identification and appreciation for the ongoing development of communication and conflict resolution skills.
- Evaluation practices that encourage leader well-being and leadership effectiveness.
- Resources established to provide individual support for leaders.

LIMITATIONS OF THE STUDY

There are several limitations of the study: (a) the lack of generalizability between the educational agencies and organizations in this study to other contexts; (b) the lack of long-term follow-up in leadership well-being for participants in this study; (c) the close relationships that were developed during data collection contributed to in-depth insights in team dynamics, but it could also have contributed to increased researcher subjectivity; and (d) the in-depth study also created a vast data set, but for the purpose of this chapter the findings are only presented in a distilled format in order to increase accessibility for leaders and researchers.

CONCLUSION

The findings presented in this chapter suggest that investing in leadership well-being may potentially have beneficial effects at the systemic level within an organization. By creating environments in which leaders can lead from the center and emphasize team culture, trust, and honesty, focus and shared core values, individual and organizational well-being can be enhanced, and efficiencies improved. Leaders tend to take on responsibilities for systemic well-being within their organizations, and sometimes they do so to the detriment of their own well-being. Investing in leadership well-being and increasing the understanding of leadership well-being may, however, initiate cycles of well-being that can motivate the well-being of all.

RESOURCES

Ebersöhn, L. (2019). *Flocking together: An indigenous psychology theory of resilience in Southern Africa*. Springer.

Fullan, M., & Campbell, D. W. (2019). *The governance core: School boards, superintendents, and schools working together*. Corwin.

Fullan, M., & Hargreaves, A. (2012). *Professional capital: Transforming teaching in every school*. Teachers College Press.

Fullan, M., & Quinn, J. (2016). Coherence making: How leaders cultivate the pathway for school and system with a shared process. *School Administrator*, 6(23), 30–34. https://www.pageturnpro.com/AASA/72631-June-2016/sdefault.html#page/34

Hattie, J. (2015). *What works best in education: The politics of collaborative expertise*. Pearson. https://www.pearson.com/content/dam/corporate/global/pearson-dot-com/files/hattie/150526_ExpertiseWEB_V1.pdf

Lencioni, P. (2014). *The five behaviors of a cohesive team: Annotated team report* (pp. 1–44). Wiley.

Lencioni, P. (2019, November 3). *The five behaviors of a cohesive team model*. DiSC Profile. https://www.discprofile.com/resources-and-tools/5behaviors-support/model/

REFERENCES

Abenavoli, R. M., Jennings, P. A., Greenberg, M. T., Harris, A. R., & Katz, D. A. (2019). The protective effects of mindfulness against burnout among educators. *The Psychology of Education Review*, 37(2), 57–69.

Al-Safran, E., Brown, D., & Wiseman, A. (2014). The effect of principal's leadership style on school environment and outcome. *Research in Higher Education Journal, 22*. http://www.aabri.com/manuscripts/131666.pdf

Anderson, D. L. (2012). *Organizational development: The process of leading organizational change*. SAGE.

Block, P. (n.d.). *The leadership toolbox: Building teams*. https://leadershiptoolbox.study/leading-teams/building-teams/

Cherkowski, S. (2018). Positive teacher leadership: Building mindsets and capacities to grow well-being. *International Journal of Teacher Leadership, 9*(1), 63–78. https://eric.ed.gov/?id=EJ1182707

Denzin, N. K., & Lincoln, Y. S. (2018). *The SAGE handbook of qualitative research*. SAGE.

DeRusso, P. A., Greeley, W. J., & St Geme, J. W. (2020). Leading from the middle: Benefits of a physician leadership program. *The Journal of Pediatrics, 219*, 4–6. https://doi.org/10.1016/j.jpeds.2019.12.016

Du, J., Shin, Y., & Choi, J. N. (2014). Convergent perceptions of organizational efficacy among team members and positive work outcomes in organizational teams. *Journal of Occupational and Organizational Psychology, 88*(1), 178–202. https://doi.org/https://doi.org/10.1111/joop.12085

DuFour, R., & Eaker, R. E. (2009). *Professional learning communities at work: Best practices for enhancing student achievement*. Hawker Brownlow Education.

DuFour, R., & Fullan, M. (2013). *Cultures built to last systemic PLCs at work*. Solution Tree Press.

Dumay, X., Boonen, T., & Van Damme, J. V. (2013). Principal leadership long-term indirect effects on learning growth in mathematics. *The Elementary School Journal, 114*(2), 225–251. https://doi.org/10.1086/673198

Eloff, I. (2013). Positive psychology and education. In M. P. Wissing (Ed.), *Wellbeing research in South Africa* (pp. 39–51). Springer.

Fiscal Crisis and Management Assistance Team. (2019). *FCMAT Annual Report 2018–2019*. https://www.fcmat.org/PublicationsReports/Annual_Report_2018-19_final.pdf

Fullan, M., & Hargreaves, A. (2012). *Professional capital: Transforming teaching in every school*. Teachers College Press.

Fullan, M., & Quinn, J. (2016). Coherence making: How leaders cultivate the pathway for school and system with a shared process. *School Administrator, 6*(23), 30–34. https://www.pageturnpro.com/AASA/72631-June-2016/sdefault.html#page/34

Garmston, R. J., & Wellman, B. M. (2009). *The adaptive school: Developing and facilitating collaborative groups*. Christopher-Gordon.

Goodwin, G. F., Salas, E., O'Shea, P. G., & Driskell, J. E. (2006). What makes a good team player? Personality and team effectiveness. *Group Dynamics: Theory, Research, and Practice, 10*(4), 249–271. https://doi.org/10.1037/1089-2699.10.4.249

Groysberg, B., & Slind, M. (2012). Leadership is a conversation. *Harvard Business Review*. June 2012. https://hbr.org/2012/06/leadership-is-a-conversation

Hackman, J. R. (2011). *Collaborative intelligence: Using teams to solve hard problems*. Berrett-Koehler.

Hawley, W. D. (Ed.). (2007). *The keys to effective schools: Educational reform as continuous improvement*. Corwin Press.

Johnson, R. B., Onwuegbuzie, A. J., & Turner, L. A. (2007). Toward a definition of mixed methods research. *Journal of Mixed Methods Research, 1*(2), 112–133. doi:10.1177/1558689806298224

Jones, J. E., & Bearley, W.L. (2001). Facilitating team development: A view from the field. *Group Facilitation, 3*(2), 56–65. http://bus378summer.pbworks.com/f/FacilitatingTeamDevelopment_ViewFromField_JonesandBearley_2001_GroupFacilitation.pdf

Katzenbach, J. R., & Smith, D. K. (2015). *The wisdom of teams: Creating the high-performance organization*. Harvard Business Review Press.

Kauffman, J. (2016). *Leading in the middle: Conversations and dialogic leadership in higher education* (Publication No. bgsu1458908710) [Doctoral dissertation, Bowling Green State University]. Bowling Green, Ohio. http://rave.ohiolink.edu/etdc/view?acc_num=bgsu1458908710

Kerns, C. D. (2019). Managing teamwork: A key leadership practice. *Journal of Leadership, Accountability and Ethics, 16*(1), 40–53. https://doi.org/10.33423/jlae.v16i1.1362

Knies, J. L. (2017). Leading from the middle: Mid-career librarians who step into take charge as needed. In B. Albitz, C. Avery, & D. Zabel (Eds.), *Leading in the new academic library*. Libraries Unlimited.

Kotter, J. (1996). *Leading change*. Harvard Business School Press.

LaFasto, F. M., & Larson, C. E. (2002). *When teams work best: 6,000 team members and leaders tell what it takes to excel*. SAGE.

Laloux, F., & Wilber, K. (2014). *Reinventing organizations: A guide to creating organizations inspired by the next stage in human consciousness*. Nelson Parker.

Lambert, L. (2003). *Leadership capacity for lasting school improvement*. Association for Supervision and Curriculum Development.

Lee, M. Y., & Edmondson, A. C. (2017). Self-managing organizations: Exploring the limits of less-hierarchical organizing. *Research in Organizational Behavior, 37*, 35–58. https://doi.org/10.1016/j.riob.2017.10.002

McGee Hewitt, M. (2019). *Sustaining leadership team effectiveness in education agencies to improve student achievement* [Unpublished doctoral dissertation, University of Pretoria]. Pretoria, South Africa.

McInerney, D. M., Dowson, M., & Van Etten, S. (Eds.). (2006). *Effective schools*. Information Age Publishing.

McMillan, J. H., & Schumacher, S. (2010). *Research in education: Evidence-based inquiry* (7th Ed.). Pearson Education.

McShane, S. L., & Von Glinow, M., A. G. (2018). *Organizational behavior*. McGraw-Hill Education.

Nickerson, J. A. (2014). *Leading change from the middle: A practical guide to building extraordinary capabilities (Innovations in leadership)*. Brookings Institution Press.

Patton, M. Q. (2015). *Qualitative research & evaluation methods: Integrating theory and practice*. SAGE.

Seligman, M. (2018). PERMA and the building blocks of well-being. *The Journal of Positive Psychology, 13*(4), 333–335.

Simmons, M., McDermott, M., Lock, J., Crowder, R., Hickey, E., DeSilva, N., Leong, R., & Wilson, K. (2019). When educators come together to speak about well-being: An invitation to talk. *Canadian Journal of Education, 42*(3), 850–872.

Sperber, S., & Linder, C. (2016). The impact of top management teams on firm innovativeness: A configurational analysis of demographic characteristics, leadership style and team power distribution. *Review of Managerial Science, 12*(1), 285–316. https://doi.org/10.1007/s11846-016-0222-z

Tan, Y. S. M., & Caleon, I. S. (2015). Exploring the process of problem finding in professional learning communities through a learning study approach. In Y. H. Cho, I. S. Caleon, & M. Kapur (Eds.), *Authentic problem solving and learning in the 21st century: Perspectives from Singapore and beyond* (pp. 3–16). Springer. https://doi.org/10.1007/978-981-287-521-1_17

Törnblom, O. (2018). Managing complexity in organizations: Analyzing and discussing a managerial perspective on the nature of organizational leadership. *Behavioral Development, 23*(1), 51–62. https://doi.org/10.1037/bdb0000068

Voelkel, R. H., & Chrispeels, J. H. (2017). Within-school differences in professional learning community effectiveness: Implications for leadership. *Journal of School Leadership, 27*(3), 424–451. https://doi.org/10.1177/105268461702700305

Yin, K. (2009). *Case study research: Design and methods.* SAGE.

SECTION II
EMPIRICAL REASONING

CHAPTER 8

PROMOTING WELL-BEING IN SCHOOL PRINCIPALS AND VICE PRINCIPALS REQUIRES STRUCTURAL CHANGE, NOT JUST SELF-CARE

Cameron Hauseman, Katrina Pollock, and Fei Wang

INTRODUCTION

Increasing attention is being paid to the well-being of principals and other school administrators. Work intensification has fundamentally altered the nature of school leadership, resulting in high levels of emotional labor, professional isolation, burnout, and stress. In this chapter, we use data derived from large-scale surveys of 1,400 principals and 862 vice principals to demonstrate how Ontario school leaders' well-being is influenced under work intensification by exploring their perceptions of work-life balance and the coping strategies they use. Ultimately, we argue that structural changes are required to promote school leaders' well-being, and the problem cannot be solved by increased self-care practices alone.

School leaders are facing a well-being crisis. Principals and vice principals are experiencing long work hours, an unrelenting workload, and a burdensome volume of email (Alberta Teachers' Association, 2014; Leithwood & Azah, 2014; Pollock, 2016; Pollock & Hauseman, 2019). Such intensified work conditions are negatively affecting their well-being and their operation of schools. Healthy schools need healthy leaders, and this makes the well-being of principals and vice principals crucially important. First, effective school leadership is a fundamental component associated with positive academic and nonacademic student outcomes (Supovitz et al., 2010; Yoon, 2016). Second, work intensification can lead to principals and vice principals experiencing high levels of emotional labor (Hauseman, 2021), professional isolation (O'Connor, 2004; Stephenson & Bauer, 2010), stress (Darmody & Smyth, 2016; Kokkinos, 2007; van der Merwe & Parsotam, 2012), and burnout (Friedman, 2002; Kokkinos, 2007; Maxwell & Riley, 2017). These undesirable aspects of the profession make the role unattractive for the next generation of principals and vice principals (Snodgrass Rangel, 2018).

Until recently, little attention has been paid to the well-being of principals and vice principals, even though they are tasked with promoting the well-being of staff, students, and other stakeholders in the school community (Devos et al., 2007; Pollock, 2016; Riley, 2015, 2016, 2018). In this chapter, we use data from large-scale surveys of principals and vice principals in Ontario, Canada, to explore school administrators' perceptions of work-life balance and their daily coping strategies to demonstrate how work intensification influences their well-being. Ultimately, we conclude that promoting the positive well-being of school leaders requires more than just improved individualized self-care practices—what is needed is structural changes at the policy and system level.

WELL-BEING

Well-being is a contested concept in the literature, as scholars have used various theoretical approaches to conceptualize and define the term (Falkenberg, 2014; Pollock et al., 2020). Some scholars make a distinction between *subjective well-being*, in which an individual relies on their own perspective to gauge their state of well-being (Steptoe et al., 2015), and *objective well-being*, in which judgments rest in the hands of others (Kahneman, 1999). For the purposes of this study, well-being describes the extent to which an individual "feels positive and enthusiastic about life. It includes the capacity to manage one's feelings and related behaviors, including the realistic assessment of one's limitations, development of autonomy, and ability to cope effectively with stress" (Manderscheid et al., 2010, p. 1). Operating from a state of positive well-being is critical for principals and vice principals to model positive practices for staff and students, and effectively manage the high levels of stress and emotional labor tied to their position (Hauseman, 2021; Maxwell & Riley, 2017; Pollock, 2016).

Well-Being of School Principals and Vice Principals

Much of the work school principals and vice principals engage in involves cultivating and promoting the well-being of staff, students, and other members of the school community. Despite being responsible for supporting the well-being of others, however, it is only recently that school administrators' own well-being has become subject to scholarly inquiry and codification in policy (Collie et al., 2020; Devos et al., 2007; Pollock, 2016; Ray et al., 2020; Riley, 2015, 2016, 2018; Walker, 2020). Understanding principals' and vice principals' perceptions of work-life balance and the strategies they use to cope with work-related stresses would be a valuable addition to the dearth of literature on principals' and vice principals' health and well-being. Although our discussion in this chapter focuses on principals and vice principals working in Ontario, Canada, the factors that influence principals' and vice principals' well-being extend beyond state and national borders (Collie et al., 2020).

Work-life balance. Principals have little control over many factors that influence the nature of their work, including the policies they must follow and initiatives they are required to implement at the school-level. Further, characterized by heavy workloads, high employer expectations, and emotional demands, work intensification has emerged as a key barrier preventing principals and vice principals from achieving a positive sense of work-life balance (Collie et al., 2020; Mahfouz, 2018). Bunner et al. (2018) define work intensification as "the process of continuously increasing job demands that have to be attended to in shorter time" (p. 2). School leaders, such as principals and vice principals, can experience work intensification as a result of several mutually inclusive factors, including an increase in the pace and complexity of one's work combined with a simultaneous extension of work hours (ATA, 2012; Green, 2004; Hauseman et al., 2017; Pollock & Hauseman, 2019). Work intensification experienced by school leaders can also be characterized by the additional work required to respond to the complexity of student needs in contemporary times, an escalation of bureaucratic requirements and an increasing reliance on email and other forms of information and communications technology (ATA, 2012; Green, 2004; Hauseman et al., 2017; Pollock & Hauseman, 2019).

Over the past 20 years, scholars have identified the negative personal and professional toll associated with principals and vice principals working long hours, answering endless emails, and engaging in new job demands. For example, research conducted in Australia (Riley, 2018), Belgium (Devos et al., 2007), Canada (Hauseman et al., 2017; Pollock, 2016), Ireland (O'Connor, 2004; Riley, 2015), the Netherlands (Kelchtermans et al., 2011), South Africa (van der Merwe & Parsotam, 2012), Turkey (Ozer, 2013), the United Kingdom (United Kingdom Department for Education,

2014; Philips et al., 2007), and the United States (Mahfouz, 2018), has indicated that work intensification is a major source of stress for contemporary principals and can foil attempts to achieve work-life balance and a sense of well-being. Similarly, Riley conducted large-scale surveys in Australia (2018), Ireland (2015), and New Zealand (2016) in which he found that principals have poorer well-being and quality of life than the general population; he also found that they experience greater levels of burnout, stress, and sleep disturbances. The same surveys indicated that principals are working too much to be able to maintain a healthy lifestyle (Riley, 2015, 2016, 2018).

The high levels of stress associated with work intensification are linked to principals and vice principals struggling with burnout (Friedman, 2002; Kokkinos, 2007; Maxwell & Riley, 2017) and professional isolation (O'Connor, 2004; Stephenson & Bauer, 2010). Difficulty managing emotions (Berkovich & Eyal, 2015; Hauseman, 2021) and emotional exhaustion (Ozer, 2013) are additional challenges that can hinder principals' and vice principals' attempts to achieve both work-life balance and a positive sense of well-being. Saddling principals and vice principals with heavy workloads may also have the unintended consequence of making school leadership less desirable for teachers to work toward (Ontario Principals' Council [OPC], 2017; Snodgrass Rangel, 2018). Although work intensification can prevent principals and vice principals from effectively balancing work and personal responsibilities, there is also emerging evidence highlighting the factors that can promote positive well-being for contemporary school leaders, including their coping strategies.

Coping. For the purposes of this chapter, coping is "defined as the thoughts and behaviors used to manage the internal and external demands of situations that are appraised as stressful" (Folkman & Moskowitz, 2004, p. 745). Evidence suggests that effective and healthy coping skills are crucial for principals and vice principals to achieve and maintain a positive sense of well-being. There are both productive and maladaptive strategies that individuals can use to cope with stressful situations. For example, maintaining a sense of humor and an optimistic mindset (Hauseman, 2021), using controlled breathing (van der Merwe & Parsotam, 2012), spending time with friends and family, and engaging in hobbies outside of work (Mahfouz, 2018; Wang et al., 2018) are all positive coping strategies identified in the literature. Although some scholars have derided mindfulness as a neoliberal response to self-care that has the potential to medicalize the emotional ebbs and flows that are part of daily life (Reveley, 2016; Sellman & Buttarazzi, 2020), mindfulness may also be an effective strategy for school leaders. Though mindfulness and meditation (Walker, 2020), self-care (Ray et al., 2020), and other internal coping mechanisms can help principals develop the resilience necessary to thrive (and survive) in contemporary school contexts (Cherkowski et al., 2020; Mahfouz, 2018; Wells & Klocko, 2018), Riley (2018) found that coping was one of several measures—including self-rated health, mental health, and well-being—where principals scored lower than the general population. While further evidence suggests that school leaders are prone to engaging in maladaptive coping strategies, such as expressive suppression, distraction, and ruminating about past events that they cannot change (Poirel & Yvon, 2014), other recent studies indicate that principals have the capacity to engage in both positive and negative coping strategies (DeMatthews et al., 2018; Hauseman, 2021; Wang et al., 2018). The participants in DeMatthews et al.'s (2018) study described engaging in reappraisal and consulting the opinions of others in an effort to cope, but they also described both experiencing emotional volatility and a habit of suppressing their true feelings. Similarly, Hauseman (2021) noted that even the most experienced and successful principals in his study demonstrated a penchant for engaging in coping strategies associated with negative outcomes.

It is important to clarify that discussing the coping skills that principals and vice principals engage in to manage emotions and tend to their well-being is not intended to suggest that self-care is an individual responsibility. The coping skills that individual principals and vice principals bring to their leadership positions can and should be buttressed and enhanced by interventions provided by government, school districts, and professional associations (Wang et al., 2018). Activities that promote principals' and vice principals' well-being include intensive professional learning opportunities, coaching and mentoring programs, and physical health assessment tools (OPC, 2017). Current research should be used to inform the design and delivery of these interventions.

METHODOLOGY

Data reported in this chapter are derived from two large-scale surveys conducted with principals and vice principals in Ontario, Canada. The surveyed principals and vice principals were members of the Ontario Principals' Council (OPC), a professional association for principals and vice principals in Ontario's public schools. At the time of data collection, all participants that responded to the surveys were current principals or vice principals. Focus groups were conducted with practicing principals and vice principals prior to launching both surveys to serve as an opportunity to refine individual questions and increase the validity and reliability of the instruments (McLeod et al., 2000; Wilkinson & Birmingham, 2003). For both the principal survey and the vice principal survey, focus group participants piloted draft versions of the data collection tools to provide feedback that influenced survey design and led to revisions of some questions and response options. All focus group participants were also members of the OPC at the time of data collection. We begin this section with a brief outline of the principal and vice principal surveys, along with descriptions of the participants in both surveys; we conclude with a description of the two-step process used to analyze data gathered from both survey instruments.

Principal Survey

The principal survey included 60 questions grouped in 12 different sections related to the work school principals engage in daily. The sections included questions on how principals spend their time, duties and responsibilities, accountability and external influences, challenges and possibilities, and well-being and job satisfaction. Additional sections of the survey include inquiring about work-life balance, supports, professional development, the Ontario Leadership Framework, community partnerships, and demographic questions about principals and their school. We focused on the well-being and work-life balance sections of this survey.

The principal survey was live for 26 days. A total of 1,434 of the 2,701 invited principals completed the survey, resulting in a response rate of 52.68%. Qualitative data that is relevant to this chapter also emerged from the principal survey. For example, 267 participants provided additional insight about the coping strategies they use to manage the stresses associated with the principalship, and 41 principals provided additional comments about work-life balance at the end of the survey.

Principals with various demographic characteristics who worked in a variety of different geographic contexts responded to the principal survey. For example, 77.3% of the sample were employed in elementary schools and 16.4% worked in secondary schools at the time of the survey. An additional 2.9% of respondents indicated that they were principals of schools serving both elementary and secondary school students. A total of 62.8% of the principal survey sample self-identified as female, while the remaining 38.2% self-identified as male. In terms of formal education, 54.3% of the participating principals had earned a master's degree and 41.6% indicated that a bachelor's degree was the highest level of formal education they had completed. Smaller percentages of participants had obtained a professional (2.4%) or doctorate (1.3%) degree. An average of 7.6 years of experience was reported in the role across the sample. A total of 92.5% of participating principals self-identified as White, 1.6% of the principal survey sample self-identified as Black, and 1.3% as South Asian.

Vice Principal Survey

The vice principal survey included a total of 77 questions related to the same 12 sections used in the principal survey; as noted in the previous section, we focused on the survey data related to work-life balance and coping. While the areas of focus are the same between the two surveys, we did make slight changes to the vice principals' survey to better reflect the work vice principals engage in. These revisions involved adding questions asking about participants' relationship with their principal as well as their plans to pursue the principalship. We also added questions and response options to the vice principals' survey based on popular responses in the "Other" section of some questions from the principals' survey. For example, the vice principals' survey included additional questions about professional learning needs as well as well-being and work-life balance, such as harassment in the workplace. Finally, we updated some questions and response options to reflect changes in the official names of policies and legislation.

The survey was live for 28 days and there were 862 surveys available for analysis after data screening, which represented a response rate of 35.6%. At the end of the survey, participants were asked to provide additional responses. Vice principal survey data also included 677 unique responses to an open-ended question that asked participants to provide advice to new vice principals about work-life balance.

The sample for the vice principal survey included a broad range of vice principals working in a variety of different contexts. For example, 46.17% of respondents were employed in elementary schools, while secondary school vice principals accounted for 36.77% of survey respondents. An additional 15.78% of participating vice principals declined to share the type of school they work in. The sample was also diverse in terms of gender, as 68.3% of respondents self-identified as female and 31.7% of vice principals self-identified as male. Just over half (50.1%) of the vice principals who participated in the survey indicated that the highest level of formal education they had completed was a bachelor's degree. A total of 46% of participating vice principals had earned a master's degree prior to data collection, while 2.4% had earned a professional degree and 1.5% had completed a doctorate. Over two thirds of the sample had less than five years of experience as a vice principal; the average years of experience participating vice principals had in the role was 4.9 years. As with the principal survey, the sample was less diverse in terms of ethnicity, as 81.5% of the sample self-identified as White or Caucasian. Only 3.5% of the sample self-identified as South Asian, with a further 3.1% self-identifying as Black. Vice principals who self-identified as First Nation, Métis, or Inuit (FNMI) comprised 1.6% of the sample. An additional 4.9% of participating vice principals selected the "Other" category when asked about ethnicity, and 3.0% indicated that they would prefer not to disclose this information.

Data Analysis

We used the same two-phase procedures to analyze data collected from both surveys. The first phase included using descriptive statistics to determine the central tendencies of variables for questions related to principals' and vice principals' work-life balance and coping strategies. We analyzed the data generated from this study using SPSS 21. The second phase of the data analysis procedures included analyzing the qualitative data gathered from the unique responses to the open-ended survey questions related to well-being found in both surveys. Our understandings of well-being (Falkenberg, 2014; Manderscheid et al., 2010; Pollock et al., 2020), work-life balance (Collie et al., 2020; Mahfouz, 2018; Riley, 2018), and coping (Folkman & Moskowitz, 2004; Hauseman, 2021; Mahfouz, 2018; Wang et al., 2018), in the context of principals' and vice principals' work, guided the qualitative analysis. We analyzed the qualitative data using the constant comparative method, which involved reading responses to identify any recurrent themes and assigning a code to each theme (Savin-Baden & Major, 2013). We then again read the qualitative responses to group together (or break apart) codes initially developed during the first stage of qualitative analysis to create categories and subcategories based on the data.

FINDINGS

Throughout this section, we report findings from large-scale surveys of 1,434 principals and 862 vice principals in Ontario, Canada, to explore how work-life balance and coping strategies influence school leaders' well-being. In each subsection, we first discuss the descriptive statistics related to principals' and vice principals' perspectives on work-life balance and coping. Then, we supplement and contextualize the quantitative data with qualitative responses from the open-ended questions found in both surveys.

Work-Life Balance

Most principals and vice principals who participated in this research indicated that work-life balance is a struggle. As displayed in Table 8.1, only 13.9% of participating principals and 15.6% of participating vice principals *often* or *always* felt they appropriately achieve balance between their work and personal lives. Similarly, work-life balance *rarely* or *never* occurred for nearly half of principals (48.9%) and vice principals (42.9%) who participated in this research.

Table 8.1

Work-Life Balance

Do you feel you have an appropriate balance between your work and your life outside of work?	Responses				
	Never	Rarely	Sometimes	Often	Always
Principal survey	13.2%	35.7%	36.8%	11.9%	2.0%
Vice principal survey	12.4%	30.5%	41.5%	13.9%	1.7%

Principals. A total of 41 principal survey participants used the Additional Comments section of the survey to voice concerns about the sustainability of their job and describe the difficulties they face in realizing an appropriate balance between work responsibilities and their personal lives. For example, one principal noted that they often prioritize work over family commitments by stating:

> I also struggle almost every day with balancing. Unfortunately, work comes first. After a stress-filled day I find it difficult not to bring those stresses home, which is not fair for my family.

Similarly, another principal mentioned they were becoming resentful of their work because it left little time for family: "I love my work but resent the time it takes away from my family and personal life. Much greater balance is needed." The participating principals also used this section to describe how their lack of work-life balance made the job unappealing for the next generation of school leaders. For example, one principal highlighted how work intensification is making school leadership unattractive and unsustainable: "The workload and stress often don't counterbalance the appeal that comes with making a difference at a system level. And so I don't know how [these] systems will be able to continue recruiting good people!" Another participating principal echoed those thoughts when pointing to the long hours expected of contemporary principals as a factor that deters teachers from pursuing administrative roles:

> The ever-increasing demands upon us as school leaders certainly would be a deterrent to individuals considering the profession. Many above us demonstrate very poor work-life balance, and expect the same from us. The 60 hours I indicated at the beginning of the survey is probably low.

Vice principals. Vice principals were asked additional questions related to work-life balance. Responses to these additional questions both support and extend the findings reported above. A total of 62% of participating vice principals indicated that their work *often* or *always* infringed on their home life, with only 4% of the sample responding *rarely* or *never*. Similarly, over half of the sample *always* (9%) or *often* (42.6%) missed home events because of work, while only 9.3% indicated that it was *rarely* or *never* an issue.

The survey also asked the participating vice principals to offer advice about work-life balance to individuals interested in school leadership. Three themes emerged when we analyzed the 677 responses to this question: (a) the importance of being able to prioritize, (b) developing and maintaining a support system outside of the school, and (c) the need to work long hours to fulfill job requirements. The vice principals in the sample noted that a heavy workload made the ability to prioritize key for success in the role. One participant noted that:

> Prioritizing your workload is very important. It is often a struggle to let things wait until the next day, but family and friendships are important. Do the things that impact on students and student learning and many other tasks can wait.

In addition to ensuring that vice principals prioritize making time for friends and family, it is important that they do not forget about themselves and their personal needs. Another vice principal responded to this question by stating: "Prioritize. Put yourself close to the top."

The need for contemporary school leaders to develop and maintain a support system outside of their school context was not lost on the vice principals who provided qualitative responses. As one vice principal noted, having a support system promotes well-being by providing opportunities to vent and share their feelings by "connect[ing] with others with whom you can share and vent and you'll see that everyone has a similar level of stress, but hearing others makes it feel more manageable." The participating vice principals also offered advice around workload expectations. For example, one vice principal stated that individuals who are new to the role should "be ready to work long hours at certain points and be ready to always be on top of your game." Finally, another participant highlighted the tensions regarding work-life balance and the need for vice principals to work long hours. They cautioned new vice principals about the importance of maintaining flexibility when making plans with family because they should "expect to work long hours and you never know when you'll be able to leave at the end of the day—never make set plans with your family." These findings demonstrate the pronounced influence that work-life balance, and a lack thereof, can have on principals' and vice principals' self-perceived well-being. Well-being can also be influenced by other factors, however, including a person's individual coping strategies.

Coping

The principals and vice principals who participated in this research reported engaging in a variety of different coping strategies to promote their own positive well-being and escape from the rigors and stresses associated with their work. The principals' and vice principals' coping strategies are displayed in Table 8.2. The response options on the two surveys are different because we used the "Other" category from the principal survey to identify additional strategies to include as potential responses when conducting the vice principal survey. Many of the more popular coping strategies across both survey samples—including spending times with friends and family, engaging in physical activity, talking with colleagues, reading, and listening to music—are generally considered healthy and associated with positive outcomes.

Table 8.2

Principals' and Vice Principals' Coping Strategies

Principal Survey		Vice Principal Survey	
Variable	Percentage of Respondents	Variable	Percentage of Respondents
Spend time with my family/friends/pets	86.2%	Time with my family/friends/pets	70.9%
Talk with colleagues	74.6%	Physical activities/exercising	62.8%
Engage in physical activities	66.2%	Watching TV/movies	56.5%
Watch TV/movies	60.3%	Talking with colleagues	56.4%
Read	43.8%	Sleeping	53.3%
Listen to music	37.0%	Eating	46.3%
Self-medicate	29.0%	Seeking solitude	38.9%
Other	13.4%	Listening to music	32.3%
Participate in professional counselling	5.6%	Alcohol use	31.9%

(Table continues on next page)

Table 8.2 (Continued)

Principals' and Vice Principals' Coping Strategies

Principal Survey		Vice Principal Survey	
Variable	Percentage of Respondents	Variable	Percentage of Respondents
		Reading	31.2%
		Talking with supervisor	30.4%
		Shopping	21.8%
		Meditating/Practicing yoga	17.8%
		Going to church/synagogue/mosque	11.1%
		Other	8.1%
		Participating in professional counselling	7.0%
		Using prescription drugs	4.4%
		Using tobacco	1.6%
		Using other drugs	0.3%

It is concerning, however, that sizable percentages of participating principals and vice principals also demonstrated a propensity for using maladaptive coping strategies. For example, 29% of the principal sample indicated that they self-medicated in an effort to cope with emotionally draining days. Coping is a very personal process, so we refrained from defining self-medication for participants and relied on their own interpretations of the term when responding to the question about coping strategies. Furthermore, 46.3% of vice principals coped by eating, while 31.9% used alcohol. Smaller numbers of vice principals also reported using tobacco and other drugs.

It is also worth mentioning that 267 participating principals provided qualitative data about their coping strategies. Most of these responses focused on specifying the type of activities they engage in with friends and family, forms of physical activity they enjoy, and favorite genres of television programs and reading material they use to cope. However, some principals described an inability to cope with the pace of work intensification. For example, one principal stated that they will be retiring early due to the demanding nature of their work: "[Coping] is the hardest part. In my case, I will be retiring early." Similarly, another principal mentioned that the pace of their work leaves little time to cope or escape from the rigors of the role: "I don't do anything to cope or escape, it just becomes tomorrow, and I forge ahead." It is troubling that some principals are either engaging in maladaptive coping strategies, such as self-medicating, or refraining from doing anything they enjoy, such as spending time with family, in an effort to keep up with their daily responsibilities.

DISCUSSION

In this chapter, we used findings from the work-life balance and coping sections of large-scale surveys of principals and vice principals to explore the well-being of school leaders in Ontario, Canada. Though this study was conducted in Ontario, the challenges these principals and vice principals experienced in terms of achieving work-life balance and engaging in positive coping strategies are ubiquitous, as work intensification is influencing the profession around the world (United Kingdom Department for Education, 2014; Devos et al., 2007; Hauseman et al., 2017). These findings support and elaborate on insights from prior research exploring how work-life balance and coping influence principals' and vice principals' well-being (e.g., Wang et al., 2018). For example, this research extends prior findings indicating that work intensification makes work-life balance a scarce commodity for school leaders and that it is detrimental to their health and well-being (Mahfouz, 2018). Principals and vice principals around the world should be commended for displaying resilience and refusing to crumble under the burden of work intensification.

Insufficient Support

At the time of the data collection, none of the participating principals or vice principals indicated being involved in jurisdictional or district-level programming or professional learning designed to promote positive well-being. This hints at employers either lacking awareness of the well-being issues facing contemporary school leaders, or lacking the conviction to support principals' and vice principals' well-being as part of their employment responsibility. Given that we know principals have a significant indirect impact on student learning (Supovitz et al., 2010; Yoon, 2016), it is in the public interest for principals and vice principals to have at least a semblance of work-life balance (Mahfouz, 2018; Wells & Klocko, 2018). There are several systemic approaches and structural changes that school districts and jurisdictions can engage in to promote principals' and vice principals' well-being, including limiting the number of initiatives they are tasked with implementing. Policy can also be a tool that promotes school leaders' well-being rather than just one more avenue that heightens the impact of work intensification. The findings of this research also highlight that school leaders need to be empowered by their employer, able to use their voice to speak about challenges in their work, and able to share information about their working conditions without fear of retribution.

Individual Strategies

Although none of the participating principals or vice principals indicated they engage in mindfulness as a strategy for promoting well-being or coping with work-related stresses, it may be one part of an effective self-care arsenal for many school leaders (Mahfouz, 2018; Wells & Klocko, 2018). For example, Walker (2020) noted that many Jamaican school principals use mindfulness meditation and prayer as coping strategy for dealing with workplace stress and anxiety. Our concern with mindfulness, however—or any other individualized coping strategy being viewed as a panacea for solving work intensification and other well-being challenges faced by principals and vice principals—is that it can be hijacked by certain political agendas (Pollock et al., 2020; Reveley, 2016; Sellman & Buttarazzi, 2020). In this way, mindfulness programs can abdicate jurisdictional ministries and/or departments of education, school districts, professional associations, and (in some cases) unions of responsibility for providing their employees and members the supports and tools necessary to do their jobs effectively while maintaining and modeling wellness. Ultimately, focusing exclusively on individualized coping strategies does not adequately get to the crux of school leaders' well-being crisis: By placing the responsibility for being well at work solely in the hand of school leaders, we fail to acknowledge the larger systemic issues—that the school leaders have no control over—contributing to principal work-life balance (Pollock et al., 2020).

Some of blame for the lack of work-life balance reported in this chapter could be cast on principals and vice principals themselves, as they demonstrate a willingness to work long hours, engage in new job demands, and manage competing priorities downloaded on to them. Perhaps these principals and vice principals internalize and/or normalize their work intensity and think that is the only way the work can get done. It can be argued that many principals and vice principals who engage in these practices do so because they believe the only way to be successful at their work is to engage in approaches to leadership that are self-sacrificing and individualistic, such as being hero leaders (Andrews, 2016; Mintzberg, 2006), lone wolves (Sugrue, 2009), or martyrs (Menkhoff, 2015; Ward, 2016). Although employers, including school districts and jurisdictional departments or ministries of education, may be taking advantage of school leaders being well intentioned, eventually individuals in these roles need to indicate when their job has become too large for one person.

CONCLUSION

In this chapter, we have discussed how the continuing intensification of principals' and vice principals' work—including the expansion of their duties and activities, as well as the increase in accountabilities—is making administration an unattractive and undesirable career path for prospective school leaders (OPC, 2017; Snodgrass Rangel, 2018). Ultimately, the current approaches for supporting principal and vice principal well-being are not working. Unless school districts and jurisdictions move away from promoting individualized approaches to self-care and policymakers enact structural change that reaches and acknowledges the root causes of work intensification and school leaders' work-life imbalance, schools and school districts as a whole will be facing a leadership crisis: Our school leaders will continue to suffer, as will students and student achievement.

POSSIBLE PRACTICES AND RESOURCES FOR PRACTITIONERS

We encourage practitioners to review the following practices and resources to further their understanding of approaches and strategies for promoting their own well-being and those of others:

- The EdCan Network has developed several fact sheets aimed at empowering school leaders in developing and maintaining safe and healthy schools for all:

Cherkowski, S., & Walker, K. (2020, March 5). *Workplace well-being in K–12 schools: What does it mean to "flourish" at work?* EdCan Network. https://www.edcan.ca/articles/flourish-at-work-fact-sheet/

Greenberg, M., Mahfouz, J., Davis, M., & Turksma, C. (2017, December 4). *Social emotional learning for principals*. EdCan Network. https://www.edcan.ca/articles/sel-for-principals/

Pollock, K., Hauseman, C., & Wang, F. (2019a, November 7). *How can education systems support principals' and vice principals' well-being?* EdCan Network. https://www.edcan.ca/articles/support-principals-well-being/

Pollock, K., Hauseman, C., & Wang, F. (2019b, November 7). *Work intensification: How the role of school leaders is changing*. EdCan Network. https://www.edcan.ca/articles/work-intensification/

- Pollock et al. (2020) edited a special issue of the *Journal of Educational Administration* on school administrators' well-being and mindfulness. This special issue contains several articles

exploring approaches for promoting well-being in principals and vice principals, factors influencing their well-being, and self-care strategies they engage in to cope with their job.
- Ontario Principals' Council (2017) provides recommendations for how school systems and professional associations can promote principal and vice principal well-being, including structural changes to school leadership roles and responsibilities.

REFERENCES

Alberta Teachers' Association. (2012). *The new work of teaching: A case study of the worklife of Calgary public teachers*. http://www.teachers.ab.ca/SiteCollectionDocuments/ATA/Publications/Research/pd-86-23%20New%20Work%20of%20Teaching%20-%20Calgary.pdf

Alberta Teachers' Association. (2014). *The future of the principalship in Canada*. https://www.teachers.ab.ca/SiteCollectionDocuments/ATA/Publications/Research/The%20Future%20of%20the%20Principalship%20in%20Canada.pdf

Andrews, M. (2016). Going beyond heroic leaders in development. *Public Administration and Development, 36*(3), 171–184.

Berkovich, I., & Eyal, O. (2015). Educational leaders and emotions: An international review of empirical evidence 1992–2012. *Review of Educational Research, 85*(1), 129–167.

Bunner, J., Prem, R., & Korunka, C. (2018). How work intensification relates to organization-level safety performance: The mediating roles of safety climate, safety motivation, and safety knowledge. *Frontiers in Psychology, 9*(Article 2575), 1–13.

Cherkowski, S., Kutsyuruba, B., & Walker, K. (2020). Positive leadership: Animating purpose, presence, passion, and play for flourishing in schools. *Journal of Educational Administration, 58*(4), 401–415.

Cherkowski, S., & Walker, K. (2020, March 5). *Workplace well-being in K–12 schools: What does it mean to "flourish" at work?* EdCan Network. https://www.edcan.ca/articles/flourish-at-work-fact-sheet/

Collie, R., Granziera, H., & Martin, A. J. (2020). School principals' workplace well-being: A multinational examination of the role of their job resources and job demands. *Journal of Educational Administration, 58*(4). 417–433.

Darmody, M., & Smyth, E. (2016). Primary school principals' job satisfaction and occupational stress. *International Journal of Educational Management, 30*(1), 115–128.

DeMatthews, D. E., Carrola, P., Knight, D., & Izquierdo, E. (2018). Principal burnout: How urban school leaders experience secondary trauma on the US-Mexico border. *Leadership and Policy in Schools, 18*(4), 681–700.

Devos, G., Bouckenooghe, D., Engels, N., Hotton, G., & Aelterman, A. (2007). An assessment of well-being of principals in Flemish primary schools. *Journal of Educational Administration, 45*(1), 33–61.

Falkenberg, T. (2014). Making sense of Western approaches to well-being in an educational context. In F. Deer, T. Falkenberg, B. McMillan, & T. Sims (Eds.), *Sustainable well-being: Concepts, issues, and educational practices* (pp. 77–94). ESWB Press.

Folkman, S., & Moskowitz, J. T. (2004). Coping: Pitfalls and promise. *Annual Review of Psychology, 55*(1), 745–774.

Friedman, I. (2002). Burnout in school principals: Role related antecedents. *Social Psychology of Education, 5*, 229–251.

Green, F. (2004). Work intensification, discretion, and the decline in well-being at work. *Eastern Economic Journal, 30*(4), 615–625.

Greenberg, M., Mahfouz, J., Davis, M., & Turksma, C. (2017, December 4). *Social emotional learning for principals*. EdCan Network. https://www.edcan.ca/articles/sel-for-principals/

Hauseman, C. (2021). Strategies secondary school principals use to manage their emotions. *Leadership and Policy in Schools, 20*(4), 630–649. https://doi.org/10.1080/15700763.2020.1734211

Hauseman, D. C., Pollock, K., & Wang, F. (2017). Inconvenient, but essential: Impact and influence of school–community involvement on principals' work and workload. *School Community Journal, 27*(1), 83–106.

Kahneman, D. (1999). Objective happiness. In D. Kahneman, E. Diener, & N. Schwarz (Eds.), *Well-being: The foundations of hedonic psychology* (pp. 3–25). Russell Sage Foundation.

Kelchtermans, G., Piot., L., & Ballet, K. (2011). The lucid loneliness of the gatekeeper: Exploring the emotional dimension in principals' work lives. *Oxford Review of Education, 37*(1), 93–108.

Kokkinos, C. M. (2007). Job stressors, personality, and burnout in primary school teachers. *British Journal of Educational Psychology, 77*(1), 229–243.

Leithwood, K., & Azah, V. (2014). *Secondary principal and vice-principal workload study: Final report*. http://www.edu.gov.ca/eng/policyfunding/memos/nov2014/FullSecondaryReportOctober7_EN.pdf

Mahfouz, J. (2018). Mindfulness training for school administrators: Effects on well-being and leadership. *Journal of Educational Administration, 56*(6), 602–619.

Manderscheid, R. W., Ryff, C. D., Freeman, E. J., McKnight-Eily, L. R., Dhingra, S., & Strine, T. W. (2010). Evolving definitions of mental illness and wellness. *Preventing Chronic Disease, 7*(1), 1–6.

Maxwell, A., & Riley, P. (2017). Emotional demands, emotional labour and occupational outcomes in school principals: Modelling the relationships. *Educational Management Administration & Leadership, 45*(3), 484–502.

McLeod, P. J., Meagher, T. W., Steinert, Y., & Boudreau, D. (2000). Using focus groups to design a valid questionnaire. *Academic Medicine, 75*(6), 671.

Menkhoff, T. (2015). Leading authentically: Overcoming the mind-boggling consequences of mindless leadership. *Catalyst Asia*, 44–47. https://ink.library.smu.edu.sg/cgi/viewcontent.cgi?article=5755&context=lkcsb_research

Mintzberg, H. (2006). Developing leaders? Developing countries? *Development in Practice, 16*(1), 4–14. https://doi.org/10.1080/09614520500450727

O'Connor, E. (2004). Leadership and emotions: An exploratory study into the emotional dimension of the role of the post-primary school principal in Ireland. *Educate*, *4*(1), 46–59.

Ontario Principals' Council (OPC). (2017). *International symposium white paper: Principal work-life balance and well-being matters*. https://www.edu.uwo.ca/faculty-profiles/docs/other/pollock/PrincipalWell-being-17-FINAL-with-Acknowledgement-1.pdf

Ozer, N. (2013). Trust me, principal, or burn out! The relationship between principals' burnout and trust in students and parents. *Alberta Journal of Educational Research*, *59*(3), 382–400.

Philips, A., Sen, D., & McNamee, R. (2007). Prevalence and causes of self-reported work-related stress in head teachers. *Occupational Medicine*, *57*(5), 367–376.

Poirel, E., & Yvon, F. (2014). School principals' emotional coping process. *Canadian Journal of Education*, *37*(3), 1–23.

Pollock, K. (2016). Principals' work in Ontario, Canada: Changing demographics, advancements in information communications technology and health and well-being. *International Studies in Educational Administration*, *44*(3), 55–74.

Pollock, K., & Hauseman, D. C. (2019). The use of email and principals' work: A double-edged sword. *Leadership and Policy in Schools*, *18*(3), 382–393.

Pollock, K., Hauseman, C., & Wang, F. (2019a, November 7). *How can education systems support principals' and vice principals' well-being?* EdCan Network. https://www.edcan.ca/articles/support-principals-well-being/

Pollock, K., Hauseman, C., & Wang, F. (2019b, November 7). *Work intensification: How the role of school leaders is changing*. EdCan Network. https://www.edcan.ca/articles/work-intensification/

Pollock, K., Wang, F., & Mahfouz, J. (2020). Guest editorial. *Journal of Educational Administration*, *58*(4), 389–399. https://doi.org/10.1108/JEA-08-2020-237

Ray, J., Pijanowski, J., & Lasater, K. (2020). The self-care practices of school principals. *Journal of Educational Administration*, *58*(4), 435–451.

Reveley, J. (2016). Neoliberal meditations: How mindfulness training medicalizes education and responsibilizes young people. *Policy Futures in Education*, *14*(4), 497–511.

Riley, P. (2015). *Irish principals and deputy principals occupational health, safety and well-being survey*. https://www.principalhealth.org/ie/2015_Final_Report_Ireland.pdf

Riley, P. (2016). *New Zealand primary school principals' occupational health and well-being survey*. https://www.healthandwell-being.org/assets/reports/NZ/2016_NZ_Final_Report.pdf

Riley, P. (2018). *The Australian principal occupational health, safety and well-being survey: 2018 data*. https://www.principalhealth.org/au/2016_Report_AU_FINAL.pdf

Savin-Baden, M., & Major, C. H. (2013). *Qualitative research: The essential guide to theory and practice*. Routledge.

Sellman, E. M., & Buttarazzi, G. F. (2020). Adding lemon juice to poison-raising critical questions about the oxymoronic nature of mindfulness in education and its future direction. *British Journal of Educational Studies*, *68*(1), 61–78.

Snodgrass Rangel, V. (2018). A review of the literature on principal turnover. *Review of Educational Research*, *88*(1), 87–124.

Stephenson, L. E., & Bauer, S. C. (2010). The role of isolation in predicting new principals' burnout. *International Journal of Education Policy & Leadership, 5*(9), 1–17.

Steptoe, A., Deaton, A., & Stone, A. A. (2015). Subjective well-being, health, and ageing. *The Lancet, 385*(9968), 640–648.

Sugrue, S. (2009). From heroes and heroines to hermaphrodites: Emasculation or emancipation of school leaders and leadership? *School Leadership and Management, 29*(4), 353–371. https://doi.org/10.1080/13632430903152039

Supovitz, J., Sirinides, P., & May, H. (2010). How principals and peers influence teaching and learning. *Educational Administration Quarterly, 46*(1), 31–56.

United Kingdom Department for Education. (2014). *Teachers' workload diary survey 2013: Research report*. https://assets.publishing.service.gov.uk/government/uploads/system/uploads/attachment_data/file/285941/DFE-RR316.pdf

van der Merwe, H., & Parsotam, A. (2012). School principal stressors and a stress alleviation strategy based on controlled breathing. *Journal of Asian and African Studies, 47*(6), 666–678.

Walker, A. R. (2020). "God is my doctor": Mindfulness meditation/prayer as a spiritual well-being coping strategy for Jamaican school principals to manage their work-related stress and anxiety. *Journal of Educational Administration, 58*(4), 467–480.

Wang, F., Pollock, K., & Hauseman, D. C. (2018). Ontario principals' and vice principals' well-being and coping strategies in the context of work intensification. In S. Cherkowski & K. Walker (Eds.), *Perspectives on flourishing schools* (pp. 287–304). Lexington Books.

Ward, S. (2016, June 22). *The most costly mistake you can make as a servant leader* [Blog post]. Claremont Lincoln University. https://www.claremontlincoln.edu/engage/ethical-leadership/costly-mistake-servant-leader/

Wells, C. M., & Klocko, B. A. (2018). Principal well-being and resilience: Mindfulness as a means to that end. *NASSP Bulletin, 102*(2), 161–173.

Wilkinson, D., & Birmingham, P. (2003). *Using research instruments: A guide for researchers*. Routledge.

Yoon, S. Y. (2016). Principals' data-driven practice and its influences on teacher buy-in and student achievement in comprehensive school reform models. *Leadership and Policy in Schools, 15*(4), 500–523.

CHAPTER 9

STUDENT ADVERSITY AND LEADER STRESS

A Critical Race Contextualization and Analysis of New York State Social Emotional Learning Policy

Melinda Lemke and Anthony L. White II

INTRODUCTION

Global capitalism, the rise of the technological society, the pace of change, the demise of traditional community support systems, and the widening gulf between rich and poor have contributed to high levels of psychological damage in society.

—Harris (2008)

Each year, across K–12 education, new problems are discovered and initiatives added, while existent challenges and tasks remain. Research details how neoliberal educational policy outside of the United States (Lemke & Zhu, 2018) and within urban American contexts (Brathwaite, 2017) buttresses rigid accountability standards, shrinks public dollars, and reproduces educational inequality. Practitioner outlets document issues that range from the financial inability to fix leaky roofs and replace old textbooks to legislation that diverts funds from already under-resourced schools to private entities (Flannery, 2010). Within a fiscally challenged environment, there is a renewed push to address adverse childhood experiences (ACE), often referred to as student trauma and/or adversity, and to institute school-based practices to reduce student stress, facilitate coping, and augment resiliency overall (Chafouleas et al., 2016). Viewed as a wider public health concern, research documents the harmful effects of contextually specific trauma on childhood and adolescent social, emotional, mental, and physical health (Lee et al., 2017; Turner et al., 2012). Research finds trauma not only impairs these aspects of the self, but also causes diminished health capacity in childhood and adolescence, with lasting negative effects in adulthood (Copeland et al., 2018; Felitti et al., 1998).

The proliferation of blogs, websites, and for-profit trainings is demonstrative of the trauma-informed zeitgeist sweeping the nation. Yet despite this, and the documented increased levels of stress experienced by Black, Indigenous, and people of color (BIPOC) communities during the COVID-19 pandemic (Quirk, 2020), we argue that it is easier to talk about student adversity within educational environments than it would be to operationalize policy to confront trauma in these same spaces. Research identifies educators as being on the frontline of intervening against violence affecting youth (i.e., commercial and sexual) and how ideologically driven policy mandates can shape such efforts (Lemke, 2019a, 2019b). This is of particular import for those populations already marginalized by economic, gender, sex, and racial status (Bay-Cheng, 2015) and underscores how neoliberal policy processes can normatively shore up deficit, pathologizing, and victim-blaming culture writ large. Furthermore, where student trauma and outcomes are at issue, the role of educators in such processes is integral yet under-examined, with more intersectional data points needed (Thomas et al., 2019; Yohannan & Carlson, 2019). Tied to the foundational concern of this chapter, research also has reviewed the ways structurally racist and White supremacist systems can affect student trauma and compromise the modalities for research and intervention on behalf of those same students (Alvarez, 2020).

As an emphasis on accountability remains (Smyth, 2011; Thompson & Allen, 2012), a competing set of policy discourses seemingly govern schools and leadership actions concerning student trauma. On one hand, leaders must work as student advocates, yet on the other, they are charged with implementing accountability policies that implicate leaders in advancing those "educational inequalities the policies were originally designed to address" (Carpenter & Brewer, 2014, p. 299). Not only does this constrain transformative leader efficacy in terms of policy, but it also detracts from an authentic response to student adversity, their own needs, and overall system well-being.

Arguably, then, expectations for educational leaders have shifted dramatically over the last three decades in ways that increase pressure on an already stressed system and on individuals experiencing a life out of balance. At a basic level, recognizing student adversity can prompt practitioner secondary traumatic stress—the emotional distress tied to knowing about trauma experienced by someone else—as well as prompting burnout, compassion fatigue, and emotional-stress responses such as depression and feelings of isolation that occur while caring for others (Aloe et al., 2014; Figley, 1995; Hydon et al., 2015). Coupled with professional development and licensure that may not be grounded in what researchers refer to collectively as cultural and linguistic responsiveness (CLR) and trauma-informed practices (TIP) (Lemke et al., 2021), these dynamics, among others, limit leader ability to understand student adversity in a transformative manner.

Given the linkages between student trauma and social emotional learning (SEL), we examined to what extent a state education policy reform effort designed to increase student SEL can, if at all, achieve the goal of "being well" for educational leaders and systems. As a framing and policy analysis tool, we utilized critical race theory (CRT), which is used elsewhere to assess existing and shape future educational policy directives (Bradbury, 2020; Buras, 2013; Gillborn, 2013). We begin with a review of interdisciplinary literature concerning student adversity within urban school spaces, as well as of research on leader stress within this same setting. We then analyze the New York State Education Department guidelines, titled *Social Emotional Learning Guide to Systematic Whole School Implementation* (New York State Education Department [NYSED], 2019), focusing on SEL to unpack the extent to which this approach can increase well-being for students and, in New York State's (NYS) goal of whole-school implementation, reciprocally support educational leader well-being. We conclude our analysis with educational policy, practice, and resource recommendations.

LITERATURE REVIEW: STUDENT ADVERSITY, URBAN SCHOOL LEADERSHIP, AND POLICY

Trauma is known to include distress tied to the experience or threat of harm, injury, or death to oneself or others. There are multiple forms and types of traumas, including but not limited to ACEs; combat; cumulative, human-made, and natural disasters; historical and/or large group trauma; political violence or torture; and sexual violence and/or rape (Substance Abuse and Mental Health Services Administration [SAMHSA], 2014). Most of what is known about student trauma is from medical research on ACE, which range from economic hardship, death of a loved one, divorce, and incarceration of a family member to forced relocation, childhood neglect, and abuse (SAMHSA, 2014).

A landmark ACE study found that at least 60% of minors experience violence in their homes, schools, or communities (Finkelhor et al., 2009).

Just under half of U.S. students have one or more ACE, with economic hardship and divorce being the most common across all states (Sacks & Murphy, 2018). Furthermore, trauma incidence, prevalence, and related health problems among some groups are higher than the U.S. average. Research found greater exposure to adversity, including violence-related trauma, among poor, racial, ethnic-minority, and LGBTQ+ subpopulations (Merrick et al., 2018), with data also indicating that urban residents with low socioeconomic status have a higher incidence of some traumas (SAMHSA, 2014). Though other studies also suggested that adverse experiences like poverty, more than violence, predict worse cognitive function (Sheridan et al., 2017), high percentages of youth experience violence-related trauma. Changing such adversity through policy and practice also increasingly includes confronting intensified discrimination and discourses of fear toward subgroups marginalized by race and refugee status (Lemke & Nickerson, 2020).

Though type, exposure, intensity, and duration vary, childhood trauma interrupts a range of human needs—(i.e., Maslow's hierarchy; see Maslow, 1943), resulting in an increased likelihood for negative social, emotional, behavioral, and physical health outcomes in adulthood (SAMHSA, 2014); there is, for example, an increased likelihood of addiction, chronic health problems, partner violence, and premature mortality (Copeland et al., 2018; Felitti, 1998). In schools, this can manifest as student attendance issues, cognitive delays, and behavioral changes, among others (Lepore & Kliewer, 2013). Thus, trauma-informed responses to students of concern aim to augment knowledge on student vulnerability, signs of distress (including within behavior), and ways to avoid triggering memories that can prompt re-traumatization (SAMHSA, 2014). Research on refugee youth, for example, found cultural responsiveness to be beneficial to development (Isakson et al., 2015). Still, even where leaders and staff aim to implement CLR and TIP, needs existed concerning staff desire for additional training on sexual violence–specific trauma, as well as ways to better address practitioner secondary trauma and attend to self-care (Lemke et al., 2021).

Compounding disproportionate rates of trauma, students of color often are concentrated in deeply segregated urban schools (Foster, 2005; Pollard, 1997) and trauma-charged learning environments. School segregation is a focal point of CRT scholarship (Ladson-Billings, 2016; Taylor, 2016), with a focus on segregation in urban schools in particular (Gooden, 2012; Khalifa et al., 2013). Additionally, students of color in urban schools face numerous challenges, including lower rates of achievement and attainment (Brown, 2005) and higher rates of push out through suspension and expulsion (Gooden, 2005), among others. Finally, research also linked the experiences of Indigenous and African American subgroups to what is referred to as historical trauma. Originally developed to explain the psychological effects of the Holocaust on family members, historical trauma encompasses the continued negative effects of prior trauma, including structural violence (i.e., institutional, policy), on current generations (SAMHSA, 2014).

This confluence of historic and ecological stressors contributes to a normative understanding of Black education as being "in crisis," which in turn can create a "rush into short-sighted fixes (reforms) that only address the symptoms of black miseducation rather than the causes" (Lozenski, 2017, p. 169)—in a phrase, what we refer to as *palliative care*. The recent push toward SEL and leader well-being, then, warrants analyses of the degree to which relevant policies are responsive to the structural factors that shape student needs, particularly African American and Latino/a/x subgroups, and leaders in urban schools. Furthermore, the current state of urban schools illustrates the seeming intractability of school segregation, thus supporting CRT's claim that racism is endemic and permanent (Taylor, 2016). Critical analyses of SEL policy implementation within these same contexts and by leaders who arguably either wittingly or unwittingly shore up barriers to equity not only are pertinent, but also are likely to remain so for the foreseeable future.

URBAN LEADER STRESS

Educational leaders in urban schools are tasked with mitigating and personally coping with an array of challenges that confront students in urban schooling. One leadership-centered approach to provide alternatives to such challenges is the practice of actively placing leaders of color into these contexts (Brown, 2005; Gooden, 2012)—with the rationale that they might be better equipped to consider the needs of students of color (Foster, 2005; Wilson et al., 2013). While this approach is responsive to the influences of race, as well as to social emotional student needs, the danger in such an approach is its potential to stop at palliative care if the structural and institutional factors that lead to disparities in educational outcomes are not simultaneously tackled. Such a circumscribed approach to urban school leadership and reform has been referred to as "the Black principal solution" (Gooden, 2012, p. 78).

Given their work in trauma-charged learning environments, urban school leaders might face higher risk for suffering from secondary trauma and burnout. In line with research discussed above, such risks likely are intensified for leaders of color when one considers that given these leaders' positioning, they have higher incidences of other forms of trauma. Acuff's (2018) work on racial battle fatigue illustrated how a leader's race influences their own experience with trauma. In particular, the demands of teaching-despite-trauma, including demands arising from the race of the leader's students, can trigger leader trauma and result in burnout (Acuff, 2018). As leader and student racial positioning intersect to shape how trauma is experienced, taught, and handled in schools, the influence of Whiteness (Gillborn, 2005, 2013) in relation to SEL policy warrants consideration. Furthermore, if urban leader and student social emotional well-being is to be achieved, then more than daily mindfulness and self-care practices are needed. However, as previously discussed, the ongoing accountability movement in public education inhibits the full realization of such an approach (Khalifa et al., 2013), as the pressure to demonstrate proficiency along traditional measures (i.e., test scores) can result in the subordination of the potentially transformative learning standards that could reverse structural inequality (Heilig et al., 2012; Lemke, 2015).

RESPONSE TO STUDENT ADVERSITY AND LEADER STRESS

Self-care and mindfulness. Those working in education, nursing, social work, and therapy constitute what is referred to as "high-touch" professions that can result in increased stress, burnout, and other health "hazards" throughout the professional lifespan (Skovholt et al., 2001, p. 169). In education, recent research documents how self-care interventions might prevent principal turnover (Mahfouz, 2018a, 2018b), with leaders, teachers, and counselors articulating specific self-care and mindfulness strategies that assist their everyday (Lemke et al., 2021). Both strategies involve self-regulation, but self-care focuses on two different aspects of the self in its aim to bridge the professional self ("training, knowledge, techniques") with the personal self ("personality traits, belief systems, and life experience)" (Dewane, 2006, p. 543); mindfulness techniques focus on awareness of the environment and internal states of being (Brown & Ryan, 2003). This is important to know given responses to student behavior not only are often punitive, but also disproportionately negatively target students of color (Skiba et al., 2014). Systematic pushout from schools also is found to affect Black girls in particular, who already face high rates of adversity, including sexual violence (Morris, 2016).

CASEL and SEL. In addition to these more individualized practices and as a mechanism to improve overall school well-being, in the 1990s policy and programming turned to student SEL. In 1994, the Collaborative for Academic, Social, and Emotional Learning (CASEL) was founded by a national leadership team comprising researchers, educators, and advocates to identify and treat issues concerning the science, programming coordination, and practice of SEL within schools. In particular, SEL was understood as a framework for discussing issues of adversity and to help coordinate a range of existent or newly emerging programming (e.g., drug prevention and sex education).

CASEL defined SEL as processes by which children and adults acquire and effectively apply the knowledge, attitudes, and skills necessary to understand and manage emotions, set, and achieve positive goals, feel and show empathy for others, establish and maintain positive relationships, and make responsible decisions (CASEL, 2019).

Since the late 1990s, CASEL has partnered with various educational leadership entities (e.g., Association for Supervision and Curriculum Development) to develop practical K–12 SEL strategies and guidelines for state policy development concerning standards and competencies (Dusenbury et al., 2018). State policy guidance to advance SEL increased steadily for reasons such as research-based evidence documenting the benefits of SEL and increased state policy flexibility under the Every Student Succeeds Act (2015) that permitted the inclusion of nonacademic factors in accountability measures; these included SEL, whole-child development, and community-based partnerships focused on integration of academic and social service provisions (Dusenbury et al., 2018).

By the end of 2017, all 50 states established baseline preschool SEL standards, and 16 states, including NYS, moved to disseminate resources that support voluntary SEL implementation. Until 2018, SEL standards in NYS existed only for pre-school age students. Since then and as the focus of our policy analysis, NYS developed K–12 SEL guidelines for "voluntary adoption by school districts, trailing early statewide adopters which use SEL standards for school improvement and accountability" (Lee et al., 2019, p. 4).

Currently, eight states have SEL standards for elementary grades and another eight have standards for K–12; no states, however, now take SEL standards beyond school settings to engage in a fully protective environment that includes multisector collaboration, intervention, and school-community partnerships toward the goal of creating safer schools, families, and communities (Lee et al., 2019). Furthermore, though most SEL standards have a shared emphasis on intrapersonal, interpersonal, and decision-making skills, state standards narrowly focus on specific competencies and fail to target "educational conditions and opportunities (or lack thereof) in and out of the school setting" that detract from whole child development (Lee et al., 2019, p. 6). Those states that adopted SEL standards also had less "racial minorities," and "no systematic pattern in terms of students in poverty or English Language Learners (ELL)," which led researchers to suggest state activism around SEL adoption was not a matter of sociodemographic factors (Lee et al., 2019, p. 8).

CRT POLICY ANALYSIS

Critical race theory (CRT) is an approach to scholarship and social activism that foregrounds race (Bell, 1995). CRT development and use in educational research has called for the centering of race to fully understand educational policy status, effects, and how identities are historically conferred, as well as the tacit agreement of racial privileging within policy processes (Apple, 1999; Gillborn, 2005). Seminal research that merged CRT and education identified race as the main construct for examining educational inequality (Ladson-Billings & Tate, 1995). While CRT is used widely in educational research (Taylor, 2016), CRT in education policy analysis remains limited (Bradbury, 2020; Buras, 2013). When utilized, some areas are highlighted as integral to analysis:

- *Colorblindness.* Colorblindness manifests in educational policy through the simultaneous inclusion and marginalization of race (Davis et al., 2015; Heilig et al., 2012) or through the crafting of race-neutral policy (Gillborn, 2016)—practices which both privilege Whiteness in educational processes, and prompt disproportionate rates of harm to students of color, regardless of policy intent (Bradbury, 2020); despite known outcomes, the policy is reauthorized or promoted. These cumulative negative policy and practice effects were termed "White supremacy" (Bradbury, 2020; Gillborn, 2005, 2016). Thus, a contribution of our analysis is that it supports findings from critical SEL literature (Hoffman, 2009; Jagers et al., 2019), noting the importance—and absence—of centering race in SEL analyses.
- *Contextualization.* The CRT tenet of historical and sociopolitical contextualization (Bell, 1995; Taylor, 2016) is central to educational policy analysis. This focus is found in research on educational policy context, reform, and actors (Buras, 2013; Heilig et al., 2012), as well as connections to broader contexts and over time (Bradbury, 2020). Again, critical analysis of trends in SEL discourse and implementation explicitly calls for contextualization in SEL research and practice (Hoffman, 2009; Jagers et al., 2019).
- *Implications of certain standards.* Finally, the content and resultant implications of student-learning and leadership-practice standards is a recurrent site of policy analyses. This includes for example, the Texas social studies curriculum standards (Heilig et al., 2012; Lemke, 2015) and the ISLLC and ELCC educational leadership standards (Davis et al., 2015).

These areas of policy consideration focus on question subsets covering racial discourse and level of neutrality or colorblindness, understanding and presentation of the policy problem, stereotype presence, varied power dynamics, policy actors and participants, and policy utility and impact, including disparity maintenance. Thus, we aligned our methodological approach with this framework, which places critiques of colorblindness and White supremacy as central to CRT scholarship overall (Gooden, 2012; Taylor, 2016). This framework was appropriate as key to emergent critical SEL literature, which condemned SEL standards as being culturally biased and built upon White cultural notions of what constitutes good or normal social emotional health (Hoffman, 2009; Jagers et al., 2019).

METHODOLOGY

The purpose of this research was to understand the extent to which the New York States' SEL policy guidance might increase well-being for students and, in the state's goal of "whole-school" implementation, reciprocally support educational leader well-being. Our analysis was concerned with how policy can manifest as both value neutral and silencing where educational inequity is concerned. It also focused on how policy operates to omit factual information and/or infuse normative and political bias into curricula.

To this end, we turned to critical educational policy studies of curriculum reform (Heilig et al., 2012; Lemke, 2015; Lemke & Zhu, 2018) as guideposts for our analysis. We also utilized Bradbury's (2020) CRT policy analysis framework that merged policy sociology and Gillborn's (2013) investigation of White supremacy in education policy. This framework asks five essential CRT-aligned questions concerned with policy context considerations including influence, text production, and practice.

To contextualize our analysis as relevant to urban school leader (and student) well-being, we used one essential question and three sub-questions from this framework as a heuristic to read and make sense of this policy guidance. These included: (a) "How does this (policy) maintain/continue/reinforce white dominance?" (essential question); (b) "How is the 'policy problem' established in the policy creation community, and how does this relate to 'race?'" (sub-question on influence); (c) "If a policy is presented as 'colorblind' or race neutral, how does this delegitimize those who challenge policy on the grounds of equity?" (sub-question on text production); and (d) "How does the absence or presence of 'race' perpetuate inequalities?" (sub-question on the context of practice) (Bradbury, 2020, p. 247). In addition, our textual analysis template included an "Other" category, which allowed us to memo and document textual considerations not otherwise neatly captured under the framework questions.

Data Collection and Analysis

We did not conduct field research, nor did we interview state board members who wrote the NYSED guidelines; thus, our data collection and analysis included a single 69-page policy text. Though limited to one policy text, our mapped theoretical framework, research process, and reflection on our individual researcher positionalities aimed to build consistency in our analyses and helped us go beyond descriptive summation toward explanation (Miles et al., 2014) and recommendations for action.

Our research process comprised three phases, which began with an individual read of the NYSED guidelines. To build structure into our process, we used the above questions to develop a template for reading and memo writing. Although we had a functional knowledge of the guidelines as a researcher and secondary practitioner working in NYS, this template guided our side-by-side readings and memo writing, and permitted us a place to reflect on researcher positionality as relevant to initial and formal findings. Next, as recommended by Charmaz (2011), we paused analysis to discuss our individual readings and compare our thinking about the policy text. Finally, we reread the text in light of the other researcher's thinking and to check for inconsistent findings, which was limited to none. In line with critical textual discourse and policy analyses, ultimately we sought to offer what we called "an interpretation" toward the goal of increasing critical dialogue and change concerning our findings.

Researcher Positionality

Commenting on racial positioning, experiential knowledge, and the responsible use of power among scholar-activists who use CRT, Bell (1995) stated:

> We emphasize our marginality and try to turn it toward advantageous perspective building and concrete advocacy on behalf of those oppressed by race and other interlocking factors of gender, economic class, and sexual orientation ... we see such identification as one of the only hopes of transformative resistance strategy. (p. 902)

Likewise, we are conscious of, and responsive to, our positionality as scholar-activists, and the ways in which race, experience, and power influence our work. As a biracial research team writing about student adversity, educational leadership, race, and social emotional well-being in urban schools, we aimed to avoid an oversimplified Black-White binary (Mutua, 2006). This enabled us to honor the varying, complex, and nuanced ways race influences student and leader social emotional experiences. In addition, the CRT tenet of using experiential knowledge to inform research and challenge dominant narratives (Ladson-Billings, 2016; Solorzano & Yosso, 2016) is employed in our work through our prior and current firsthand experience serving as educators and equity advocates for often marginalized students.

Together, we have more than 25 years of experience in urban school teaching, and have been active in educational leadership practice from classroom to international policy levels. We also are educators (assistant professor and adjunct, respectively) in a large state university graduate school of education, where we focus our energies on considering inequity through critical analyses of educational policy and practice. The lead author is a White, cisgender, and queer woman whose research examines how social policies address structural violence to improve the well-being and human rights of young women and girls. Her research is informed by ongoing work in sexual assault prevention and a career in a Texas urban, public school district that serves predominantly racially and ethnically minoritized student groups. The second author is an African American male who has taught for 13 years exclusively in one large urban district—in schools primarily serving students of color. Prior to this research, the author's undergraduate and graduate coursework were singularly focused upon the study of African American history, culture, and education, resulting in a current doctoral focus on African American education, achievement in urban schools, and CRT.

WELL-BEING FOR LEADERS AND STUDENTS IN NEW YORK STATE

We begin our discussion with overall findings on the NYSED guidelines, and then turn to specific findings related to the questions listed previously. The NYSED guidelines aimed to consider leader well-being, including, for example, "encouraging self-care opportunities for all school staff" (NYSED, 2019, p. 16), auditing and potentially removing staff's preexisting responsibilities, providing professional development resources, and, most notably, signaling the potential of SEL to reduce leader "burnout" (p. 35). Yet, these were the only mentions of leader well-being, with limited attention given to the increasing leader responsibility regarding implementation. Concepts found in the text but not used to discuss equity issues and leadership practices included, for example, the term *inclusion* (two mentions). Terms of relevance, but with minimal to no discussion as relevant to *race* (four mentions) included, for example, *diversity* (four mentions), and *trauma* (12 mentions). It is significant that the term *race* was incorporated only via citations from three external documents.

Regarding student well-being, while there was one direct link between SEL and TIP, the remaining mentions of trauma focused on all students as opposed to issues specific to race and/or racial trauma, with most mentions also tied to supplemental recommended resources. A number of concepts not found in the guidelines included, for example, structural inequality, inequity, and poverty. Finally, while certain resources were listed, there was neither a discussion of nor resources included on CLR and TIP.

HOW POLICY MAINTAINS WHITE DOMINANCE AND LEADER STRESS

Endemic to U.S. society are White, heteropatriarchal social norms, which generally include intolerance and acts of oppression, including racism (Collins, 1997, 2004; Mutua, 2006). As Gillborn (2016) stated, "[A] deliberate intention to discriminate is by no means a necessary requirement in order to recognize that an activity or policy may be racist in its consequences" (p. 54). Our first indication of the existence of White dominance was through the identified guideline goal that students, "act in accordance with social norms" (NYSED, 2019, p. 8). As SEL was argued to be constructed using White middle-class culture as a normative reference (Hoffman, 2009), we found that this goal translated to student achievement being contingent upon the successful adoption of White cultural practices and the directive that leaders drive instruction from this paradigm. Thus, White cultural practice was held as the educational standard, which equates to White supremacy and compels students and leaders into the act of maintaining White dominance. While this competency was not explicitly phrased as alignment with White normative culture, the implied use of White social norms as the de facto educational standard is itself the act of colorblindness in this policy text—an act that, while an unintended policy consequence, maintains racism (Bradbury, 2020; Buras, 2013).

The second indication of racism is that the failure to acknowledge structural racism and White supremacy within this text ultimately limits leader preparation and effectiveness in implementing proposed programming, which prevents achieving some of SEL's most fundamental goals (e.g., resolving conflict, understanding others' perspectives). Failure to include both does not encourage the "mindset change necessary for effective SEL implementation" (NYSED, 2019, p. 35), as explicitly mentioned in some early sections of the implementation guide. This is particularly concerning for urban school leaders as it fails to prepare and assist leaders already engaged in these conversations with providing remedies for the detrimental impact of White supremacy on the social emotional well-being of students of color. It also does not support leaders in efforts to assist these same students to combat White supremacy in their own lives and communities—practices that align to stated SEL goals of "self-efficacy," "ethical decision-making," and "facilitating community well-being" (p. 15). The failure to directly name structural inequities linked to student SEL suggests that resultant educational challenges that arise from these same inequities will continue unabated, thus guaranteeing continued or increased leader stress.

HOW THE POLICY PROBLEM IS ESTABLISHED AND RELATES TO RACE

While consideration is given to the inclusion of diverse student groups throughout the NYSED guidelines, we found that one of the most important references to such inclusion was in the use of students of color as members of school-wide SEL implementation teams, whereby students are to function powerfully as advocates for their own SEL needs. We concluded that here the phrase "unique populations" meant "all students of color groups" (NYSED, 2019, p. 22), given the ambiguous student labels (e.g., "diverse") (p. 13) in other parts of the document and given that more direct qualifiers related to race, gender, class, and language were not used. The use of ambiguous terminology leads to an approach to SEL conceptualization, planning, and implementation whereby undefined subgroups are merged and the unique needs of all students can be neither meaningfully considered nor addressed. This undermines goals of inclusivity and the potential for cultural responsiveness.

The inclusion of students of color on SEL implementation teams was problematic in another way, as these students' inclusion occurs in tandem with the proposed inclusion of intervention staff, including social workers, school psychologists, and nurses. Such inclusion operates to reinforce the practice of approaching students of color through a deficit lens, rendering them abnormal and perpetually in need of intervention and remediation (Wilson et al., 2013). For us, this constitutes racism within the guidelines, and we turned to Wilson et al. (2013), who challenged such approaches through strengths-based transformative leadership, which rejects deficit views. This is accomplished by abandoning the "at-risk" label and its common application to students of color, which notably was used in the guidelines (NYSED, 2019, p. 10) and contradicts the aim of a "strengths-based" perspective stated in other text sections. Thus, we found that the policy problem for "implementing SEL among diverse student populations" (p. 22) was inherently understood as a problem to be fixed—which also could further leader stress in the policy limitations placed on authentic learning and dialogue about student needs.

RACE NEUTRALITY AND DELEGITIMIZING THOSE WHO CHALLENGE COLORBLIND POLICIES

The education of African American students should comprise both academic learning goals and the explicit sociopolitical goal of overcoming racism (Wilson et al., 2013). Throughout the NYSED guidelines, we found that the use of a colorblind approach to policy implementation minimizes not only the ability of SEL to facilitate educational equity for African American students, but also limits the potential of the learning environment to overcome broader societal inequality. By failing to consider race, fundamental terms, learning goals, and competencies become ambiguous, thus ill-preparing leaders to implement an SEL that can meaningfully speak to student well-being and potentially render SEL usable by students of color. To begin with, the guideline expectations that students demonstrate "ethical decision-making skills and responsible behaviors in personal, school, and community contexts" and "self-efficacy" (NYSED, 2019, p. 15)—which, interestingly, is illustrated with a reference to the African American civil rights movement (p. 28)—are unachievable if leaders are neither encouraged to consider nor properly trained to deal with the detrimental impact of racism on the well-being of students of color.

Second, the limits of a colorblind approach were further compounded when aligned with the discussed goal of "acting in accordance with social norms" (NYSED, 2019, p. 8). A colorblind approach prevents achievement of important SEL goals related to interpersonal understanding and communication such as "demonstrate understanding of another perspective" and "resolve conflict" (p. 15). Assuming, as demonstrated, that SEL social norms refer to White supremacist social norms (Hoffman, 2009; Jager et al., 2019), then achieving this competency demands that countering racism not be pursued. Though the text stated that "even more than academic skills, they (SEL skills) must develop in the context of daily life as social challenges . . . arise" (p. 9), we found that a colorblind rendering of SEL places clear limitations on leadership attentiveness to the well-being of students of color—and their own.

Finally, even if the NYSED recommendations directly confronted SEL through a racial equity lens, this text made assumptions about policy actor (i.e., a school leader) positionality, knowledge base, levels of bias, and racial animus—and the ability for the public to challenge shortcomings in these areas. By failing to state race and such factors directly, the SEL guidelines assumed leaders to be current in their training on race and that they have a critical orientation toward dynamics involving race (i.e., linkages between student race, trauma, and discipline). For example, connections were not made between student social emotional well-being and poverty, which disproportionately negatively affects African American students and is tied to broader societal issues such as health, housing, and job opportunities. The guidelines also assumed that leaders would take authentic responsibility for learning about the community they lead and will ethically use interactions with students and families concerning SEL as a basis for learning to become more critically conscious.

THE PRESENT ABSENCE OF RACE

SEL policy implementation has been critiqued for its unintentional focus on student misbehavior, as opposed to fostering relationships between groups of students and between students and leaders (Hoffman, 2009). There was an unequivocal absence of race within the NYSED guidelines and the overall approach was "student-focused," meaning it attempted to change student behavior as opposed to looking at structural factors (NYSED, 2019, p. 40). Such a colorblind approach to SEL and behavior management does not encourage leaders to consider how leader bias in misinterpreting student behavior is tied to disproportionate rates of suspension and expulsion of African American students, thereby allowing inequitable practices to continue.

Second, behavior management was such a significant guideline component that it received its own section, "Approach to Discipline" (NYSED, 2019). In this section, which had subsections and was longer than other sections—including those on equity, trauma, and professional development—leader reflection on discipline was encouraged through the use of data; yet, a focus on inequitable discipline was found in one sentence that stated, "It *may* also be beneficial to review all the previous year's behavioral incidents together to ascertain patterns of behavior and disproportionalities and determine SEL strategies to address them" (NYSED, 2019, p. 40, emphasis added). Though "contextual factors" (p. 47) concerning student misbehavior was suggested, such factors were tied only to the school setting (e.g., grade levels and times of the school day or school year). The lack of a discussion of race is notable given that within NYS and across the United States, disproportionate rates of African American students are suspended and/ or classified as "emotionally disturbed." Thus, one could correctly assume that policy aimed at teaching SEL skills would examine the factors leading to this disproportionality and how SEL learning can focus on learner needs in particular—neither of which option was found in the guidelines. The text did state that discipline should be used as a "teachable moment" and attempted via "restorative practices" (p. 40). Yet, the current absence of any discussion of race and what might be "restored" led us to question how such moments would occur, to what ends, and the ways they would differ based on demographic groups.

Finally, the lack of a discussion of race in student behavior management implementation could prompt increased leader stress. The recommended approach encouraged teaching students to avoid misbehaviors (preventive), yet also detailed how leaders should respond to misbehaviors (reactive). Thus, it failed to offer guidance on how to improve relationships between leaders and students. Furthermore, though restorative practices are found to be beneficial, as discussed in the guidelines, they were additive and failed to bring out root causes of student misbehavior (e.g., structural racism, poverty, leader bias, and poor leader-student relationships). Failing to consider the role of race in discipline practices (i.e., colorblindness) seemingly means that SEL benefits to student and leader well-being could go unrealized—that is, "the ability to recognize the thoughts, feelings and perspectives of other individuals, including ideas and viewpoints that are different from one's own, and to empathize with others from diverse backgrounds ... and constructively resolve conflicts with others" (NYSED, 2019, p. 15).

DISCUSSION

> There would be no lynching if it did not start in the classroom
>
> —Woodson (1933, p. 8).

States vary in their social norms and thus positions on equity, and the corresponding creation, implementation, or blockage of rights-based legislation, including the advent of policies focused on social emotional well-being, also can vary. Given the influence of neoliberalism and retrenchment of rights-driven solutions since the 1970s, arguably much found within educational policy and programming today—and even in states traditionally thought of as progressive—is little more than Band-Aid solutions to racial and economic inequality. The good intentions of SEL policies and programming are not enough, and actually could stand as little more than an example of "roll-out" neoliberalism; whereas "roll-back" neoliberalism was described as the dismantling of key elements of public systems that serve the public good, "roll-out" involves construction and consolidation, which engenders, through policy, new markets that previously did not exist (Peck & Tickell, 2002).

As found in our analysis, such policies fail to motivate concern about those forces that shore up structural inequality (i.e., neoliberalism, heteropatriarchy, White supremacy, and neocolonialism) and corresponding negative short- and long-term health effects, as well as champion the voices of those historically disenfranchised—here, African American students and other students of color. In other words, these policies are not authentically concerned with the social emotional well-being of all students, staff, or leaders, but rather just some. Furthermore, they do little more than contribute to the development of new for-profit TIP. What therefore is required where student SEL and leader well-being is concerned is an approach to educational policy and practice that: (a) is responsive to the role of structural inequalities—including racism—in producing such challenges as student achievement gaps and leaders' secondary trauma and burnout; and (b) values supporting each of these challenges equally and simultaneously.

Our analysis of the NYSED guidelines revealed a lack of deep understanding of how race, structural racism, and the specific needs of African American students, leaders, and community members is relevant to SEL. Instead, the policy recommendations offer a so-called "neutral" perspective, which in reality have "raced" (and "classed" and "gendered") undercurrents. These value-laden dynamics have serious implications for leaders and students (i.e., the ignoring, silencing, and undermining of specific demographics and relevant needs historically underserved by the system). Akin to critiques of social justice "light" policy and programming, the guidelines are SEL "light": embedded White and normalized understandings of student SEL needs and thus how leaders should fulfill them, which ultimately fails students and does not alleviate leader stress—and even could increase it. In much the same way that "grit" discourses are a misnomer for financially insecure students and students of color, the discussion of SEL in the guidelines fails to identify the world behind the student—the raw lived experiences that they walk into school with—which in many respects sets leaders up for failure.

Ultimately, SEL as relevant to student of color trauma (i.e., specific acts of violence against African American bodies and within African American communities) and its relationship to school leaders was not considered. Not only does this work against African American and other historically underserved students, contributing to an inability to build generational wealth and face loss of talent and health disparities, but such efforts also fail to prepare White students for life within a multiracial nation. Our findings echo landmark CRT scholarship, which argued that the violence perpetrated against the African American community was never explicitly presented in the formal curriculum because such trauma was made ordinary, mundane, and normal (Bethune, 1938; Cooper, 1892; Dubois, 1903; Watkins, 2001; Woodson, 1933). Our findings also offer another answer to "the question of what is distinct about a CRT policy analysis" (Bradbury, 2020, p. 242). By identifying the ways in which racial inequality hampers SEL and well-being for students and urban school leaders, and by offering suggestions for future educational policy and practice, we help fulfill the CRT call to "expose racism in education *and* propose radical solutions for addressing it" (Ladson-Billings, 2016, p. 28; italics in original).

CONCLUSION

Knowing more about student-educator feedback loops concerning trauma and intervention strategies within specific state and local policy contexts is needed. Given the previously discussed tensions between neoliberal accountability, student trauma, and increased leader stress, we argue that applying palliative care to systemic and overt symptoms is not sufficient. At a minimum, ensuring individual and systemic well-being necessitates a conscious effort to untangle factors like childhood neglect, abuse, and poverty from structural racism, sexism, and other forms of identity-driven discrimination. As it is the foundational concern of this chapter, it means that educational policies must remove structural barriers that detract from student social emotional agency, including anti-Blackness and White supremacy. Awareness of power and privilege matters to how attention to overall system well-being positions students, and thus educational leader competency, development, and health also must simultaneously and authentically be a part of this equation.

RESOURCES

¡Colorín Colorado! (2021). *Talking about racism and violence: Resources for educators and families*. WETA Public Broadcasting. https://www.colorincolorado.org/talking-about-racism-and-violence-students-resources-educators

Learning for Justice. (2020). *Affirming Black lives without inducing trauma*. Southern Poverty Law Center. https://www.learningforjustice.org/the-moment/may-8-2020-affirming-black-lives-without-inducing-trauma?fbclid=IwAR276l4wLsnNCsPdoVl_FjPN-ZTjsPv4t-D9vXwroEGmvDlQi9aOuI7mnP0

National Association of School Psychologists. (2021). *Social justice resources*. https://www.nasponline.org/social-justice

#SayHerName. (2021). *Initiatives*. African American Policy Forum. https://www.aapf.org/initiatives

U.S. Department of Health and Human Services, Center for Disease Control and Prevention. (2021). *Adverse Childhood Experiences resources*. National Center for Injury Prevention, Division of Violence Prevention. https://www.cdc.gov/violenceprevention/aces/resources.html?CDC_AA_refVal=https%3A%2F%2Fwww.cdc.gov%2Fviolenceprevention%2Facestudy%2Fresources.html

REFERENCES

Acuff, J. (2018). Confronting racial battle fatigue and comforting my blackness as an educator. *Multicultural Perspectives, 20*(3), 174–181. https://doi.org/10.1080/15210960.2018.1467767

Aloe, A. M., Shisler, S. M., Norris, B. D., Nickerson, A. B., & Rinker, T. W. (2014). A multivariate meta-analysis of student misbehavior and teacher burnout. *Educational Research Review, 12*, 30–44. https://doi.org/10.1016/j.edurev.2014.05.003

Alvarez, A. (2020). Seeing race in the research on youth trauma and education: A critical review. *Review of Educational Research, 90*(5), 583–686. https://doi.org/10.3102/0034654320938131

Apple, M. W. (1999). The absent presence of race in educational reform. *Race Ethnicity and Education, 2*(1), 9–16.

Bay-Cheng, L. Y. (2015). The agency line: A neoliberal metric for appraising young women's sexuality. *Sex Roles, 73*(7), 279–291. https://doi.org/10.1007/s11199-015-0452-6

Bell, D. (1995). Who's afraid of critical race theory? *University of Illinois Law Review, 1995*(4), 893–910.

Bethune, M. M. (1938). Clarifying our vision with the facts. *Journal of Negro History, 7*(2), 10–15.

Bradbury, A. (2020). A critical race theory framework for education policy analysis: The case of bilingual learners and assessment policy in England. *Race Ethnicity and Education, 23*(2), 241–260. https://doi.org/10.1080/13613324.2019.1599338

Brathwaite, J. (2017). Neoliberal education reform and the perpetuation of inequality. *Critical Sociology, 43*(3), 429–448. https://doi.org/10.1177/0896920516649418

Brown, F. (2005). African Americans and school leadership: An introduction. *Educational Administration Quarterly, 41*(4), 585–590. https://doi.org/10.1177/0013161X04274270

Brown, K. W. & Ryan, R. M. (2003). The benefits of being present: Mindfulness and its role in psychological well-being. *Journal of Personality and Social Psychology, 84*(4), 822–848. https://doi.org/10.1037/0022-3514.84.4.822

Buras, K. (2013). Let's be for real: Critical race theory, racial realism and education policy analysis (toward a new paradigm): The policy of inequity. In M. Lynn & A. D. Dixson (Eds.), *Handbook of critical race theory in education* (pp. 129–139). Taylor & Francis.

Carpenter, B., & Brewer, C. (2014). The implicated advocate: The discursive construction of the democratic practices of school principals in the USA. *Discourse: Studies in the Cultural Politics of Education, 35*(2), 294–306. https://doi.org/10.1080/01596306.2012.745737

Chafouleas, S. M., Johnson, A. H., Overstreet, S., & Santos, N. M. (2016). Toward a blueprint for trauma-informed service delivery in schools. *School Mental Health, 8*, 144–162. https://doi.org/10.1007/s12310-015-9166-8

Charmaz, K. (2011) A constructivist grounded theory analysis of losing and regaining a valued self. In F. J. Wertz, K. Charmaz, L. M. McMullen, R. Josselson, R. Anderson, & E McSpadden (Eds.), *Five ways of doing qualitative analysis: Phenomenological psychology, grounded theory, discourse analysis, narrative research, and intuitive inquiry* (pp. 165–204). Guilford Press.

Collaborative for Academic, Social, and Emotional Learning [CASEL]. (2019). *What is SEL?* https://casel.org/what-is-sel/

Collins, P. H. (1997). Defining Black feminist thought. In L. Nicholson (Ed.), *The second wave: A reader in feminist theory* (pp. 241–259). Routledge.

Collins, P. H. (2004). Learning from the outsider within: The sociological significance of Black feminist thought. In S. Harding (Ed.), *The feminist standpoint theory reader: Intellectual and political controversies* (pp. 103–126). Routledge.

Cooper, A. J. (1892). *A voice from the south (by a black woman from the south)*. Aldine Printing House.

Copeland, W. E., Shanahan, L., Hinesley, J., Chan, R. F., Aberg, K. A., Fairbank, J. A., van den Oord, E. J. C. G., & Costello, J. (2018). Association of childhood trauma exposure with adult psychiatric disorders and functional outcomes. *JAMA Network Open, 1*(7), 1–11. https://doi.org/10.1001/jamanetworkopen.2018.4493

Davis, B., Gooden, M., & Micheaux, D. (2015). Color-blind leadership: A critical race theory analysis of the ISLLC and ELCC standards. *Educational Administration Quarterly, 51*(3), 335–371. https://doi.org/10.1177/0013161X15587092

Dewane, C. J. (2006). Use of self: A primer revisited. *Clinical Social Work Journal, 34*(4), 543–558. https://doi.org/10.1007/s10615-005-0021-5

DuBois, W. E. B. (1903). *The souls of Black folk*. McClurg.

Dusenbury, L., Dermody, C., & Weissberg, R. P. (2018). *State scorecard scan: More states are supporting social and emotional learning*. Collaborative for Academic, Social, and Emotional Learning.

Every Student Succeeds Act. (2015). U.S. Department of Education. https://www2.ed.gov/policy/elsec/leg/essa/index.html

Felitti, V. J., Anda, R. F., Nordenberg, D., Williamson, D. F., Spitz, A. M., Edwards, V., Koss, M. P., & Marks, J. S. (1998). Relationship of childhood abuse and household dysfunction to many of the leading causes of death in adults: The Adverse Childhood Experiences (ACE) study. *American Journal of Preventive Medicine, 14*(4), 245–258. https://org.doi:10.1016/s0749-3797(98)00017-8

Figley, C. R. (Ed.). (1995). *Compassion fatigue: Coping with secondary traumatic stress disorder*. Routledge.

Finkelhor, D., Turner, H., Ormrod, R., & Hamby, S. L. (2009). Violence, abuse, and crime exposure in a national sample of children and youth. *Pediatrics, 124*(5), 1411–1423. https://doi.org/10.1542/peds.2009-0467

Flannery, M. (2010, September 13). Top eight challenges teachers face this school year. *National Education Association*. http://neatoday.org/2010/09/13/top-eight-challenges-teachers-face-this-school-year-2/

Foster, L. (2005). The practice of educational leadership in African American communities of learning: Context, scope, and meaning. *Educational Administration Quarterly, 41*(4), 689–700. https://doi.org/10.1177/0013161X04274276

Gillborn, D. (2005). Education policy as an act of white supremacy: Whiteness, critical race theory and education reform. *Journal of Education Policy, 20*(4), 485–505. https://doi.org/10.1080/02680930500132346

Gillborn, D. (2013). The policy of inequity. In M. Lynn & A. D. Dixson (Eds.), *Handbook of critical race theory in education* (pp. 129–139). Taylor & Francis.

Gillborn, D. (2016). Education policy as an act of white supremacy. In E. Taylor, D. Gillborn, & G. Ladson-Billings (Eds.), *Foundations of critical race theory in education* (pp. 43–59). Routledge.

Gooden, M. (2005). The role of an African American principal in an urban information technology high school. *Educational Administration Quarterly, 41*(4), 630–650. https://doi.org/10.1177/0013161X04274273

Gooden, M. (2012). What does racism have to do with leadership? Countering the idea of color-blind leadership: A reflection on race and the growing pressures of the urban principalship. *The Journal of Educational Foundations, 26*(1&2), 67–84.

Harris, B. M. (2008). *Supporting the emotional work of school leaders*. SAGE.

Heilig, J., Brown, K., & Brown, A. (2012). The illusion of inclusion: A critical race theory textual analysis of race and standards. *Harvard Educational Review, 82*(3), 403–424. https://doi.org/10.17763/haer.82.3.84p8228670j24650

Hoffman, D. (2009). Reflecting on social emotional learning: A critical perspective on trends in the United States. *Review of Educational Research, 79*(2), 533–556. https://doi.org/10.3102/0034654308325184

Hydon S., Wong M., Langley, A. K., Stein, B. D., Kataoka, S. H. (2015). Preventing secondary traumatic stress in educators. *Child and Adolescent Psychiatric Clinics of North America, 24*(2), 319–333. https://doi.org/10.1016/j.chc.2014.11.003

Jagers, R., Rivas-Drake, D., & Williams, B. (2019). Transformative social and emotional learning (SEL): Toward SEL in service of educational equity and excellence. *Educational Psychologist: Social and Emotional Learning, 54*(3), 162–184. https://doi.org/10.1080/00461520.2019.1623032

Isakson, B., Legerski, J., & Layne, C. M. (2015). Adapting and implementing evidence-based interventions for trauma-exposed refugee youth and families. *Journal of Contemporary Psychotherapy, 45*(4), 245–253. https://doi.org/10.1007/s1087 9-015-9304-5

Khalifa, M., Dunbar, C., & Douglasb, T. (2013). Derrick Bell, CRT, and educational leadership 1995–present. *Race Ethnicity and Education, 16*(4), 489–513. https://doi.org/10.1080/13613324.2013.817770

Ladson-Billings, G. (2016). Just what is critical race theory and what's it doing in a *nice* field like education? In E. Taylor, D. Gillborn, & G. Ladson-Billings (Eds.), *Foundations of critical race theory in education* (pp. 15–30). Routledge.

Ladson-Billings, G., & Tate, W. F. (1995). Toward a critical race theory of education. *Teachers College Record 97*, 4–68.

Lee, E., Larkin, H., & Esaki, N. (2017). Exposure to community violence as a new Adverse Childhood Experience category: Promising results and future considerations. *Families in Society, 98*(1), 69–78. https://doi.org/10.1606/1044-3894.2017.10

Lee, J., Kim, N., Cobanoglu, A., & O'Connor, M. (2019). *Moving to educational accountability system 2.0: Socioemotional learning standards and protective environments for whole children.* The Rockefeller Institute of Government.

Lemke, M. (2015). (Un)making the neoliberal agenda in public education: A critical discourse analysis of Texas high school social studies policy processes and standards. In K. M. Sturges (Ed.), *Neoliberalizing educational reform: America's quest for profitable market colonies and the undoing of public good* (pp. 53–77). Sense.

Lemke, M. (2019a). Educators as the "front line" of human trafficking prevention: An analysis of state-level educational policy. *Leadership and Policy in Schools, 18*(3), 284–304. https://doi.org/10.1080/15700763.2017.1398337

Lemke, M. (2019b). The politics of "giving student victims a voice": A feminist analysis of state trafficking policy implementation. *American Journal of Sexuality Education, 14*(1), 74–108. https://doi.org/10.1080/15546128.2018.1524805

Lemke, M., & Nickerson, A. (2020). Educating refugee and hurricane displaced youth in troubled times: Countering the politics of fear through culturally responsive and trauma-informed schooling. *Children's Geographies, 18*(5), 529–543. https://doi.org/10.1080/14733285.2020.1740650

Lemke, M., Nickerson, A., & Saboda, J. (2021). Global displacement and local contexts: A case study of U.S. urban educational policy and practice. *International Journal of Leadership in Education.* (Online first). https://doi.org/10.1080/13603124.2021.1884747

Lemke, M., & Zhu, L. (2018). Successful futures? New economy business logics, child rights, and Welsh educational reform. *Policy Futures in Education, 16*(3) 251–276. https://doi.org/10.1177/1478210317751269

Lepore, S. J., & Kliewer, W. (2013). Violence exposure, sleep disturbance, and poor academic performance in middle school. *Journal of Abnormal Child Psychology, 41*(8), 1179–1189. https://doi.org/10.1007/s10802-013-9709-0

Lozenski, B. D. (2017). Beyond mediocrity: The dialectics of crisis in the continuing miseducation of Black youth. *Harvard Educational Review, 87*(2), 161–185. https://doi.org/10.17763/1943-5045-87.2.161

Mahfouz, J. (2018a). Mindfulness training for school administrators: effects on well-being and leadership. *Journal of Educational Administration, 56*(6), 602–619. https://doi.org/10.1108/JEA-12-2017-0171

Mahfouz, J. (2018b). Principals and stress: Few coping strategies for abundant stressors. *Educ. Management Administration & Leadership, 48*(3), 440–458. https://doi.org/10.1177/1741143218817562

Maslow, A. H. (1943). A theory of human motivation. *Psychological Review, 50,* 370–396. https://doi.org/10.1037/h0054346

Merrick, M. T. Ford, D. C., Ports, K. A., & Guinn, A. S. (2018). Prevalence of adverse childhood experiences from the 2011–2014 Behavioral Risk Factor Surveillance System in 23 states. *JAMA Pediatrics, 172*(11), 1038–1044. https://doi.org/10.1001/jamapediatrics.2018.2537

Miles, M. B., Huberman, A. M., & Saldaña, J. (2014). *Qualitative data analysis: A methods sourcebook* (4th ed.). SAGE.

Morris, M. W. (2016). *Pushout: The criminalization of Black girls in schools.* The New Press.

Mutua, A. (2006). The rise, development and future directions of critical race theory and related scholarship. *Denver University Law Review, 84*(2), 329–394.

New York State Education Department (NYSED). (2019). *Social emotional learning guide to systematic whole school implementation.* http://www.p12.nysed.gov/sss/documents/GuideToSystemicWholeSchoolImplementationFINAL.pdf

Peck, J., & Tickell, A. (2002). Neoliberalizing space. *Antipode, 34*(3), 380–404. https://doi.org/10.1111/1467-8330.00247

Pollard, D. (1997). Race, gender, and educational leadership: Perspectives from African American principals. *Educational Policy, 11*(3), 353–374. https://doi.org/10.1177/0895904897011003005

Quirk, A. (2020, July 28). Mental health support for students of color during and after the Coronavirus pandemic. *Center for American Progress.* https://www.americanprogress.org/issues/education-k-12/news/2020/07/28/488044/mental-health-support-students-color-coronavirus-pandemic/

Sacks, V., & Murphey, D. (2018). The prevalence of adverse childhood experiences, nationally, by state, and by race or ethnicity. *Child Trends.* https://www.childtrends.org/publications/prevalence-adverse-childhood-experiences-nationally-state-race-ethnicity

Sheridan, M. A., Peverill, M., Finn, A. S, & McLaughlin, K. A. (2017). Dimensions of childhood adversity have distinct associations with neural systems underlying executive functioning. *Development & Psychopathology, 29*(5), 1777–1794 https://doi.org/10.1017/S0954579417001390

Skiba, R. J., Arredondo, M. I., & Williams, N. T. (2014). More than a metaphor: The contribution of exclusionary discipline to a school-to-prison pipeline. *Equity & Excellence in Education, 47*(4), 546–564. https://doi.org/10.1080/10665684.2014.958965

Skovholt, T. M., Grier, T. L., & Hanson, M. R. (2001). Career counseling for longevity: Self-care and burnout prevention strategies for counselor resilience. *Journal of Career Development, 27*(3), 167–176. https://doi.org/10.1023/A:1007830908587

Smyth, J. (2011). The disaster of the 'self-managing school': Genesis, trajectory, undisclosed agenda, and effects. *Journal of Educational Administration and History, 43*(2), 95–117. https://doi.org/10.1080/00220620.2011.560253

Solorzano, D., & Yosso, T. (2016). Critical race methodology: Counter-storytelling as an analytical framework for educational research. In E. Taylor, D. Gillborn, & G. Ladson-Billings (Eds.), *Foundations of critical race theory in education* (pp. 43–59). Routledge.

Substance Abuse and Mental Health Services Administration (SAMHSA). (2014). *Trauma-informed care in behavioral health services.* Treatment Improvement Protocol (TIP) Series 57. HHS Publication No. (SMA) 13-4801. Substance Abuse and Mental Health Services Administration.

Taylor, E. (2016). The foundations of critical race theory in education: An introduction. In E. Taylor, D. Gillborn, & G. Ladson-Billings (Eds.), *Foundations of critical race theory in education* (pp. 1–12). Routledge.

Thomas, M. S., Crosby, S., & Vanderhaar, J. (2019). Trauma-informed practices in schools across two decades: An interdisciplinary review of research. *Review of Research in Education*, *43*(1), 422–452. https://doi.org/10.3102/0091732X18821123

Thompson, G., & Allen, T. (2012). Four effects of the high-stakes testing movement on African American K-12 students. *The Journal of Negro Education*, *81*(3), 218–227. https://doi.org/10.7709/jnegroeducation.81.3.0218

Turner, H. A., Finkelhor, D., Ormrod, R., Hamby, S., Leeb, R. T., Mercy, J. A., & Holt, M. (2012). Family context, victimization, and child trauma symptoms: Variations in safe, stable, and nurturing relationships during early and middle childhood. *American Journal of Orthopsychiatry*, *82*(2), 209–219. https://doi.org/10.1111/j.1939-0025.2012.01147.x

Watkins, W. H. (2001). *The white architects of Black education: Ideology and power in America 1865–1954*. Teachers College Press.

Wilson, C., Douglas, T., & Nganga, C. (2013). Starting with African American success: A strength-based approach to transformative educational leadership. In L. C. Tillman & J. J. Scheurich (Eds.), *The handbook of research on educational leadership for equity and diversity* (pp. 111–133). Routledge.

Woodson, C. G. (1933). *The mis-education of the Negro* (Reprint). Africa World Press.

Yohannan, J., & Carlson, J. S. (2019). A systematic review of school-based interventions and their outcomes for youth exposed to traumatic events. *Psychology in the Schools*, *56*(3), 447–464. https://doi.org/10.1002/pits.22202

SECTION III

MODELS FOR WELL-BEING

CHAPTER 10

THRIVE

A Guiding Model for Facilitating School Leader Well-Being

Connor M. Moriarty, Kimberly J. Rushing, and Lisa A. W. Kensler

Those who invest in educational leadership through practice, research, or policy understand that schools need to be places where students not only learn, but also flourish and thrive. The school environment can serve as a replenishing system that connects and grows the lives and minds of the young people who enter and engage within it. This aspiration is at the heart of school leadership, and it is the collective and individual responsibility of educational leaders to direct their efforts towards such a result, as called for in our *Professional Standards for Educational Leaders* (Murphy, 2016). This level of student success and well-being is achievable, but as leaders work to ensure that the needs of others are met, attending to their own self-care and well-being is essential.

The concept of well-being can be understood as a state of human flourishing where individuals have positive experiences in the areas of "emotion, engagement, relationships, meaning, and achievement" (Cherkowski & Walker, 2013). Well-being is described as happiness (Diener et al., 2003); the sense of life satisfaction that comes from a person's emotions and judgments in the present and over time (Diener et al., 2003; Fischer & Boer, 2011). Research shows that the demands of school leadership are intensifying, and that school principals' work can negatively impact their well-being (Wang et al., 2018). In fact, the level of well-being in school leaders has been found to be lower than in the general public (Maxwell & Riley, 2017),

---

Supporting Leaders for School Improvement Through Self-Care and Well-Being, pp. 177–199
Copyright © 2024 by Information Age Publishing
www.infoagepub.com
All rights of reproduction in any form reserved.

and so prioritizing self-care should become a norm for principals. Self-care is a necessary effort of "self-preservation and self-empowerment" to counteract burnout and despair (Kruger, 2018). Because principals both directly impact teachers and indirectly influence students (Lambersky, 2016), a leader's positive investment into his or her own well-being will permeate throughout the entire learning community. However, many principals, encumbered by the pressures and requirements of their role, appear to forgo their own replenishment.

Currently, there is little research on principal well-being, and strategic models for improving well-being of school leaders are also lacking. Yet, there is evidence showing that school leaders experience high levels of stress (Fuller et al., 2018; Mahfouz, 2020), including chronic stress (Maxwell & Riley, 2017) and that coping with stress unsuccessfully leads to burnout (Federici & Skaalvik, 2012), to physical, psychological, social problems, and to attrition in school principals. Principal turnover is linked to negative school outcomes (Bartanen et al., 2019), and retaining effective principals is a widespread challenge (Fuller et al., 2017). Because of these issues, the need to equip school leaders with ways to increase their well-being is critically important.

Fortunately, steps to increase personal well-being do not need to be exacting, expensive, or exclusive. As strategies for self-care and minimizing the risk of burnout in high stress workplaces are considered, spending time in and connecting with nature is an effective and accessible approach for all school leaders, even those leaders situated in highly developed neighborhoods with limited access to swaths of open, natural spaces. Research explicating links between individual well-being and connection with/time spent in nature has been growing rapidly over the past decade (see, e.g., Bratman et al., 2019; Kuo, 2015). This chapter represents a synthesis of this body of literature, with specific application to those leading schools. We present this practical synthesis as the THRIVE model.

The THRIVE model offers activity and reflective tools that enable principals to improve their physical, emotional, and mental states even while the complex demands of school management mount. For each element of the THRIVE model (Thoughts, Health, Resilience, Interdependence, Vitality, and Empathy), we present a brief review of the literature that demonstrates a positive association between time in and/or connecting with nature and that particular element of the model. Following the research, we also offer practical suggestions for school leaders to monitor and cultivate their own well-being. Research shows that the associated outcomes of even just a few minutes immersed in nature are powerful, and the THRIVE model captures the collective essence of these multifaceted outcomes associated with spending time in and connecting with nature (Moriarty, 2020). Immersion in nature may mean a walk in a forest or some other undeveloped ecosystem. However, immersion in nature may also include focused attention on indoor plants, aquariums, or even just looking at the day's sky outside one's window. We offer the following definitions as a brief overview of the THRIVE model prior to addressing each individually.

> T—Thoughts. Looking out a window at the landscape or even simply images of nature in one's office can restore one's attention and focus. Taking a walk in the park is even better (Berman et al., 2008; Stevenson et al., 2018).
>
> H—Health. Time in nature is associated with a broad range of health and well-being benefits (Capaldi et al., 2015; Kuo, 2015).
>
> R—Resilience. One's ability to bounce back after physical, emotional, and mental challenges is improved with time spent in nature (Capaldi et al., 2015; Ingulli & Lindbloom, 2013).
>
> I—Interdependence. Interdependence speaks to social connections as well as our connection with nature. Research tells us that our perceptions of social cohesion, social interdependence, are positively associated with time spent in nature (Shanahan et al., 2016).
>
> V—Vitality. Vitality goes beyond being healthy. It is a powerful combination of energy and confidence; it is the confidence of knowing we can face any challenge on our path. Vigor and vitality increase with time spent in nature (Hyvönen et al., 2018; Korpela et al., 2017).
>
> E—Empathy. Empathy, the capacity to feel with others and consider their perspectives, plays a critical role in leadership, organizations, and local and global communities. As our society takes on challenges such as climate change, empathy for nature is also important. Spending time in nature with fellow humans is associated with increased empathy for others and also for nature (Brown et al., 2019; Zhang et al., 2014).

We offer readers a free download of THRIVE model reflective tool at https://www.resetoutdoors.com/resources. This handout provides an opportunity to record what one notices about their personal well-being along each aspect of the THRIVE model. If used regularly, patterns of well-being may appear that will help guide continued practice.

THRIVE: THOUGHTS

At any given time, school leaders must make quick, correct decisions and accurate, ethical judgements in a variety of complex situations that impact the lives of others in profound ways. Consider how a principal must immediately address and simultaneously solve problems with student discipline, behavior and learning, conflicting requests from teachers, hostile complaints from parents, time consuming directives from central office, questions from school board members, social media misinformation, discrepancies in accountability data, building repairs, budget and funding constraints, legal mandates, and ongoing health and safety concerns. These daily issues demand high levels of attention and focus, and yet they are only a segment of what a school leader must think about and consider on a continuous basis. This multilayered level of mental pressure puts stress on a school principal's cognitive functions to an extent that even the most experienced, qualified, and competent school leaders are at risk of chronic mental fatigue. Yet, leaders must be able to think clearly and correctly in order to effectively navigate the needs of the school in creative, insightful, and sensitive ways.

One's ability to think, and to think well, is crucial in school leadership and also to the well-being of the leader as a person. One's thoughts are ever present and powerful; not only are thoughts an indispensable tool for helping one achieve his or her goals, but thoughts are a critical part of what makes a person who he or she is as an individual. Because cognitive functioning is central to one's efforts and identity, much like the muscles in the body must rest prior to and after intense exercise, it is necessary to experience regular times of refreshment and rejuvenation to restore healthy thinking. To function in a place of mental wellness, leaders must allow their thoughts the opportunity to rest in order to reset their attention, focus, creativity, and overall cognitive abilities.

Nature provides this opportunity. Research shows that spending time in nature replenishes cognitive functioning, particularly in the areas of working memory, cognitive flexibility, and attention control (Stevenson et al., 2018). Natural stimuli require effortless attention and enable mental recovery by way of providing patterns of "soft fascination" to the onlooker that capture attention "in an undramatic fashion" and "leave ample opportunity for thinking about other things" (Kaplan, 1995, p.174). The passive mental state afforded by natural surroundings enables one's directed attention, a limited resource, to be refilled. In nature, "[a]s the brain engages externally driven and effortless attention, capacity to direct attention in an effortful manner is restored" (Stevenson et al., 2018, p. 231). Fatigued and depleted mental resources recover in natural settings as the mind is allowed the opportunity to settle into a state of easy reflection. Based on attention restoration theory, "[a]fter an interaction with natural environments, one is able to perform better on tasks that depend on directed-attention abilities" (Berman et al., 2008, p. 1207). By permitting the highly taxed, directed attention to rest, one can return to mental tasks refreshed and ready to make decisions with renewed clarity and focus. Notably, the benefits of nature on mental functioning come not only from actual outdoor experiences, but also, although possibly to a lesser extent, from simply viewing images of nature. Walking in nature or resting by observing pictures of nature have both been found to improve mental performance and provide the perception of refreshment (Berman et al., 2008; Lymeus et al., 2018).

Nature also improves one's thought process by supplying a sense of "being away" from problems and infusing a feeling of being in the present experience (Lymeus et al., 2017, p. 5). Immersion in nature rebuilds mental fortitude as "[p]resence in a safe natural environment can also relieve worries and other strains on self-regulatory capabilities" (Lymeus et al., 2017, p. 6). This feeling of mental distance from stress provides mental space for positive thoughts to flow into one's thinking. While many have perceived this to be true from personal experience, there is now documentation that "[n]ature can promote improved cognitive functioning and overall well-being" (Berman et al., 2008, p. 1207), and "encountering nature exposures day after day will increase the likelihood of [experiencing] continuously high well-being" (Korpela et al., 2017, p. 40).

Because of nature's positive impact on the mind's ability to function well, spending time in or even just observing green spaces can be a supplement to one's current self-care practices. For those who need a simple place to start, a few minutes with nature is an accessible, inexpensive, and risk-free way to meet their mental well-being needs in the present. Connecting to nature for a few minutes via time outdoors or by viewing natural settings (images or through windows) is something every leader can do to receive the direct and immediate benefit of better thinking.

REFLECTION

- In general, do you feel you are aware of your thoughts? Does bringing your attention to the specific thoughts you are having in this moment feel familiar or foreign?
- As you bring your awareness to this moment, what patterns can you identify in the ways in which you think?
- Do your thoughts generally feel clear, focused, and purposeful? Or, do they feel disorganized, disjointed, and fuzzy?
- Are you able to think clearly in some circumstances and yet struggle to achieve clarity in others? What helps you achieve clarity and what gets in the way?
- Who or what in the environment around you inspires helpful, positive thoughts?

- Who or what in the environment around you produces unhelpful, distracting thoughts?

ACTION

1. Survey your thoughts throughout the day. Pick a time (for example: every hour on the hour) or set a reminder alarm on your watch or phone and spend two minutes breathing and simply noticing your thoughts. Just notice what you are thinking—resist the urge to diagnose or analyze. Are your thoughts calm, clear, and focused? Distracted, jumbled, and chaotic? Are you comfortable with how your thoughts are in this moment? If so, take a few seconds to appreciate that feeling! If not, consider a break and take a stroll outdoors or rest your gaze on a nature scene.
2. Using the THRIVE Compass tool (you may download this free tool at https://www.resetoutdoors.com/resources), rate your thoughts on the scale from unclear or distracted (low score) to clear and focused (high score). Take 10–30 minutes to sit in nature or even just observe a natural view. Let your eyes rest this view—a field, a forest, a pond, the ocean. Take in the beauty and just be still. Then reassess. What shifts were you able to notice?

THRIVE: HEALTH

Leading from a position of well-being requires both mental and physical health in order to fully engage in and enjoy one's work and personal life. Without health, the school leader's impact and efforts can be greatly hindered by the additional distraction and struggle to feel and function well (Beisser et al., 2014). The weighty role of school leadership demands a considerable investment of one's personal well-being into the lives of others, and it is understood that a feeling of poor mental or physical health limits not only the individual, but, ultimately, the larger school community. Most likely, leaders are not intentionally disconnecting from nature or unwilling to spend time outdoors, but in their commitment to long, indoor workdays, time in nature can dwindle. Inadvertently, school leaders may sacrifice this opportunity for well-being and consequently be challenged by health issues simply because they have underestimated how their surroundings are influencing their condition. By increasing one's awareness of the ways in which nature directly contributes to their health, educational leaders can prioritize effective efforts to reengage with green spaces and reap healthful benefits.

Nature's vast and far reaching benefits on human health are well documented (Barton & Pretty, 2010), and yet, people may be overlooking this link in their lives (Capaldi et al., 2015). Nevertheless, "[t]ime spent in and around tree-lined streets, gardens, parks, and forested and agricultural lands is consistently linked to objective, long-term health outcomes. The less green a person's surroundings, the higher their risk of morbidity and mortality" (Kuo, 2015, p. 1). Nature based interventions have been found to improve overall health as well as prevent and treat specific medical conditions (Shanahan et al., 2016). The remarkable ability of nature to realign the body and mind is partly attributed to the chemical and biological agents present in natural settings that work to enhance immune function and to curb the onset of certain diseases (Kuo, 2015). The health benefits of nature are not replicated in urban venues, nor in the offices and halls of traditional school buildings. However, many school properties include open or forested natural areas, even if relatively small. These schoolyards can be improved for everyone's well-being (van Dijk-Wesselius et al., 2018).

In addition to the defense against illness and disease, natural environments are able to generate "a variety of stress-reducing psychophysiological responses" (Capaldi et al., 2015, p. 3) in ways that promote overall mental health. Research finds that interaction with natural environments can lower rates of depression and improve social relationships (Shanahan, 2016), both of which significantly contribute to a healthy mental state. Capaldi et al. (2015) add that people are "happier when in natural environments than when in urban ones" (p. 4), further affirming that one's mental health is indeed impacted by contact with nature or lack thereof. Considering its health benefits, the choice to engage with natural stimuli is a simple, but significant way to increase one's life satisfaction and "provide a buffer against mental distress" (Capaldi et al., 2015, p. 4).

As expected, frequent and extended interactions with nature have the best health outcomes (Shanahan et al., 2016; Kuo, 2015). Yet, there is plenty of evidence to show even a brief interaction with nature will activate healing effects (Capadi et al., 2015). Five minutes of "green exercise," defined as "activity in green places (in the presence of nature)," has been shown to have an immediate effect on a participant's mood (Barton & Pretty, 2010, pp. 3947, 3950). Mood impacts both mental and physical health, and here we see that outdoor activity can quickly improve mental health while also countering the physical health risks of a modern, sedentary life. In a unique way, nature proves to be an efficient health intervention because "a single intervention can affect people in multiple ways and, therefore, potentially improve well-being across a range of domains" (Shanahan et al., 2016, p. 10). Leaders who take a few minutes to exercise in a green space or who even step outside the school building during the day for a few minutes may be able to improve their health while meeting the demands inherent in school leadership.

REFLECTION

- Considering the complexity of your health, how healthy do you feel right now in this moment?
- What factors contribute to you feeling healthy? Physically? Mentally? Emotionally? Socially? Spiritually? What takes away from your overall health and well-being?
- How does your health impact the ecosystem/community around you? How does the health of your ecosystem/community impact your health?

ACTION

1. Using the THRIVE compass, write down an assessment of your overall health and well-being (possibly use your reflections above as a starting point). Consider all aspects of your health—physical, mental, emotional, social, and spiritual.
2. In what ways do you feel healthy? Why? Appreciate these successes and commit to continuing to nurture them.
3. Identify which areas might benefit from more careful attention. Rank them from easiest to address to the most difficult to address. Develop your plan for improving your health and, of course, speak with appropriate professionals as needed.
4. Take a 10 to 30-minute walk outdoors, preferably in a park or along a tree-lined street and note any shifts that may occur. After your walk, consider what steps you can take to improve the areas you identified as needing some additional attention and care.

THRIVE: RESILIENCE

Regardless of their different school contexts, principals universally face challenging circumstances that draw upon the leader's personal repertoire of well-being. In the ebb and flow of workplace pressure, there are those who become overwhelmed, discouraged, and depleted, while other leaders encounter similar problems and are able to reframe setbacks, adjust, and thrive. The latter not only come out stronger on the other side of challenge, but they lead in such a way that the entire school community moves ahead despite difficult experiences. Instead of quitting, these leaders are resilient. They view hardship realistically and frame trouble as an opportunity for learning and growth, and in doing so, these leaders inspire hope and strength in others. "To lead at one's best over time requires everyday resilience. It is an essential everyday quality because of the variety, intensity and complexity of the worlds which principals inhabit" (Day, 2014, p. 641). Ultimately, the resilient school leader has the will to find a way through daily conflict and struggle so that greater well-being is achieved for those involved.

Resilience gives a leader the flexibility to move and shift through trying circumstances. It contributes to confidence that allows for risk-taking that results in improvement (Allison, 2012). In the context of leadership, resilience can be demonstrated as "the ability to recover, learn from, and developmentally mature when confronted by chronic or crisis adversity" (Reed & Blaine, 2015, p. 460). While typically referred to as the ability to recover well and to "bounce back" after loss, resilient leaders actually position themselves and their school community to be ahead after a challenge (Allison, 2012). Resilience can be thought of as recovery and sustainability, but in addition because resilience suggests a move forward, "a strong future orientation is also required" (Fillery-travis et al., 2006 p. 13). As a personal attribute, resilience is not innate (Day, 2014); it can be both learned and improved (Turk & Wolfe, 2019). Research shows that resilience is "in our habits of mind—habits we can cultivate and change" (Zolli & Healy, 2013, p. 14). Because it can be gained, school leaders need to know how to strengthen their own resilience and how to help others to do the same (Lane et al., 2013; Turk & Wolfe, 2019). Not only can leaders build the quality in themselves, but they can also promote resilience in those they lead (Day, 2014). "Adversity provides educational leaders with the opportunity to model in context the very behaviors that they seek to develop in their subordinates" (Farmer, 2010, p. 7). Recognizing the connection between self-care practices and a resilient mindset is a step towards greater well-being for leaders and for those they influence.

One strategy for building and maintaining resilience is through renewal and refreshment (Castro et al., 2010). This is where nature proves to be a critical complement to resilience; natural environments provide holistic replenishment and promote health (Kuo, 2015). Health fuels the capacity for resilience, and the connection works the other ways as well. "Resilient leaders demonstrate the ability to maintain their emotional, physical, and spiritual health when adversity strikes" (Reed & Blaine, 2015, p. 463). While a principal's schedule is heavy laden with demands, taking time for self-care has compounding benefits. "Resilient leaders who are happy and doing meaningful work make time for activities that revitalize them physically, emotionally, spiritually, and intellectually. Personal renewal generates the energy leaders need to show up for demanding work" (Allison, 2012, p. 81). "Natural environments can ... trigger deep reflection" (Hyvönen et al., 2018, p. 2), and time in nature provides an ongoing opportunity for self-care by revitalizing a person's entire system. Building resilience and maintaining health can happen by creating a lifestyle that regularly contacts and connects with natural environments. The level of connection with the natural world is positively associated with perceived levels of resilience (Ingulli & Lindbloom, 2013), and as resilience is a facet of positive mental health (Ingulli & Lindbloom, 2013), time in nature contributes both to one's personal well-being and leadership capacity.

REFLECTION

- Think back to a time when you encountered an important/intimidating challenge and successfully made it through. What helped you? How did your talents and strengths help you?
- Think back to a challenge that you encountered that you felt you were unable to navigate well? What got in your way? What did you learn? How can those lessons be applied now?
- Who or what boosts your confidence? Why do these people or activities help you feel more confident and able to persevere and more than bounce back, but grow and thrive?

ACTION

1. Using the THRIVE compass, write down an assessment of your sense of resilience (possibly use your reflections above as a starting point). List past successes. Note any strengths you exhibited and/or any points of pride/appreciation. List examples of challenges where you feel you came up short. Note any specific lessons learned and any insight that can be applied to this current challenge/set of challenges.
2. Make a list of people in your life who you feel embody resilience (start with people you know and love—then move further away towards people you do not know personally). How, from your perspective, how have these people been able to navigate and overcome challenges? What hardships do you think they encountered? Who and what do you think helped them bounce back and look forward?
3. Spend 10–30 minutes outdoors. Take notice of the ecosystem around you ... where can you see resilience in action? What

challenges are there in the ecosystem around you, and in what ways are the organisms bouncing back and growing because of, or despite, their circumstances?

THRIVE: INTERCONNECTION

The ability to connect and interact in social networks is vital to one's well-being, and for school leaders, the importance of building healthy, mutually beneficial relationships is also central to the school community's ability to thrive (Murphy & Louis, 2018). Research continues to show that webs of social dependence, collaborative cultures, and distributed leadership allow a school's system to promote work and life satisfaction for administrators and faculty as well as to improve outcomes for students (Lambersky, 2016; Owen, 2016). While leaders recognize that their commitment to community is critical, the effort to create and sustain these supportive relationships may not come easily for many who hold superordinate roles in schools (Howard & Mallory, 2008). The current model of education positions the principal in such a way as to carry burdens for those in the building, often creating conditions of isolation and feelings of loneliness in the individual (Howard & Mallory, 2008; Mahfouz, 2020). To mitigate this imbalance as well as the drift towards disconnection with its detrimental consequences to leaders and their schools, a growing awareness of one's need to connect with others and to a larger system is necessary. Educational leadership research has had much to say on the importance of social connection (Murphy & Louis, 2018), but what is emerging now is how socioecological connections also influence one's practice and well-being.

Human beings need dense, networking webs, and the natural world is the model for this. Social networks are nested in natural systems, and we understand that fresh air, clean water, and nourishing food contribute to our wellness; environmental elements are weaved into the human experience. Because of this, noticing how the natural world cycles and flows in systems that touch and depend upon each other shows us what interconnected relationships can and should be. Capra (2009) explains, "This is the profound lesson we need to learn from nature. The way to sustain life is to build and nurture community" (p. 2). Leaders benefit from building and nurturing both their social and natural connections because, as ecopsychology reminds us, "the natural world is not separate from humanity; but it is at the very core of humanity, even if we live in a material and cultural world which may attempt to deny recognition of this fact" (Martyn & Brymer, 2016, p. 1438). Interacting with nature and becoming attuned to its balance and feedback is a way for leaders to understand and better participate in their own opportunities for interconnection.

Brief and casual contact with nature certainly brings a level of benefit to one's thinking, health, and resilience levels, yet it is depth of immersion and appreciation that produces connection, a deep sense of understanding of one's ties to others and to the living world. These are two different experiences. "The theme of connection reflects being connected to something larger and revolve[s] around feeling immersed, being part of something bigger, at one with, or connecting with what [is] important" (Martyn & Brymer, 2016, p. 1442). Nature connectedness is "one's subjective sense of connection with the natural world" (Capaldi et al., 2015, p. 2). At this level, nature helps us connect socially. "[W]hen people are in contact with natural scenes or living objects they will demonstrate a more intrinsic value set, orienting them to greater connection and a focus on others" (Weinstein et al., 2009, p. 1316). Immersion in nature "brings individuals closer to others, whereas human-made environments orient goals toward more selfish or self-interested ends" (Weinstein et al., 2009, p. 1327). Outdoor activities create higher social contact (Ryan et al., 2010), and nature fosters social cooperation by cultivating motivation for relationship and community goals in those who immerse themselves in outdoor environments. Natural environments, particularly beautiful nature, create prosocial behavior that corresponds to social acceptance and social well-being (Zhang et al., 2014), and those who spend time in green spaces show greater social cohesion (Shanahan et al., 2016). Although many forms of connection impact our ability to thrive, notably, it is one's sense of nature relatedness that predicts "happiness independently of other subjective connections" (Zelenski & Nisbet, 2014, p. 16). Deepening one's connection with nature creates an understanding of our own human need to thrive within the various communities one interacts within.

REFLECTION

- Think about all the people, places, and things that comprise your community, your socioecological ecosystem. Picture them and try to identify each individual stakeholder.
- Who do you depend on daily? Who depends on you?
- What value do you offer to the people who rely on you? What do you gain from the people on whom you rely?

ACTION

1. Using the THRIVE compass, write down an assessment of your interdependence (possibly use your reflections above as a starting

point). Make a list with two columns. In column "A "list all the people on whom you depend. In column "B" list all the people who depend on you. If possible, try to identify any connections between the different people listed in column A with the people in column B.
2. Pick two people from column A (those on whom YOU depend). Make a list of bullet points of things they could do better to help you AND make a list of ways that you could help them.
3. Pick two people from column B (those who depend on you). Make a list of bullet points of ways in which you can better support and nurture them, and then, make a list of ways in which they can more effectively support you.
4. Spend 10–30 minutes outdoors:

   a. How many connections can you notice between different organisms in the green space around you? (For example: a fallen tree branch feeds insects, which may then be eaten by a frog. The tree is connected to the insects which are connected to the frog.) Have fun with this! Try to see how many connections it takes to come full circle OR how many connections it takes to get to you or someone you know.
   b. What about the natural world supports and nurtures you? Be as specific as possible. Then consider the ways that you help to nurture and support the ecosystem around you. How do you contribute to its health and well-being?

5. Consider holding a leadership team meeting outside in a comfortable space. How does meeting outside enliven the meeting? What if you also made the time to play outside together? What opportunities in your community exist for team building outside? Could you schedule some time to connect more intentionally with your team while also being outside?

THRIVE: VITALITY

Leaders who successfully accomplish their work efforts and personal endeavors are able to draw from an inner source of healthy energy that enables them to bound ahead in their pursuits. This energy source is recognized as vitality, a component of well-being commonly described as liveliness, alertness, and strength. Above baseline health and wellness, vitality represents a condition of thriving that is expressed through inner buoyancy and fortitude. It is referred to as the fuel that enables one to exert productivity (Baruch et al., 2014), and "has been empirically associated with behavioral and health outcomes" (Ryan et al., 2010, p. 159). For the school leader, vitality, or vigor, shows up as excitement to achieve goals and an enduring passion to contribute to education in deep and meaningful ways. "Vigor is a key dimension of work engagement and refers to high levels of energy and mental resilience while working" (Korpela et al., 2017, p. 40); it is associated with positive organizational and career outcomes as well as with life satisfaction (Baruch et al., 2014).

Developing vitality is particularly important for leaders because those who have heavy workloads are prone to fatigue. School employees face continuous demands that deplete their cognitive, physical, and emotional energies (Ilies et al., 2015), and this toll drains those without a sustainable source of replenishment. While principals may be tempted to forgo self-care and focus solely on work outcomes, "[b]oth achievement and well-being are equally as critical to the school improvement process" (Zaharris et al., 2017, p. 91). Investing in one's energy ensures the leader has the capacity and endurance to thrive in his or her role. A way to experience greater vitality is by connecting with nature (Capaldi et al., 2015; Ryan et al., 2010). Research shows that regularly participating in physical activity in nature contributes to one's vitality (Hyvönen et al., 2018), and this is "a potential strategy for enhancing employee vitality across time" (Korpela et al., 2017, p. 38). Yet, even without exercise, one's sense of vitality has been shown to increase with nature connectedness (Capaldi et al., 2014), and this enhanced vitality was even found in those who "merely imagined themselves in an outdoor setting" (Capaldi et al., 2015, p. 5; Ryan et al., 2010).

In addition to replenishing one's energy, connecting to nature impacts vitality by tapping into the human spirit and awaking wonderment and reverence. The beauty and grandeur of nature has the capacity to create awe in those who connect to it and perceive it (Capaldi et al., 2015; Zhang et al., 2014), and this nourishes our spiritual health. The sense of awe and wonder that comes from taking in natural surroundings revives our spiritual intelligence, "the universally accepted spiritual values of hope, faith, altruistic love and caring for the well-being of the human spirit" (Zaharris et al., 2017, p. 81). While not often a topic in educational leadership, "[s]piritual leadership may be the catalyst that empowers exemplary school leaders to perform in meaningful, productive ways that link the caring aspect of leadership with the need to increase student achievement (Zaharris et al., 2017, p. 90). Using one's reserve of inner fuel and leading with deep insight benefits leaders and those under their care. The leader who will embrace opportunities to build their vitality by attending to this inner source of well-being will have energy to meet the needs in a school community in such a way that people are able to thrive.

REFLECTION

- What comes to mind when you think about the idea of vitality?
- When was the last time you felt vitality? What was the situation? How did the feeling of vitality impact you?
- What factors help you feel more physically and mentally capable, productive, vigorous?
- Name two to three people you know who, in your opinion, embody vitality. How do you see them express their vitality? Be as specific as you can.

ACTION

1. Using the THRIVE compass, mark your assessment of your vitality (possibly use your reflections above as a starting point). When you think of instances when you felt capable, productive, positively alive, what emotions can you identify? Do you feel this vitality in your body? If so, where and how?
2. Walk around your neighborhood/your school/your community and assess its vitality. Make note of the things that contribute to its vigor, its liveliness, its vibrancy, and note what takes away from or inhibits its vitality.
3. Spend 10–30 minutes outdoors in green space. Take notice of the ecosystem around you and see how many examples of vitality you observe. Can you identify any similarities between the natural space you are in and your school/community/neighborhood? Any similarities between the natural world and your own vitality?

THRIVE: EMPATHY

There are few organizations that include the scope of diversity of need, development, and experiences as those found in public school systems. Not only in the students, but also in the faculty and staff, a simultaneous expression of different abilities, values, beliefs, and levels of well-being exist in every office, classroom, and athletic space (Maxwell & Riley, 2017). Because of this, leaders need to access their inner resources to help them understand and connect with those they serve (Ilies et al., 2015). It is well documented that a leader's emotions influence the emotions and affective tone of followers (Johnson, 2008), and so attempting to manage others through a state of emotional distance risks a drift towards a school culture of indifference and apathy. Yet, the principal who sees through the cacophony of the crowd and cares for people as individuals will be better able to discern how to meet needs and create desirable school outcomes for such a profoundly divergent group. With empathy, school leaders can use both emotions and intellect to buffer against insensitivity and help those under their care to feel connected and comfortable at school.

Empathy is an emotional and cognitive response (Brown et al., 2019) that allows for multiple perspectives. "Empathy means taking the perspective of the other and feeling an emotional bond with that other" (Brown et al., 2019, p. 55). It is the ability to comprehend the unique experiences of people and to extend compassion towards them. Inversely, it is also the willingness to give oneself the same sensitive care and grace given to others. "Empathy requires passion, understanding, and interconnectedness" as well as an authentic understanding of differences among people (Boske et al., 2017, p. 364). This quality plays a role in those who are leading through collaboration and maintaining responsiveness in the culturally diverse setting of a school (Hartman et al., 2017); it enables leaders to be change agents who are willing and able advocates for the students and teachers in their community (Wang, 2019). Often empathy in a leader is connected to efforts in social reform (Boske et al., 2017), and when paired with discernment and agency, empathy helps buffer against bias and inaction (Brown et al., 2019). Furthermore, because emotions impact decision making (Wang, 2019), as an emotion, a leader's empathy contributes to improving school outcomes (Eldor & Shoshani, 2016). Creating cultures of empathy protects administrators, teachers, and staff from negative emotions and job dissatisfaction. Specifically, when empathy is expressed as compassion from school principals towards teachers, it lessens the effect of workplace stress and appears to increase an array of positive emotions, vitality, and organizational commitment (Eldor & Shoshani, 2016).

Understanding the importance of developing empathy as a school leader, one can cultivate this quality naturally by connecting and learning to appreciate the wonder of the outdoor world. Evidence shows that those who notice the beauty of nature report a greater tendency towards empathy (Zhang et al., 2014). Notably, this happens automatically in the observer as the beauty in nature activates regions of the brain known to be linked with empathy (Zhang et al., 2014). "[N]ature-related people tend to be open to experience, agreeable, and conscientious" (Howell et al., 2011, p. 732), and because empathy can be understood as a quality that transcends different kinds of boundaries (Brown et al., 2019), the ability of nature to help one feel open and present may also contribute to one's deepening empathy. Boske et al. (2017) suggests, "[b]eing present is grounded in the capacity to understand, recognize, and authentically respond to another person's emotional state" (p. 366), and time in nature encourages one to be present (Van Gordon et al., 2018). Furthermore, immersion in nature evokes generous decision making (Weinstein et al., 2009) which, along with a sense of openness and being present, supports dimensions of empathy.

REFLECTION

- How do you see and experience empathy in your life? Who are some people you know who consistently understand you and your emotional experience? Who is someone that you feel like you just get what they are going through?
- In what ways does empathy help you in your role? Where could there be more empathy? Where is there, perhaps, too much empathy? What does "balanced" or "effective" empathy feel like internally AND look like in practice to you?
- What steps can you take to regularly practice effective, balanced empathy?

ACTION

1. Using the THRIVE compass, write down an assessment of your sense of empathy (possibly use your reflections above as a starting point). Write down positive examples of your empathy in action, as well as your experience of others' empathy in action (Note: The same example may work for both—just make note of how you gave and received effective empathy paying attention to similarities and differences.) Write down an example or two of instances when empathy did not work, backfired, or was not fully present. Can you identify factors that limit the balanced and effective use of empathy?
2. Think of a situation where you were able to understand someone's emotional experience and extend compassion. Write an exhaustive list of the emotions you can name that were in that experience. As you recall this experience, try to remember if you felt any physical sensations and identify where in your body you felt them.
3. Spend 10–30 minutes outdoors, maybe watching a sunrise or sunset. If you want to catch the most beautiful colors, head out about thirty minutes or so before the time of sunrise listed in your weather app. Take notice of the ecosystem around you ... and pay close attention to any emotions that you experience. Then, see if you can feel any physical sensations when these

emotions are appearing. If you can notice and identify "good" emotions, what in the natural world sparked them into your consciousness? Can you increase their intensity? If you can notice and identify uncomfortable emotions, what triggered them? What will help you decrease their intensity?

SUMMARY

The school environment has the potential to function as a replenishing system for students, educators, and leaders alike. For this to happen, though, it is necessary that principals attend to their own well-being and model their example to those they lead. Utilizing practical, simple strategies proven to increase physical, emotional, and psychological wellness is extremely important for principals because research repeatedly documents the unique demands placed on those in the school principal profession. In order to overcome the daily drain on personal resources, school leaders can use the THRIVE model (Moriarty, 2020) to intentionally restore themselves and to be better equipped to promote the well-being of students and staff. THRIVE offers a research-based solution for self-care by showing leaders how spending time in and connecting with nature brings healing and refreshment. By reflecting and acting upon ways to increase and reinvigorate one's thoughts, health, resilience, interconnections, vitality, and energy through nature immersion, either by spending time outside or even just resting one's gaze on nature pictures or views, a leader will function in greater wellness and be better able to ensure that those in his or her school system will also thrive.

REFERENCES

Allison, E. (2012). The resilient leader. *Educational Leadership*, *69*(4), 79-82.

Bartanen, B., Grissom, J. A., & Rogers, L. K. (2019). The impacts of principal turnover. *Educational Evaluation and Policy Analysis*, *41*(3), 350–374. https://doi.org/10.3102/0162373719855044

Barton, J., & Pretty, J. (2010). What is the best dose of nature and green exercise for improving mental health? A multi-study analysis. *Environmental Science and Technology*, *44*(10), 3947–3955. https://doi.org/10.1021/es903183r

Baruch, Y., Grimland, S., & Vigoda-Gadot, E. (2014). Professional vitality and career success: Mediation, age and outcomes. *European Management Journal*, *32*(3), 518–527. https://doi.org/10.1016/j.emj.2013.06.004

Beisser, S. R., Peters, R., & Thacker, V. M. (2014). Balancing passion and priorities: An investigation of health and wellness practices of secondary school principals. *NASSP Bulletin*, *98*(3), 237–255. https://doi.org/10.1177/0192636514549886

Berman, M. G., Jonides, J., & Kaplan, S. (2008). The cognitive benefits of interacting with nature. *Psychological Science*, *19*(12), 1207–1212. https://doi.org/10.1111/j.1467-9280.2008.02225.x

Boske, C., Osanloo, A., & Newcomb, W. S. (2017). Exploring empathy to promote social justice leadership in schools. *Journal of School Leadership*, *27*(3), 361–391.

Bratman, G. N., Anderson, C. B., Berman, M. G., Cochran, B., De Vries, S., Flanders, J., Folke, C., Frumkin, H., Gross, J. J., Hartig, T., Kahn, P. H., Kuo, M., Lawler, J., Levin, P. S., Lindahl, T., Meyer-Lindenberg, A., Mitchell, R., Ouyang, Z., Roe, J., Scarlett, L., Smith, J. R., Bosch, M. V. D., Wheeler, B. W., White, M. P., Zheng, H., & Daily, G. C. (2019). Nature and mental health: An ecosystem service perspective. *Science Advances*, *5*(7), 1–14.

Brown, K., Adger, W. N., Devine-Wright, P., Anderies, J. M., Barr, S., Bousquet, F., Butler, C., Evans, L., Marshall, N., & Quinn, T. (2019). Empathy, place and identity interactions for sustainability. *Global Environmental Change*, *56*, 11–17. https://doi.org/10.1016/j.gloenvcha.2019.03.003

Capaldi, C. A., Dopko, R. L., & Zelenski, J. M. (2014). The relationship between nature connectedness and happiness: a meta-analysis. *Frontiers in Psychology*, *5*(976), 1–15. https://doi.org/10.3389/fpsyg.2014.00976

Capaldi, C. A., Passmore, H. A., Nisbet, E. K., Zelenski, J. M., & Dopko, R. L. (2015). Flourishing in nature: A review of the benefits of connecting with nature and its application as a wellbeing intervention. *International Journal of Wellbeing*, *5*(4), 1–16. https://doi.org/10.5502/ijw.v5i4.449

Capra, F. (2009). *The new facts of life. Center for Ecoliteracy.* Center for Ecoliteracy website: https://www.ecoliteracy.org/article/new-facts-life

Castro, A. J., Kelly, J., & Shih, M. (2010). Resilience strategies for new teachers in high-needs areas. *Teaching and Teacher Education*, *26*(3), 622–629. https://doi.org/10.1016/j.tate.2009.09.010

Cherkowski, S., & Walker, K. (2013). Schools as sites of human flourishing: Musings on efforts to foster sustainable learning communities. *Journal of Educational Administration and Foundations*, *23*(2), 139–154.

Day, C. (2014). Resilient principals in challenging schools: The courage and costs of conviction. *Teachers and Teaching*, *20*(5), 638–654. https://doi.org/10.1080/13540602.2014.937959

Diener E., Oishi S., & Lucas, R. E. (2003). Personality, culture, and subjective wellbeing: Emotional and cognitive evaluations of life. *Annual Review of Psychology*, *54*, 403–425. https://doi.org/10.1146/annurev.psych.54.101601.145056

Eldor, L., & Shoshani, A. (2016). Caring relationships in school staff: Exploring the link between compassion and teacher work engagement. *Teaching and Teacher Education*, *59*, 126–136. https://doi.org/10.1016/j.tate.2016.06.001

Farmer, T. A. (2010, October 23). *Overcoming adversity: Resilience development strategies for educational leaders* [Paper presentation]. The annual meeting of the Georgia Educational Research Association, Savannah, Georgia.

Federici, R. A., & Skaalvik, E. M. (2012). Principal self-efficacy: Relations with burnout, job satisfaction and motivation to quit. *Social Psychology of Education*, *15*(3), 295–320. https://doi.org/10.1007/s11218-012-9183-5

Fillery-travis, A., & Lane, D. (2006). Does coaching work or are we asking the wrong question? *International Coaching Psychology Review, 1*(1), 23–36. https://doi.org/10.53841/bpsicpr.2006.1.1.23

Fischer, R., & Boer, D. (2011). What is more important for national wellbeing: money or autonomy? A meta-analysis of wellbeing, burnout, and anxiety across 63 societies. *Journal of Personality and Social Psychology, 101*(1), 164. http://dx.doi.org.spot.lib.auburn.edu/10.1037/a0023663

Fuller, E. J., Hollingworth, L., & Pendola, A. (2017). The Every Student Succeeds Act, state efforts to improve access to effective educators, and the importance of school leadership. *Educational Administration Quarterly, 53*(5), 727–756. https://doi.org/10.1177/0013161X17711481

Fuller, E. J., Young, M. D., Richardson, S., Pendola, A., & Winn, K. (2018). *The pre-K–8 school leader in 2018: A 10-year study.* National Association of Elementary School Principals and University Council for Educational Administration. Available at https://www.naesp.org/sites/default/files/NAESP%2010-YEAR%20REPORT_2018.pdf

Hartman, R. J., Johnston, E., & Hill, M. (2017). Empathetic design: A sustainable approach to school change. *Discourse and Communication for Sustainable Education, 8*(2), 38–56. https://doi.org/10.1515/dcse-2017-0014

Howard, M. P., & Mallory, B. J. (2008). Perceptions of isolation among high school principals. *Journal of Women in Educational Leadership, 32*, 7–27. http://digitalcommons.unl.edu/jwel/32

Howell, A. J., Dopko, R. L., Passmore, H. A., & Buro, K. (2011). Nature connectedness: Associations with well-being and mindfulness. *Personality and Individual Differences, 51*(2), 166–171. https://doi.org/10.1016/j.paid.2011.03.037

Hyvönen, K., Törnroos, K., Salonen, K., Korpela, K., Feldt, T., & Kinnunen, U. (2018). Profiles of nature exposure and outdoor activities associated with occupational well-being among employees. *Frontiers in Psychology, 9*(754). https://doi.org/10.3389/fpsyg.2018.00754

Ilies, R., Huth, M., Ryan, A. M., & Dimotakis, N. (2015). Explaining the links between workload, distress, and work–family conflict among school employees: Physical, cognitive, and emotional fatigue. *Journal of Educational Psychology, 107*(4), 1136–1149. http://dx.doi.org/10.1037/edu0000029

Ingulli, K., & Lindbloom, G. (2013). Connection to nature and psychological resilience. *Ecopsychology, 5*(1), 52–55. https://doi.org/10.1089/eco.2012.0042

Johnson, S. K. (2008). I second that emotion: Effects of emotional contagion and affect at work on leader and follower outcomes. *The Leadership Quarterly, 19*(1), 1–19. https://doi.org/10.1016/j.leaqua.2007.12.001

Kaplan, S. (1995). The restorative benefits of nature: Toward an integrative framework. *Journal of Environmental Psychology, 15*(3), 169–182.

Korpela, K., De Bloom, J., Sianoja, M., Pasanen, T., & Kinnunen, U. (2017). Nature at home and at work: Naturally good? Links between window views, indoor plants, outdoor activities and employee well-being over one year. *Landscape and Urban Planning, 160*, 38–47. https://doi.org/10.1016/j.landurbplan.2016.12.005

Kuo, M. (2015). How might contact with nature promote human health? Promising mechanisms and a possible central pathway. *Frontiers in Psychology*, *6*(1093). https://doi.org/10.3389/fpsyg.2015.01093

Kruger, E. (2018). A grounded theory of ECD principals' self-care and workplace wellness-promotion practices. *Bulgarian Comparative Education Society Conference Books*, *16*, 112–118. https://files.eric.ed.gov/fulltext/ED586158.pdf

Lambersky, J. (2016). Understanding the human side of school leadership: Principals' impact on teachers' morale, self-efficacy, stress, and commitment. *Leadership and Policy in Schools*, *15*(4), 379–405. https://doi.org/10.1080/15700763.2016.1181188

Lane, K. E., McCormack, T. J., & Richardson, M. D. (2013). Resilient leaders: Essential for organizational innovation. *International Journal of Organizational Innovation (Online)*, *6*(2), 7–25. Available here: https://search.proquest.com/docview/1446441747/fulltextPDF/6B9E208EF9624CF7PQ/1?accountid=8421

Lymeus, F., Lindberg, P., & Hartig, T. (2018). Building mindfulness bottom-up: Meditation in natural settings supports open monitoring and attention restoration. *Consciousness and cognition*, *59*, 40–56. https://doi.org/10.1016/j.concog.2018.01.008

Lymeus, F., Lundgren, T., & Hartig, T. (2017). Attentional effort of beginning mindfulness training is offset with practice directed toward images of natural scenery. *Environment and Behavior*, *49*(5), 536–559. https://doi.org/10.1177/0013916516657390

Mahfouz, J. (2020). Principals and stress: Few coping strategies for abundant stressors. *Educational Management Administration & Leadership*, *48*(3), 440–458. https://doi.org/10.1177/1741143218817562

Martyn, P., & Brymer, E. (2016). The relationship between nature relatedness and anxiety. *Journal of health psychology*, *21*(7), 1436–1445. https://doi.org/10.1177/1359105314555169

Maxwell, A., & Riley, P. (2017). Emotional demands, emotional labour and occupational outcomes in school principals: Modelling the relationships. *Educational Management Administration & Leadership*, *45*(3), 484–502. https://doi.org/10.1177%2F1741143215607878

Moriarty, C. (2020, May). *What Kant missed about human nature: And finding it in nature*. TEDx Lehigh River Conferences. https://www.youtube.com/watch?v=JB1bq8X9paI

Murphy, J. F. (2016). *Professional standards for educational leaders: The empirical, moral, and experiential foundations*. Corwin Press.

Murphy, J., & Louis, K. S. (2018). *Positive school leadership*. Teachers College Press.

Owen, S. (2016). Professional learning communities: Building skills, reinvigorating the passion, and nurturing teacher wellbeing and "flourishing" within significantly innovative schooling contexts. *Educational Review*, *68*(4), 403–419. https://doi.org/10.1080/00131911.2015.1119101

Reed, D. E., & Blaine, B. (2015). Resilient women educational leaders in turbulent times: Applying the leader resilience profile® to assess women's leadership strengths. *Planning & Changing, 46*(3/4), 459–468. http://web.b.ebscohost.com/ehost/pdfviewer/pdfviewer?vid=0&sid=22f44c84-f565-4d48-b536-80e3507ea97d%40sessionmgr103

Ryan, R. M., Weinstein, N., Bernstein, J., Brown, K. W., Mistretta, L., & Gagne, M. (2010). Vitalizing effects of being outdoors and in nature. *Journal of Environmental Psychology, 30*(2), 159–168. https://doi.org/10.1016/j.jenvp.2009.10.009

Shanahan, D. F., Bush, R., Gaston, K. J., Lin, B. B., Dean, J., Barber, E., & Fuller, R. A. (2016). Health benefits from nature experiences depend on dose. *Scientific Reports, 6*(February), 1–10. https://doi.org/10.1038/srep28551

Stevenson, M. P., Schilhab, T., & Bentsen, P. (2018). Attention restoration theory II: A systematic review to clarify attention processes affected by exposure to natural environments. *Journal of Toxicology and Environmental Health, Part B, 21*(4), 227–268. https://doi.org/10.1080/10937404.2018.1505571

Turk, E. W., & Wolfe, Z. M. (2019). Principal's perceived relationship between emotional intelligence, resilience, and resonant leadership throughout their career. *International Journal of Educational Leadership Preparation, 14*(1), 147–169. https://files.eric.ed.gov/fulltext/EJ1218931.pdf

van Dijk-Wesselius, J. E., Maas, J., Hovinga, D., van Vugt, M., & van den Berg, A. E. (2018). The impact of greening schoolyards on the appreciation, and physical, cognitive and social-emotional well-being of schoolchildren: A prospective intervention study. *Landscape and Urban Planning, 180*, 15–26. https://doi.org/10.1016/j.landurbplan.2018.08.003

Van Gordon, W., Shonin, E., & Richardson, M. (2018). Mindfulness and nature. *Mindfulness, 9*, 1655–1658. https://doi.org/10.1007/s12671-018-0883-6

Wang, Y. (2019). Pulling at your heartstrings: Examining four leadership approaches from the neuroscience perspective. *Educational Administration Quarterly, 55*(2), 328–359. https://doi.org/10.1177/0013161X18799471

Wang, F., Pollock, K. E., & Hauseman, C. (2018). School principals' job satisfaction: The effects of work intensification. *Canadian Journal of Educational Administration and Policy, 185*, 73–90. https://ir.lib.uwo.ca/cgi/viewcontent.cgi?article=1129&context=edupub

Weinstein, N., Przybylski, A. K., & Ryan, R. M. (2009). Can nature make us more caring? Effects of immersion in nature on intrinsic aspirations and generosity. *Personality and Social Psychology Bulletin, 35*(10), 1315–1329. https://doi.org/10.1177/0146167209341649

Zaharris, M., Sims, P., Safer, L., Hendricks, A., Sekulich, K., & Glasgow, D. (2017). The impact of spirituality on school leadership. *ICPEL Education Leadership Review, 18*(1), 81–95. https://files.eric.ed.gov/fulltext/EJ1162588.pdf

Zelenski, J. M., & Nisbet, E. K. (2014). Happiness and feeling connected: The distinct role of nature relatedness. *Environment and behavior, 46*(1), 3–23. https://doi.org/10.1177/0013916512451901

Zhang, J. W., Howell, R. T., & Iyer, R. (2014). Engagement with natural beauty moderates the positive relation between connectedness with nature and psychological well-being. *Journal of Environmental Psychology, 38*, 55–63. https://doi.org/10.1016/j.jenvp.2013.12.013

Zhang, J. W., Piff, P. K., Iyer, R., Koleva, S., & Keltner, D. (2014). An occasion for unselfing: Beautiful nature leads to prosociality. *Journal of Environmental Psychology*, *37*, 61–72. https://doi.org/10.1016/j.jenvp.2013.11.008

Zolli, A., & Healy, A. M. (2013). *Resilience: Why things bounce back*. Simon and Schuster.

CHAPTER 11

SCHOOL ADMINISTRATORS' WELL-BEING AND MINDFULNESS AS CRITICAL COMPONENTS OF LEADERSHIP AND BUILDING HEALTHY TEAMS

Nancy Norman, Adrienne Castellon, and David D. Stinson

INTRODUCTION

This chapter explores the intersectionality of administrators' and educators' well-being within the context of a school community and presents a personal and organizational wellness model, the Stinson Wellness Model (Lee & Stinson, 2013, 2014, 2015, 2017a; Stinson, 2015) that schools can leverage for greater effectiveness and human flourishing. The model argues that an important role of administrators is to create professional environments that enhance educators' confidence, will, and capacity to contribute positively in a volatile, uncertain, chaotic, and ambiguous world. While capacity building in education is traditionally associated with professional development, this chapter goes beyond and explores ways to inform and build expert knowledge within school teams through a holistic approach of personal and professional well-being. The Stinson Wellness Model takes into consideration inclusive dispositions to enhance well-being and mindfulness by transforming school personnel's worldview, mindset, and self-concept (Dillon & Bourke, 2016; Hendel-Giller, 2017).

The Stinson Wellness Model is a theoretical framework by which those using the model can assess decisions and fit based on criteria that they apply using the model. Because holistic wellness involves all of life, the Stinson Wellness Model draws from vastly different bodies of work—for example, from authors like Kahneman (2011), Kahneman and Klein (2009), and Duke (2018) in relation to the decision-making element of the model; the alignment aspect of the model draws on literature from authors like Palmer (1999) and the fields of appreciative inquiry and positive psychology. Although the model has been in use for approximately 10 years as an innovative approach to wellness and decision making, empirical research needs to be done to validate its premise.

The purpose of this chapter is twofold: first, to present the Stinson Wellness Model as both a theoretical framework for understanding personal and organizational wellness and a tool for school leaders to guide practice; and second, to connect the Stinson Wellness Model to three distinct dispositions that support well-being and mindfulness—reflective, appreciative, and collaborative leadership.

The Stinson Wellness Model Framework

The primary premise of the Stinson Wellness Model is that for people to live well, they need to make wise decisions that align with their identity. Within the context of leadership, well-being is challenging particularly because it is not simply an individual pursuit but also includes the context in which educators live and lead. In effect, there are two key aspects to well-being in leadership. The first is related to developing healthy individual lifestyles with clear personal boundaries. The second focuses on how to lead the development of healthy teams and school communities that prioritize inclusive practices.

There is a positive connection between healthy individuals who breathe life into their school and those who lead in ways that facilitate health for everyone in the school. When leaders make wise decisions both personally and professionally, they fulfill their role as leaders by initiating healthy systems and behaviors. Consider the juxtaposition of a healthy leader leading in a healthy organization, and that same healthy leader functioning in a toxic environment. The toxic environment will have a negative impact on the health of the leader, despite their level of health.

The Stinson Wellness Model focuses on two significant processes that can be applied personally to the leader and professionally to the context of the school. The first is *wise decision-making;* the second is *alignment*. This framework can be used on a personal level to organize thoughts and personalize solutions that fit the identity and goals of individual leaders. On an organizational level, the model offers a framework to organize, plan, and execute strategic decisions that enhance the health of the school.

Figure 11.1

The Stinson Wellness Model

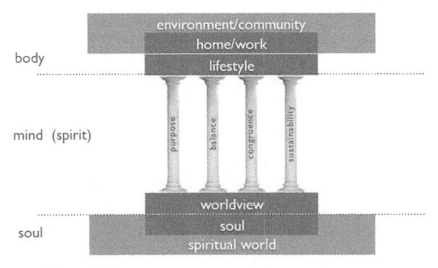

Source: Stinson (2015).

WISE DECISION-MAKING

We make many decisions each and every day. Some are routine, while others are incredibly complex and challenging. By using the four pillars of wellness shown in Figure 11.1—purpose, balance, congruence, and sustainability—the user evaluates possible solutions with the goal of making wise decisions. Each pillar has a starter question that helps practitioners begin to design the essential questions that should be answered to make an assessment about the strength of a solution. This is done not only on a personal basis for each leader, but also on an organizational basis for the health and well-being of the school.

Purpose

There should be a fundamental reason or reasons one might choose to make a given decision. The question associated with the purpose pillar is: *Does this take me in the direction I want to go?* Identifying a direction to move in and the strategy associated with that movement is no simple endeavor. It is very common that people feel pressured into making decisions that may not fit for them, so it is worthwhile identifying what the pressures are, where they come from, and then to determine whether it is a decision that takes them in the direction they need to go. We should not be pressured by the urgent but take the time to make strategic decisions based on principles and values we ascribe to in order to make purposeful movement toward our chosen goals.

Balance

Good decisions are based on quality, broad-based data, and information. In addition, seeing the big picture also helps a person understand the context of a situation, which enables wise decision making. The essential question associated with balance is: *Have I taken a balanced approach?* Balance is not simply positioning two opposing variables; instead, it is the ability to balance many variables at the same time. A metaphor illustrating this complexity is dancers who use all of their senses and muscle memory to pull off amazing moves that look incredibly off balance, but due to their skill, land with perfect control. Great dancers practice intensely to perfect their skills, but also dance with organic enthusiasm. The combination of routine practice and organic enthusiasm allows for artistic expression with full control. For schools to be balanced, there needs to be a system where balance is practiced alongside an organic respect and value for people within the school.

Congruence

This pillar focuses on making aligned decisions based on the identity of the person. For example, a person may have a clear vision of where they want to go, but to get there in ethical and principled ways can be challenging. This pillar requires commitment to the values and beliefs they stand for, and then to live them to the full within their community. As educational leaders we need to lead others in identifying the core values of our organization and how they might be demonstrated to others through our policy and procedures. The question for the congruence pillar is: *Do my values and actions match?*

Sustainability

One of the ways to ensure that we are able to continue to live balanced lives going forward is to ask: *Can I do this long term?* This pillar compels us to look at the long-term outcome of a solution we are considering. Even though it might take us in the direction we want to go, and it is a balanced decision that fits who we are, if we think we cannot support it long term, we need to consider how that sustainability might be achieved. A lot of very good decisions have resulted in failure simply because the pillar of sustainability has not been considered. Organizationally, leaders need to build sustainability into the school so it will thrive through the challenging phases that every school encounters.

ALIGNMENT

Alignment refers to the extent to which the pillars of wellness—purpose, balance, congruence, and sustainability—are aligned with personal values and goals. On Figure 11.1, you will see several rectangles depicting an important part of personal wellness. The goal is that by being mindful of each rectangle layer, individuals will grow their own understanding of who they are. The darker gray rectangles are related to the individual while the lighter rectangles provide the broader context.

Environment/Community and Home/Work

We all live within a community. For many of us, our immediate community is our family and workplace. More broadly, we have the opportunity to have an impact on our community and the environment in which we live. What is most important here is that leaders live within a community that gives them both positive and negative feedback on how they are doing—both at home and in the workplace. Leaders need to consider what these responses say about the impact of their leadership on their family and colleagues.

Lifestyle

On a personal basis, lifestyle is the external reflection of a person's internal world. Values, beliefs, and talents all find expression within our community in how we live and lead. Lifestyle is the concrete expression of personal values but also organizational values as they are expressed by schools within the communities in which we live.

Worldview

The term *worldview* has been chosen to represent the idea that every person understands life through their own eyes and experience (Gray, 2011). They have a view of the world that is personal and somewhat different from those around them because of their experiences, values, and beliefs. Thus, everyone has a personal worldview that is particular to them, but they operate in a world full of differing worldviews representing other people, groups, organizations—and even countries.

On an organizational level, there are many competing worldviews that may or may not align well with an individual's personal worldview or with organizational worldviews in which they participate. We live in an inherently incongruent world. The challenge of leadership is to find ways to align the many personal worldviews connected to the various constituents with the larger worldview and values of the school (also organization/institution). This is no small leadership task.

Spirituality and Soul

There are many views related to spirituality—what it is, how it works, what is believed. The goal is not to push anyone in one direction or another but simply to have each individual consider what they believe and value. Obviously, if a person has strong spiritual beliefs, those beliefs should figure prominently in their understanding of who they are. On the other hand, if a person does not subscribe to any spiritual views, then this layer is simply left out of the equation.

For the purposes of the Stinson model, soul is defined as a person's personal identity in the spiritual world. For those who do not believe in a spiritual world, the term *soul* can represent the core, or essence, of who they are, whatever they believe that to be.

On an organizational level, while the impact of spirituality may be less obvious, it is common for schools to be inclusive of religious/spiritual viewpoints but not to endorse one over another. As a result, however this view is expressed within the context of any given school, the impact of spirituality ought to be considered.

Similarly, language that describes organizations often includes identifying the soul of the organization. Organizations have a soul—that is, an ethos or culture—that is the core of who they are, whether directly cultivated or derived by chance. The mission, vision, and value statements that are often found on lobby walls and websites of many organizations may or may not reflect the culture of an organization. In school settings, some schools may be known for their compassion and social justice values, which are highlighted by their support systems and programs. Other schools may be known for athletics, where a culture of competition and supporting the school's teams is central to their identity. While the use of spiritual language may be somewhat unusual, we believe that there is room to consider these ideas when strategizing about how an organization can live well within the context of their community.

PERSONAL APPLICATION OF THE STINSON WELLNESS MODEL

Who Is a Healthy Educational Leader?

We would contend that good leaders lead authentically. In order to be authentic, leaders need to grow their understanding of who they are as people. They need to have a good idea of their strengths and problem areas, along with what fuels their passion and what does not. What they value should be reflected in how they live, and their words should match their actions. The leader's goals should reflect who they are, their interests and strengths, values, and beliefs. Their ethos should also align with the values of the school they lead.

Most people would agree that aligning various aspects of life so that they harmonize makes perfect sense. Who does not want peace, amity, and meaning in life? But aligning life on both a personal level and a professional level is very challenging. Much of the discord that we see in our world has to do with misalignment. On a personal level, a leader may think that they are doing a good job being responsible to the school by taking on more at work. The flip side of this alignment may be the negative impact on the leader's family and friends. It is rare to find a satisfactory work-life balance in leadership roles. This is because they are often misaligned.

Misalignment is also at the root of many organizational and social issues. When we look below the surface, we find differing values, dysfunctional and offensive behaviors, and subcultures that have little or no trust in the leadership of a school. The problem is that most would agree that alignment is important, but few stop to see how misaligned we are in so many ways. Good leaders seek to align their school so that there is care and understanding—the essential components that provide adequate resolution of conflict so that trust is maintained—and to provide flexibility so that employees can find alignment between their workplace and their personal values. Leaders should look for places where their values and expertise can be used in order to help a school flourish. There needs to be some agreement at core levels between the leader and the organizational context of the school in order for that leader to lead authentically.

Application of the Stinson Wellness Model

This chapter is focused primarily on processes and tools that will help leaders navigate their complex world in meaningful ways. Below is a leadership grid (Table 11.1) that has been created with educational leaders in mind. You will note that the top category set asks questions about personal well-being, the middle category set is related to evaluating options and next steps, and the bottom category set has questions that fit contextually within the category of professional leadership. Even though a person might feel very comfortable where they currently are, they always need to be looking forward to where they hope to lead others in the near future. Whether a leader is feeling comfortable in their leadership role or encountering burnout, the Personal Wellness Grid for School Leaders is a helpful tool to support reflection.

THE STINSON WELLNESS GRID FOR SCHOOL LEADERS

What Is a Healthy School?

The Stinson Decision-Making Grid for School Leaders (Table 11.2) provides a helpful structure for evaluating the strengths and weaknesses of any school initiative. By asking questions designed around the four wellness pillars (purpose, balance, congruence, sustainability) and social license (explained below), input on a decision can be gathered from key informants on the impact the initiative will have on their constituents.

An application of the Stinson Wellness Model within the context of a school (or School Board) is the context for the creation of a second wellness grid. School leaders have responsibilities to ensure that decisions they make are in the best interest of the stakeholders within their scope of leadership. At the center of decision making is the student; however, there are other stakeholders with demanding agendas. Administrators are concerned about budgets; teachers feel overworked, and parents have varying views on what is good for their children in the school. On an elemental level, school leaders need to consider and follow respected educational protocol and appropriate educational learning strategies to meet learning outcome goals. The context of leading in educational venues is extremely challenging. As leaders use the framework in the Stinson model to evaluate their situation and potential solutions, better decisions and greater alignment will result.

Table 11.1

The Stinson Wellness Model: Personal Wellness Grid for School Leaders

	Purpose	**Balance**	**Congruence**	**Sustainability**
Personal	What's my purpose in life? Am I moving in a direction that uses my passions, skills, and talents? Do I find meaning and fulfillment in what I am doing? How does the role I currently play align with other aspects of life? (i.e., family and other aspects of life I value)	Am I living a balanced lifestyle? What am I neglecting? Are there ways to rebalance? Normally I have already tried the easy solutions, so what difficult solutions need to be considered? How close to a crisis am I? Who else needs to be considered?	Am I able to live congruently? Do my beliefs and values bubble into my lifestyle in a relevant way? How much peace and harmony do I feel internally? Are those around me able to live congruently in the current situation? (family)	Can I keep doing this long-term? What kinds of solutions would make my life and work more sustainable? Are those around me able to live sustainably given my situation? What is the impact of my level of sustainability on those I care about most?
Possible Options/ Next Steps	If I do feel satisfied with where I'm at and the direction I'm going, what's the next step? If I don't feel satisfied with the situation I'm in, what options might take me in the direction I want to go?	As I look at various options, what do I need to be aware of in order to ensure that I am taking a balanced approach (information, advice)? Does the option I am looking at bring greater balance? If not, how might balance be maximized during the implementation process?	Which options that I am looking at fit best? Which of my gifts and talents will be used to a greater extent if I choose this option? Which options fit best for those closest to me? What would it take to make it congruent for them as well?	How would the option(s) I'm considering affect my ability to thrive long-term? If there is an initial outlay of energy to make the change, what strategies do I have to replenish my energy? How might I make this option sustainable for those around me?

(Table continued on next page)

Table 11.1 (Continued)

The Stinson Wellness Model: Personal Wellness Grid for School Leaders

	Purpose	Balance	Congruence	Sustainability
Professional Leadership	How does my personal purpose play out within the context of the school? Do I feel that I can make a meaningful contribution in a space that I value? Can I see movement in a direction that I believe is helpful organizationally?	As a leader, am I able to live a balanced life? What is the impact on those around me if I'm not balanced? When I am balanced, what is the impact? Do I regularly seek a balanced perspective on situations and decisions that I make as a leader?	In my role as a leader, am I able to lead congruently using the beliefs and values that are at the core of who I am? Does the context of leadership encourage authenticity for both the leader and the follower? How are challenging disagreements resolved?	Can I as a leader continue leading long term? What assists me or hinders me from sustainability? If sustainability is an issue for me and others, what needs to change in order for sustainability to be increased?

Stakeholders

The purpose of this grid is to gather perspectives from the various stakeholders of a decision. At the top is the School Board. The grid flows down throughout the organization to external stakeholders at the bottom. You will see that many stakeholders have been identified; however, for each decision you may want to customize the layers of stakeholders and the questions that are asked in each column. What you see in the grid are samples of how questions might be designed to help evaluate the quality of a decision. Feel free to change the questions to suit your needs.

Social License

The concept of social license is about public support for initiatives beyond legal contracts and licenses. The term has been used in business literature for years (see MacDonald Laurier Institute, 2020), but it can also be used in the fields of social services such as education. In this context, for example, social license may refer to stakeholder support for curriculum initiatives or special projects; in other words, a school does not need only the typical professional and government licenses to operate but also the support and goodwill of those in the community in which it is located. Understanding the impact that decisions can have on the goodwill of various constituents should be factored into wise decision-making.

There are times, of course, when the right decision may not be well understood by constituents and as a result they are against the decision. Do not let that wariness deflect you from making the hard but necessary decision in the circumstances—the one best for the most in the long run.

Table 11.2

The Stinson Wellness Model: Organizational Wellness Grid for School Leaders

	Purpose	Balance	Congruence	Sustainability	Social License (+/–)
School Board	From a system administration perspective, why would we choose to do this? Does it fit the mandate of the School Board?	Does this initiative bring or reduce balance at the School Board level? Is the rationale for this initiative broad-based and does it represent the views of the majority of people within the district?	How does this initiative fit with the ethos and ethics of the School Board? Is it a comfortable fit?	From the perspective of the School Board, is this strategy sustainable over time? Is it something that the public will continue to value and commit resources to?	At the School Board level, does this initiative have a lot of support or will it test the goodwill of those on the board?

(Table continued on next page)

Table 11.2 (Continued)

The Stinson Wellness Model: Organizational Wellness Grid for School Leaders

	Purpose	Balance	Congruence	Sustainability	Social License (+/−)
Principal	Does this strategy fit well with the direction the school is going? How does it strengthen or weaken the development of the school?	Within the school, does this initiative seem balanced? Are there enough resources committed where they are needed?	Does this solution fit well with the DNA of the school? As a principal, do you sense that this initiative feels good? Does it make sense?	Is this solution sustainable for the school? Are there enough resources (finances, HR, administrative structures) to keep it going long term?	How will this initiative affect you as the leader? How much social capital will be needed in order for it to be successful?
Teachers and Support Staff	Will teachers view this initiative as purposeful? Will teachers feel that it is moving the school in a good direction?	What would the impact be on the teacher's workload? Will teachers feel this is a balanced approach?	Is this solution congruent for those in the teaching profession? How does it complement or derail key teaching strategies and principles?	Can this strategy be managed well within the classroom for a long period of time? Will extra resources need to be added to ensure sustainability?	How much social capital and hard work will this require from teachers for it to be successful? Do they see this initiative to be valuable for students and families?
Students	What will the impact be on the students and the development of their purpose and identity?	How will the decision affect the balance a student feels?	Will students be able to see that the decision is congruent with the values of the school?	Will students be able to count on this decision being in place for a significant amount of time?	How will students feel about the change? Do they see it as purposeful and meaningful?

(Table continued on next page)

Table 11.2 (Continued)

The Stinson Wellness Model: Organizational Wellness Grid for School Leaders

	Purpose	Balance	Congruence	Sustainability	Social License (+/−)
Parents	Will the parents see this approach as meeting their goals for their children? Will they feel that the school is doing what is best for their children?	Will parents feel that it balances the needs of the different stakeholders, including their desires for their children?	Will parents feel that this approach fits them and their children? Does it align with their values and expectations?	Will parents feel that this strategy is sustainable over time? Do they feel that the resources will meet the needs of those involved?	Will the parents be supportive of the efforts the school has made for their children?
Community	Will the community be supportive? Does the community feel that this initiative supports the direction they are going?	What are the key concerns that need to be balanced within the community in order for this initiative to be endorsed? Who are the major players?	What ideals embedded in the community support this initiative? How and why does this initiative fit within the community?	Would the community value this deeply enough to engage and support the initiative over time?	What is the cost/benefit as viewed by the community? How will challenges be managed? Will they step up to support this financially and in other ways?
Union(s) *Note: There could be multiple unions involved and alignment may be a challenge.*	Will the union see this as a helpful initiative that they support? Does it move their interests forward?	Will the union see this as a balanced approach? If not, how will the School Board work out the problems?	Does this initiative align with union contracts? How will these issues be dealt with?	Will the union see this initiative as being sustainable?	What is the cost/benefit for the union? To what extent can the union claim victory if this initiative was approved?

Source: Adapted from Lee and Stinson (2017b).

SOCIOCOGNITIVE MINDFULNESS

The Stinson Wellness Model incorporates concepts of sociocognitive mindfulness (also called Langerian mindfulness) within a context of working with others. Sociocognitive mindfulness emphasizes an open and accepting stance, one that allows for nonjudgmental acceptance of novel experiences in the present moment, with sensitivity to context. This practice allows for deep understanding of self and others from multiple perspectives, and promotes empathy and compassion (Davenport & Pagnini, 2016; Langer & Moldoveanu, 2000). The next section describes key leadership dispositions that promote self-awareness and mindfulness, with the goal of individual and community wellness.

Leadership Dispositions That Support Well-Being and Mindfulness

It is hard to separate the model from the leader. With this in mind, there are three leadership dispositions described here that support well-being and mindfulness and extend our understanding of the Stinson Wellness Model applied in education. Together, these dispositions can be remembered by the acronym RAC: *reflective, appreciative,* and *collaborative.* The education leader who fosters these dispositions will be better prepared to pursue individual growth and community wellness in authentic and sustainable ways. What is clear is that wellness begins with an individual commitment for growth, which leads to support and growth of school communities.

Reflective. A primary disposition for educational leaders is to foster a reflective or contemplative approach. In order to reflect and to think deeply, one needs time and stillness. The fragmented role of a leader, however, with its time constraints, proclivity toward action as well as the expectation to be transparent and interactive both on- and offline, often means that finding time for self-reflection can be challenging for the busy educational leader. Nevertheless, these challenges only serve to amplify the need for a leader to schedule time to think about these and similar questions: How do I process what's going on? What are my ways of gaining the big picture? What are my practices for restoring a sense of peace and possibility (Wheatley, as cited in Goldman Schuyler et al., 2016)? Such questions speak to a leader's alignment of personal and professional purpose. When the necessary alignment is achieved, greater individual and communal wellness results.

It is not difficult to conclude that if a leader has the ability to notice, choose, perceive, and integrate, their effectiveness and the community's overall wellness are likely to benefit. This can be understood by considering the effects of the absence of such competencies: limited patience, increased distractibility, preoccupation, and decreased ability to be fully present and recognize others' needs. Ying Gao (2018) identified the following organizational benefits of such inner work for the individual: more respect, collegiality, collaboration, openness, willingness to listen and empathize; and a safe atmosphere free from fear, suspicion, back-stabbing, and hostility. Clearly, a leader's ability to hone their reflective capacities nurtures a healthy and purposeful atmosphere in the workplace.

Appreciative. A second disposition for school leaders to foster is an appreciative lens that focuses on potential and resilience rather than a deficit approach. The main idea behind an appreciative disposition (what Stavros et al., 2015, call appreciative inquiry) is to focus on strengths:

> At its heart, AI [appreciative inquiry] is about the search for the best in people, their organizations, and the strengths-filled, opportunity-rich world around them. AI is not so much a shift in the methods and models of organizational change, but AI is a fundamental shift in the overall perspective taken throughout the entire change process to "see" the wholeness of the human system and to "inquire" into that system's strengths, possibilities, and successes. (p. 97)

Ryan et al. (1999) state: "It is important to stress that appreciative inquiry can be used to guide school reform within any school community—public or private, from the elementary through the secondary level" (p. 164). While appreciative inquiry is an established research approach used in school-based research (Bergmark & Kostenius, 2018; Calabrese, 2015; Gordon, 2016; Zepeda & Ponticell, 2018), it can also be characterized as an individual disposition that leaders can foster through recognizing and working from a strengths-based perspective.

Collaborative. The third disposition for school leaders to foster is a commitment to authentic pursuit of community actualization rather than individual goals alone. This is based on a commitment to the idea that leadership is not an individual pursuit but rather presumes a collective effort whereby an individual uses influence to work with and through others to achieve organizational goals. Fostering a collective leadership approach is both freeing and healthy. Identifying the work that needs to be done to reach shared goals and then doing that work with others can increase both humility and confidence in the sense of "I can't do this alone but with others I feel more assured and will consider taking a risk I wouldn't have on my own." In addition, collaborative work can be enjoyable, leading to innovative ideas, less defensiveness, and a sense of shared purpose and responsibility. When we collaborate, we may experience important aspects of wellness, including the reassurance, belonging, and purpose that come from contribution.

This collaborative, interdependent approach is one that is supported in diverse literatures, including Indigenous (Boler, 2004; Kress, 2015), gender (Bohnet, 2016; Longman et al., 2018), social thinking, psychology, and education (Allen et al., 2004; Kress-White, 2009) as well as in the leadership/management literature (Eckert, 2018; Giambatista et al., 2020; Wheatley, 2017).

Educational leaders who foster dispositions that are reflective, appreciative, and collaborative create professional environments that enhance educators' confidence, will, and the capacity to contribute in a volatile, uncertain, chaotic, and ambiguous world. It is necessary to realize that fostering dispositions takes time and involves persistent focus and commitment to incremental changes of attitudes and habits. Knowing what should be done and having the means to do it are useless without personal commitment. Whether it ss articulated in a Zen training path, monastic rule, fitness regime, or corporate code of ethics, personal transformation takes effort and consistent individual commitment to an often nonlinear path. The Stinson Wellness Model is a framework that embeds the use of these dispositions as a way of knowing and developing a sense of self-awareness and identity. Making wise decisions that align with a person's core identity leads to meaning, emotional wellbeing, and fulfillment in life.

FINAL WORDS

School leaders encounter many challenges in their day-to-day interactions with students, teachers, staff, families, and the broader community. In the hurry of meetings, preparations for events, responding to requests from teachers, staff, families, central office, and local and provincial/state government there is not much time to think, process, discern, or evaluate from diverse standpoints. Purpose, balance, alignment, sustainability, and good decisions can be hard to clarify and achieve. Often, we have a sense that something may be wrong but struggle to identify the core problem. Without the time to reflect, it is difficult for anyone—particularly educational leaders—to go beyond the unsettled feeling and untangle the issues at a deeper level. The Stinson Wellness Model presented in this chapter can help identify underlying causes and explain the thinking behind a decision, providing a framework for reflecting and acting that can be tailored to the needs of each individual and each school.

RESOURCES

Boyatzis, R., & McKee, A. (2005). *Resonant leadership: Renewing yourself and connecting with others through mindfulness, hope, and compassion.* Harvard Business School Press. This book presents the emotional regulation and management of self and others as central.

Brown, B. (2018). *Dare to lead: Brave work. Tough conversations. Whole hearts.* Random House. This book emphasizes the importance of authentic leadership through vulnerability, self-awareness, and courage.

Goleman, D. (2006). *Emotional intelligence.* Bantam. The seminal book provides a foundational understanding of the rational and emotional mind, and highlights how both determine individual and collective success.

Goleman, D., & Senge, P. (2014). *The triple focus: A new approach to education—More than sound.* This book explains and promotes social and emotional learning in terms of the interconnections between the inner focus (self-awareness/self-management), other focus (social awareness/relationship skills), and system focus (responsible decision-making/system thinking within organizations).

Stinson, D., D. (2015). *Aligning life: The Stinson Wellness Model.* Stinson Education. The book presents a comprehensive discussion of the Stinson Wellness Model, which helps people build wellness into their lives by encouraging wise decision making and authentic living help a person contribute their talents and uniqueness to society.

REFERENCES

Allen, T. D., Eby, L. T., Poteet, M. L., Lentz, E., & Lima, L. (2004). Career benefits associated with mentoring for proteges: A meta-analysis. *Journal of Applied Psychology, 89,* 127–136.

Bergmark, U., & Kostenius, C. (2018). Appreciative student voice model: Reflecting on an appreciative inquiry research method for facilitating student voice processes. *Reflective Practice, 19*(5), 623–637.

Bohnet, I. (2016). *What works: Gender equality by design.* Belknap Press of Harvard University Press.

Boler, M. (2004). *Democratic dialogue in education: Troubling speech, disturbing silence.* Lang Publishing.

Calabrese, R. (2015). A collaboration of school administrators and a university faculty to advance school administrator practices using appreciative inquiry. *International Journal of Educational Management, 29*(2), 213–221.

Davenport, C., & Pagnini, F. (2016). Mindful learning: A case study of Langerian mindfulness in schools. *Frontiers in Psychology, 7*(1372), 1–5. https://doi.org/10.3389/fpsyg.2016.01372

Dillon, B., & Bourke, J. (2016). *The six signature traits of inclusive leadership: Thriving in a diverse new world.* Deloitte Insights. https://www2.deloitte.com/us/en/insights/topics/talent/six-signature-traits-of-inclusive-leadership.html

Duke, A. (2018). *Thinking in bets: Making smarter decisions when you don't have all the facts*. Penguin.

Eckert, J. (2018). *Leading together: Teachers and administrators improving student outcomes*. Corwin.

Giambatista, R., McKeage, R., & Brees, J. (2020). Cultures of servant leadership and their impact. *The Journal of Values-Based Leadership 13*(1), 1–16.

Goldman Schuyler, K., Baugher, J. E., & Jironet, K. (2016). *Creative social change: Leadership for a healthy world*. Emerald Group.

Gordon, S. P. (2016). Expanding our horizons: Alternative approaches to practitioner research. *Journal of Practitioner Research 1*(1), 1–17. http://doi.org/10.5038/2379-9951.1.1.1030

Gray, A. J. (2011). Worldviews. *International Psychiatry: Bulletin of the Board of International Affairs of the Royal College of Psychiatrists, 8*(3), 58–60.

Hendel-Giller, R. (2017, August). *Vertical development for leaders*. Actionable Blog. https://actionable.co/blog/2017/08/vertical-development-leaders/

Kahneman, D. (2011). *Thinking fast and slow*. Farrar, Straus and Giroux.

Kahneman, D., & Klein, G. (2009). Conditions for intuitive expertise: A failure to disagree. *American Psychologist, 64*(6), 515–526.

Kress, M. (2015). *Mental health strategy and feasibility study for a wellness, health and recovery centre for the Lac La Ronge Indian band*. Lac La Ronge Indian Band.

Kress-White, M. (2009). *The quest of inclusion: Understandings of ableism, pedagogy and the right to belong*. [Unpublished master's thesis, Department of Educational Foundations, College of Education, University of Saskatchewan]. Saskatoon, Saskatchewan.

Langer, E. J., & Moldoveanu, M. (2000). The construct of mindfulness. *Journal of Social Issues, 56*(1), 1–9. https://doi.org/10.1111/0022-4537.00148

Lee, M., & Stinson, D. D. (2017a). Finding your personal and organizational voice: A holistic approach to developing authentic leaders and organizations. *International Journal of Business Research, 17*(4), 29–40.

Lee, M., & Stinson, D. (2017b). Organizational governance: Using the Stinson Organizational Wellness Model as a governance model. *International Journal of Business Research, 17*(1), 30–42.

Lee, M., & Stinson, D. (2013). Sustaining corporate performance through employee well-being: Applying the Stinson Wellness Model in a business environment. *International Journal of Strategic Management, 13*(3), 67–78.

Lee, M., & Stinson, D. (2014). Organizational decision-making models: Comparing and contrasting to the Stinson Wellness Model. *European Journal of Management, 14*(3) 13–28.

Lee, M., & Stinson, D. (2015). The discipline of leading through empowerment: Implementing the Stinson Organizational Wellness Model. *European Journal of Management, 15*(3) 31–40.

Longman, K., Daniels, J., Lamm-Bray, D., & Liddell, W. (2018). How organizational culture shapes women's leadership experiences. *Administrative Sciences, 8*, 1–16. https://doi.org/10.3390/admsci8020008

MacDonald Laurier Institute. (2020). *Social license and Canadian democracy*. https://www.macdonaldlaurier.ca/social-licence-and-canadian-democracy/

Palmer, P. J. (1999). *Let your life speak: Listening for the voice of vocation*. Wiley.

Ryan, F. J., Soven, M., Smither, J., Sullivan, W. M., & Van Buskirk, W. R. (1999). Appreciative inquiry: Using personal narratives for initiating school reform. *The Clearing House, 7*(3), 164–167.

Stavros, J., Godwin, L., & Cooperrider, D. (2015). Appreciative inquiry: Organization development and the strengths revolution. In W. Rothwell, R. Sullivan, & J. Stavros (Eds.), *Practicing organization development: A guide to leading change and transformation* (4th ed.). Wiley.

Stinson, D. D. (2015). *Aligning life: The Stinson Wellness Model*. Stinson Education.

Wheatley, M. (2017). *Who do we choose to be? Facing reality, claiming leadership, restoring sanity*. Berret-Koehler.

Ying Gao, C. Y. (2018). *A narrative inquiry into contemplative leadership: Concepts, characteristics, challenges, opportunities* [Unpublished doctoral dissertation, Dublin City University]. Dublin, Ireland.

Zepeda, S. J., & Ponticell, J. A. (2018). *The Wiley handbook of educational supervision*. Wiley-Blackwell.

CHAPTER 12

POSITIVE LEADERSHIP FOR FLOURISHING LEARNING COMMUNITIES

Sabre Cherkowski, Benjamin Kutsyuruba, and Keith Walker

INTRODUCTION

This chapter is a compilation and synthesis of writing from our previously published body of articles, chapters, and books that share what we have learned from our participants and the research literature. We offer a conceptual model of positive leadership, grounded within the values of purpose, passion, play, and presence in the belief that these value have been and are useful for school leaders as they continue to create conditions for flourishing in their schools. We suggest that these values animate the work of those formal leaders who make space for and facilitate conditions for themselves and others to flourish in their work. The model is built on the extant literature and our research findings that illustrate what it means to work from the standpoint of those values that prompt, animate, or bring to life the work of leading and learning such as encourage flourishing for all in the learning community. The model emphasizes the embeddedness of these concepts and their potential for all in the flourishing of school cultures and especially for school leaders who wish to pay attention to the vitality, goodness, and possibilities that are latent but inherent in our school systems. As a way of bringing to life the model and the various components within it, we offer a series of reflective questions that leaders may use to adapt and animate these four values within their particular contexts.

LEADER INFLUENCE

Formal leaders, such as principals and vice principals, have a strong influence in shaping school culture (Leithwood et al., 2008). Lee and Louis (2019) made positive associations between school culture constructs and the levels of school performance in which leaders were found to play a critical role in the complex process of reculturing schools; this occurs mainly by their paying attention to developing cultures of organizational learning and professional community. In our research on flourishing in schools, we found that administrators were key agents in fostering cultures of well-being (Cherkowski et al., 2020) and that a positive organizational perspective for noticing and nurturing leadership for flourishing in schools offered benefits for sustainable school improvement efforts that are grounded in and focused on well-being as a priority for all. This positive organizational approach is supported by research that shows how attending to positive capacities such as compassion and resilience at work results in improved engagement, innovation, and creativity, among other benefits, and fewer sick days and leaves from work (Bakker & Schaufeli, 2008; Carmeli & Spreitzer, 2009; Lillius et al., 2008). Research on positive leadership reflects a shift away from the more typical approach of focusing research on deficits, gaps, and shortcomings (Cameron, 2012; Murphy & Louis, 2018).

STUDY PURPOSE

The purpose of the research described in this chapter, which we conducted in Canada, was to examine school leader well-being through taking a broader perspective, beyond stress-management approaches (Lim & Pollock, 2019; Mahfouz, 2018; Maxwell & Riley, 2016); we did this in order to offer a positive and complementary organizational perspective and analysis on school leader well-being. This positive focus does not deny the existence of very real challenges, struggles, hardships, and trauma that can lead to stress and burnout among administrators. Instead, within the reality of the work, we were interested in studying aspects of the well-being continuum that stretches toward a sense of flourishing (Keyes, 2002).

Data Collection

As part of our research project, we carried out several data collection activities. First, we conducted case studies to learn what it meant for school administrators to flourish in their work, gaining an understanding of well-being from their perspective. We also organized a multiday Positive

Leadership for Flourishing Schools forum in Kingston, Ontario. For this event we invited researchers, practitioners, graduate students, and interested community stakeholders to learn about the research and practices of flourishing in schools and discuss research findings. Each of these data collection activities were designed from an appreciative-inquiry perspective (Whitney & Trosten-Bloom, 2010) that opened spaces for reflection and analysis on what had worked well and created vitality, engagement, connection, and meaning. Among these and other positive qualities we noted how important these affordances are for building and sustaining positive organizational cultures. Collected data were qualitatively examined through a reflective and interpretative process. Our overall aim was to better understand how school administrators foster and sustain a sense of well-being for self and others in their learning communities.

Four Values

In our research, we found four values that permeated the stories of well-being at work for principals and vice principals: purpose, presence, passion, and play (see Figure 12.1). We suggest that these values form a

Figure 12.1

Positive Leadership for Flourishing: Leading from Purpose, Presence, Passion, and Play

foundation for positive leadership that fosters and supports the conditions for individuals and groups to work together toward constant improvement in their teaching and learning. Applying an appreciative, comprehensive, living-systems approach to organizing, the concept of flourishing for self and others means paying attention to the possibilities for reaching the collective agency that together creates the desired well-being and more preferred futures (Cherkowski et al., 2020).

CREATING CONDITIONS FOR FLOURISHING IN SCHOOLS

The work of cultivating flourishing learning communities is often about learning to see and then activate and nurture existing positive potential in particular contexts and moments. We have observed that principals and vice principals in flourishing schools are both aware and unwitting agents of this cultivating work—working together to grow more of what is wanted and desired through engaging in the work from and through the promotion of a sense of well-being.

Our research on leadership for growing and sustaining well-being as a foundation for learning communities in schools is aligned with research in the fields of positive psychology and positive organizational scholarship. With this approach we have aimed to establish an interdisciplinary theoretical framework that provides new ways of thinking about, inquiring into, and reflecting on well-being in schools. Knowing the importance of well-being for learning, teaching, and leading, we aim to provide an alternate perspective on well-being as more than surviving the challenges and being able to withstand the hardships of the work of the principal and vice principal. The reality of this work is that it is difficult, stressful, and often overwhelming. Within this reality of leadership work in schools, we wondered if there were opportunities to share how these school leaders found enjoyment, experienced a sense of achievement, and demonstrated resilience. Research in positive psychology encourages the development of positive outlooks, habits, and mental models with a focus on describing and building positive qualities in individuals; rather than a deficit-model approach which tries to repair the negative and destructive aspects of circumstances (Achor, 2011; Ben-Shahar, 2008; Keyes et al., 2012; Seligman & Csikszentmihalyi, 2000). From this, we understood that there are benefits to paying attention to what moves us feel engaged, connected, and alive in our lives. Findings from positive organizational scholarship (POS) showed that these benefits and advantages are brought to the forefront in our work lives when we focus on the goodness, virtuousness, and vitality found in organizations and the people who work within them (Bakker & Schaufeli, 2008; Cameron & Caza, 2004; Cameron et al., 2003; Roberts & Dutton,

2009). For example, research on high-quality connections and relationships at work are linked to team resilience (Dutton & Heaphy, 2003; Stephens et al., 2013). Expressing and receiving compassion at work have been found to increase retention and organizational commitment (Lillius et al., 2008) and positive psychological capital (representative of hope, optimism, resilience, and efficacy) is a strong predictor of other positive organizational outcomes such as commitment, performance and organizational citizenship (Luthans & Youssef, 2004). With our research, we certainly recognize the negative aspects and challenges of the work of school leaders; however, within these realities that ought not to be trivialized, we have explored the strengths, virtues and positive human capacities of school leaders that create conditions for flourishing learning communities where all may thrive.

Flourishing in schools is an ecological metaphor for imagining growth, interconnection and well-being. The metaphor encourages us to think about the heliotropic nature of plant life, turning and stretching toward the sun to grow, shifting our attention toward the capacities that promote vitality, interdisciplinary, well-being in schools, prompting us to see the system from the perspective of what is working well, what makes us feel whole, connected, engaged and alive (Cherkowski & Walker, 2018). The conceptual model that we present in this chapter reflects this ecological metaphor of flourishing in living systems (Wheatley, 1999). As we have seen in our research and in the extant research literature on positive leadership, school leaders are key agents in the creation of conditions for individuals and groups to work together toward constant learning and growth from a strengths-based and positive perspective. Flourishing for self and others within such an appreciative, living systems metaphor means paying attention to the possibilities for collective agency for creating desired futures of well-being together. With this model, we aim to highlight the importance of positive leadership for teachers, students, and their families and communities to thrive when leaders cultivate and grow conditions for the four values in and through their work—purpose, presence, passion, and play (Cherkowski et al., 2020). Although they are seemingly distinct values, the model demonstrates an important synergy, symbiosis and synchronicity interwoven into the dynamics of their influence on all aspects of the work and life of school principals. Through our research we have found that teaching, learning, and leading in the kind of environment created by and with these animated values offers a sense of flourishing—where educators and their students feel a sense of being engaged, connected, alive, and enjoying their time with each other as they contribute their strengths to building the well-being of the entire learning community. Positive leaders are key agents in animating these values and binding the community together through modeling and encouraging these values to grow, over time and with consistency, in generating personal and collective well-being and in stimulating a sense of flourishing for all within the school community.

Having reviewed the literature from studies on positive organizations, it became clear that the four values—purpose, presence, passion, and play—were important for animating leadership toward flourishing cultures, where positive emotions, engagement, relationships, and a sense of meaning and accomplishment are regularly experienced (Seligman, 2011). From the research on positive organizations, we noticed a lexicon of key characteristics that are associated with the four values of purpose, passion, presence, and play, including terms like creativity, curiosity, courage, collaboration, compassion, integrity, humility, optimism, vitality, meaningfulness, and exhilaration that are important to organizational well-being (Cameron et al., 2003). Our research is underpinned with the assumption that examining these positive concepts is critical to understanding what it means to flourish for school communities. Though the animating values are rarely experienced or stimulated in isolation, for coherence and analysis purposes we have presented them individually.

The Animating Value of Purpose

Positive leadership was described by the participants in our study as a strong sense of purpose; one that strives for sustainability, meaningfulness, and a sense of authenticity in their own work. When we asked the administrators to relate moments and experiences in their work when they felt alive, engaged, connected, and that they were expressing their best—our way of asking them to recount their experiences of flourishing—they provided rich descriptions of times at work where they felt happy, energetic, on purpose, and having fun. From our analysis of their stories, we determined that experiencing purpose was important for these principals to feel a sense of well-being in their work. This sense of purpose was slightly different or unique for each of them; however, they all expressed that they felt that they were at their best when they were living out their intentions toward a specific purpose that they were able to identify and articulate. These descriptions were often shared in relation to how they felt they were able to positively influence and inform the work of teachers toward helping them to grow stronger and deeper learning relationships with students. While all the values are connected to and experienced within relationships at work with colleagues, purpose was the value that resonated the strongest with relationally-based approaches to leadership. As we shared in previous writing (Cherkowski et al., 2018, 2020), purpose seemed to be animated through working together, taking collective action and shared ownership, and feeling a sense of contribution, meaning, and fulfillment of one's work.

This was especially so as these principals and vice principals noticed the collective impact of a shared sense of purpose. As these educators worked together and experienced positive emotions of fulfilment through collective movement toward shared purpose, this seemed to produce positive emotions that further created resources for overcoming adversity, invigorating motivation, and ultimate transformation (Cooperrider & Sekerka, 2003); what might be described as broadening and building resources and capacities from positive emotional experiences (Fredrickson, 2003). Living out a sense of purpose together also created conditions for growing positive organizational culture when positive personal traits and organizational virtues converged to create a positive "person-in-organization" (Park & Peterson, 2003, p. 34). Living out a sense of organizational virtues, such as purpose, can build and promote capacities for success across different levels of the organization and promote resiliency at work (Seligman & Csikszentmihalyi, 2014; Sutcliffe & Vogus, 2003).

In our research, the school leaders felt a sense of thriving when they were able to experience moments of connections with teachers and students; in turn, such experiences led to growing a culture of improvement in teaching and learning for all. These moments of working from purpose, of feeling that they were in service to and with others and had some agency for contributing to a greater good in the school, seemed to provide a cumulative sense of energy, of sustainability, and of resilience. Purpose was about working together, taking collective action and shared ownership, and achieving a sense of contribution, meaning, and fulfillment in their work.

Being able to articulate their sense of purpose helped administrators to maintain their focus, especially when times were hard, allowing for a view of the bigger picture within the particularities that are an ever-present, and sometimes overwhelming, part of the work of leadership in schools. As an opportunity for leaders to develop a more solid articulation of their purpose, the questions below were designed from an appreciative-inquiry perspective to encourage administrators to reach for experiences and values that they can use to develop and deepen their purpose at work.

Reflecting on Leadership for Flourishing: Animating Purpose

Spend a moment reflecting on your purpose as a leader.

- Think to a time when you were living out your higher purpose in your work or life. What did you notice was happening for you at that time that made you feel alive, engaged, and/or connected?

- In what ways do experiences at work resonate with what you feel are deeply held values about what makes life meaningful? List as many of these experiences as you can and connect them to your values of meaningfulness.
- In what ways do you see your own purpose connected to and infusing the purpose of the learning communities into your school or district? How can you create opportunities for bringing together purpose across and within the school?
- Consider what you want to keep doing in order to further achieve your purpose as a leader, and also consider what you want to avoid getting caught up in. In what ways can you build a statement of purpose that has opportunities for growth and opportunities for letting go?

The Animating Value of Presence

Educational leaders who are positively present cultivate cultures of connection, active being and listening, trust, acceptance, and understanding (Barner & Barner, 2013; Langley, 2012; Van Maele et al., 2014). Presence encompasses positively attending to the emotional lives of others and to the larger truth of who people are and what they are capable of (Cook-Sather & Curl, 2014; Tschannen-Moran & Tschannen-Moran, 2010). Presence is a "state of awareness, in the moment, characterized by the felt experience of timelessness, connectedness, and a larger truth" (Silsbee, 2008, as cited in Tschannen-Moran & Tschannen-Moran, 2010, p. 29); as the heart of mindfulness, presence involves not only attending in the moment but also assuming engagement with others through a nonjudgmental attitude and being fully aware of experiences, thoughts, and feelings (Barner & Barner, 2013). Reflective capacity is important to mindful leading, which Kopelman et al. (2012) described as "a state of mind that allows objective observation and accepting one's thoughts and feelings in the moment" (p. 167). Growing a virtuous cycle of positive relationships often starts with the leader who extends and affirms presence in ways for others to feel heard, acknowledged, valued, and understood (Starratt, 2013).

The stories from our participants affirmed the importance of sustaining a level of presence in the workplace. For our participants, presence meant more than just being visible in school throughout the day; this meant being approachable, available, able to sense the pulse of the school, and ready to handle any issues that may arise. They expressed the importance of being present at times throughout the day to what makes them feel well and brings them moments of contentment in their work. Building trust and relationships were also key to how these participants experienced a sense of presence in their approach to work and their classes. We heard stories about the importance of leaders' mindful awareness, manifested by their being present to the full story of others, and to know more about how and what they needed to proceed effectively. Their stories highlighted how these school leaders had built connections and relationships through being physically present and available, and then their being present to the stories that made up their schools through knowing and understanding the teachers and how they work best with their students.

From an appreciative, strength-based, living-systems approach to organizations, flourishing for self and others means paying attention to the possibilities for collective agency for creating desired futures of well-being together. From the stories of the administrators in our study, this often seemed to happen through presence (i.e., a mindful and attentive approach to their work and taking care to make and keep connections with those in their workplaces). Connecting and attending to the needs and well-being of teachers, staff, and the stakeholders in the learning community requires a level of presence to context. The stories of positive leadership highlighted the central role of formal school leaders in cultivating and sustaining practices steeped in presence to establish a sense of connecting, of mindfulness, and of attention to how processes and structures are affecting and influencing the diversity of cultures that make up our school communities. The questions below offer opportunities to reflect on how presence may be established and play a positive role in the work of leading schools.

Reflecting on Leadership for Flourishing: Animating Presence

Think to a time when you would say you were experiencing your work from a stance of presence, in which you were fully attentive to the moment, the work, and the people around you. As you think about that time, reflect on the following questions to learn more about how to engage in your work with and from the value of presence.

- How can mindful attention be a useful approach for you in your leadership?
- What strategies from a mindfulness perspective would help you to pay attention to small details or subtle differences in your work context?
- As you reflect on the importance of presence in your work, what opportunities do you see for strengthening or building in more of these in your daily/weekly/monthly routines?

The Animating Value of Passion

The concept of passion emerges in the literature as encompassing elements of love, virtuousness, and people using their strengths and gifts in the pursuit of collective endeavors. Often passion is positively associated with outcomes and performance that exceed expectations and purposely illuminates strengths, capabilities, and possibilities (Cameron et al., 2011). Virtuousness is synonymous with the best of the human condition, the essence of humankind, and the highest aspirations humans achieve (Cameron, 2003). In this way, passion is linked to excellence and characteristics that allow people to attain and even exceed their potential. Emmons (2003) contended that passion, referring to love and sharing gifts, is embedded in gratefulness, which is exemplified in the three components of gratefulness (i.e., benefactor, gift or benefice, and beneficiary). As such, passion is an individual quality that nurtures human capacity, cultivates positivity, and leads to social betterment.

The construct of passion resonated with, and is permeated through, the stories of the school leaders in our research through their sense of agency from building capacities for seeing and encouraging strengths, gifts, and talent in others and in themselves. These capacities entailed passion, as they actively sought ways of seeing and working from a strengths orientation and helped others to do the same. In this way, collective agency was built for growing more passion. Through their stories, we noticed that school leaders who shared their strengths, nurtured virtues, and rose to the situations that had moved them closer to fulfilling their potential felt like they had been flourishing at work. These administrators shared the importance of kindling their passions over and over again; as they worked with educators, they encouraged them to do the same. They were open to growing and engaging in ongoing self-reflection in the pursuit of their personal and professional development. Passion was linked to achieving excellence and supporting educators in reaching their full potential. It was their passionate mindsets that had allowed these leaders to nurture their capacity and the capacities and virtues of their colleagues and students. They believed that this would ultimately evolve into a flourishing school culture. With further reflection on our participants' stories, we noted that passion was understood as a collective expression of strengths and talents that had been observed to foster an environment of care, where colleagues felt a sense of connection, appreciation, and valuing of their talents and gifts. Caring school leadership is critical for the well-being of teachers and all in the learning community (Louis et al., 2016), contributing to cultures of flourishing where colleagues who feel cared about seem to engage with colleagues in growing their passion and learning together (Cherkowski & Walker, 2018). We suggest that working from passion animates and enlivens a sense of autonomy, trust, and authenticity as colleagues work together to build and grow their strengths and talents.

As with the other animating values, working and articulating for others a sense of passion at work seemed to encourage and grow more of the same agentic benefits for leaders and for those who they served in their schools and communities. Passion is often connected with stories of love and romance, but it can also be linked at work to ideas of virtuousness and using strengths and gifts in the pursuit of collective endeavors (Park & Peterson, 2003). Passion is often at the heart of learning, of wanting to continue to grow and improve in bringing our best efforts to our work and to even exceeding our potential. As with all the animating values, these administrators reflected on passion as both an individual and collective value—one in which they had learned to recognize their strengths and gifts as a leader such that they could contribute to growing the learning community. This sense of framing their work within what one leader called "my own lane" of talents allowed them to seek out complementary gifts and talents among their staff, in order to build a robust and rich learning community. The set of questions below offers reflective opportunities to notice strengths among self and others toward growing the talents of many in the community.

Reflecting on Leadership for Flourishing: Animating Passion

Imagine someone is watching you at work when you are at your best, when you are feeling engaged, connected, energized, and doing well—all working from your talents and strengths.

- In what ways have you felt that sense of passion in your work this week and why do you think that happened? What small steps can you take each week to empower yourself to work from passion more often?
- What are the gifts and talents of the teacher you most relate to or connect with? How do these align with your own ideas or values about what it means to teach and work well in your school? Now, think to a teacher with whom you might be more challenged to relate. What are their gifts and strengths?
- In what ways can you support the variety of gifts and strengths toward a common goal?
- In what ways do you need further support to be able to empower all teachers and staff to work from their strengths in your context?

The Animating Value of Play

Positive organizational scholars have demonstrated that play embedded in work may be the best-kept secret of organizational success. This may be because of its numerous happy outcomes, ranging from the well-being of workers to organizational success (Bono & Ilies, 2006). Play brings about eudaimonia (a word from the Greek language meaning "happiness"), leading to flow and joy that "can be transformational and fuel upward spirals toward optimal individual and organizational functioning" (Fredrickson, 2003, p. 163). Furthermore, Park and Peterson (2003) identified the following character strengths that they determined were linked to play or to outcomes of playing: creativity, originality, ingenuity, curiosity, interest, industry, perseverance, diligence, social intelligence, appreciation of beauty and excellence, awe, wonder, playfulness, and humor. Based on these strengths, play can be framed as "a developmental perspective [that] recognizes both the possibility of fallibility and the probability of successful coping" (Sutcliffe & Vogus, 2003, p. 97). In addition, play and fun are important aspects of well-being in alleviating stress and depressive symptoms (Sin & Lyubomirsky, 2009).

The stories of the school leader research participants demonstrated that flourishing was often experienced as moments of delight, fun, laughter, and amusement, moments that were often shared experiences with colleagues. They found ways to embed these moments of joy and fun in their work, and had made sure to enjoy these in the moment. As with the other values, play had not happened in a vacuum, apart from purpose, passion, and presence, but instead were amplified when associated with other values. As we have emphasized, a positive organizational perspective does not deny the traumas and struggles of the work, but rather honors the full range of human experiences, with a focus on noticing positive capacities and values. Our participants acknowledged the challenges and hardships they had faced in their line of work, but within these stories of struggles they identified opportunities for crafting their work that had allowed them to experience the humor and good feeling in it and to model those same or similar opportunities for staff members and students. Administrators shared the importance of framing the work for their colleagues in ways that opened them to the possibility of enjoying their work and of having fun in their workplaces, all the while acknowledging the blunt and often daunting reality that schools are often places of stress and challenge.

Play can also be a catalyst for school improvement as leaders learn to pay attention to processes and opportunities for engaging teachers in creative approaches to innovation and job crafting, doing so in ways that open space for moments of lightness and connection where learning can happen (Cherkowski et al., 2018). In our research, we found that participants used humor and moments of fun to model for others the permission for play in their work, to not take themselves too seriously, and to enjoy connecting with colleagues in laughter as important to how they work. They seemed to enjoy recounting the moments of joy they find in their work day as opportunities for experiencing positive emotions even while they navigate the challenges and difficult circumstances in their leadership work. Educational leaders who feel a sense of joy resulting from their work are likely to have increased well-being, energy, and performance. The resulting positive emotions contribute to creating safe spaces in which community connection and collaboration can grow a sense of wellness, resilience, and opportunities for growth and connection (Fredrickson, 2003; Tugade & Fredrickson, 2007). The questions below are designed to help identify and reflect upon the parts of one's day that bring joy, so that the reflective practitioner is able to grow more personal joy and model for others how to create conditions in work for play, humor, laughter, and fun as essential components of flourishing at work.

Reflecting on Leadership for Flourishing: Animating Play

Think to a time at work that you thoroughly enjoyed—that you may have described as fun. Bring to mind as many details as you can from that experience to notice what was happening, what were you doing, who were you with, and what else was going on that may have contributed to this sense of enjoyment.

- Where do you most often experience this sense of enjoyment? How can you create daily or weekly experiences that fill up your joy bucket at work?
- What routines, practices, and habits do you have in your school that promote, encourage, and make room for adults to enjoy their time together?
- In what ways do you see connections between creativity and innovation in your school? How can you support creativity and play for yourself and your staff?
- What aspects of your personal life provide you a level of creativity, fun, enjoyment, and restoration? As you make space for fun in your personal life, notice what happens in your work life and then move forward based on what you notice in a way that grows more of what you want in your work and life.

CONCLUSION

Increasingly, well-being has become an important consideration for improvements within organizational contexts (Cameron, 2012; Lencioni, 2012; Seligman, 2011). This perspective is supported by research showing that attention to positive capacities, such as positive relationships, happiness, and resilience will result in such benefits as improved engagement, higher levels of well-being and happiness, and fewer sick days and leaves from work (Bakker & Schaufeli, 2008; Harter et al., 2003).

Our research on flourishing in schools (Cherkowski & Walker, 2018; Cherkowski et al., 2018, 2020) reflects an increasing international awareness of the need for attention to broader measures of success in school (Hayward et al., 2007; Kim, 2016). Indeed, schools are systems to be managed and led; but schools are also living systems (Capra, 2002; Hargreaves & Fink, 2006) that may be nourished and sustained through a focus on the life-giving attributes of flourishing school organizations. We build on findings from our recent research to suggest that a positive organizational lens for noticing and nurturing leadership for flourishing offers benefits for sustainable school improvement efforts that are grounded in, and focused on, well-being as a priority for all.

Through our research, we offer a conceptual model of positive leadership for flourishing in schools that highlights four animating values: purpose, presence, passion, and play. We see each of these as a helpful guide for school leaders aiming to grow and sustain well-being for themselves, their colleagues, their staff members, and their students—all who make up their learning communities. In the conceptual model of positive leadership for flourishing in schools, the four animating values interact and combine through the work of leading in a complex living system made up of dynamic relationships. The model emphasizes the embeddedness of these concepts in school cultures and positions flourishing as a potential for all, and especially school leaders, to pay attention to the vitality, goodness, and possibilities that are inherent in our school systems. The work of cultivating flourishing learning communities is often about learning to see and then activate and nurture existing positive potential in particular contexts and moments. As indicated, we have seen that principals and vice principals of flourishing in schools are both aware and unwitting agents of this cultivating work. Working together to grow more of what is wanted and desired through engaging in the work from and through recognized values for flourishing can promote a deep and relatable sense of well-being.

REFERENCES

Achor, S. (2011). *The happiness advantage: The seven principles of positive psychology that fuel success and performance at work.* Crown Business.

Ben-Shahar, T. (2008), *Happier.* McGraw-Hill.
Bakker, A. B., & Schaufeli, W. B. (2008). Positive organizational behavior: Engaged employees in flourishing organizations. *Journal of Organizational Behavior, 29*(22), 147–154.
Barner, R. W., & Barner, C. P. (2013). The role of mindfulness in fostering transformational learning in work settings. In A. B. Bakker (Ed.), *Advances in positive organizational psychology* (Vol. 1, pp. 189–210). Emerald.
Bono, J. E., & Ilies, R. (2006). Charisma, positive emotions and mood contagion. *The Leadership Quarterly, 17*(4), 317–334.
Cameron, K. S. (2003). Organizational virtuousness and performance. In K. S. Cameron, J. E. Dutton, & R. E. Quinn (Eds.), *Positive organizational scholarship: Foundations of a new discipline* (pp. 48–65). Berrett-Koehler.
Cameron, K. S. (2008). Paradox in positive organizational change. *The Journal of Applied Behavioral Science, 44*(1), 7–24.
Cameron, K. S. (2012). *Positive leadership: Strategies for extraordinary performance.* Berrett-Koehler.
Cameron, K. S., & Caza, A. (2004). Introduction: Contributions to the discipline of positive organizational scholarship. *The American Behavioral Scientist, 47*(6), 731–739.
Cameron, K. S., Dutton, J. E., & Quinn, R. E. (2003). *Positive organizational scholarship: Foundations of a new discipline.* Berrett-Koehler.
Cameron, K. S. (2012). *Positive leadership: Strategies for extraordinary performance.* Berrett-Koehler.
Cameron, K. S., Mora, C., Leutscher, T., & Calarco, M. (2011). Effects of positive practices on organizational effectiveness. *The Journal of Applied Behavioral Science, 47*(3), 266–308. https://doi.org/10.1177/0021886310395514
Capra, F. (2002). *The hidden connections: A science for sustainable living.* Random House.
Carmeli, A., & Spreitzer, G. M. (2009). Trust, connectivity, and thriving: Implications for innovative behaviors at work. *The Journal of Creative Behavior, 43*(3), 169–191.
Cherkowski, S., Hanson, K., & Walker, K. (2018). Flourishing in adaptive community: Balancing structures and flexibilities. *Journal of Professional Capital and Community, 3*(2), 123–136.
Cherkowski, S., Kutsyuruba, B., & Walker, K. (2020). Positive leadership: Animating purpose, presence, passion and play for flourishing in schools. *Journal of Educational Administration, 58*(4), 401–415.
Cherkowski, S., & Walker, K. (2018). *Teacher well-being: Noticing, nurturing, and sustaining flourishing.* Word and Deed.
Cook-Sather, A., & Curl, H. (2014). I want to listen to my students' lives: Developing an ecological perspective in learning to teach. *Teacher Education Quarterly, 41*(1), 85–103.
Cooperrider, D. L., & Sekerka, L. E. (2003), Toward a theory of positive organizational change. In K. S. Cameron, J. E. Dutton, & R. E. Quinn (Eds.), *Positive organizational scholarship: Foundations of a new discipline* (pp. 225–240). Berrett-Koehler.

Dutton, J. E., & Heaphy, E. (2003). The power of high-quality connections. In K. S. Cameron, J. E. Dutton, & R. E. Quinn (Eds.), *Positive organizational scholarship: Foundations of a new discipline* (pp. 263–278). Berrett-Koehler.

Emmons, R. A. (2003). Acts of gratitude in organizations. In K. S. Cameron, J. E. Dutton, & R. E. Quinn (Eds.), *Positive organizational scholarship: Foundations of a new discipline* (pp. 81–93). Berrett-Koehler.

Fredrickson, B. L. (2003). Positive emotions and upward spirals in organizations. In K. S. Cameron, J. E. Dutton, & R. E. Quinn (Eds.), *Positive organizational scholarship: Foundations of a new discipline* (pp. 163–175). Berrett-Koehler.

Hargreaves, A., & Fink, D. (2006). *Sustainable leadership*. Wiley.

Harter, K., Schmidt, F. L., & Keyes, C. (2003). Well-being in the workplace and its relationship to business outcomes: A review of the Gallup studies. In C. L. M. Keyes & J. Haidt (Eds.), *Flourishing: The positive person and the good life* (pp. 205–224). American Psychological Association.

Hayward, K., Pannozzo, L., & Colman, R. (2007). *Developing indicators for the educated populace domain of the Canadian Index of Well-Being*. A report prepared for the Atkinson Charitable Foundation.

Keyes, C. (2002). The mental health continuum: From languishing to flourishing in life. *Journal of Health and Social Research*, *43*(2), 2017–2022.

Keyes, C., Fredrickson, B. L., & Park, N. (2012). Positive psychology and the quality of life. In C. L. M. Keyes, B. L. Frederickson, & N. Park (Eds.), *Handbook of social indicators and quality of life research* (pp. 99–112). Springer.

Kim, G. J. (2016). *Happy schools: A framework for learner well-being in the Asia Pacific*. A report prepared for UNESCO.

Kopelman, S., Feldman, E. R., McDaniel, D. M., & Hall, D. T. (2012). Mindfully negotiating a career with a heart. *Organizational Dynamics*, *41*(2), 163–171.

Langley, S. (2012). Positive relationships at work. In S. Roffey (Ed.), *Positive relationships: Evidence based practice across the world* (pp. 163–180). Springer.

Lee, M., & Louis, K. S. (2019). Mapping a strong school culture and linking it to sustainable school improvement. *Teaching and Teacher Education*, *81*, 84–96.

Leithwood, K., Harris, A., & Hopkins, D. (2008). Seven strong claims about successful school leadership. *School Leadership & Management*, *28*(1), 27–42.

Lencioni, P. (2012). *The advantage: Why organizational health trumps everything else in business*. Jossey-Bass.

Lillius, J. M., Worline, M. C., Maitlis, S., Kanov, J., Dutton, J. E., & Frost, P. (2008). The contours and consequences of compassion at work. *Journal of Organizational Behaviour*, *29*, 193–218.

Lim, L., & Pollock, K. (2019). Secondary principals' perspectives on the impact of work intensification on the secondary vice principal role. *Leading & Managing*, *25*(9), 80–98.

Louis, K. S., Murphy, J., & Smylie, M. (2016). Caring leadership in schools: Findings from an exploratory analysis. *Educational Administration Quarterly*, *52*(2), 310–348.

Luthans, F., & Youssef, C. M. (2007). Emerging positive organizational behavior. *Journal of Management*, *33*(3), 321–349.

Mahfouz, J. (2018). Principals and stress: Few coping strategies for abundant stressors. *Educational Management Administration & Leadership*, *48*(3), 440–458.

Maxwell, A., & Riley, P. (2016). Emotional demands, emotional labour and occupational outcomes in school principals. *Educational Management Administration & Leadership, 45*(3), 484–502.
Murphy, J. F., & Louis, K. S. (2018), *Positive school leadership: Building capacity and strengthening relationships*. Teachers College Press.
Park, N., & Peterson, C. M. (2003). Virtues and organizations. In K. S. Cameron, J. E. Dutton, & R. E. Quinn (Eds.), *Positive organizational scholarship: Foundations of a new discipline* (pp. 33–47). Berrett-Koehler.
Roberts, L., & Dutton, J. (2009), *Exploring positive identities and organizations: Building theoretical and research foundation*. Routledge.
Seligman, M. (2011). *Flourish: A visionary new understanding of happiness and well-being*. Free Press.
Seligman, M., & Csikszentmihalyi, M. (2000). Positive psychology: An introduction. *American Psychologist, 55*(1), 5–14.
Sin, N. L., & Lyubomirsky, S. (2009). Enhancing well-being and alleviating depressive symptoms with positive psychology interventions: A practice-friendly meta-analysis. *Journal of Clinical Psychology, 65*(5), 467–487.
Starratt, R. J. (2013). Presence. In M. Fullan & M. Grogan (Eds.), *The Jossey-Bass reader on educational leadership* (pp. 55–76). Wiley.
Stephens, J. P., Heaphy, E. D., Carmeli, A., Spreitzer, G. M., & Dutton, J. E. (2013). Relationship quality and virtuousness: Emotional carrying capacity as a source of individual and team resilience. *Journal of Applied Behavioral Science, 49*(1), 13–41.
Sutcliffe, K. M., & Vogus, T. J. (2003). Organizing for resilience. In K. S. Cameron, J. E. Dutton, & R. E. Quinn (Eds.), *Positive organizational scholarship: Foundations of a new discipline* (pp. 94–110). Berrett-Koehler.
Tschannen-Moran, B., & Tschannen-Moran, M. (2010). *Evocative coaching: Transforming schools one conversation at a time*. Jossey-Bass.
Tugade, M. M., & Fredrickson, B. L. (2007). Regulation of positive emotions: Emotional regulation strategies that promote resilience. *Journal of Happiness Studies, 8*, 311–333.
Van Maele, D., Forsyth, P. B., & Van Houtte, M. (2014). *Trust and school life: The role of trust for learning, teaching, leading, and bridging* (1st ed.). Springer.
Wheatley, M. J. (1999). Bringing schools back to life: Schools as living systems. In F. M. Duffy & J. D. Dale (Eds.), *Creating successful school systems: Voices from the university, the field, and the community* (pp. 3–19). Christopher-Gordon Publishers.
Whitney, D., & Trosten-Bloom, A. (2010). *The power of appreciative inquiry: A practical guide to positive change*. Berrett-Koehler.

CHAPTER 13

EDUCATIONAL LEADERSHIP AS EMOTIONAL LABOR

A Framework for the Values-Driven Emotion Work of School Leaders

Kristina N. LaVenia, Christy Galletta Horner, and Judy Jackson May

The reality is that organizations are places of emotion, ranging from anger to joy to sorrow, from love to hate, with characteristic emotional climates and cultures—

—Hearn and Parkin (1995, p. 136)

INTRODUCTION

Emotions are an integral part of the human experience, both in and out of the workplace. Although leadership theories have acknowledged that emotions matter for successful leadership, traditional views typically support the idea that cognition and emotion are separate, and that cognitive activity is *the stuff* of leadership. Scholarship aimed at building our knowledge of what makes for effective leadership has naturally focused on understanding effective decision making as well as leader behaviors associated with organizational success. Important for our discussion here is that recent research from psychology and neuroscience rejects the ideas that emotion and cognition are separate, and that cognition is more important in our decision making (Barrett, 2017); scientists from multiple fields are building consensus that emotion and cognition are deeply intertwined and likely inseparable. Moreover, as our knowledge base around leadership is evolving, emotions are moving from backstage to front-and-center as being worthy of investigation and understanding. The spirit and plan for this chapter is to offer readers a broad conceptual framework that incorporates constructs related to leadership theory and the emotional demands of educational leadership in hopes that we spark interest in more—and perhaps novel—educational research and practitioner dialogue focused on understanding leadership as emotional labor.

RELEVANCE OF EMOTION IN EDUCATION

Exploring the critical role of emotion in school leadership is a relatively recent research endeavor (Beatty, 2000). Beatty and Brew (2004) note that "There are inextricable links among emotion, learning, and leading. Yet the effective integration of emotional meaning making as professional practice remains outside the norm in most professional discourse in schools" (p. 2). As noted, the evolution of leadership theory is characterized by approaches emphasizing more cognitive rather than emotional perspectives. Twentieth-century schools of thought, from trait theories of the 1920s to more systems-oriented theories of the 2000s, have yet to authentically meld emotion and cognition for effective school leadership. Recognizing the limitations inherent to trait-based theories, research perspectives began to consider the significance of other factors such as the environment, the task, and the person. Seminal research emerging from the Ohio State University leadership studies (Hemphill & Coons, 1957) initiated the scholarly discussion on the link between task- and relationship-oriented leader behaviors. Halpin (1966) asserts that effective leaders appropriately merge the competing dimensions of consideration for the structure of the task and consideration for the authenticity of the connections between leader and follower.

Task and Relationship

The nexus between task and relationship serves as the foundation for many ensuing schools of thought, such as the concepts of transformational and transactional leadership. While Burns (1978) receives acclaim for introducing the concept in a political context, Bass's (1985) notable expansion of the model finds applications to social contexts such as educational administration leadership. Contingency theories attempt to consider external contexts by noting that no one style of leadership is appropriate for all situations. Most notable is Fiedler's Contingency Model (1967), which suggests the effectiveness of leader behavior depends on three components: leader-member relations, task structure, and position power. Fiedler's model assumes that when considering these three components, some circumstances will favor more relationship-oriented leaders, and some will favor more task-oriented leaders. Contemporary approaches attempt to consider the collective leadership experience in a world hit by social, political, economic, and global demands mediated by culture and dynamic systemic change (Hersey & Blanchard, 1970; Kotter, 2001; Senge et al., 2015; Sergiovanni, 2006). As noted, however, research on the emotional demands of leadership is still in the early stages.

The Role of Well-Being

The responsibilities of school leaders is unparalleled in this age of increasing federal, state, and local demands coupled with management of all organizational functions. These responsibilities encompass creating and nurturing strong relationships with multiple publics, ensuring effective instructional leadership, maintaining financial solvency, and leadership that contextualizes the culture of the students and staff. Current priorities in U.S. education include an emphasis on student well-being. The Aspen Institute, in their report *From a Nation at Risk to a Nation at Hope*, states, "The promotion of social, emotional, and academic learning is not a shifting educational fad; it is the substance of education itself" (Aspen Institute, 2018, p. 6).

This emphasis on well-being has implications for educational leaders and leadership preparation, especially around new leadership preparation standards (i.e., National Educational Leadership Preparation [NELP]) and the increased focus on social emotional learning (SEL) for PK–12 at the national, state, and local levels (e.g., American Institutes for Research [AIR], 2020; The Collaborative for Academic, Social, and Emotional Learning [CASEL], 2020). Both AIR and CASEL are working to drive a policy conversation focused on increased attention to, and resources for, implementation of interventions, training, and curricula focused on improved SEL for both teachers and students. Additionally, the 2015 reauthorization of the No Child Left Behind Act (NCLB) to the Every Student Succeeds Act (ESSA) reflects the importance of the relationship between SEL and student success by adding stipulations requiring districts receiving federal funds to include a nonacademic measure of accountability. ESSA specifically supports the use of school-wide positive behavioral interventions and supports (Every Child Succeeds Act [ESSA], 2015; von Ravensberg & Blakely, 2017), which promotes attention to and evaluation of SEL.

As educational leadership preparation transitions from the Educational Leadership Constituent Council (ELCC) standards to NELP, a key difference is that NELP "expands ELCC's concern for supporting 'the success of every student' to promoting the 'current and future success and well-being of each student and adult'" (National Policy Board for Educational Administration [NBPEA], 2018, p. 5). This change seeks to prepare leaders to focus on each individual in the building—students, support staff, and instructional staff—to meet the needs of all stakeholders. Though a focus on the well-being of everyone in the building is not new for school leaders, making it a central component in each of the NELP leadership preparation standards sends a clear message that today's school leaders are expected to support the development of the whole person(s) and be responsible for much more than the cognitive and academic success of students. This evolution toward a stronger emphasis on well-being is observable not only in the NELP standards, but also in the field of SEL as well. In October 2020, Karen Niemi, president and CEO of CASEL, offered an update on CASEL's definition of SEL, in which she outlined the emphasis on equity in education, students' agency, and recognition that students' home life (e.g., where and how they live) cannot be considered as separate from their social, emotional, and academic success (Niemi, 2020). These calls for practitioners to support the well-being of students, and for school leaders to support the well-being of all persons in their building sites, rest on a tacit understanding that educators can—and should—be prepared to support SEL and wellness in addition to academic success.

The expectation that educators can be trusted to facilitate well-being and SEL is grounded in the fact that educators are members of what have been termed the helping professions (van Dernoot Lipsky & Burk, 2009, p. 11; Skaalvik & Skaalvik, 2018). People drawn to education often self-identify as nurturing, supportive, and eager to make a difference in the lives of others (Pereira et al., 2015). Educational leaders in particular are thought to be motivated in part because of their desire to help both adults and students reach their potential (Faulkner, 2017); to help both adults and students thrive, school leaders need strong interpersonal skills. Research findings highlight the importance of quality relationships between leaders and followers for successful school outcomes (e.g., Leithwood, 2010; Riggio & Lee, 2007). Relationships between principals and teachers that rest on successful communications as well as high levels of trust are particularly important for administering high-performing schools (Eilers & Camacho, 2007; Skrla et al., 2000; Skrla & Scheurich, 2001).

Schools are highly emotional institutions, and as the demands on school leaders intensify researchers studying educational leadership (e.g., Wang,

2020) are increasingly aware that understanding the emotional demands of leadership is needed if we are to fully support leaders' development and success. Ample literature reflects the significance of quality relationships; there is less evidence, however, specifying what it means to practice as a relational leader. According to Fletcher (2001), relational practice "requires a number of relational skills such as empathy, mutuality, reciprocity, and a sensitivity to emotional contexts" (p. 84). While educational leadership researchers refer to school leadership as an emotional venture (Goleman et al., 2002; Leithwood, 2007), the focus on the routine tasks of leadership frequently overshadow dialogue relative to managing the emotional demands (Fletcher, 2001).

EMOTIONAL LABOR

This chapter aims to draw attention to a framework for understanding the emotional work of educational leaders and situate this framework within a broader context of leader well-being. Sociologist Arlie Hochschild introduced the term "emotional labor" (EL) (Hochschild, 2012, p. 7) as a way of understanding the emotion work employers require of employees, with a particular focus on service industry employer-employee dynamics. At the most fundamental level, EL is the expression, suppression, and adjustment of emotions in response to workplace goals and professional expectations (Hargreaves, 2000a; Hochschild, 2012), and leaders in various fields report performance of EL as a critical part of their day-to-day work (Iszatt-White, 2013). According to a study by Downs (2013):

> A significant amount of the work we do, as school leaders, entails managing our emotions and the emotions of others. Intellectualizing emotional labor as the work administrators do with the emotional-self and the emotional-other may enhance relational skills with others and diminish the strain on self. (p. iii)

In the decades since Hochschild put EL forward, researchers have used this framework to explore how emotion work matters for the "caring professions" (e.g., nurses, social workers, and teachers), but studies of educational leaders' EL, especially in the U.S. context, are lacking. In Hochschild's original conception, EL was viewed as one-sided and exploitive of employees because of its focus squarely on the employer's aims and the assumption that any benefit to the employee was wholly financial (Hochschild, 1983, 2012). Costs to employees from that practice are well documented, and include both burnout and attrition (Yilmaz et al., 2015; Yin et al., 2013). As EL has been adapted for use in understanding a broader range of employee experiences, however, we now recognize that

EL is more complex—particularly in the case where employees come to their careers with the employers' values already internalized, and it is likely that what makes work meaningful and rewarding for an employee includes emotional labor (Price, 2001)—that is, EL for professions, especially helping professions, may function quite differently than in work roles that involve lower levels of organizational attachment and professional identity.

EMOTIONAL LABOR IN EDUCATIONAL SETTINGS

Educating is an emotional process marked by frustration, jubilation, compassion, and even heartbreak. Yet, as one teacher bluntly put it: "[I]f I told my students how they make me feel when they do certain things on a daily basis, I would lose my job, probably" (Horner et al., 2020, p. 8). For Hochschild, emotional labor (EL) was a way to understand the emotion work employers require of employees—which she viewed as essentially exploitive— and offered a careful examination of emotion work in service-industry positions such as flight attendants, fast-food servers, and call-center workers; in a workplace setting, it is a framework that describes and explains emotion regulation and its three main components—expectations about emotions in a particular workplace, strategies employees use to meet these expectations (emotional acting), and relevant organizational goal—are observed across employment sectors (Hargreaves, 2000b; Hochschild, 1983).

Though research on EL has its deepest roots in the service industry, such as customer service, it is observed in all occupations where work requires social interaction (Beatty, 2000; Gronn, 2003; Hargreaves, 2000a). Recent research has focused on adapting the EL framework for use specifically in educational settings with an emphasis on teachers' EL, where the clients are students and their families, organizational goals are learning rather than profit-oriented, and relationships unfold over months or years rather than minutes or hours (Horner et al., 2020).

For purposes of our discussion here, where we promote EL as a framework applicable to educational leadership, it is important to note that teachers report their principals hold and communicate, or fail to communicate, expectations about emotion work in their schools (Brown, et al., 2015; LaVenia & Horner, in press). Moreover, given that school leaders are presumably the people responsible for the operationalization of employers' expectations within their school buildings, we see EL as a promising—and exciting—framework that is ready for application in exploring not only how school leaders perform EL, but also how they influence others' (e.g., teachers') performance. Figure 13.1 shows the components of the EL framework as applied to educational settings. We describe and discuss the contents of each column across the top: expectations, emotional acting, and goals.

Figure 13.1

Emotional Labor in K–12 Education

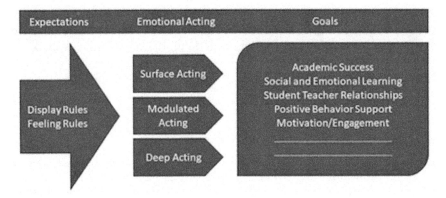

Expectations

Expectations about emotions in the workplace come in two different forms: display rules and feeling rules (Hochschild, 1983). Should a teacher yell at students in frustration or anger? The answer to this question (whatever it may be) is a display rule, or an expectation about whether and how educators should display emotions within their professional capacities. Should teachers feel compassion for their students? The answer to that question (again, whatever it may be) is a feeling rule, or an expectation about how educators should authentically experience emotions in their professional capacity. Though much EL research only includes display rules, educators have described feeling rules as prevalent in their profession as well.

What Are the Rules?

There is no fixed list of display rules or feeling rules. These expectations may vary by culture at the macro level, such as between different countries, or at the micro level, such as between two schools in the same district. Furthermore, teachers in the same school might perceive different expectations even though they have the same administrators (Brown et al., 2015). This could be, for example, because they developed different beliefs about emotions in their childhood and adolescence, and view their experiences in schools through different lenses (Horner et al., 2016). Also, although these expectations are sometimes communicated directly, teachers and teacher candidates have described learning about school-based display rules in more complicated and implicit ways, such as through observing how others behave while inferring how they feel (Brown et al., 2015; Horner et al., 2018).

By pointing out that display rules exist as sociocultural phenomena, we are neither advocating nor condemning them. Rather, it is likely that some display rules are generally harmful while others are generally beneficial, and still others do not make much of a difference either way. And, certain display rules could prove helpful in some settings and not in others.

Emotional Acting

Often, educators' experience emotions they believe would violate display rules if expressed and emotions that are out of alignment with the feeling rules they perceive. In addition, sometimes educators do not feel an emotion that they perceive the need to express, such as excitement about a lesson. As one teacher told us in a recent interview,

> [T]hese kids are depending on me being as best as I can be. And even when I don't feel like it, they need to see it. And it's hard and it's stressful and draining on me. But it'd be more draining if I stood in front of my class and cried. (LaVenia & Horner, in press)

In such situations, a measure of emotional performance is often the solution to the misalignment between emotions and expectations.

The EL framework identifies three different types of acting that educators use to align with expectations and work toward goals: surface acting, modulated acting, and deep acting (Hargreaves, 2000a; Hochschild, 1983; Horner et al., 2020).

Surface acting. In many different situations, educators might decide to hide an emotion or express an emotion that they are not really feeling. Creating a mismatch between internal experience and outward expression is called surface acting. Surface acting includes misrepresenting the display of emotion (Naring et al., 2011). For educators, this often involves hiding anger or frustration or pretending to be excited, but varies widely; some educators have described pretending to be angry and hiding excitement (Brown et al., 2015; Horner et al, 2020).

Modulated acting. Other times, educators may decide to express their authentic emotion, but in a purposeful rather than spontaneous way. For example, an educator may feel frustrated and want to curse and slam a door, but instead express that frustration by saying "I'm very frustrated. I need to take a moment." This is modulated acting (Horner et al., 2020).

Deep acting. Finally, educators might shift their emotional state to align with expectations reflective of deep acting. Unlike surface acting, deep acting finds the educator purposely engineering their inner feeling to feel a certain emotion (Naring et al., 2011). Hochschild (2012) asserts that the effect of deep acting is "deceiving oneself as much as deceiving others" (p. 33). A common example of deep acting is when an educator initially experiences anger in response to challenging student behavior, and then shifts to feeling empathy by calling to mind trauma that the student has experienced (Brown et al., 2015).

Goals

Organizational goals are a key component of the EL framework. Ideally, expectations about emotions in an organization should function to drive behavior within the organization in ways that meet these goals. The list of goals included in Figure 13.1 was adapted from research conducted with educators about their emotional labor (Horner et al., 2014). We invite those in education to include their own priorities when using the EL framework to reflect on and work with EL in their setting. Thus, we included blank spaces in the final column of Figure 13.1 to indicate that the list of goals is both context-dependent and dynamic. Keep in mind that, ideally, school leaders can not only work to articulate their own EL but also help teachers and other staff members reflect on and develop their EL practice, including the identification of individual and organizational goals.

A FRAMEWORK FOR SUPPORTING SCHOOL LEADERS

There are many compelling reasons to explore the emotional demands of school leadership, including the fact that school leaders are required to successfully engage multiple stakeholder groups across all ages and stages of development (e.g., youth, novice teachers, experienced teachers, parents, community members); the concomitant communication demands can be highly stressful (Berkovich & Eyal, 2015). Successful school leadership requires knowledge of not only what to communicate to whom, but also how to calibrate emotional communications in order to achieve organizational goals. Recent findings (Maxwell & Riley, 2017) suggest school leaders' EL is associated with well-being, with results supporting the notion that surface acting, in particular, is associated with higher rates of burnout and decreased leader well-being.

Managing Emotions

Emotions, or affective processes, are at play across all domains—including politics, decision-making, and working as a member of an organization (Fineman, 2003); emotions also drive our motivations and engagement in the workplace, in particular when we are working on projects or problems about which we care deeply (Barsade & Gibson, 2007). Findings from various fields, including psychology and economics, indicate that emotions are important for decision-making (Lerner et al., 2015; Wang, 2020). Moreover, the quality of leader-follower relationships is predictive of employees' commitment to the organization/intent to leave as well as employee well-being (Brunetto et al., 2010; Rodwell et al., 2009). To the extent that leader success requires strong relationships with followers, leadership is emotional, and effective leaders are, in large part, skilled at motivating and engaging followers. We posit that EL is a useful framework for understanding—and thereby supporting—school leadership because it provides a lens through which we can investigate how leaders manage emotions in the workplace.

From a review of the most popular cases over the past three years from the *Journal of Cases in Educational Leadership* two of the nine most read cases—(a) Murray-Johnson and Guera (2018), Ready for Change? Emotions and Resistance in the Face of Social Justice Leadership"; and (b) Tenuto et al. (2016): "Leaders on the Front Line—Managing Emotion for Ethical Decision Making: A Teaching Case Study for Supervision of School Personnel"—it is clear that emotional labor and preserving relationships are central to the work of school leaders. However, training programs often prepare novice leaders to monitor their emotions to the extent that Marshall and Greenfield (as cited in Jeffery & Beatty, 2006) note that school leaders' proclivity to conceal and falsify their actual emotions is often "treated as evidence of suitability for school administration" (p. 4). Contrary to actual practice, leadership preparation programs, and organizational change literature in particular, often focus on the logic and rationality of a leader's decision-making. Theories of emotion are not central to leadership preparation, likely more out of convention than the on-the-ground reality of leadership practice.

Rationale

Exploring school leadership as emotional labor allows us to ask questions about when, how, and why school leaders express or suppress specific emotions (e.g., anger, sadness, satisfaction). For example, we can envision a school leader in a new placement who is working to understand the school culture while actively suppressing negative emotions (e.g., confusion, disapproval) provoked by observing practices and behaviors that the school leader finds problematic. Alternatively, we might find a school leader in a new placement who is intentionally displaying confusion or disapproval in response to practices and behaviors the leader does not endorse. Using the lens of EL, we seek to explore the leaders' perspectives and sense making around their emotional displays as well as followers' responses to these leader moves. Because school leaders work to *influence* followers, especially teachers, we can use emotional labor to understand when, how, and why school leaders influence followers to display and/or feel certain emotions. Each of the major components of the EL model map onto some aspect of school leaders' work, not only as employee-as-follower (i.e., reporting to their superintendent) but also as employee-as-leader. Later in this chapter, we will revisit this aspect of school leaders' emotional labor. For now, it is worth noting that emotional labor as a frame for understanding school leadership can support successful leadership vis-à-vis a clearer understanding of school leaders' dual (and perhaps competing) roles as emotional laborers and emotional-labor-drivers. For example, when teachers report that they often do not know what a particular feeling rule and/or display rule is in their school until they have broken a rule, we see that principals are, in fact, behaving as referees for teachers' emotional labor. Reports of teachers' experiences when they are reprimanded—*We don't cry in front of students here*—or *You never tell a parent that we made a mistake*—offer some insight into how school leaders work to shape teachers' emotional displays.

DISCUSSION AND IMPLICATIONS

One of the most fascinating things we have noticed in our conversations with educators across studies is that almost everyone immediately identifies emotional labor as an integral part of their daily work, but few people have the language to describe it until we introduce this framework. We also find educators have a complex relationship with EL. Teachers have all but apologized for performing it (Horner et al., 2020); novice teachers have described confusion around implicit and unclear (but ubiquitous) EL expectations (Brown et al., 2015); preservice teachers have worried aloud that they will not be able to show their students that they are "human" (Horner et al., 2020, p. 8). We believe the time is right for EL as a framework for educational leadership research and practice to move front and center.

In *Communicating Emotion at Work*, Vincent Waldron (2012) describes leaders as emotional orchestrators who work to define and model the appropriate emotional displays for their followers, boost employee morale, sustain motivation, and induce lower-performing team members to either improve their work or exit the organization. Teachers, according to Waldron, are emotional prescribers, who help students to understand what is appropriate with regard to emotional displays and experiences. While we have some evidence of school leaders functioning as referees for teachers' emotional labor, we know less about how principals might work to act as emotional labor coaches. And although there is evidence of the performative nature of teaching and leading (e.g., "you put your mask on"), we have not yet clarified what this performance costs educators and students. What, for example, might happen if we trained educators to behave more authentically? Would this require changes in our willingness to be vulnerable in the workplace? Might we see improvements in the quality of relationships between school leaders, teachers, and students if we normalize school cultures of transparency around emotions?

When we think about people we know—even ourselves—who are former educators or school leaders who chose a different career, what are the reasons for exiting? Do people report leaving practitioner roles because of cognitive and/or intellectual strain? In our experience, the reasons for exiting are more reflective of emotional strain and burnout. As a field, we have much to learn about the emotional labor of leading and teaching. This chapter seeks to convince readers that this is an area ripe for exploration in our research agendas, professional practice in schools, and leadership preparation coursework.

IDEAS FOR RESEARCHER-PRACTITIONER COLLABORATION

In preparing this chapter, we worked to identify areas where educational researchers might focus investigations of educational leadership as emotional labor. This list offers just a few ideas we have and is by no means comprehensive:

- Gender and leadership in schools: There is evidence that women are not granted the same authority and status in leadership positions that men can expect. Gender differences in workplace communication exist, as do gender differences in emotion expression (e.g., Karpowitz & Mendelberg's (2014) *The Silent Sex*). What are the implications for school leaders' EL when we consider gender as a variable of interest? How might gender match between leader and follower dyads (e.g., female leader and follower) matter for EL and job satisfaction, burnout, trust, organizational citizenship behaviors, and self-efficacy?

- Expectations associated with emotional labor vary according to settings and persons. School leaders likely have some ability—perhaps even responsibility—to shape what is expected with regard to emotional labor in their schools. Currently, research on culturally sustaining and responsive EL practice is absent in the literature. We invite all educators and educational researchers to consider how school leaders may either maintain the status quo or disrupt current practices that privilege white, middle-class emotion communications.
- What is the role of threat in educational leaders' EL? Studies of socialization and group norms (e.g., Gelfand, 2018) demonstrate that adherence to rules and norms is culturally driven, and varies not only between persons but also across cultures. Threat appears to be an important predictor of *loose* vs. *strict* adherence to rules and norms, with groups that have experienced more threat (e.g., natural disasters, invasion, and war) skewing toward more strict rule following. In a sociopolitical climate in which schools increasingly face accountability pressures, threats to funding, and heightened demands around school safety, what is the relation between threat/safety and school leaders' EL?
- How does the practice of EL vary according to individual differences around these factors: person-role fit, professional identity, beliefs about emotions, distress tolerance, compassion fatigue, empathy, and collegial trust?
- How and where does EL overlap with SEL? How and where are these frameworks at odds? As we learn more about both EL and SEL for school leaders, which changes to these models are necessary so that practice informs theory more significantly?
- Are there ways to develop what we conceptualize as *communities of emotional practice* that can support practitioners' EL development? Much the same way that communities of instructional practice, professional learning communities, or lesson study allow practitioners to reflect on—and refine—their instructional practices, how can we facilitate *communities of emotional practice* around improved EL for personnel?

POSSIBLE PRACTICES AND RESOURCES FOR PRACTITIONERS

- The model for EL presented in Figure 13.1 provides an overview of the major components of EL. Practitioners are encouraged

to reflect on their thoughts, experiences, and questions about expectations, emotional acting, and goals related to EL.
- School leaders and teachers can think about creating a *community of emotional practice* in which practitioners reflect on and improve EL in their school sites. Use Figure 13.1 as a guide for your reflections.
- Invite a group of colleagues to engage in a study of *Communicating Emotion at Work* by Vincent Waldron (2012). This interesting and accessible text offers insight into how and why better understanding of emotions in the workplace are critically important for employee well-being. Think about how you and your colleagues can center issues of equity in communicating emotion at work.

REFERENCES

American Institutes for Research (AIR). (2020, October 15). *Social and emotional learning.* https://www.air.org/topic/social-and-emotional-learning

Aspen Institute. (2018). *From a nation at risk to a nation at hope: Recommendations from the national commission on social, emotional, and academic development.* https://nationathope.org/wp-content/uploads/2018_aspen_final_report_full_webversion.pdf

Barrett, L. F. (2017). *How emotions are made: The secret life of the brain.* Harcourt.

Barsade, S. G., & Gibson, D. E. (2007). Why does affect matter in organizations? *Academy of Management Perspectives, 21*(1), 36–59.

Bass, B. M. (1985). *Leadership and performance.* Free Press.

Beatty, B. R. (2000, December 3-8). *Emotion matters in teacher-administrator interactions: Teachers speak about their leaders* [Paper presentation]. The Annual Conference of the Australian Association for Research in Education. Sydney, Australia.

Beatty, B., & Brew, C. (2004, November 28–December 2). *Examining and developing emotional epistemologies: A foundational issue for leadership preparation programmes* [Paper presentation]. The Annual Conference of the Australian Association for Research in Education. Melbourne, Australia. https://www.aare.edu.au/data/publications/2004/bea04599.pdf

Berkovich, I., & Eyal, O. (2015). Educational leaders and emotions: An international review of empirical evidence 1992–2012. *Review of Educational Research, 85*(1), 129–167.

Brown, B., Horner C. G., Scanlon, C., & Kerr, M. M. (2015). United States teachers' emotional labor and professional identities. *KEDI Journal of Educational Policy, 11*(2), 205–225.

Brunetto, Y., Farr-Wharton, R., & Shacklock, K. (2010). The impact of supervisor–subordinate relationships on public and private sector nurses' commitment. *Human Resource Management Journal 20*(2), 206–225.

Burns, J. M. (1978). *Leadership*. Harper & Row.

Collaborative for Academic, Social, and Emotional Learning (CASEL). (2020, October 20). *SEL policy*. https://casel.org/policy/

Downs, P. H. (2013). *Dealing with feelings: Perspectives on the emotional labor of school leadership* [Unpublished doctoral dissertation, University of Hull]. Yorkshire, England. https://hydra.hull.ac.uk/resources/hull:8623

Eilers, A. M., & Camacho, A. (2007). School culture change in the making: Leadership factors that matter. *Urban Education, 42*(6), 616–637.

Every Student Succeeds Act (ESSA). (2015). *Every Student Succeeds Act Summary*. https://www.ed.gov/essa?src=rn

Faulkner, S. (2017). *The influence of effective principal leadership on teacher job satisfaction framed within Maslow's theory of motivation* (Publication No. 10280399) [Doctoral dissertation, Lamar University–Beaumont]. ProQuest Dissertations and Theses Global.

Fiedler, F. E. (1967). *A theory of leadership effectiveness*. McGraw-Hill.

Fineman, S. (2003). *Understanding emotion at work*. SAGE.

Fletcher, J. K. (2001). *Disappearing acts: Gender, power, and relational practice at work*. MIT Press.

Gelfand, M. J. (2018). *Rule makers, rule breakers: How tight and loose cultures wire our world* [First Scribner hardcover ed.]. Scribner, an imprint of Simon & Schuster.

Goleman, D., Boyatzis, R., & McKee, A. (2002). *Primal leadership*. Harvard Business School Press.

Gronn, P. (2003). *The new work of educational leaders*. Paul Chapman.

Halpin, A. W. (1966). *Theory and research in administration*. Macmillan.

Hargreaves, A. (2000a, April 24-28). *Emotional geographies: Teaching in a box* [Paper presentation]. American Educational Research Association Annual Conference. New Orleans, LA, United States.

Hargreaves, A. (2000b). Mixed emotions: Teachers' perceptions of their interactions with students. *Teaching and Teacher Education, 16*(8), 811–826.

Hearn, J., & Parkin, W. (1995). *Sex at work: The power and paradox of organization sexuality*. St. Martin's Press.

Hemphill, J. K., & Coons, A. E. (1957). Development of the leader behavior description questionnaire. In R. M. Stogdill & A. E. Coons (Eds.), *Leader behavior: Its description and measurement* (PAGES?). Bureau of Business Research, Ohio State University.

Hersey, P., & Blanchard, K. H. (1970). Cultural changes: Their influence on organizational structure and management behavior. *Training and Development Journal, 24*(10), 2–3.

Hochschild, A. R. (1983). *The managed heart: Commercialization of human feeling*. University of California Press.

Hochschild, A. R. (2012). *The managed heart: The commercialization of human feeling*. University of California Press.

Horner, C. G., Brown, E. L., Kerr, M. M., & Scanlon, C. (2014, April 3–7). *Teachers' selection of emotional acting strategies in pursuit of classroom goals* [Paper presentation]. Classroom Management SIG, Annual Conference of American Educational Research Association, Philadelphia, PA.

Horner, C. G., Brown, E. L., & Valenti, M. W. (2016, April 8–12). *The roles of educators' beliefs about emotions and perceptions of display rules in emotional acting* [Paper presentation]. The Lives of Teachers SIG, Annual Conference of American Educational Research Association, Washington, D.C.

Horner, C. G., LaVenia, K. L., & Vostal, M. (2020, April 17–21). *Teacher candidates wonder: Can emotional labor and authentic student-teacher relationships coexist?* [Paper presentation]. AERA Annual Meeting, San Francisco, CA. http://tinyurl.com/tjfajn3 (Conference canceled)

Horner, C. G., LaVenia, K. L., Vostal, M., & Ishola, O. (2018, October). *Preservice teachers' introduction to the emotional regulation demands of the teaching profession* [Paper presentation]. Northeastern Educational Research Association Annual Conference, Trumbull, CT, United States.

Iszatt-White, M. (2013). *Leadership as emotional labour: Management and the "managed heart."* Routledge.

Jeffery, P., & Beatty, B. (2006). *Leaning into our fears: A new master's course prepares principals to engage with the emotions of leadership.* Semantic Scholar. https://www.semanticscholar.org/paper/Leaning-Into-Our-Fears%3A-A-new-masters-course-to-the-Jeffery-Beatty/2d71cdb644fa3f8db49b20710d23d15d5b3b4064

Karpowitz, C. F., & Mendelberg, T. (2014). *The silent sex: Gender, deliberations, & institutions.* Princeton University Press.

Kotter, J. P. (2001). What leaders really do. *Harvard Business Review, 79*(11), 85–96.

LaVenia, K. N., & Horner, C. G. (in press). *School leaders' expectations for teachers' emotion work: Exploring perceptions of leader influence.*

Leithwood, K. (2007). The emotional side of school improvement: A leadership perspective. In T. Townsend (Ed.), *International handbook of school effectiveness and improvement* (Vol. 17, pp. 615–634). Springer.

Leithwood, K. (2010). Characteristics of school districts that are exceptionally effective in closing the achievement gap. *Leadership and Policy in Schools, 9*(3), 245–291.

Lerner, J. S., Li, Y., Valdeso, P., & Kassam, K. S. (2015). Emotion and decision-making. *Annual Review of Psychology, 66,* 799–823.

Maxwell, A., & Riley, P. (2017). Emotional demands, emotional labour and occupational outcomes in school principals: Modelling the relationships. *Educational Management, Administration & Leadership, 45*(3), 484–502.

Murray-Johnson, K., & Guerra, P. L. (2018). Ready for change? Emotions and resistance in the face of social justice leadership. *Journal of Cases in Educational Leadership, 21*(3)3–20.

Naring, G., Vlerick, P., & Van de Ven, B. (2011). Emotion work and emotional exhaustion in teachers: The job and individual perspective. *Educational Studies, 38*(1), 63–72.

National Policy Board for Educational Administration (NPBEA). (2018). *National Educational Leadership Preparation (NELP) Program Standards—Building Level*. www.npbea.org.

Niemi, K. (2020). *A reintroduction to SEL: CASEL's definition and framework* [Video]. YouTube. https://www.youtube.com/watch?v=0N_Y34tjQm8&feature=youtu.be

Pereira, F., Lopes, A., & Marta, M. (2015). Being a teacher educator: Professional identities and conceptions of professional education. *Educational Research, 57*(4), 451–469.

Price, H. (2001). Emotional labor in the classroom: A psychoanalytic perspective. *Journal of Social Work Practice, 15*(2), 161–180.

Riggio, R. E., & Lee, J. (2007). Emotional and interpersonal competencies and leader development. *Human Resource Management Review, 17*(4), 418–426.

Rodwell, J., Noblet, A., Demir, D., & Steane, P. (2009). Supervisors are central to work characteristics affecting nurse outcomes. *Journal of Nursing Scholarship 41*, 310–319.

Senge, P., Hamilton, H., & Kania, J. (2015, Winter). The dawn of system leadership. *Stanford Social Innovation Review*, 1–9.

Sergiovanni, T. J. (2006). *The principalship: A reflective practice*. Allyn & Bacon.

Skaalvik, E. M., & Skaalvik, S. (2018). Job demands and job resources as predictors of teacher motivation and well-being. *Social Psychology of Education, 21*(5), 1251–1275.

Skrla, L., & Scheurich, J. J. (2001). Displacing deficit thinking in school district leadership. *Education and Urban Society, 33*(3), 235–259.

Skrla, L., Scheurich, J. J., & Johnson, J. F. (2000). Equity-driven achievement-focused school districts. http://www.utdanacenter.org.

Tenuto, P. L., Gardiner, M. E., & Yamamoto, J. K. (2016). Leaders on the front line—managing emotion for ethical decision making: A teaching case study for supervision of school personnel. *Journal of Cases in Educational Leadership, 19*(3), 11–26.

van Dernoot Lipsky, D., & Burk, C. (2009). *Trauma stewardship: An everyday guide to caring for self while caring for others*. Berrett-Koehler.

von Ravensberg, H., & Blakely, A. W. (2017, June). *Guidance for states on ESSA state plans: Aligning the school climate indicator and SW-PBIS*. https://eric.ed.gov/?id=ED591247

Waldron, V. R. (2012). *Communicating emotion at work*. Polity Press.

Wang, Y., (2020). What is the role of emotions in educational leaders' decision making? Proposing and organizing framework. *Educational Administration Quarterly, 18*(3), 1–11.

Yilmaz, K., Altinkurt, Y., Guner, M., & Sen, B. (2015). The relationship between teachers' emotional labor and burnout level. *Eurasian Journal of Educational Research, 59*, 75–90.

Yin, H. B., Lee, J. C. K., & Zhang, Z. H. (2013). Exploring the relationship among teachers' emotional intelligence, emotional labor strategies and teaching satisfaction. *Teaching and Teacher Education, 35*, 137–145.

CHAPTER 14

AN URBAN DISTRICT'S APPROACH TO SCALING UP SOCIAL-EMOTIONAL LEARNING COMPETENCIES THROUGH A LEADERSHIP LENS

Delia Estrada, Marco A. Nava, and Susan Ward-Roncalli

INTRODUCTION

The Large Urban School District (LUSD), was founded in the mid-1800s, and currently enrolls more than 600,000 students in preschool through adult education at over 1,200 centers and schools. Geographically, the LUSD covers an area totaling 700 square miles and is a diverse global community consisting of approximately 30 smaller municipalities. In its schools, 94 languages other than English are spoken, and 74% of students are Latino, 10% White, 9% African American, and 8% Asian. Of this population, over 75% of students come from low-income households. The LUSD employs over 60,000 teachers, administrators, and support staff with an annual operating budget of over $7.5 billion. The demands on school leaders to meet the needs of this community and the people who serve them is ever growing and persistently urgent.

Recent research highlights that the school leadership challenge is even greater within the complex cultures of persistently low-performing and underserved schools. Inequitable funding formulas, variance in content

Supporting Leaders for School Improvement Through Self-Care and Well-Being, pp. 257–275
Copyright © 2024 by Information Age Publishing
www.infoagepub.com
All rights of reproduction in any form reserved.

257

coverage, low student support, and a lack of autonomy at the school site level exacerbate these challenges (Schmidt & McKnight, 2012). Described in these terms, such schools are considered to be lacking, low-performing, and powerless in meeting student needs—a negative narrative that discourages educators from acknowledging assets inherent within the communities they serve and reinforces deficit thinking.

In order to successfully take on these challenges, educators must recognize their own capacity to adapt, change, and create flourishing communities of learning (Cherkowski & Walker, 2013). The LUSD has a great need for high-quality, equity-driven leaders who can guide school communities to implement a positive, trauma informed, asset-based approach that challenges deficit thinking and provides culturally proficient and responsive school environments (Lindsey et al., 2018).

To this end, serving the needs of this diverse population requires the LUSD to actively prepare, support, and recruit school leaders who can foster belongingness, connectedness, and well-being—in sum, lead schools where human capacity for creativity, learning, resiliency is encouraged and supported (Cherkowski & Walker, 2014). This work is integral to maintaining healthy school communities where children and staff can flourish academically and emotionally. Central to this mission is the promotion and institutionalization of social-emotional learning (SEL).

School leaders are in a unique position to promote SEL through intentional, comprehensive practices (Cherkowski & Walker, 2014). To maximize their good effect on school culture and improve student outcomes, school districts must invest in building administrator leadership capacity, and their leaders required to have a solid understanding of SEL constructs, practices, and self-care. One way to accomplish this is through systemic change management rooted in a framework of professional learning standards for social justice (Furman, 2012). School leaders should be intentional in building educator capacity to create SEL-friendly and trauma-sensitive ecologies within their school (California Department of Education [CDE], 2018).

This mixed method study used both quantitative and qualitative data to analyze the actions that the LUSD employed to elevate SEL as part of daily practice in schools. These actions included, but were not limited to:

- Incorporating the four unified SEL competencies shown in Figure 14.1—a growth mindset, self-efficacy, self-management, and social awareness—for students and adults.
- Adding the SEL competencies to the LUSD school leadership framework.
- Investing in professional development for school leaders on SEL, self-care, and mindfulness strategies.

Figure 14.1

LUSD Social-Emotional Learning Competencies

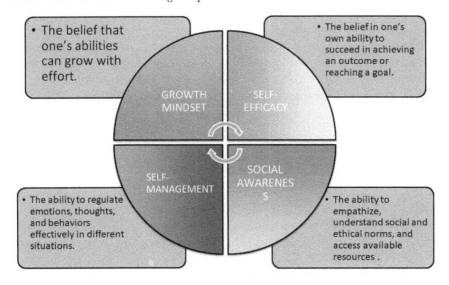

The research questions are:

- What do school site leaders perceive as their role in implementing effective SEL practices and ecologies? What supports and resources do they need?
- How does a district build capacity and scale up SEL leadership competencies for over 2,900 school site administrators?
- What impact will targeted professional development have on administrator knowledge and application of SEL practices?

LITERATURE REVIEW

Our professional development plan evolved, driven by research in the literature. Recent events have brought the need for social-emotional learning to the forefront. Advances in our understanding of the importance of inter- and intrapersonal skills support the need for schools to seek to hire and train for these abilities. What follows is a brief exploration of recent research that examines the importance of SEL and a summary of recent advances in brain research that have demonstrated the need to counter trauma in students and educators through self-care and SEL practices.

Many studies support the need for SEL. Gabrieli et al.'s (2015) *Ready to Be Counted* was significant in that this white paper looked at the research base through the lens of the impact of social-emotional skills on life outcomes. The paper links the findings from a number of pivotal studies conducted by economists, psychologists, physicians, and education researchers onto a framework organized around the domains of academics, career, and well-being. Among other benefits, positive health effects associated with stronger noncognitive skills include reduced mortality and lower rates of obesity, smoking, substance abuse, and mental health disorders (Gabrieli et al., 2015).

Heckman and Kautz (2012) assert that investing in emotional skills is a cost-effective approach to increasing the quality and productivity of the workforce through fostering workers' motivation, perseverance, and self-control A literature review published in 2012 by the Institute of Education in London looked at eight factors comprising noncognitive skills that are thought to improve life outcomes: self-perception, motivation, perseverance, self-control, metacognitive strategies, social competencies, resilience/coping, and creativity. The authors of the review then looked at correlational evidence, malleability, and causal evidence for each factor, and concluded that these factors are, for the most part, malleable, and that improving abilities in these areas could improve overall quality of life (Gutman & Vorhaus, 2012). This research makes the case for the importance of persisting with SEL in working with both children and adults.

TRAUMA AND NEUROSCIENCE

Advances in many fields, including neuroscience and psychology, have moved the work in social-emotional learning forward over the last 15 years. We have learned that the brain continues to grow and change throughout life, and that this neuroplasticity is crucial to utilizing SEL to improve outcomes for individuals who have experienced trauma (Tovar-Moli & Lent, 2016).

There is increasing evidence that neuroplasticity is disrupted by stress, which is observed on both the structural and molecular levels (Holmes & Wellman, 2009; Pittenger & Durnan, 2008). Stressful early experiences alter neural functioning and connectivity within and between the areas of the brain responsible for coordinating thoughts and actions and regulating the stress response. Stress causes the release of the neurotransmitter cortisol, and constant stress can cause what is known as the "cortisol cascade effect" (Carpenter et al., 2011, p. 370). This occurs when stress is unresolved, and can lead to mood and behavior issues, and disruptions in memory and recall. This was also found to be predictive of attention deficit hyperactivity disorder (ADHD) (Durlak et al., 2015). Links between childhood trauma and anxiety disorders, suicidal ideation, and depression have been established (Binder, 2009; Heim et al., 2008; Krishnan & Nestler, 2008; Roy et al., 2010).

Research in neuroscience informs trauma-informed educational practices, and many individuals who have experienced trauma need to develop social emotional competencies (Carello & Butler, 2015). We understand that as the brain develops, neural pathways are created. These connections are shaped over time by experience (Fox et al., 2010). By providing opportunities for individuals to practice and develop these skills, we can help them to rebuild neural pathways that may have been damaged in childhood.

We also understand that as the brain develops, neural pathways are created. These connections are shaped over time by experience (Fox et al., 2010). By providing opportunities for individuals to practice and develop these skills, we can help them to rebuild neural pathways that may have been damaged in childhood.

ADVERSE CHILDHOOD EXPERIENCES AFFECTING THE BRAIN

Early experiences shape a child's developing neurological and biological systems for better or worse, and the types of "stressful experiences that are endemic to families living in poverty can alter children's neurobiology in ways that undermine their health, their social competence, and their ability to succeed in school and in life" (Thompson, 2004, p. 45). Felitti et al.'s (1998) study found a strong relationship between exposure to abuse or dysfunction and multiple health risk factors later in life.

Felitti et al. (1998) developed the adverse childhood experience (ACE) questionnaire from their determination to use the ACE score as a measure of cumulative childhood trauma, hypothesizing a dose response relationship of the ACE score to selected outcomes. They found a convergence between epidemiologic and neurobiological evidence of the effects of childhood trauma. Tyrka et al. (2010) found that stress caused lasting damage on a chromosomal level. Complex trauma impairs development, specifically executive functioning (ventromedial prefrontal cortex) and creating academic challenges. ACEs that are prolonged and repeated reveal themselves in more detrimental effects across multiple developmental domains; in addition, trauma results in changes to the emotional processing areas of the brain in the ventromedial prefrontal cortex (De Brito et al., 2013).

Executive functions encompass a variety of skills responsible for self-regulation, goal setting, and engagement. Emerging evidence points to specific developmental windows and specificity of ACE subtypes in the development of neurobiological alterations, including volume and functional changes in the amygdala and hippocampus in adulthood, these changes can result in complex clinical profiles with several co-occurring mental and somatic disorders such as posttraumatic stress disorder, depression, borderline personality disorder, obesity, and diabetes (Herzog & Schmahl, 2018). Based upon this evidence, our district realizes that both early intervention that provides social-emotional skill building for students and resources that support healing and self-care for adults are indispensable supports.

FACILITATOR TEAM AND WORKSHOP

Our sense of urgency prompted the LUSD to dedicate resources to this effort. This began in 2015, with the formation of a team of wellness facilitators whose work sat in the Division of Student Health and Human Services. The facilitators were, by and large, social workers who provided guidance to schools around strategies to increase student well-being. In 2016, the work was moved to the Division of Instruction; the work then was adapted to a more universal Tier 1 approach; this meant that social-emotional well-being would be taught within classrooms by teachers as a part of whole-class instruction. New staff hired were teachers who could speak about how to integrate SEL into direct instruction. The team provided professional development and technical support to schools to help them develop and implement school-wide social-emotional learning plans. The requests for services in the schools quickly outpaced the team's ability to meet them.

A structure was developed that would catalyze a shift in the culture of LUSD schools. A collaboration was formed among colleagues from Health and Human Services, the Division of Instruction, and Human Resources to develop a six-hour Saturday professional development workshop for teachers. This workshop introduced social-emotional learning, explored the California Office to Reform Education (CORE) competencies, and considered how we as a district measure them. An overview of ACEs and trauma-informed practices was included. This was followed by providing information about, and practice with, the evidence based SEL curricula that the district provides for teachers. Though the focus of the training workshop was on teachers and classroom practice, it was discovered that many school site administrators were interested in attending as well. At the same time, there was a realization that it was important to expand the workshop offerings and include additional strategies for self-care. Participants connected with the work on both a professional and a personal level.

SEL AND SCHOOL LEADERSHIP TRAINING

The need to provide differentiated SEL content to school leaders became apparent; possible implications for classroom and schoolwide practices were also noted. A social-emotional development team was established to ensure the professional development was designed to meet the specific needs of school leaders. The team, which included personnel from human resources, the Division of Instruction, labor leadership, a state administrator association representative, and the leadership development branch, designed the SEL professional development training for school leaders to focus on SEL competencies, leadership standards, and adult learning.

The team followed this program because it recognized that school leaders are in the unique position of influencing not only academic instruction, but also the culture and climate of an entire school community. Leadership is second only to teaching as the most important school-based factor in student academic achievement, and there are as yet few examples of where troubled schools managed a positive turnaround without effective leaders (Mendels, 2012).

An understanding of SEL can lead to deeper reflection on the healthy— or unhealthy—effects of current school personnel's beliefs, assumptions, and procedures because it has the potential to transform school community perspectives on many school practices, such as discipline, intervention, and referral services (Nava & Nava, 2020). In addition, such understanding can facilitate discussion of the possible barriers and opportunities that exist in acknowledging these effects; moreover, it can lead to courageous conversations that reconstruct a school community's vision of itself and how it fosters capacity and resilience in its students and faculty; and it can be used to steer conversations away from what students "can't" to what a school *can* foster and support.

SEL can be a powerful tool in steering from deficit thinking to asset-based thinking, and building the foundation for culturally proficient and flourishing communities (Cherkowski & Walker, 2014; Lindsey et al., 2018). In order to succeed in this work, it is imperative for school leaders to work collaboratively with teachers to implement a clear and strategic vision for school success (University of Chicago, n.d.). School leaders would not only need to understand SEL but also how to guide a community in implementing these concepts in their daily practices.

The SEL team recognized that school leaders are typically trained in management choices but not the profound challenges of human dynamics that play out in our public schools—especially around issues of race, class, language, and disability. Research has shown that university-based administrative preparation programs have been found to lack the rigor, curriculum, real-world experiences, and prerequisite screening that will prepare principals for the unrelenting and varied demands of the job; surveys of school administrators show that many of them did not feel adequately prepared by their administrative preparation programs (Clifford, 2010). While current administrative programs have begun to integrate SEL into their curricula, current school leaders likely did not have this incorporated into their preparation experience. In recognition of this gap, the SEL team aimed at providing what school leaders need to know in its SEL professional development training.

Earlier training for health and human services personnel and teachers had used the four SEL competencies adopted by the CORE districts in 2015—a growth mindset, self-efficacy, self-management, and social awareness. These competencies were adopted by the Division of Instruction within the LUSD, providing a powerful opportunity to create cohesive and common language across the district regarding SEL.

The SEL leadership team used these competencies as a foundation to build understanding, analyze current practices, and facilitate discussions. Throughout the LUSD, school leaders needed the ability to communicate to district teachers' concepts that had previously been introduced and needed reinforcement, as well as the motivation to share examples, artifacts, and insights on the work accomplished to date by district teachers. Participating school leaders were exposed and given access to the available curriculum and resources to support SEL efforts.

LEADERSHIP STANDARDS

For several years before this SEL effort, the LUSD had adopted standards for teaching and learning intended to describe clear expectations for effective teaching and to identify exemplary practices that enhanced the success of all students. It was a base by which school leaders could observe, discuss, and support teachers in their growth as instructors. The inception of the teaching and learning standards for the district revealed the need to develop aligned administrator standards to foster genuine instructional and educational leadership. Developed by the Human Resources Division, the standards acknowledge that leadership is an essential component of school success.

Leadership Categories

Just as the teaching and learning standards help build instructional capacity, the professional leadership standards were aimed at building leadership capabilities. The standards describe the knowledge, skills, dispositions, and actions that leaders take to develop teacher effectiveness and improve student achievement. Six leadership categories were adopted: leadership and professional growth, change management, instruction, culture of learning and positive behavior, family and community engagement, and systems and operations. School administrators are guided and mentored using the categories to reflect on their own growth as leaders. The categories are reviewed each year for relevance and effectiveness.

In the year prior to the offering of the SEL professional development, recognition of the importance of SEL was acknowledged. It was explicitly included in the leadership standards and directly included under two categories: leadership and professional growth, which refers to a leader's own self-learning, and culture of learning and positive behavior, part of a path to building teacher capacity in SEL. The inclusion of SEL language acknowledged its importance in the development and daily work of school leaders and positioned SEL as an inherent, pivotal concern for school leaders, indicating that supporting SEL work needed to be an ongoing commitment.

Skill Development

Though successful leadership cannot be reduced to a single style or personality type, leadership skills can be developed and expanded over time—they are not innate or fixed. Successful leaders are interested in developing additional skills and are open to adapting their leadership style when necessary. To do so, leaders need to reflect on their actions, their perceptions, and the ways in which they are reacting to challenges. These characteristics became essential in informing the activities chosen for professional development. The link to the leadership standards became a grounding feature in the design of this training opportunity.

METHODOLOGY

Context

This mixed-method study on leading SEL took place during the 2018–2020 school years. The professional development days were originally offered in face-to-face settings. Due to the COVID-19 school and office closures, however, the model switched to a synchronous virtual classroom setting. School site administrators who served at schools designated as Title I were invited to participate in the training. The sessions were designed to deepen school leader understanding of SEL in order to proactively engage and sustain positive school cultures.

The professional development day covered six hours of content. Five different Saturday training dates were made available where school administrators selected one to participate in. The first session occurred in a face-to-face format, and the remaining four were conducted on a virtual platform. The content included an overview of trauma-informed practices, a deeper dive into the social-emotional learning competencies, reflection, and drafting a commitment to leading SEL at their school sites. A total of 204 school site administrators participated in the SEL leadership professional development.

Data Sources

SEL leadership activities included lecture time, readings, group work, small-group work, reflection, and an actionable commitment item. Data sources include 4-point Likert scale items, coded chat box responses and an open-ended SEL leadership consideration exercise.

The Likert scale items captured some school demographic data, pre- and post-training comparison items measuring SEL knowledge growth, and participant perceptions of the value of SEL competencies on student learning and positive school culture.

Data Analysis

To measure SEL content growth, a 4-point Likert scale was developed. In order to develop a composite index measuring attitudes (Joshi et al., 2015), the four points were placed in a logical sequence (Strongly Agree, Agree, Disagree, and Strongly Disagree) and there was enough differentiation among them for participants to more readily make a selection. The open-ended questions and action plan items were coded, grouped into categories, and then connected to a thematic concept (Creswell & Creswell, 2017).

Results

SEL leadership participants were asked to complete a pre-survey at the beginning of the professional development session and a post-survey at the end of the session. Although a few participants had some issues connecting to the online pre-survey, most did complete it, and a slightly higher number completed the post-survey.

Table 14.1 shows SEL leadership participants indicated a high level of satisfaction with the training, with 98% of respondents rating it Excellent/

Very Good. There is growing interest among school site leaders to grow their own understanding of SEL practices and the desire to support teachers in incorporating this into daily practice. What has been missing in the LUSD is an intentional-capacity-building piece for school site administrators in leading this work. The training incorporated adult learning theory and engagement strategies to keep the six-hour session interactive and meaningful. The session proved to prepare school leaders to fulfill their administrative role of integrating SEL into daily teaching practice, as evidenced in Table 14.2.

Table 14.1

Survey Results from School Leaders Regarding How They Would Rate the SEL Professional Development

How would you rate today's session?	School Site Administrators f	%
Excellent	163	79.9
Very Good	37	18.1
Good	4	2
Fair	0	0
Poor	0	0
	$n = 204$	

Table 14.2 (Likert Scale)

Survey Results From School Leaders Regarding Their Ability to Teach Teachers How to Integrate SEL Into Daily Teaching Practice

I am confident in my ability to teach teachers how to integrate SEL strategies into their teaching practice.	School Site Administrators Pre-Survey[a] f	%	Post-Survey[b] f	%
Strongly Agree	7	3.8	50	24.5
Agree	98	52.7	141	69.1
Disagree	78	41.9	3	6.4
Strongly Disagree	3	1.6	0	0

[a]$n = 186$; [b]$n = 204$

At the beginning of the session, only 56.5% of participants were confident in their ability to support teachers to integrate SEL strategies into their teaching practice. At the end of the session, the percentage of school site leaders feeling confident about leading the work rose to 93.6%.

The increased rate of the self-reported degree of confidence came in part from a higher level of understanding the LUSD social-emotional competencies. Overall, participants indicated that the training increased their understanding of the SEL competencies, reporting a growth of 0.45 point between the pre- and post-survey. Participants responded to a pre- and post-survey questionnaire indicating their knowledge level on each of the four SEL competencies. The largest increase was in the self-management competency, with a growth of 0.54 point. Notably, on the pre-survey, 100 total responses across the four competencies reported "Disagree" or "Strongly Disagree" to these statements. On the post-survey, the number of responses in these categories dropped to 9.

Throughout the sessions, the chatbox feature was open, and participants were encouraged to post their thoughts, reactions, comments, and responses to prompts. The chatbox information was saved, and the transcripts were coded for emergent concepts. The themes from the chatbox transcripts were:

Figure 14.2

School Administrator Knowledge

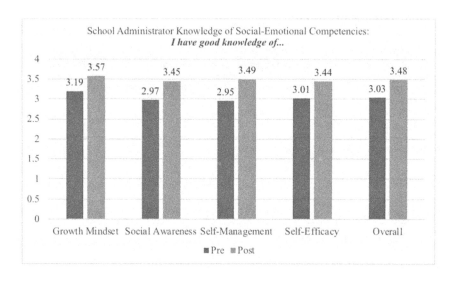

- Administrators need to understand the importance of self-care in order to maintain health and be able to move teaching and learning work forward.
- School site leaders must understand and model the SEL competencies in order for adults and students to more readily adopt them.
- In order to fully realize social-emotional learning, it must be embedded in diverse cultures.
- At the same time, school leaders cannot be expected to know all and do all. Demonstrating vulnerability and establishing boundaries are leadership assets, not weaknesses.

At the end of the session participants were asked to complete an SEL consideration exercise intended as a brainstorming and reflection piece that would help them process their commitment to SEL at their school sites. The responses were coded, and the following emerging commitment themes surfaced:

- Make SEL materials and curriculum more readily accessible for teachers. Responses stated a need for additional resources on self-care for students and adults.
- Learn to engage in challenging conversations across a school community, as SEL challenges common assumptions and beliefs about students and accepted practice.
- Expand and strengthen an understanding of SEL across school services, including but not limited to attendance, discipline, intervention, special education services, and restorative justice practices. Inviting parents and community members into the discussion was also emphasized.

The responses showed school leaders' perception of their role in leading SEL work. They expressed the need to work collaboratively with colleagues to successfully implement SEL strategies; they also expressed the necessity to integrate this capacity into all facets of school policy and practice. In addition, they specifically wanted data tools to plan and monitor their progress. The responses acknowledged their vital role in building an entire community's capacity to understand and implement SEL.

ADULT LEARNING

The SEL team also embedded the tenets of adult learning theory (Vella, 2016) within the training activities. These tenets include but are not limited to:

- Knowing why: Understanding why they are learning the topic.
- Tailoring to learning needs: Using scenarios, case studies, and other formats to meet the individual learning needs of students.
- Learning preparedness: Immediacy and relevance of applying learned knowledge.
- Enthusiasm for learning: Motivating student learning through engagement and inclusion.
- Freedom of choice: Creating a safe learning environment where risk-taking is encouraged through small-group work, debates/discussions, self-selected research.

The design was also influenced by work of Drago-Severson's (2008) pillars of growth for adults, which include:

- Engaging in teamwork to question assumptions and beliefs about the work of educational leaders.
- Experiencing leadership roles and sharing in the decision-making process of authority.
- Engaging in collegial inquiry to learn and reflect on building personal and system-wide capacity.
- Mentoring to foster leadership development for each candidate.

Using the SEL competencies, the school leadership framework, and adult learning theory, the SEL team constructed a six-hour experience for school leaders. Within these six hours there were opportunities for participants to:

- Understand the moral and scientific reasons for SEL and the implications for the school communities they serve.
- Develop a deeper understanding of each of the four SEL competencies (many of the participants may have been introduced to SEL at a session intended for teachers). The four competencies were explored for both implications for instruction and school-wide culture and climate.
- Process their learning through interactive activities, discussion, and small-group work.

- Reflect on their own assumptions and beliefs about their work as educational leaders, specifically around SEL.
- Connect with other school leaders about SEL's relevance to their current work.
- Construct an initial plan and considerations for SEL at their school sites.
- Consider how SEL work aligns with building their own professional capacity as school leaders.

IMPLICATIONS AND NEXT STEPS

The researchers acknowledge that the SEL training was only a start in the journey of institutionalizing SEL practices into schools. Even as they were participating, school leaders were requesting future opportunities to work collaboratively on SEL. The following are recommendations of the SEL team who collaborated on this project, and are based on observations, research, and participant and partner feedback.

- Capacity continues to be built, and their explorations and experimentations need to be encouraged.
- Support the use of a variety of data, both quantitative and qualitative, to deepen participants' understanding of establishing and maintaining an SEL-conducive environment.
- Utilize SEL to build understanding regarding issues of access, social justice, and racial equity.
- Explore Improvement Science (Bryk et al., 2015) to support school leaders' disciplined inquiry and implementation of SEL.
- Ensure the focus stays on the work of those closest to students and ensure the leaders have networking opportunities.

The one persistent cornerstone of this work is that we must continue to build understanding of SEL, leadership capacity development, and adult learning theory. The partnerships that began the work must continue, and be used to regularly assess its effectiveness, relevance, and purpose for school leaders. The most pertinent learning from this research has revealed the urgency and importance of this work, which has only been exacerbated and expanded by the onset of COVID-19.

CONCLUSION

The SEL leadership training was designed to build the capacity of 200 Title 1 school site administrators on leading SEL practices. The intent was to expand SEL understanding across a district that serves more than 600,000 students. The results revealed that school leaders view understanding SEL as pivotal and urgent in their current roles. This study offers two major conclusions from this two-year inquiry.

Reconsidering Measures of Student Success

As their understanding of SEL grew, school leaders were able to acknowledge other measures of student success and flourishing. Participants recognized that simply looking at academic measures is limiting. By considering SEL competencies participants were able to look at other aspects of the school experience for students and allow for a deeper analysis of school practices/policies (CDE, 2018). It allows school communities to assess if current practices help, or hinder, children to realize their capacities. SEL provides the opportunity to look at the climate and culture of a school through a holistic lens that builds leadership capacity to serve diverse populations.

A Popular Presentation

Participation in professional development was not mandated or required. School leaders chose to attend, even during COVID-19 school closures. The workshop provided the opportunity to work on a relevant problem with their peers. To expand district wide, the authors learned to begin with the people who are closest to the work, in this case teachers, then to school leaders.

The SEL sessions were very well received. After the second workshop was completed, the requests to attend increased significantly. District leadership and nonschool site administrators were also requesting to attend. The SEL team was then asked to present at the district-wide training regarding online learning and leadership; it reached approximately 15,000 participants. In August 2020, the SEL presentation was given to 12,000 paraprofessionals, and 90 principal supervisors received professional development on SEL. In the fall of 2020, the SEL presentation was given to regional leadership. The lesson is clear: to underscore the importance and relevance of this work, begin with those who have the greatest impact on student learning—their teachers—and then move to school site administrators, letting it grow from there.

We are "primed to advance SEL throughout the state but the urgency of the moment demands bold and immediate action" (Education First, 2020 p. 35). This report reemphasizes the need for educators to seize the moment to assert and live up to our ideals as educators and enact who we say we are. It is an opportunity to make school what it has always been meant to be: a place where everyone, student, teachers, parents, regardless of race, color, creed, socioeconomic or sexual orientation, or trauma they face, can acknowledge their capacity and flourish in the world.

REFERENCES

Binder, E. B. (2009). The role of FKBP5, a co-chaperone of the glucocorticoid receptor in the pathogenesis and therapy of affective and anxiety disorders. *Psychoneuroendocrinology, 34*(suppl. 1), S186–S195. https://doi.org/10.1016/j.psyneuen.2009.05.021

Bryk, A. S., Gomez, L. M., Grunow, A., & LeMahieu, P. G. (2015). *Learning to improve: How America's schools can get better at getting better.* Harvard Education Press.

Carello, J., & Butler, L. D. (2015). Practicing what we teach: Trauma-informed educational practice. *Journal of Teaching in Social Work, 35*(3), 262–278. https://doi.org/10.1080/08841233.2015.1030059

California Department of Education (CDE). (2018). *California's social and emotional learning guiding principles.* https://www.cde.ca.gov/eo/in/socialemotionallearning.asp

Carpenter, L. L., Shattuck, T. T., Tyrka, A. R., Geracioti, T. D., & Price, L. H. (2011). Effect of childhood physical abuse on cortisol stress response. *Psychopharmacology, 214*(1), 367–375. https://doi.org/10.1007/s00213-010-2007-4

Cherkowski, S., & Walker, K. (2013). Schools as sites of human flourishing: Musings on efforts to foster sustainable learning communities. *EAF Journal, 23*(2).

Cherkowski, S., & Walker, K. (2014). Flourishing communities: Re-storying educational leadership using a positive research lens. *International Journal of Leadership in Education, 17*(2), 200–216.

Clifford, M. (2010). *Hiring quality school leaders: Challenges and emerging practices.* Learning Point Associates.

Creswell, J. W., & Creswell, J. D. (2017). *Research design: Qualitative, quantitative, and mixed methods approaches.* SAGE.

De Brito, S. A., Viding, E., Kumari, V., Blackwood, N., & Hodgins, S. (2013). Cool and hot executive function impairments in violent offenders with antisocial personality disorder with and without psychopathy. *PLoS ONE, 8,* e65566. https://doi.org/10.1371/journal.pone.0065566

Drago-Severson, E. (2008). Pillars for adult learning. *Journal of Staff Development, 29*(4), 60–63.

Durlak, J. A., Domitrovich, C., Weissberg, R., & Gullotta, T. (2015). *Handbook of social emotional learning: Research and practice.* The Guilford Press.

Education First. (2020). *Advance SEL in California final report and recommendations.* https://education-first.com/library/publication/advance-sel-in-california-final-report-and-recommendations/

Felitti, V. J., Anda, R. F., Nordenberg, D., Williamson, D. F., Spitz, A. M., Edwards, V., & Marks, J. S. (1998). Relationship of childhood abuse and household dysfunction to many of the leading causes of death in adults: The Adverse Childhood Experiences (ACE) study. *American Journal of Preventive Medicine, 14*(4), 245–258. https://doi.org/10.1016/S0749-3797(98)00017-8

Fox, S. E., Levitt, P., & Nelson, C. A., III. (2010). How the timing and quality of early experiences influence the development of brain architecture. *Child Development, 81*(1), 28–40. https://doi.org/10.1111/j.1467-8624.2009.01380.x

Furman, G. (2012). Social justice leadership as praxis: Developing capacities through preparation programs. *Educational Administration Quarterly, 48*(2), 191–229.

Gabrieli, C., Ansel, D., & Krachman, S. B. (2015). *Ready to be counted: The research case for education policy action on non-cognitive skills.* Transforming Education.

Gutman, L. M., & Vorhaus, J. (2012). *The impact of pupil behaviour and wellbeing on educational outcomes.* Institute of Education, University of London Childhood Wellbeing Research Centre.

Heckman, J. J., & Kautz, T. (2012). Hard evidence on soft skills. *Labor Economics, 19,* 451–464. https://doi.org/10.1016/j.labeco.2012.05.014

Heim, C., Newport, D. J., Mletzko, T., Miller, A. H., & Nemeroff, C. B. (2008). The link between childhood trauma and depression: Insights from HPA axis studies in humans. *Psychoneuroendocrinology, 33,* 693–710. https://doi.org/10.1016/j.psyneuen.2008.03.008

Herzog, J. I., & Schmahl, C. (2018). Adverse childhood experiences and the consequences on neurobiological, psychosocial, and somatic conditions across the lifespan. *Frontiers in Psychiatry, 9,* 420.

Holmes, A., & Wellman, C. L. (2009). Stress-induced prefrontal reorganization and executive dysfunction in rats. *Neuroscience and Behavioral Reviews, 33*(6), 773–783. https://doi.org/10.1016/j.neubiorev.2008.11.005

Joshi, A., Kale, S., Chandel, S., & Pal, D. K. (2015). Likert scale: Explored and explained. *Current Journal of Applied Science and Technology, 7*(4), 396–403.

Krishnan, V., & Nestler, E. J. (2008). The molecular neurobiology of depression. *Nature, 455*(7215), 894–902. https://doi.org/10.1038/nature07455

Lindsey, R. B., Nuri-Robins, K., Terrell, R. D., & Lindsey, D. B. (2018). *Cultural proficiency: A manual for school leaders.* Corwin Press.

Mendels, P. (2012). The effective principal. *Journal of Staff Development, 33*(1), 54–58.

Nava, M. A., & Nava, I. L. (2020). Partnerships in practice. In F. Kochan & D. M. Griggs (Eds.), *Creating school partnerships that work: A guide for practice and research* (pp. 27+). Information Age Publishing.

Pittenger, C., & Duman, R. S. (2008). Stress, depression, and neuroplasticity: A convergence of mechanisms. *Neuropsychopharmacology, 33*(1), 88–109. https://doi.org/10.1038/sj.npp.1301574

Roy, A., Gorodetsky, E., Yuan, Q., Goldman, D., & Enoch, M.A. (2010). Interaction of FKBP5, a stress-related gene, with childhood trauma increases the risk for attempting suicide. *Neuropsychopharmacology, 35*, 1674–1683. https://doi.org/10.1038/npp.2009.236

Schmidt, W. H., & McKnight, C. C. (2012). *Inequality for all: Why America's schools are failing our children*. Teachers College Press.

Thompson, R. A. (2004). Stress and child development. *Future Child, 24*(1), 41–59. https://doi.org/10.1353/foc.2014.0004

Tovar-Moll, F., & Lent, R. (2016). The various forms of neuroplasticity: Biological bases of learning and teaching. *Prospects, 46*(2), 199–213. https://doi.org/10.1007/s11125-017-9388-7

Tyrka, A. R., Price, L. H., Kao, H. T., Porton, B., Marsella, S. A., & Carpenter, L. L. (2010). Childhood maltreatment and telomere shortening: Preliminary support for an effect of early stress on cellular aging. *Biological Psychiatry, 67*(6), 531–534. https://doi.org/10.1016/j.biopsych.2009.08.014

University of Chicago. (n.d.). *5 essentials framework*. https://uchicagoimpact.org/sites/default/files/5eframework_outreach%26marketing%20%281%29.pdf

Vella, J. (2016). The power of dialogue in adult learning. *Reflective Practice: Formation and Supervision in Ministry*. https://journals.sfu.ca/rpfs/index.php/rpfs/article/view/456

CHAPTER 15

COLLECTIVE LEADERSHIP FOR WELL-BEING AND SUSTAINABLE SCHOOL IMPROVEMENT

Jonathan Eckert

Isolation is exhausting. If nothing else, 2020 taught us this.

However, we have known that the superhero teacher/principal narrative, long popularized in movies (e.g., *Dead Poets Society*, 1989; *Freedom Writers*, 2007; *Lean on Me*, 1989; *Stand and Deliver*, 1988) is fictionalized and unsustainable. These movies leave out the amazing colleagues that make the work of the great teacher or administrator possible. Leading schools is far too complex to do by ourselves. Certainly, education draws idealists who want to teach and lead for justice, change trajectories for students, and inspire. These passions are fuel for work that is often underappreciated; however, they can also sap us of our strength as we push beyond our limits and move beyond the support of our collective professional community.

For *sustainable* school improvement, school leaders must change the cultures of schools in two ways: the way we do leadership work and the way we address the well-being of leaders and others. Consideration of well-being should be seamlessly integrated into the way school improvement work is done for that improvement to be sustainable. Leaders need to become catalysts. In a chemical reaction, a catalyst is not the focus of the reaction, it simply accelerates the reaction. Catalysts who develop collective leadership are what schools need to improve.

Perhaps a superhero movie could be instructive here. In *Spider-Man Homecoming* (2017), Spider-Man depends on Ned, his "guy in the chair,"

Supporting Leaders for School Improvement Through Self-Care and Well-Being, pp. 277–293
Copyright © 2024 by Information Age Publishing
www.infoagepub.com
All rights of reproduction in any form reserved.

to catalyze his superhero efforts. Ned is his catalyst by telling him where to go, what to do, and how to think differently. We need more catalysts like Ned if we are going to address well-being and improvement.

This chapter poses three questions: what is collective leadership, how do we lead collectively for the well-being of others, and how does collective leadership lead to sustainable school improvement?

WHAT IS COLLECTIVE LEADERSHIP?

Collective leadership encompasses the practices through which teachers and administrators influence colleagues, policymakers, and others to improve student outcomes (Eckert, 2018, 2019). Simply put, leadership work consists of functions (Firestone, 1996) that support shared goals. Collective leadership is built on the premise that leadership work should be shared and performed by those most capable of leading well.

Collective leadership emphasizes joint goal setting and strategic implementation of those goals in the service of the mission at the core of schools—teaching and learning. There have been numerous calls for distributed, shared, layered, or collective leadership (Day et al., 2016; Hargreaves & Fullan, 2012; Leithwood, 2010; Leithwood & Mascall, 2008; Seashore-Louis et al., 2010; Spillane et al., 2001). These types of leadership require teachers and administrators to work together toward shared organizational goals. However, terms such as distributed leadership have been reduced to task delegation from administrators to teachers, so for this framework, we use collective leadership. Collective leadership has been found to have a greater influence on student outcomes than individual leadership (Seashore-Louis et al., 2010). Collective leadership is increasingly important because collective teacher efficacy, a subset of this type of leadership, is the most influential factor influencing student learning (Hattie, 2012, 2015a).

The collective leadership framework is based on work redesign literature (e.g., Campion et al., 2005; Hackman & Oldham, 1980; Humphrey et al., 2007), leadership development across organizational type and sector (e.g., Avolio, 2010; Conger, 1992; Day et al., 2004; Van Velsor et al., 2010; Yukl, 2013) and teacher leadership (e.g., Berg, 2018; Lieberman & Miller, 2004; Mangin & Stoelinga, 2008; Murphy, 2005; Wenner & Campbell, 2017; York-Barr & Duke, 2004). This theory views leadership functionally (Firestone, 1996), as redesigned work to be performed rather than as a particular role to be assumed (Mayrowetz et al., 2007; Smylie, 1994).

The theory frames collective leadership development as a blending of the work of teachers and administrators to identify and advance shared goals that will benefit students. The entire model is an iterative process of improvement based on seven conditions that support or constrain development efforts resulting in increased capacity, improved leadership practice, and results in improved student outcomes (see Figure 15.1).

Figure 15.1

Model for Collective Leadership Development

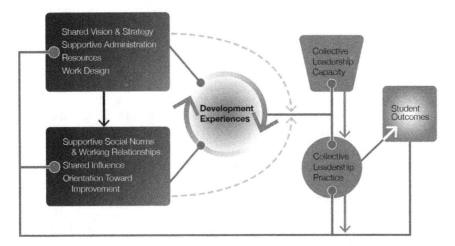

The seven conditions for collective leadership are comprehensive and interrelated.

1. Collective leadership requires vision and strategy that are supported by dynamic, strategically "ambidextrous" leadership development (Fullan, 2005; Hargreaves & Fink, 2006; McCauley, 2008; Mumford et al., 2007; Smylie, 2010; Tushman & O'Reilly, 1996) that is democratic, participative inclusive leadership(Bryk et al., 2010; Leithwood & Louis, 2012; Light, 1998). Top-down, hierarchical leadership structures are not conducive to collective leadership; instead, clear vision combined with strategies that move beyond buy-in to the collective expertise of teachers and administrators are particularly important for improvement particularly in teaching and learning (Smylie & Eckert, 2018).
2. Supportive administration that believes in teacher leadership (Birky et al., 2006; Camburn et al., 2008; Murphy et al., 2009; Smylie & Brownlee-Conyers, 1992; Van Velsor et al., 2010) recalibrates authority relationships (Murphy, 2005). Administrators who support the leadership of others do not see the sharing of leadership work as diminishing their power; instead, they see

the leadership and expertise of teachers and other administrators as increasing the efficacy of their efforts toward shared goals (Eckert, 2018, 2019).
3. Resources and initial leadership capacity that provide the necessary talent, time, and space to lead together (Avolio & Hannah, 2008; Bond et al., 2008; Conger, 1992; Martineau, 2004) facilitate collective leadership. Resources include money, facilities that foster collaboration, and human capital. Human capital includes administrative and teaching expertise, resources to develop and spread that expertise, and time and space for teachers and administrators to expand their influence through shared leadership work. In schools with adequate resources and leadership capacity, teachers and administrators have the opportunity and support to improve with others (Eckert, 2018, 2019).
4. Closely connected to resources is adequate work design that facilitates collaboration, improvement, and the spread of teaching expertise (Campion et al., 2005; Hackman & Oldham, 1980; Margolis, 2012; Smylie & Denny, 1990). Adequate work design includes opportunities for teachers to see others teaching, the opportunity to give and receive feedback, plan together, and analyze student work with other teachers and administrators. Feedback for improvement, rather than evaluation and judgment, drives this type of work design (Eckert, 2018, 2019).
5. Supportive social norms and working relationships that foster relational trust (Bryk & Schneider, 2002; Hargreaves & O'Connor, 2018; Muijs & Harris, 2007; Van Velsor & McCauley, 2004) are precipitating factors for collective leadership as well as results of that type of leadership when enacted. In schools with supportive social norms and working relationships, teachers and administrators walk alongside others when they lead. Students, teachers, and administrators generate ideas, and others come alongside to help the ideas come to fruition. Survey results for schools engaging in collective leadership often demonstrate significant increases in this condition as leadership work spreads to more leaders (Eckert, 2018, 2019).
6. Related to norms and relationships, shared influence of administrators and teachers on themselves and others (Day et al., 2004; Lai & Cheung, 2015; Muijs & Harris, 2007) is critical for the development and spread of collective leadership. In fact, school improvement is contingent on teachers and administrators spreading practices, mindsets, and strategies that work in a school. The power of shared influence within a school is that the

ideas offered for improvement are contextualized and designed for that particular student population.
7. Orientation toward improvement that facilitates growth (Eckert & Daughtrey, 2019; Smylie & Eckert, 2018) and reflective risk-taking (Eckert, 2016) are necessary hallmarks of collective leadership. Chip and Dan Heath (2017) remind us that, "A risk is a risk. If risks always paid off, they wouldn't be risks. The promise of stretching is not success. It's learning" (p. 131). Schools that understand this prioritize reflective risk-taking because they realize this is essential as a learning organization (Eckert, 2018, 2019).

Of the seven conditions, the first four are antecedent to the other three, but there are systemic interactive relationships among all seven (Bass, 1990; Firestone, 1996; Smylie, 2010; Yukl, 2013). In ideal contexts, these seven conditions support development experiences. These development experiences can be formal or informal but typically revolve around shared goals for school improvement. In the model, the dotted lines that extend from the seven conditions beyond the development experiences represent the influence these conditions have after development experiences. Again, in ideal contexts, these seven conditions support and accelerate the work that comes out of development experiences. In less ideal contexts, these conditions might constrain the work. For example, an administrator who might have been supportive initially might withdraw support after feeling threatened by leadership work that comes out of the development experience. However, the development experiences should contribute to increased leadership capacity of teachers and administrators which should in turn improve collective leadership practice. Because collective leadership practice is typically focused on instructional improvement, student learning outcomes should improve. As those outcomes improve, they will improve collective leadership practice and influence the seven conditions.

HOW DO WE LEAD COLLECTIVELY FOR THE WELL-BEING OF OTHERS?

No amount of self-care or individual well-being exercises can make up for isolation or the expectations educators place on themselves to be superhuman in their support of student needs. Teachers and administrators fall victim to the tyranny of the urgent due to the many student needs they see each day. No matter how physically, mentally, socially, spiritually, or emotionally healthy an individual might be, she cannot do this work alone—at least not for long. "Self-care is a necessary but insufficient response to worker burnout.... An over-reliance on self-care to resist work-related distress is aligned with problematic yet prevailing discourse about the amelioration of stress and its negative outcomes" (Bressi & Vaden, 2017, p. 37). This is especially true for outstanding teachers and administrators who continue to take on responsibilities because they see urgent needs, they are competent, and they operate in an environment of scarce resources. Many believe, probably rightly so, that if they do not step into the gap, the need will go unmet. However, continually adding to her proverbial professional plate will likely lead to burnout (Eckert et al., 2016).

Leaders are particularly influential in the way organizations think about and respond to stress. In a review of empirical research of leaders' influence on employee stress and affective well-being, leaders' stress affects employee stress and well-being (Skakon et al., 2010). Two takeaways: (1) we cannot do all that is increasingly required of educators alone, and (2) leaders are particularly important to consider. Leaders need to think more about how to say "no" to innovation that will simply stretch their teams too thin. As David Brooks (2019) writes, "A life of commitment requires a thousand noes for the sake of a few precious yeses" (p. 18). This is particularly important in schools where a "yes" to one idea or program likely means hundreds of "yeses" in the future—specific yeses that cannot be anticipated at the initial yes but should be considered generally before agreeing to initiate something new.

The word "innovate" cannot be spelled without the word "no." School leaders especially need to be disciplined with how they say "no." Typically, school leaders end initiatives in one of two ways that stifle innovation:

1. Impatient abandonment: We are not patient enough to wait for results.
2. Overwhelmed abandonment: We lack the resources, primarily emotional energy, to persist.

Many great initiatives at schools have the potential to improve student outcomes but that potential is unrealized because of the urgent desire for immediate progress. Schools drop a reading initiative, a schedule change, a new assessment system that could have improved student outcomes after a few years of implementation when they do not see results within the first two months of the school year. Alternatively, schools drop innovations because federal, state, and district requirements simply overwhelm them by their sheer volume. Schools require "organized abandonment"—the acknowledgment that organizations cannot do everything well (Drucker, 1999). Therefore, school leaders should thoughtfully abandon those things that fail to serve students well (Eckert, 2017).

Two concepts are essential for organized abandonment: collective leadership and feedback. An award-winning principal of a South Carolina middle school is a strong believer in innovation. The school's mission statement is: "Learn by doing. Leading by example." The leadership team of teachers and administrators use a filter to determine what they will say "yes" to, and what will get an automatic "no." The principal says, "If it is not in one of the three buckets that are part of our core mission, then we don't do it."

With the three "buckets" or dimensions of achievement as a filter, the leadership team determines how they will innovate based on what they will do and, maybe more importantly, what they will not do. These buckets encompass a great deal, but they also provide direction for when to say "no." The school is organized into "houses" that support the collaboration of teachers and students so that teams can generate ideas that support their specific needs. Collective leadership that prioritizes shared vision, supportive administration, resources, work design, relationships, shared influence, and a strong orientation toward improvement requires a disciplined approach innovation (see Table 15.1). To be successful and manage educator and student well-being, school leaders have to say "no" to good ideas. They simply cannot do them all. Having rules in place that allow them to automatically say "no" to initiatives that take them off mission is equally important to saying "yes."

Table 15.1

Collective Leadership and the "No" in Innovate

Collective Leadership Conditions	School's Approach
Shared vision and strategy	Three buckets
Supportive administration	A principal and team who listen to possible ideas
Resources	Limiting "yeses" to protect scarce resources and limited capacity
Work design	House system for collaboration
Supportive norms and working relationships	Ideation flourishes within clear parameters
Shared influence	Ideation of educators and students with principled decisions made by teachers and administrators
Orientation toward improvement	Improvement within the three buckets drives learning by doing

The most important aspect of collective leadership for innovation that protects well-being is feedback. In contexts where collective leadership is practiced, school leaders report increased collegiality, improved relational trust, reduced stress, stronger orientations toward improvement, and reduced teacher and administrator burnout (Eckert, 2018, 2019). We know that relational trust is essential for school improvement (Bryk & Schneider, 2002) and can reduce teacher burnout (Van Maele & Van Houtte, 2015). Collective leadership with an eye toward leader well-being could also address factors that lead to principal burnout (Gmelch & Gates, 1998; Mahfouz, 2018). Without collective leadership, even effective administrators or teacher leaders burnout due to being overwhelmed by work tasks as they continue to increase commitments due to the needs they see around them (Eckert et al., 2016). To avoid burnout, school leaders need to be disciplined in giving and receiving feedback.

Over the past few years, educators have become increasingly aware of the importance of feedback for student learning. John Hattie (2012, 2015a, 2015b) has highlighted that feedback is one of the most influential factors affecting student learning and that it is also one of the most variable. To determine what schools should be doing, everything should be predicated on what is working for students. This is mutually reinforcing (see Figure 15.2). For students to flourish, educators have to support their well-being first. Maslow's hierarchy of needs for security, physical, and emotional well-being are foundational to any educational endeavor. The next level of the pyramid is engagement because learning does not happen if students are not actively engaged. Once students are engaged, then teachers can assess and provide feedback on how to improve. Feedback flows from assessment. Assessment is not primarily about evaluation and judgment. The word "assessment" is from the Latin root word "assidere" which means "to sit beside." Therefore, assessment is about feedback for improvement.

This pyramid also applies to school leaders. Leading collectively requires focusing on the well-being of ourselves and others first. To illustrate, in the spring of 2020, with emergency remote learning happening in his school, one principal set aside two times each week for teachers to Zoom with him to answer his only two questions: "How are you doing? What do you need?" Their well-being came first. To lead collectively and build on the collective expertise of a team, many leaders must be engaged. The work that needs to be done dictates who leads and therefore, who need to be engaged. Finally, as we have learned from the emerging knowledge-based of networked improvement communities (Bryk et al., 2015), feedback toward our shared goals determines the next steps for growth within and across learning organizations.

HOW DOES COLLECTIVE LEADERSHIP LEAD TO SUSTAINABLE SCHOOL IMPROVEMENT?

Increasing research-practice partnerships and networked improvement communities connect leadership efforts to continuous school improvement.

Figure 15.2

Well-Being, Engagement, and Feedback

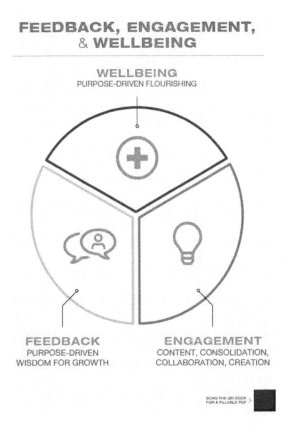

Research-practice partnerships are a model for organizing the improvement of practitioners and researchers around common problems of practice (Coburn & Penuel, 2016). Similar to research-practice partnerships, networked improvement communities (Bryk et al., 2015) operate on principles that support continuous improvement through iterative processes of design, implementation, and evaluation contingent upon school contexts in ways that promote empirical research and insights from practice. Additionally, design thinking increasingly informs schools and improvement communities through its emphasis on empathy and perspective-taking for deeper understanding (Nash, 2019). While continuous improvement in schools is certainly not a new concept (e.g., Murphy, 2005; Smylie, 2010), the emphasis on design thinking and tools of improvement science offers connecting points between collective leadership and school improvement in meaningful ways. In fact, researchers are identifying "cultures of improvement" (e.g., Dolle et al., 2013; Harrison et al., 2019) that permeate learning organizations that both tolerate and encourage reflective risk-taking (Eckert, 2016; Heath & Heath, 2017). In a recent study, I found these cultures of improvement to be especially prevalent in schools that emphasize science, technology, engineering, and mathematics (STEM) in large part because the engineering mindset that permeated the schools prioritized design thinking, prototyping, and iterative processes of improvement (Eckert, 2020; Eckert & Teisan, 2020). Additionally, collective leadership leads to collective teacher efficacy, which has one of the largest effect sizes on student learning (Hattie, 2015a) making it a primary lever for school improvement. Collective teacher efficacy refers to educators believing they positively influence student learning by examining students' work together and monitoring progress.

How do we spread school improvement while making it sustainable? Moving from theoretical to practical reality, here are three examples from extensive case studies conducted in three different states.

Urban High School: Illinois

With a total enrollment of approximately 2000 students, over 75% of those students qualifying for free and reduced-price meals (FARM), and 20% of students classified as English language learners, on the surface, this school looks like many urban high schools. Due in large part to the humility of a principal who arrived seven years earlier, the school is improving. Teachers and administrators are engaged in professional learning communities, the principal is listening, and leadership is spreading.

The school recently received national recognition as a Positive Behavior Intervention Supports (PBIS) model school. This was due in large part to the work of a special education teacher at the school who saw a need for developing a more positive school culture. Although the Universal Team was supported by the administration, administrators do not lead the team. The principal serves as a member of the team. Six teachers, the principal, a school security officer, a parent, and two students meet monthly in a windowless basement room of the school to discuss issues that range from reducing the number of office referrals to positive reinforcement of desired behaviors. This diverse team of leaders has helped dramatically reduce the number of office referrals and improve the overall culture of the school. Two tangible results of their problem solving are illustrative.

The main entrance to the school is directly across from the cafeteria. When students enter the building, there is a brick wall that rises about halfway up to a 15-foot-high ceiling that separates the entrance from the cafeteria. A team of leaders identified the hot spot for fights as just past the end of the eight-foot wall between the entrance and the cafeteria. Students would enter the school in the morning or at lunchtime when large numbers of students were in the cafeteria and fights would ensue where there was a large audience. To reduce the possibility of an audience for fights as soon as students entered the building, the wall was extended to the end of the cafeteria.

On the other side of the cafeteria was a courtyard. To create a more peaceful environment, resources were allocated to build a Koi pond that serves as a type of outdoor classroom. Financial resources dedicated to this project have paid dividends in school pride and created a different atmosphere in one of the most challenging areas of the building. The wall extension and the Koi pond did not solve school problems on their own. School leaders altered entry and exit patterns at the school, increased lunch supervision, and school culture was more positive in general. However, the physical changes did make a difference and are tangible reminders of how the school is changing. Administrator, teacher, and student well-being are much improved, and students are better supported in their learning.

Suburban Middle School: New York

With a total enrollment of over 700 students, nearly 50% of who qualify for FARM, this suburban middle school is similar to many others. However, collective leadership makes them different. An eighth-grade team consisting of four teachers and 96 students have fundamentally changed the way the school operates. Over the last decade, the team has developed a strong reputation for collaboration with STEM as the vehicle. The eighth-grade science teacher teams with an English, math, and social studies teacher to integrate STEM into all aspects of student work. They have partnered with NASA, multiple foundations, and other local organizations to develop innovative curriculum, STEM projects, and programs that extend learning beyond the school day and school year. They have transformed the way students and teachers collaborate across eighth grade and the entire school.

In fact, the collaborative philosophy of the eighth-grade team is reflected in the redesigned building that reopened in 2016–2017. Each middle school team has a four-classroom pod with collaborative space between the rooms. The teams have control of their schedule for most of the days, in a bell-free environment where they can combine the whole team into one class of 96, two classes of 48, or four classes of 24. This type of flexible grouping facilitates interdisciplinary inquiry where teachers can coteach as students engage real-world problems from multiple perspectives. The entire building now reflects the flexible use of spaces, the lack of a bell schedule, and the ability to access outside resources that teams have adopted after learning how the eighth-grade team was using their time, space, and resources. The principal said, "Teams just needed to know that they had the flexibility and resources to do what they wanted to do. They can take risks because I can take risks because [the superintendent] lets me take risks."

Rural Elementary School: South Carolina

Serving nearly 600 students, with nearly 65% of those students qualifying for FARM, this rural elementary school has been engaged in a three-year statewide initiative to develop collective leadership. The new principal recognized the need for collective leadership and volunteered the school for the South Carolina Department of Education's Collective Leadership Initiative (CLI, 2020). Through this initiative, a leadership team of teachers and the principal learned alongside other schools across the state and with the support of the Center for Teaching Quality (2019). After two years in the initiative using no additional resources, the leadership team created space for teams of teachers to conduct grade-level learning walks to assess what was working around the school, and every teacher has at least five hours of collaboration and professional learning time each week.

Both teachers and administrators report that these changes have improved working relationships, shared influence, and reflective risk-taking. They see collective leadership as a process and not a program that improves the culture of teaching and learning at the school because they can address the holistic needs of educators and students. As compared to the other 17 schools that have participated in CLI and completed the collective leadership survey, this school is significantly higher on nearly every construct than the other schools.

Teachers reported increased teacher efficacy which appears to be resulting in more distal improvement in student learning. Grade retentions have decreased, school culture has improved, and students have demonstrated significant improvement in state achievement in mathematics and literacy and received the distinguished Palmetto's Finest award for school improvement in 2020.

IMPLICATIONS

Collective leadership can support increased self-care and human flourishing. The design of administrators' and teachers' work must make space for collaboration, reflection, and team building that develops a range of leaders for leadership work instead of repeatedly relying on the same leaders. The well-being of leaders is enhanced in a culture that prioritizes collective leadership which will support sustainable school improvement. Theoretically, this is established in the literature on leadership development, work design, and teacher leadership and now synthesized in collective leadership. More importantly, collective leadership improves the well-being of leaders through shared goals, expertise, and work. States like South Carolina, districts, and schools are recognizing the potential for collective leadership to lead to sustainable school improvement. In different contexts, and at the elementary, middle, and high school levels, leaders are growing together in ways that benefit students. No longer are leaders isolated and attempting superhero leadership feats; instead, they are accelerating the work of others as catalysts that do not burn themselves out.

PRACTICES AND RESOURCES

Center for Teaching Quality. (2019). *Collective leadership playbook*.
Eckert, J. (2018). *Leading together: Teachers and administrators improving student outcomes*. Corwin Press.
Eckert, J. (2020). *Exemplary STEM learning: Lessons from outstanding New York schools and teachers*. National Network of State Teachers of the Year.
Eckert, J., & Teisan, J. (2020). *Exemplary STEM learning: Teacher leader fellowship toolkit*. National Network of State Teachers of the Year.
South Carolina Department of Education. (2020). *Collective Leadership Initiative*.

REFERENCES

Avildsen, J. G. (1989). *Lean on me*. Warner Bros.
Avolio, B. J. (2010). *Full range leadership development* (2nd ed.). SAGE.
Avolio, B. J., & Hannah, S. T. (2008). Developmental readiness: Accelerating leader development. *Psychology Journal: Practice and Research, 60*(4), 331–347.
Bass, B. M. (1990). *Handbook of leadership: Theory, research, and managerial applications* (3rd ed.). Free Press.
Berg, J. H. (2018). *Leading in sync: Teacher leaders and principals working together for student learning*. ASCD.
Birky, V. D., Shelton, M., & Headley, S. (2006). An administrator's challenge: Encouraging teachers to be leaders. *90*(2), 87–101.
Bond, F. W., Flaxman, P. E., & Bunce, D. (2008). The influence of psychological flexibility on work redesign: Mediated moderation of a work reorganization intervention. *Journal of Applied Psychology, 93*(3), 645–654.
Bressi, S. K., & Vaden, E. R. (2017). Reconsidering self care. *Clinical Social Work Journal, 45*(33), 33–38. https://doi.org/0.1007/s10615-016-0575-4
Brooks, D. (2019). *The second mountain: The quest for a moral life*. Random House.

Bryk, A. S., Gomez, L. M., Grunow, A., & LeMahieu, P. G. (2015). *Learning to improve: How America's schools can get better at getting better*. Harvard Education Press.

Bryk, A. S., Sebring, P. B., Allensworth, E., Luppescu, S., & Easton, J. Q. (2010). *Organizing schools for improvement: Lessons from Chicago*. University of Chicago Press.

Bryk, A., & Schneider, B. (2002). *Trust in schools: A core resource for improvement*. Russell Sage Foundation.

Camburn, E. M., Kimball, S. M., & Lowenhaupt, R. (2008). Going to scale with teacher leadership: Lessons learned from a districtwide literacy coach initiative. In M. M. Mangin & S. R. Stoelinga (Eds.), *Effective teacher leadership: Using research to inform and reform* (pp. 120–143). Teachers College Press.

Campion, M. A., Mumford, T. V., Morgeson, F. P., & Nahrgang, J. D. (2005). Work redesign: Eight obstacles and opportunities. *Human Resource Management*, 44(4), 367–390.

Coburn, C. E., & Penuel, W. R. (2016). Research–practice partnerships in education: Outcomes, dynamics, and open questions. *Educational Researcher*, 45(1), 48–54. https://doi.org/10.3102/0013189X16631750

Conger, J. (1992). *Learning to lead: The art of transforming managers into leaders*. Jossey-Bass.

Day, C., Gu, Q., & Sammons, P. (2016). The impact of leadership on student outcomes. *Educational Administration Quarterly*, 52(2), 221–258. https://doi.org/10.1177/0013161X15616863

Day, D. V., Zaccaro, S. J., & Halpin, S. M. (2004). *Leadership development for transforming organizations: Growing leaders for tomorrow*. Psychology Press.

Dolle, J. R., Gomez, L. M., Russell, J. L., & Bryk, A. S. (2013). More than a network: Building professional communities for educational improvement. In *Yearbook of the National Society for the Study of Education* (Vol. 112, pp. 443–463). Teachers College.

Drucker, P. (1999). *Management challenges for the 21st century*. HarperCollins.

Eckert, J. (2016). *The novice advantage: Fearless practice for every teacher*. Corwin Press.

Eckert, J. (2017). The "no" in innovate. *Edutopia*. https://www.edutopia.org/article/no-innovate

Eckert, J. (2018). *Leading together: Teachers and administrators improving student outcomes*. Corwin Press.

Eckert, J. (2019). Collective leadership development: Emerging themes from urban, suburban, and rural high schools. *Educational Administration Quarterly*, 55(3), 477–509. https://doi.org/10.1177/0013161X18799435

Eckert, J. (2020). *Exemplary STEM learning: Lessons from outstanding New York schools and teachers*. National Network of State Teachers of the Year. http://www.nnstoy.org/wp-content/uploads/2020/05/NNSTOY-Report2020_Final.pdf

Eckert, J., & Daughtrey, A. (2018). *Conditions for teacher leadership: Findings from one district's implementation of Iowa's Teacher Leadership and Compensation System*. American Education Research Association, New York, NY.

Eckert, J., & Daughtrey, A. (2019). Teacher leadership development: Tracking one district's progress over three years. *Education Policy Analysis Archives*, 27(42), 1–22. http://dx.doi.org/10.14507/epaa.27.4130

Eckert, J., & Teisan, J. (2020). *Exemplarly STEM learning: Teacher leader fellowship toolkit*. National Network of State Teachers of the Year. http://www.nnstoy.org/wp-content/uploads/2020/05/NNSTOY-Toolkit2020_final.pdf

Eckert, J., Ulmer, J., Khachatryan, E., & Ledesma, P. (2016). Career pathways of teacher leaders in the United States: Adding and path-finding new professional roles. *Professional Development in Education*, *42*(5), 687–709.

Firestone, W. A. (1996). Leadership: Roles or functions? In K. Leithwood, J. Chapman, D. Corson, P. Hallinger, & A. Hart (Eds.), *International handbook of educational leadership and administration, Part I* (pp. 395–418). Kluwer.

Fullan, M. (2005). *Leadership and sustainability: System thinkers in action*. Corwin Press.

Gmelch, W. H., & Gates, G. (1998). The impact of personal, professional and organizational characteristics on administrator burnout. *Journal of Educational Administration*, *36*(2), 146–159.

Hackman, J. R., & Oldham, G. R. (1980). *Work redesign*. Addison-Wesley.

Hargreaves, A., & Fink, D. (2006). *Sustainable leadership*. Jossey-Bass.

Hargreaves, A., & Fullan, M. (2012). *Professional capital: Transforming teaching in every school*. Teachers College Press.

Hargreaves, A., & O'Connor, M. T. (2018). *Collaborative professionalism: When teaching together means learning for all*. Corwin Press.

Harrison, C., Wachen, J., Brown, S., & Cohen-Vogel, L. (2019). A view from within: Lessons learned from partnering for continuous improvement. *Teachers College Record*, *121*(9).

Hattie, J. (2012). *Visible learning for teachers: Maximizing impact on learning*. Routledge.

Hattie, J. (2015a). The applicability of visible learning to higher education. *Scholarship of Teaching and Learning in Psychology*, *1*(1), 79–91. http://dx.doi.org/10.1037/stl0000021

Hattie, J. (2015b). *What works best in education: The politics of collaborative expertise* (Open Ideas). Pearson. https://www.pearson.com/content/dam/corporate/global/pearson-dot-com/files/hattie/150526_ExpertiseWEB_V1.pdf

Heath, C., & Heath, D. (2017). *The power of moments*. Simon & Schuster.

Humphrey, S. E., Nahrgang, J. D., & Morgeson, F. P. (2007). Integrating motivational, social, and contextual work design features: A meta-analytic summary and theoretical extension of the work design literature. *Journal of Applied Psychology*, *92*(5), 1332–1356.

LaGravenese, R. (2007). *Freedom writers*. MTV Films.

Lai, E., & Cheung, D. (2015). Enacting teacher leadership: The role of teachers in bringing about change. *Educational Management Administration & Leadership*, *43*(5), 673–692. https://doi.org/10.1177/1741143214535742

Leithwood, K. (2010). Characteristics of school districts that are exceptionally effective in closing the achievement gap. *Leadership and Policy in Schools*, *9*, 245–291. https://doi.org/10.1080/15700761003731500

Leithwood, K., & Louis, K. S. (2012). *Linking leadership to student learning*. Jossey-Bass.

Leithwood, K., & Mascall, B. (2008). Collective leadership effects on student achievement. *Educational Administration Quarterly*, *44*(4), 529–561.

Lieberman, A., & Miller, L. (2004). *Teacher leadership*. Jossey-Bass.

Light, P. C. (1998). *Sustaining innovation: Creating nonprofit and government organizations that innovate naturally*. Jossey-Bass.

Mahfouz, J. (2018). Principals and stress: Few coping strategies for abundant stressors. *Educational Management Administration & Leadership, 20*(10), 1–19.

Mangin, M. M., & Stoelinga, S. R. (2008). *Effective teacher leadership: Using research to inform and reform*. Teachers College Press.

Margolis, J. (2012). Hybrid teacher leaders and the new professional development ecology. *Professional Development in Education, 38*(2), 291–315.

Martineau, J. W. (2004). Evaluating the impact of leader development. In C. D. McCauley & E. Van Velsor (Eds.), *The Center for Creative Leadership handbook of leadership development* (2nd ed., pp. 234–267). Jossey-Bass.

Mayrowetz, D., Murphy, J., Louis, K. S., & Smylie, M. A. (2007). Distributed leadership as work redesign: Retrofitting the job characteristics model. *Leadership and Policy in Schools, 6*, 69–101.

McCauley, C. D. (2008). *Leader development: A review of research*. Center for Creative Leadership.

Menendez, R. (1988). *Stand and deliver*. American Playhouse.

Muijs, D., & Harris, A. (2007). Teacher leadership in (in)action: Three case studies of contrasting schools. *Educational Management, Administration, and Leadership, 35*(1), 111–134.

Mumford, M. D., Hunter, S. T., Eubanks, D. L., Bedell, K. E., & Murphy, S. T. (2007). Developing leaders for creative efforts: A domain-based approach to leadership development. *Human Resource Management Review, 17*(4), 402–417.

Murphy, J. (2005). *Connecting teacher leadership and school improvement*. Corwin Press.

Murphy, J., Smylie, M. A., Mayrowetz, D., & Louis, K. S. (2009). The role of the principal in fostering the development of distributed leadership. *School Leadership and Management, 29*, 181–214.

Nash, J. B. (2019). *Design thinking in schools: A leader's guide to collaborating for improvement*. Harvard Education Press.

Seashore-Louis, K., Leithwood, K., Wahlstrom, K., & Anderson, S. (2010). *Learning for leadership: Investigating the links to improved student learning*. Educational Research Service.

Skakon, J., Nielsen, K., Borg, V., & Guzman, J. (2010). Are leaders' well-being, behaviours and style associated with the affective well-being of their employees? A systematic review of three decades of research. *Work & Stress, 24*(2), 107–139. https://doi.org/10.1080/02678373.2010.495262

Smylie, M. A. (1994). Redesigning teachers' work: Connections to the classroom. In L. Darling-Hammond (Ed.), *Review in research in education* (Vol. 20, pp. 129–177). American Educational Research Association.

Smylie, M. A. (2010). *Continuous school improvement*. Corwin Press.

Smylie, M. A., & Brownlee-Conyers, J. (1992). Teacher leaders and their principals: Exploring the development of new working relationships. *Educational Administration Quarterly, 28*, 150–184.

Smylie, M. A., & Denny, J. W. (1990). Teacher leadership: Tensions and ambiguities in organizational perspective. *Educational Administration Quarterly, 26*(3), 235–259.

Smylie, M. A., & Eckert, J. (2018). Beyond superheroes and advocacy: The pathway of teacher leadership development. *Educational Management Administration & Leadership*, *46*(4), 556–577. https://doi.org/10.1177/1741143217684893

Spillane, J. P., Halverson, R., & Diamond, J. B. (2001). Investigating school leadership practice: A distributed perspective. *Educational Researcher*, *30*(3), 23–38.

Tushman, M. L., & O'Reilly, C. A. (1996). Ambidextrous organizations: Managing evolutionary and revolutionary change. *California Management Review*, *38*(4), 8–30.

Van Maele, D., & Van Houtte, M. (2015). Trust in school: A pathway to inhibit teacher burnout? *Journal of Educational Administration*, *53*(1), 93–115.

Van Velsor, E., & McCauley, C. D. (2004). *Our view of leadership development*. Jossey-Bass.

Van Velsor, E., McCauley, C. D., & Ruderman, M. N. (Eds.). (2010). *The center for creative leadership handbook of leadership development* (3rd ed.). Jossey-Bass.

Watts, J. (2017). *Spider-man: Homecoming*. Columbia Pictures.

Wenner, J. A., & Campbell, T. (2017). The theoretical and empirical basis of teacher leadership: A review of the literature. *Review of Educational Research*, *87*(1), 134–171. https://doi.org/10.3102/0034654316653478

Wier, P. (1989). *Dead poets society*. Touchstone Pictures.

York-Barr, J., & Duke, D. (2004). What do we know about teacher leadership? Findings from two decades of scholarship. *Review of Educational Research*, *74*(3), 255–316.

Yukl, G. (2013). *Leadership in organizations* (8th ed.). Pearson.

SECTION IV

WELL-BEING PRACTICES AND FRAMEWORKS FOR PRACTITIONERS TO USE

CHAPTER 16

APPLYING BRAIN RESEARCH AND POSITIVE PSYCHOLOGY TO PROMOTE THE WELL-BEING OF PRINCIPALS

Kent Divoll and Angelica Ribeiro

INTRODUCTION

The role of the school principal is extremely important. Principals have an influence on teaching practices—for example, the curriculum taught at the school, methods used to teach, which teachers teach which classes, and where funding in the school is allocated (Cohen et al., 2009; Leithwood et al., 2004; Valentine & Prater, 2011). Principals also have an impact on teacher outcomes—for example, school climate, teacher retention, teacher morale, teacher training, and teacher induction (Allen et al., 2015; Coelli & Green, 2012; Divoll et al., 2019; Gulsen & Gulenay, 2014; Hirsch et al., 2008; Johnson, 2006). Furthermore, student outcomes, e.g., graduation rates, school climate, student morale, and student achievement, are affected by principals (Allen et al., 2015; Branch et al., 2012; Coelli & Green, 2012; Dhuey & Smith, 2014; Grissom et al., 2015; Gulsen & Gulenay, 2014; Lambersky, 2016; Leithwood et al., 2004, 2008). Given all of the aspects of administration that a school principal has an influence over, it would be difficult for one to argue against the importance of a principal to the school they oversee.

Supporting Leaders for School Improvement Through Self-Care and Well-Being, pp. 297–316
Copyright © 2024 by Information Age Publishing
www.infoagepub.com
All rights of reproduction in any form reserved.

Despite being such an important role, being a principal today has become increasingly more demanding and stressful (Darmody & Smyth, 2016; Markow et al., 2013; Wang et al., 2018). Wicher (2017) encapsulates the principal's role and stress in the following quote about the position: "Instructional leader, human resource manager, financial planner, strategic advisor, counsellor, staff and parent mediator, mentor, coach and keynote speaker; the role of the school principal is as challenging and emotionally demanding as it is rewarding" (p. 25). Principals are "constantly worried as to the repercussions of their decisions and actions which could have an impact on staff, job satisfaction, on the school climate in general and, ultimately on student learning" (Poirel & Yvon, 2014, p. 16). Principals of today, unlike their predecessors of 20 years ago, have to worry about such additional factors as school accountability ratings, school choice, and student achievement scores. Each of these factors can result in negative ramifications for the school and principal, including: (a) the principal losing their job, (b) (b) losing students and funding, and (c) lower teacher and student morale. Despite all of the stress that principals face, however, they are often focused on the well-being of the school and those in the school more so than on their own well-being (Wicher, 2017).

Not surprisingly, compared to the general population, principals have higher levels of emotional demands, issues with work-life balance, burnout, difficulty sleeping, and stress (Riley et al., 2020). The stress caused by being a principal can result in principals leaving the school or leaving the field altogether (Goldring & Taie, 2018; Levin & Bradley, 2019). Principals who leave the profession or change districts suggest that there are five common reasons for their decision: (a) lack of preparation or professional development, (b) issues with working conditions, (c) salaries that do not match the requirements of the position, (d) lack of autonomy in decision-making, and (e) national, state, and local accountability policies (Levin & Bradley, 2019). All of these stressors result in a turnover rate that is between 15% and 30% (DeAngelis & White, 2011; Goldring & Taie, 2018; Levin & Bradley, 2019). In addition, as a result of the increased challenges for principals in high-poverty areas, the turnover rates for such schools are usually above those of other types of schools (Beteille et al., 2012; DeAngelis & White, 2011; Goldring & Taie, 2018; Levin & Bradley, 2019; Markow et al., 2013). Given the influence of a principal on their school, principal turnover can be problematic for that school. For example, research has shown a direct link between principal turnover and student scores on achievement tests (Beteille et al., 2012; Burkhauser et al., 2012; DeAngelis & White, 2011; Kearney et al., 2012; Miller, 2013). Although all of these stressors are present for principals, how the principal perceives these issues and their capacity to deal with demands of the position are significant in managing stress (Greenberg, 2017; McGonigal, 2016). Thus, one way to accommodate the stress of the position is to focus on the well-being of principals.

PRINCIPALS' WELL-BEING

Cherkowski and Walker (2014) advocated for moving away from research that focuses on school administrators as influencers of achievement toward an emphasis on their emotional well-being. Yet, several years later, very little research has been focused specifically on the well-being of school principals (Wicher, 2017); instead, much of the research on well-being is concentrated on students, teachers, or the school as a whole. Some of these studies include research on mindfulness (Abenavoli et al., 2013; Frank et al., 2013; Roeser et al., 2013), the Cultivating Awareness and Resilience in Education (CARE) program (Jennings et al., 2013; Schussler et al., 2016), and Leading Together (LT) (Leis et al., 2017; Rimm-Kaufman et al., 2014). Moreover, there are a number of organizations that focus directly or indirectly on the well-being of those in schools, but are not specifically designed for principals. Some of these organizations include the Center for Courage and Renewal, PERMA training programs, and the VIA Institute (links to each website are given in the Programs list on page 307).

Until recently, though, much of the research that has been conducted about the well-being of principals comes from countries outside the United States. For example, there is research in Canada (Poirel & Yvon, 2014) that centers on principals' emotional coping and in Australia that focuses on surveying principals to learn about their well-being and the demands of the position as well as about using activities that encourage gratitude (Riley et al., 2020; Waters & Stokes, 2015). In addition, there are additional organizations in Australia that have their own well-being programs: the National Excellence in School Leadership Institute's (NESLI) Principals' Wellbeing Program and the Victoria State Government's Department of Education and Training program called the Principal Health and Wellbeing Strategy (a link to each program's website is included in the program's listing). Recently, there has been a recent push to focus on the well-being of principals in the United States. This includes training principals in mindfulness using the CARE professional development program, which was adapted to specifically focus on principals (Mahfouz, 2018). Moreover, again in the United States, recent research assessed the stress and social-emotional competencies of preservice building leaders and suggested that future principals might not have the capacity to deal with the stress of the position (Mahfouz & Richardson, 2020).

Strategies to Promote the Well-Being of Principals

Among other interventions, the call for principals' well-being has resulted in an emphasis on research that includes mindfulness, coping strategies for stress, resilience, and emotional skills (Jennings et al., 2017; Mahfouz, 2018; Wells & Klocko, 2018; Wicher, 2017). Each of the aforementioned interventions has shown promise in assisting principals with their well-being and reducing their stress. However, many of these interventions have combined activities typically resulting in intensive programs that are lengthy and cost thousands of dollars. For example, the version of the CARE program that was adapted for principals included hour-long sessions over the course of five weeks, with an additional session four weeks later (Mahfouz, 2018); in addition, NESLI's Principals' Wellbeing Program, which can be presented in online modules or face-to-face sessions, is conducted over the course of four months (NESLI, 2019). Out of all of the aforementioned programs, the Principal Health and Wellbeing Strategy is the most complex and involved because it integrates multiple layers of support such as mentoring, professional development, and support networks (Victoria, Australia: State Department of Education and Training, 2018). Although we recognize that having these professional development programs for principals occur over time is more likely to result in the strategies being implemented (Desimone, 2009; Garet et al., 2001; Patton et al., 2015), the size of the program, the time needed to initiate and maintain the program, and the cost can limit the number of school districts that implement well-being strategies for principals. As a result, few principals are likely to receive the support recommended by these programs and will continue to struggle with the demands of the position and the associated stress that negatively shapes their well-being.

Thus, although we recognize the benefits of the aforementioned programs to improve principal well-being, we argue for simpler, less involved practices that can be easily incorporated into a principal's routine. Our hope is that, with strategies that are simple to implement and inexpensive, more principals can improve their well-being. The practices for which we advocate integrate aspects of understanding of just two elements: (a) how the brain reacts to and is influenced by stress (Doyle & Zakrajsek, 2018; Jensen, 2008; Sousa, 2016; Wilson & Conyers, 2013) and (b) how to apply strategies from positive psychology. Each of these ideas has demonstrated individually the potential to relieve stress and thus can be combined and adapted for principals to improve their well-being (Achor, 2011; Ben-Shahar, 2012; Ribeiro, 2018; Waters & Stokes, 2015).

UNDERSTANDING STRESS AND THE BRAIN

Given all of the issues that principals face in their profession, it is safe to say that they are under a great deal of stress (Carpenter & Brewer, 2014; Chaplain, 2001; Darmody & Smyth, 2016; Wang et al., 2018). McGonigal (2016) argues that stress can be good for someone and that how a person perceives stress influences the effect it has on that person. However, much of the current research on the impact of stress on teachers and principals focuses on the negative results of that stress. Unfortunately, a principal's job satisfaction, tendency for burnout, and level of self-efficacy are all intertwined with the decision to remain in the profession (Federici & Skaalvik, 2012). Similar to teachers (Divoll, 2022; Divoll & Ribeiro, 2021, 2022a; Sutton et al., 2009), a principal's stress has the potential to distort daily decision making. Stressful situations can prompt a release of chemicals such as cortisol that, among other effects, result in: (a) being more likely to overreact to situations, (b) a decrease in one's ability to apply higher order thinking, and (c) a loss of ability to recall information (Greenberg, 2017; Jensen, 2008).

Not understanding how the brain, stress, and emotions interrelate can have a negative impact on a principal. Feeling constantly stressed creates a cyclical effect that is more likely to result in difficulty returning to a normal state of mind. When a principal is stressed, they are more likely to think negatively and recall negative memories (Doyle & Zakrajsek, 2018; Sousa, 2016; Wilson & Conyers, 2013). This has the potential to result in principals reacting differently to a situation when they feel stressed. If, in the stressful situation, the principal feels threatened professionally, emotionally, or physically (which often happens in such situations), then the amygdala in the brain is activated and a memory encoded with emotion is created (Doyle & Zakrajsek, 2018). The amygdala regulates how a person handles a situation (Greenberg, 2017; Jenson, 2008). The activation of the amygdala results in the memory being encoded with an emotional response that is stored in the hippocampus. Such memories are more easily recalled (Zull, 2011).

Dealing with stress becomes more complicated because the next time that the principal is in a similar stressful situation, the brain's hippocampus subconsciously recalls memories that relate to the stressful situation and consequently the principal is more likely to react in a negative way. Thus, a cycle of stress is created—that is, a principal is stressed, chemicals are released in the brain, the principal is more likely to think negatively and recall negative situations and be more likely to react negatively, which creates a negative environment and future troublesome interactions (Divoll, 2022; Greenberg, 2017). Given all of the interactions and important decisions that a principal makes in a day and their impact on the school climate

(Allen et al., 2015; Gulsen & Gulenay, 2014), reacting to a situation in a harsh manner or making a decision that would not normally be made when not stressed has the potential to be problematic. Because the nature of a principal's interactions with teachers is an elemental component of a school climate, and teachers who do not feel supported by their administrators tend to leave the school, such interactions can result in additional stress for the principal (Carver-Thomas & Darling-Hammond, 2019; Sutcher et al., 2016, 2019). Teachers leaving the school can result in a change in the school climate and decreased student achievement (Coleman, 2018; Ingwalson, 2016; Kraft et al., 2016)—and this can certainly increase principal stress.

Without understanding the cycle of stress and how the brain, emotions, memories, and negative thoughts interact, a principal will not notice the triggers, tend to remain under stress, and be more likely to experience burnout, which may lead to unintended consequences for the school (for a more detailed explanation of the brain's influence on stress and emotion, see Greenberg, 2017). Although there is a call for principals to learn about the brain (Conyers & Wilson, 2016; Lyman, 2016), much of this call is in relation to learning about how the brain can mold teaching practices, student development, and teacher development. Thus, we advocate for training principals about how the brain and emotions can affect their decisions and reactions while stressed (Doyle & Zakrajsek, 2018; Greenberg, 2017; Sousa, 2016; Wilson & Conyers, 2013). Implementing such training allows principals to feel as if they are more in control of their stress, consequently reducing its impact and limiting inappropriate or harsh reactions to situations. By taking control of their stress, principals have the potential to change their mindset about stress and view their job differently (Greenberg, 2017; McGonigal, 2016).

POSITIVE PSYCHOLOGY STRATEGIES

Positive psychology is "the scientific study of the strengths that enable individuals and communities to thrive" (Positive Psychology Center, n.d., para. 2). Positive psychology strategies are important because they can help people "develop a positive state of mind" (Lyubomirsky, 2007, p. 3), which can lead them to a "happier, more fulfilled life" (Ben-Shahar, 2007, p. xi). More specifically, a positive mindset has the potential to benefit principals. For example, principals with a positive mindset are more likely to recognize positive realities, which they would probably not see without that favorable attitude (Dweck, 2016). Recognizing positive realities helps principals focus on possible solutions instead of fielding complaints or creating more problems. As a result, they become more productive, "improve their response to stress at work and decrease [their] fatigue symptoms" (Achor,

2013, p. 26). Additionally, a positive mindset can increase intelligence, energy, and creativity, making the brain work 31% better than a neutral or negative mindset (Achor, 2011, p. 58).

In this chapter, we focus on positive psychology strategies that can help principals: (a) develop a positive mindset and therefore reduce stress and improve their well-being, and (b) make their schools a more positive learning and work environment (Allen et al., 2015; Gulsen & Gulenay, 2014). When principals apply positive psychology strategies, they spread positivity into the school environment (Divoll & Ribeiro, 2022b). That means that they inspire those around them to perform helpful actions as well, leading others toward the benefits of having a positive state of mind, such as being able to better manage stress (Patti et al., 2015).

Unfortunately, negativity is contagious too. As Achor (2018) states, "[B]eing surrounded by only negative and stressed-out people very quickly tips our balance from motivated and positive to frazzled and negative" (p. 149), which can negatively influence the school environment. Therefore, it is paramount that principals create "a culture of support instead of stress" (p. 99). Persuading school staff, teachers, and students to change their behavior in order to create a more positive environment and therefore a less-stressful learning and workplace can be difficult, because "humans are habitual creatures and can be resistant to ideas that feel new and different" (p. 100). However, when a principal models positive actions, it helps people "see *why* they should want the change, [which] activates a sense of ownership, turning indifference or inertia into potential" (p. 100). In this way, principals can encourage school staff, teachers, and students to develop a supportive environment by applying positive psychology strategies themselves.

Several strategies of positive psychology can build a positive mindset. We next describe three simple strategies that can be easily incorporated in a school principal's routine without taking much of their time: (a) express gratitude, (b) write down two happy moments, and (c) perform random acts of kindness (Ribeiro, 2018).

Express Gratitude

Studies have proven that practicing gratitude is simple, yet very powerful. For example, Emmons and McCullough (2003) investigated the impact of gratitude on psychological and physical well-being in daily life. Based on their randomly assigned experimental condition, for 10 weeks, participants had to write five things for which they were grateful or thankful (gratitude condition), list five hassles that happened to them (hassle condition), or write five events that made an impression on them (life-event condition).

Participants also had to rate their mood, physical symptoms, coping and health behaviors, and overall life appraisal. Results demonstrated that the gratitude condition had positive benefits for well-being. Compared to the hassle and life-event groups, participants from the gratitude group were more optimistic about their experiences in the coming days and felt better regarding their lives in general. Moreover, they spent more time exercising and had fewer physical complaints.

In another study, Grant and Gino (2010) discovered that gratitude expressions promoted cooperation by making people feel socially valued. The researchers divided the participants, who were fundraisers at a university, into two conditions: control and gratitude. Both groups received feedback on their work. However, only the participants in the gratitude group received an expression of gratitude from the fundraiser director: "I am very grateful for your hard work. We sincerely appreciate your contributions to the university" (p. 951). Grant and Gino measured the participants' prosocial behavior and their perceptions of self-efficacy and social worth. Results showed that, compared to the control group, the fundraisers in the gratitude condition improved the prosocial behavior as they increased their weekly calls to help the university by more than 50%. The gratitude expressions that the participants received strengthened their feelings of social worth, which made them want to contribute even more.

As indicated in the studies above, expressing gratitude can bring physical, psychological, and social benefits to people, including school leaders. As Emmons (2010) stated, people who practice gratitude have "stronger immune systems, lower blood pressure, and higher levels of positive emotions" (Why Gratitude Is Good section, para. 4, bullet points), while people who are stressed tend to have higher blood pressure (Moya-Albiol et al., 2010; Waters & Stokes, 2015). Gratitude can lead people to experience more joy, optimism, and happiness, as well as be more alert, alive, helpful, generous, and compassionate (Divoll & Ribeiro, 2022b; Emmons, 2010; Ribeiro, 2018; Waters & Stokes, 2015). Such benefits of gratitude help principals reduce stress and improve their well-being, which positively spreads throughout their workplace to reach staff, teachers, and students.

Principals need only a few minutes to express gratitude and can practice it anywhere, including at work. Modifying the study requirements set by Emmons (2010), we propose that every day, principals should simply write down or share out loud with a colleague, friend, or family member three (instead of Emmons's five) things for which they are grateful. They can express gratitude for big or small things, from their jobs (big) to a morning cup of coffee (relatively small!) (Ribeiro & Divoll, 2020). This practice "consciously, intentionally focuses [their] attention on developing more grateful thinking and on eliminating ungrateful thoughts" (Emmons, 2010, Cultivating Gratitude section, para. 3). Therefore, what matters is to show appreciation. If principals want to challenge themselves when cultivating gratitude, they should focus only on the last 24 hours and avoid repeating what they may have already written on a previous day. By doing so, they force themselves to scan for even more good things in their everyday lives, which helps them create a positive mindset. In short, as Emmons (2010) stated, gratitude is:

> an affirmation of goodness. We affirm that there are good things in the world, gifts and benefits we've received. This doesn't mean that life is perfect; it doesn't ignore complaints, burdens, and hassles. But when we look at life as a whole, gratitude encourages us to identify some amount of goodness in our life. (Why Gratitude Is Good section, para. 6)

Such practice encourages us to appreciate our experiences, the people around us, and what we have (Waters & Stokes, 2015). Most important, it helps us, including principals, be more resistant to stress.

Write Down Two Happy Moments

Writing down two happy moments is supported by empirical studies conducted on the connection between writing about positivity and well-being. Research has found that writing about happy moments or positive experiences increases well-being. For example, Seligman et al. (2005) examined the happiness intervention called *Three Good Things in Life*, in which participants were asked to "write down three things that went well each day and their causes every night for one week. In addition, they were asked to provide a casual explanation for each good thing" (p. 416). As a result of this intervention, participants felt happier and less depressed at the one-, three-, and six-month follow-ups. Participants were also more optimistic, suggesting that the practice of writing down three good things improved their ability to scan for positive events.

Burton and King (2004) also found that writing about positive experiences brings psychological and health benefits. In their study, they asked participants from the intervention group to write about an intensely positive experience for 20 minutes every day for three consecutive days. Results showed that writing about such deep experiences enhanced the participants' well-being. Compared to the control group, the intervention participants improved their immediate mood. Three months after the intervention, they also had fewer symptoms of illness.

Knowing that school principals have a busy schedule, an adapted version of the writing activities described above is writing down two happy moments. To practice the happy moment strategy, during or by the end of the day principals should write down two sentences describing two happy moments (one sentence for each happy moment) that occurred during the last 24 hours. This strategy can help principals create a positive mindset because it encourages them to scan for good experiences, notice positive situations that happened to them, and identify their happiness boosters. Furthermore, writing down two happy moments makes principals relive those events, bringing the same good feeling they enjoyed when they first experienced them (Ribeiro, 2018).

This strategy can reduce principals' stress for two reasons: it creates happiness and transforms their state of mind. First, this strategy creates happiness because when school principals scan for good moments and relive positive experiences, their brains release feel-good chemicals such as dopamine and endorphins. The brain does not distinguish present from past; therefore, when school leaders think of a good situation that happened earlier in the day, their brains believe they are actually living it at the moment they are describing it, which makes them feel good (Achor, 2013). Second, writing down two happy moments can transform a principal's general state because it helps them identify what makes them happy. Ben-Shahar (2007) calls "these brief but transforming experiences *happiness boosters*—activities, lasting anywhere from a few minutes to a few hours, that provide us with both meaning and pleasure, both future and present benefits" (p.130, italics in the original), which then inspire and energize principals to face stressful situations through the perspective of being a problem-solver. Being aware of the resulting happiness boosters allows principals to apply them whenever they want to improve their state of mind.

Perform Random Acts of Kindness

Performing acts of kindness promotes positive emotions for not only the person who performs the act but also the person who receives it (Fredrickson, 2009). As Achor (2011) suggests, "Acts of altruism—giving to friends and strangers alike—decrease stress and strongly contribute to enhanced mental health" (p. 52). Research shows doing acts of kindness increases well-being and happiness. Lyubomirsky (2007) describes a study that she and her colleagues conducted to examine the effects of kindness on well-being. They assigned the participants to either the treatment or control group. The treatment group was asked to perform five acts of kindness per week for six weeks. The acts of kindness (e.g., writing a thank-you note) could be practiced on one day or over the whole week. The control group was not asked to perform acts of kindness. When participants self-reported their well-being, the researchers found that, while the control group reduced their well-being, the treatment group increased their well-being as a result of performing acts of kindness. Furthermore, results indicated that the participants who performed the five weekly acts of kindness on the same day increased their well-being even more than those who practiced kindness on different days. The researchers explained that performing several acts of kindness in one single day might have made them more distinguishable from participants' usual kind behavior. As this study's findings show, doing acts of kindness positively affects well-being.

Another study found that simply counting kindness leads to happiness. Otake et al. (2006) investigated how keeping track of acts of kindness affects people's feelings of happiness. Participants were divided into two conditions: counting kindness intervention and control. The participants from the intervention condition were asked to keep track of the acts of kindness they practiced every day for one week. The researchers measured all participants' happiness level one month before the intervention and one month after the end of the intervention. Results showed that, compared to the control group, the happiness level of the participants from the intervention group was higher after performing the one-week intervention. This finding suggests that counting acts of kindness increases happiness. As Otake et al. concluded, "[K]indness is an important human strength that influences subjective well-being" (p. 366).

To practice the strategy of acts of kindness, principals simply have to perform at least one random act of kindness a day. The act of kindness can be to compliment, help, or genuinely thank someone. Examples of kind acts are a principal: (a) complimenting a teacher on how they handled a disciplinary issue, (b) taking some time to help the librarian put books back on the shelves, and (c) thanking a teacher for completing a task. Principals—like most of us—can perform acts of kindness on anyone and anywhere. As Ben-Shahar (2012) stated, "Our behavior toward other people—colleagues, family members, friends—sends out ripples that impact those we meet, and beyond" (p. 203). Having that in mind, when performing acts of kindness at work, principals should encourage staff, teachers, and students to do the same. Such a ripple effect may well result in creating a more positive workplace and learning environment and reducing teachers' and students' levels of stress.

CONCLUSION

Being a principal is a stressful profession, but an important one. Without strategies to assist principals with their stress levels, there can be negative consequences for the school, teachers, students, and the principal. In this chapter, we argue that principals can benefit from learning about how the brain, emotions, stress, and reactions to situations are all connected. In addition, we advocate for principals to implement simple positive psychology strategies that reduce stress and do not take a lot of time or money, that is, (a) expressing gratitude, (b) writing down two happy moments, and (c) performing random acts of kindness. All of the strategies mentioned in this chapter are designed to empower principals to take control of their stress. Many additional practices and resources can help principals with stress. Thus, we have included a list of additional resources that are also beneficial.

LIST OF STRATEGIES FROM THIS CHAPTER

- **Training about stress, the brain, emotions, and reactions:** Principals need to learn about how the brain, emotions, and stress impacts reactions to situations. Doing so has the potential to empower principals to feel in control of their stress and reactions.
- **Express gratitude:** Principals write down two or share out loud with a college, friend, or family member three things for which they are grateful.
- **Write down two happy moments:** Principals write down two sentences describing two happy moments that occurred to them during the last 24 hours.
- **Perform acts of kindness:** Principals perform at least one random act of kindness a day. The act of kindness can be to compliment, help, or genuinely thank someone.

RESOURCES RELATED TO THIS CHAPTER

Activities

Accomplishments log. Principals take a few minutes to log at least one accomplishment they had that day.
Best-loved self story: Writing a best-loved self story can help principals reduce stress and re-energize them. See Divoll and Ribeiro (2022b).
Emotional intelligence: Training in emotional intelligence helps participants be more aware of and control one's emotions.
Exercise: Incorporating physical exercise into a principal's day has been shown to reduce stress.
Gratitude diary: The strategy of having a principal write a daily diary of their gratitude.
Gratitude letter: The strategy of having a principal write and deliver a gratitude letter.
Meditation: Meditating on one's own or in a group has been shown to reduce teachers and administrator stress.

Mindfulness for teachers and principals: Mindfulness is a type of meditation that trains school personnel to be more aware of the moment that they are in.

Yoga: A number of schools are using yoga as a method to reduce teacher and administrator stress.

Readings

Emotional intelligence: Why it can matter more than IQ: Daniel Goleman.
Exploring your past to strengthen your best-loved self: Kent Divoll and Angelica Ribeiro.
How to create happiness at work: Seven evidence-based strategies to enjoy your day. Angelica Ribeiro.
Keeping your sanity: 6 strategies to promote well-being. Angelica Ribeiro and Kent Divoll.
Mindful teacher, mindful school: Improving wellbeing in teaching and learning: Kevin Hawkins.
Mindfulness and yoga in schools: A guide for teachers and practitioners: Catherine Cook-Cottone.
Mindfulness for teachers: Simple skills for peace and productivity in the classroom: Patricia Jennings.
Mindfulness training for school administrators: Effects on well-being and leadership: Julia Mahfouz.
My happiness habit journal: Angelica Ribeiro.
Positive education for school leaders: Exploring the effects of emotion-gratitude and action-Gratitude. Lea Waters and Helen Stokes.
Positive psychology: A pathway to principal wellbeing and resilience: Marcus Wicher.
Strategies to overcome middle school teachers' management stress: Kent Divoll and Angelica Ribeiro.
The ability to model emotional intelligence: Principles and updates: John Mayer, David Caruso, and Peter Salovey.
The mindful school leader: Practice to transform: Valerie Brown and Kirsten Olson.
The myths of happiness: What should make you happy, but doesn't, what shouldn't make you happy, but does. Sonja Lyubomirsky.
The new psychology of success: Carol Dweck.
The new science of learning: How to learn in harmony with your brain (2nd ed.): Terry Doyle and Todd Zakrajsek.
The stress-proof brain: Master your emotional response to stress using mindfulness and neuroplasticity: Melanie Greenberg.
The upside of stress: Why stress is good for you, and how to get good at it: Kelly McGonigal.

Programs

Center for Courage and Renewal. http://www.couragerenewal.org/approach/

Cultivating Awareness and Resilience in Education (CARE) professional development program: A professional development program that incorporates mindfulness, emotional skills, and caring and compassion skills into a training for teachers and principals.

National Excellence in School Leadership Institute (NESLI) Principals' Wellbeing Program. https://wtaa.edu.au/pr/nesli/19/The-Principals-Wellbeing-Program.pdf

PERMA Training Programs. https://ppc.sas.upenn.edu/learn-more/perma-theory-well-being-and-perma-workshops

VIA Institute. https://www.viacharacter.org/

Victoria, Australia: State Government Department of Education and Training Program—Principal Health and Wellbeing Strategy. https://www.education.vic.gov.au/hrweb/Documents/PrincipalHWB-Strategy-2018-2021.pdf

REFERENCES

Abenavoli, R. M., Jennings, P. A., Greenberg, M. T., Harris, A. R., & Katz, D. A. (2013). The protective effects of mindfulness against burnout among educators. *Psychology of Education Review, 37*(2), 57–69.

Achor, S. (2011). *The happiness advantage: The seven principles that fuel success and performance at work*. Virgin Books.

Achor, S. (2013). *Before happiness: The 5 hidden keys to achieving success, spreading happiness, and sustaining positive change*. Crown Business.

Achor, S. (2018). *Big potential: Five secrets of reaching higher by powering those around you*. Virgin Books.

Allen, N., Grigsby, B., & Peters, M. L. (2015). Does leadership matter? Examining the relationship among transformational leadership, school climate, and student achievement. *International Journal of Educational Leadership Preparation, 10*(2), 1–22.

Ben-Shahar, T. (2007). *Happier: Learn the secrets to daily joy and lasting fulfillment*. McGraw-Hill.

Ben-Shahar, T. (2012). *Choose the life you want: The mindful way to happiness*. The Experiment.

Beteille, T., Kalogrides, D., & Loeb, S. (2012). Stepping stones: Principal career paths and school outcomes. *Social Science Research, 41*(4), 904–919.

Branch, G., Hanushek, E., & Rivkin, S. (2012). *Estimating the effect of leaders on public sector productivity: The case of school principals*. NBER Working Paper No. 17803. National Bureau of Economic Research. http://dx.doi.org/10.3386/w17803

Burkhauser, S., Gates, S. M., Hamilton, L. S., & Ikemoto, G. S. (2012). *First-year principals in urban school districts: How actions and working conditions relate to outcomes*. Rand Corporation. https://www.rand.org/pubs/technical_reports/TR1191.html

Burton, C., & King, L. (2004). The health benefits of writing about intensely positive experiences. *Journal of Research in Personality, 38*(2), 150–163.

Carpenter, B. W., & Brewer, C. (2014). The implicated advocate: The discursive construction of the democratic practices of school principals in the USA. *Discourse: Studies in the Cultural Politics of Education, 35*(2), 294–306.

Carver-Thomas, D., & Darling-Hammond, L. (2019). The trouble with teacher turnover: How teacher attrition affects students and schools. *Education Policy Analysis Archives, 27*(36), 1–32. http://dx.doi.org/10.14507/epaa.27.3699

Chaplain, R. P. (2001). Stress and job satisfaction among primary headteachers: A question of balance? *Educational Management & Administration*, *29*(2), 197–215.

Cherkowski, S., & Walker, K. (2014). Flourishing communities: Re-storying educational leadership using a positive research lens. *International Journal of Leadership in Education*, *17*(2), 200–216. http://dx.doi.org/10.1080/13603124.2013.827240

Coelli, M., & Green, D. A. (2012). Leadership effects: School principals and student outcomes. *Economics of Education Review*, *31*(1), 92–109. https://doi.org/10.1016/j.econedurev.2011.09.001

Cohen, J., McCabe, L., Michelli, N. M., & Pickeral, T. (2009). School climate: Research, policy, practice, and teacher education. *Teachers College Record*, *111*(1), 180–213. https://www.researchgate.net/profile/Jonathan-Cohen-11/publication/235420504_School_Climate_Research_Policy_Teacher_Education_and_Practice/links/59d67f050f7e9b42a6aa0145/School-Climate-Research-Policy-Teacher-Education-and-Practice.pdf

Coleman, K. T. (2018). *Optimal conditions to support school climate and increase teacher retention in middle school classrooms* [Doctoral dissertation, Gardner-Webb University]. Boiling Springs, North Carolina. https://digitalcommons.gardner-webb.edu/education_etd/292

Conyers, M., & Wilson, D. (2016). *Smarter teacher leadership: Neuroscience and the power of purposeful collaboration*. Teachers College Press.

Darmody, M., & Smyth, E. (2016). Primary school principals' job satisfaction and occupational stress. *International Journal of Educational Management*, *30*(1), 115–128.

DeAngelis, K. J., & White, B. R. (2011). Principal Turnover in Illinois Public Schools, 2001–2008. Policy Research: IERC 2011-1. *Illinois Education Research Council*. https://files.eric.ed.gov/fulltext/ED518191.pdf

Desimone, L. M. (2009). Improving impact studies of teachers' professional development: Toward better conceptualizations and measures. *Educational Researcher*, *38*(3), 181–199. https://journals.sagepub.com/doi/pdf/10.3102/0013189X08331140

Dhuey, E., & Smith, J. (2014). How important are school principals in the production of student achievement? *Canadian Journal of Economics*, *47*(2), 634–663. https://onlinelibrary.wiley.com/doi/pdf/10.1111/caje.12086

Divoll, K. (2022). Teacher aggression and classroom management. In E. J. Sabornie & D. Espelage (Eds.), *Handbook of classroom management: Research, practice, and issues* (3rd ed., pp. 415–435). Routledge.

Divoll, K., Gauna, L., & Ribeiro, A. (2019). Career changers' experiences as neophyte middle school ESL teachers. In D. McDonald (Ed.), *Facing challenges and complexities in retention of novice teachers* (pp. 179–260). Information Age Publishing.

Divoll, K., & Ribeiro, A. (2021). Strategies to overcome middle school teachers' management stress. In C. Gaines & K. Hutson (Eds.), *Promoting positive learning experiences in middle school education* (pp. 217–235). IGI Global. https://doi.org/10.4018/978-1-7998-7057-9.ch012

Divoll, K., & Riberio, A. (2022a). Strategies to overcome middle school teachers' classroom management stress. In Information Resources Management Associates (IRMA) (Ed.), *Research anthology on instructions in student behavior and misconduct* (pp. 822–840). IGI Global.

Divoll, K., & Ribeiro, A. (2022b). Exploring your past to strengthen you best-loved-self. In C. Craig, D. McDonald, & G. Curtis. (Eds.), *Best-loved self: Learning and leading in teaching and teacher education* (pp. 145–169). Palgrave Macmillan.

Doyle, T., & Zakrajsek, T. (2018). *The new science of learning: How to learn in harmony with your brain* (2nd ed.). Stylus Publishing.

Dweck, C. (2016). *Mindset: The new psychology of success*. Random House.

Emmons, R. (2010, November 16). *Why gratitude is good*. Greater Good Magazine: Science-Based Insights for a Meaningful Life. https://greatergood.berkeley.edu/article/item/why_gratitude_is_good

Emmons, R., & McCullough, M. (2003). Counting blessings versus burdens: An experimental investigation of gratitude and subjective well-being in daily life. *Journal of Personality and Social Psychology, 84*(2), 377–389.

Federici, R. A., & Skaalvik, E. M. (2012). Principal self-efficacy: Relations with burnout, job satisfaction, and motivation to quit. *Social Psychological Education, 15*, 295–320. https://www.researchgate.net/publication/257665097_Principal_self-efficacy_Relations_with_burnout_job_satisfaction_and_motivation_to_quit

Frank, J. L., Jennings, P. A., & Greenberg, M. T. (2013). Mindfulness-based interventions in school settings: An introduction to the special issue. *Research in Human Development, 10*(3), 205–210. https://www.researchgate.net/publication/242329947_Mindfulness-Based_Interventions_in_School_Settings_An_Introduction_to_the_Special_Issue_INTRODUCTION

Fredrickson, B. (2009). *Positivity: Top-notch research reveals the upward spiral that will change your life*. Three Rivers Press.

Garet, M. S., Porter, A. C., Desimone, L., Birman, B. F., & Suk Yoon, K. (2001). What makes professional development effective? Results from a national sample of teachers. *American Education Research Journal, 38*(4), 915–945.

Goldring, R., & Taie, S. (2018). Principal attrition and mobility: Results from the 2016–2017 principal follow-up survey first look (NCES 2018-066). U.S. Department of Education National Center for Education Statistics. https://nces.ed.gov/pubs2018/2018066.pdf

Grant, A., & Gino, F. (2010). A little thanks goes a long way: Explaining why gratitude expressions motivate prosocial behavior. *Journal of Personality and Social Psychology, 98*(6), 946–955. https://www.umkc.edu/facultyombuds/documents/grant_gino_jpsp_2010.pdf

Greenberg, M. (2017). *The stress-proof brain: Master your emotional response to stress using mindfulness and neuroplasticity*. New Harbinger Publications.

Grissom, J. A., Kalogrides, D., & Loeb, S. (2015). Using student test scores to measure principal performance. *Educational Evaluation and Policy Analysis, 37*(1), 3–28. https://journals.sagepub.com/doi/pdf/10.3102/0162373714523831

Gulsen, C., & Gulenay, G. B. (2014). The principal and healthy school climate. *Social Behavior and Personality: An International Journal*, *42*(1), 93S–100S. https://www.researchgate.net/publication/272208109_The_Principal_and_Healthy_School_Climate https://www.principalhealth.org/au/reports/2019_AU_Final_Report.pdf

Hirsch, E., Freitas, C., Church, K., & Villar, A. (2008). *Massachusetts Teaching, Learning and Leading Survey: Creating school conditions where teachers stay and students thrive.* https://www.nysut.org/~/media/files/nysut/resources/2013/april/ted/mass_tlc_survey_finalreport.pdf?la=en

Ingwalson, G. (2016). Mentoring and induction. In S. B. Mertens, M. M. Caskey, & N. Flowers (Eds.), *The encyclopedia of middle grades education* (pp. 250–253). Information Age Publishing.

Jennings, P. A., Brown, J. L., Frank, J. L., Doyle, S., Oh, Y., Davis, R., Rasheed, D., DeWeese, A., DeMauro, A. A., Cham, H., & Greenberg, M. T. (2017). Impacts of the CARE for Teachers program on teachers' social and emotional competence and classroom interactions. *Journal of Educational Psychology*, *109*(7), 1–19. https://doi.org/10.1037/edu0000187

Jennings, P. A., Frank, J. L., Snowberg, K. E., Coccia, M. A., & Greenberg, M. T. (2013). Improving classroom learning environments by Cultivating Awareness and Resilience in Education (CARE): Results of a randomized controlled trial. *School Psychology Quarterly*, *28*(4), 374–390.

Jensen, E. (2008). *Brain-based learning: The new paradigm of teaching* (2nd ed.). Corwin Press.

Johnson, S. M. (2006). *The workplace matters: Teacher quality, retention, and effectiveness.* [Working paper]. National Education Association Research Department. www.nea.org/assets/docs/HE/mf_wcreport.pdf

Kearney, W. S., Valdez, A., & Garcia, L. (2012). Leadership for the long-haul: The impact of leadership longevity on student achievement. *School Leadership Review*, *7*(2), 24–33. https://scholarworks.sfasu.edu/cgi/viewcontent.cgi?article=1103&context=slr

Kraft, M. A., Marinell, W. H., & Yee, D. (2016). *Schools as organizations: Examining school climate, teacher turnover, and student achievement in NYC.* Research Alliance for New York City Schools.

Lambersky, J. (2016). Understanding the human side of school leadership: Principals' impact on teachers' morale, self-efficacy, stress, and commitment. *Leadership and Policy in Schools*, *15*(4), 379–405. http://dx.doi.org/10.1080/15700763.2016.1181188

Leis, M., Rimm-Kaufman, S. E., Paxton, C. L., & Sandilos, L. E. (2017). Leading together: Strengthening relational trust in the adult school community. *Journal of School Leadership*, *27*(6), 831–859. https://files.eric.ed.gov/fulltext/ED580950.pdf

Leithwood, K., Harris, A., Hopkins, D. (2008). Seven strong claims about successful school leadership. *School Leadership and Management*, *28*(1), 27–42.

Leithwood, K., Seashore Louis, K., Anderson, S., & Wahlstrom, K. (2004). *Review of research: How leadership influences student learning.* The Wallace Foundation. https://www.wallacefoundation.org/knowledge-center/documents/how-leadership-influences-student-learning.pdf

Levin, S., & Bradley, K. (2019). *Understanding and addressing principal turnover: A review of the research*. National Association of Secondary School Principals. https://learningpolicyinstitute.org/sites/default/files/product-files/NASSP_LPI_Principal_Turnover_Research_Review_REPORT.pdf

Lyman, L. L. (Ed.). (2016). *Brain science for principals: What school leaders need to know*. Rowman & Littlefield.

Lyubomirsky, S. (2007). *The how of happiness: A new approach to getting the life you want*. Penguin Books.

Mahfouz, J. (2018). Mindfulness training for school administrators: Effects on wellbeing and leadership. *Journal of Educational Administration, 56*(6), 602–619. https://doi.org/10.1108/JEA-12-2017-0171

Mahfouz, J., & Richardson, J.W. (2020). At the crossroads: Wellbeing and principalship preparation. *Journal of Research on Leadership Education, 57*(5), 540–553. https://doi.org/10.1177/1942775120933914

Markow, D., Macia, L., & Lee, H. (2013). *The MetLife survey of the American teacher: Challenges for school leadership*. Metropolitan Life Insurance Company.

McGonigal, K. (2016). *The upside of stress: Why stress is good for you, and how to get good at it*. Penguin.

Miller, A. (2013). Principal turnover and student achievement. *Economics of Education Review, 36*, 60–72. https://doi.org/10.1016/j.econedurev.2013.05.004

Moya-Albiol, L., Serrano, M. A., & Salvador, A. (2010). Burnout as an important factor in the psychophysiological responses to a work day in teachers. *Stress and Health: Journal of the International Society for the Investigation of Stress, 26*(5), 382–393. https://onlinelibrary.wiley.com/doi/pdf/10.1002/smi.1309

National Excellence in School Leadership Institute (NESLI). (2019). *Principal's Wellbeing Program*. https://wtaa.edu.au/pr/nesli/19/The-Principals-Wellbeing-Program.pdf

Otake, K., Shimai, S., Tanaka-Matsumi, J., Otsui, K., & Fredrickson, B. (2006). Happy people become happier through kindness: A counting kindnesses intervention. *Journal of Happiness Studies, 7*(3), 361–375. https://doi.org/10.1007/s10902-005-3650-z

Patti, J., Senge, P., Madrazo, C., & Stern, M. (2015). Growing school leaders who can grow learning cultures. In J. A. Durlak, C. E. Domitrovich, R. P. Weissberg, & T. P. Gullotta (Eds.), *Handbook of social and emotional learning: Research and practice* (pp. 395–405). Guilford Publications.

Patton, K., Parker, M., & Tannehill, D. (2015). Helping teachers help themselves: Professional development that makes a difference. *NASSP Bulletin, 99*(1), 26–42. https://doi.org/10.1177/0192636515576040

Poirel, E., & Yvon, F. (2014). School principals' emotional coping process. *Canadian Journal of Education, 37*(3), 1–23.

Positive Psychology Center. (n.d.). *Welcome*. https://ppc.sas.upenn.edu/

Ribeiro, A. (2018). *Running into happiness: How my happiness habit journal created lasting happiness in the midst of a crazy-busy semester*. CreateSpace Independent Publishing Platform.

Ribeiro, A., & Divoll, K. (2020). Keeping your sanity: 6 strategies to promote wellbeing. *The Teacher Advocate, Winter*, 14–15. https://www.kdp.org/resources/pdf/covid19/TA-W20-Ribeiro.pdf

Riley, P., See, S. M., Marsh, H., & Dicke, T. (2020). *The Australian Principal Occupational Health, Safety and Wellbeing Survey* (IPPE Report). Institute for Positive Psychology and Education, Australian Catholic University.

Rimm-Kaufman, S. E., Leis, M., & Paxton, C. (2014). *Innovating together to improve the adult community in schools: Results from a two-year study of the initial implementation of Leading Together.* The Center for Courage & Renewal. https://www.couragerenewal.org/PDFs/UVA_LeadingTogether_July_11_2014_Final_Full_Report.pdf

Roeser, R. W., Schonert-Reichl, K. A., Jha, A., Cullen, M., Wallace, L., Wilensky, R., Oberle, E., Thomson, K., Taylor, C., & Harrison, J. (2013). Mindfulness training and reductions in teacher stress and burnout: Results from two randomized, waitlist-control field trials. *Journal of Educational Psychology, 105*(3), 787–804. https://www.researchgate.net/publication/263919667_Mindfulness_Training_and_Reductions_in_Teacher_Stress_and_Burnout_Results_From_Two_Randomized_Waitlist-Control_Field_Trials

Schussler, D. L., Jennings, P. A., Sharp, J. E., & Frank, J. L. (2016). Improving teacher awareness and well-being through CARE: A qualitative analysis of the underlying mechanisms. *Mindfulness, 7*(1), 130-142. https://link.springer.com/article/10.1007/s12671-015-0422-7

Seligman, M. E. P., Steen, T. A., Park, N., & Peterson, C. (2005). Positive psychology progress: Empirical validation of interventions. *American Psychologist, 60*(5), 410–421.

Sousa, D. A. (2016). *How the brain learns* (5th ed.). Corwin Press.

Sutcher, L., Darling-Hammond, L., & Carver-Thomas, D. (2016). *A coming crisis in teaching? Teacher supply, demand, and shortages in the US.* Learning Policy Institute. https://learningpolicyinstitute.org/sites/default/files/product-files/A_Coming_Crisis_in_Teaching_REPORT.pdf

Sutcher, L., Darling-Hammond, L., & Carver-Thomas, D. (2019). Understanding teacher shortages: An analysis of teacher supply and demand in the United States. *Education Policy Analysis Archives, 27*(35), 1–40. https://files.eric.ed.gov/fulltext/EJ1213618.pdf

Sutton, R. E., Mudrey-Camino, R., & Knight, C. C. (2009). Teachers' emotion regulation and classroom management. *Theory into Practice, 48*(2), 130–137. https://doi.org/10.1080/00405840902776418

Valentine, J. W., & Prater, M. (2011). Instructional, transformational, and managerial leadership and student achievement: High school principals make a difference. *NASSP Bulletin, 95*(1), 5–30. https://doi.org/10.1177/0192636511404062

Victoria, Australia: State Department of Education and Training (2018, April). *Principal Health and Wellbeing Strategy 2018–2021.* https://www.education.vic.gov.au/hrweb/Documents/PrincipalHWB-Strategy-2018-2021.pdf

Wang, F., Pollock, K. E., & Hauseman, C. (2018). School principals' job satisfaction: The effects of work intensification. *Canadian Journal of Educational Administration and Policy, 185*, 73–90. https://files.eric.ed.gov/fulltext/EJ1179195.pdf

Waters, L., & Stokes, H. (2015). Positive education for school leaders: Exploring the effects of emotion-gratitude and action-gratitude. *Australian Educational and Developmental Psychologist, 32*(1), 1–22. https://doi.org/10.1017/edp.2015.1

Wells, C. M., & Klocko, B. A. (2018). Principal well-being and resilience: Mindfulness as a means to that end. *NASSP Bulletin, 102*(2), 161–173. https://doi.org/10.1177/0192636518777813

Wicher, M. (2017). Positive psychology: A pathway to principal wellbeing and resilience. *Education Today, 17*(1), 24–26. https://www.pesa.edu.au/wp-content/uploads/2017/08/Positive-Psychology-Principal-Wellbeing-and-Resilience.pdf

Wilson, D., & Conyers, M. (2013). *Five big ideas for effective teaching: Connecting the mind, brain, and education research classroom practice*. Teachers College Press.

Zull, J. (2011). *From brain to mind using neuroscience to guide change in education*. Stylus.

CHAPTER 17

CULTIVATING AWARENESS AND RESILIENCE IN EDUCATION

Caring for Yourself So You Have the Resources to Care for Others

Sebrina L. Doyle Fosco

Leading is high-stress work. There is no way to avoid stress when you are responsible for people, organizations, outcomes, and managing the constant uncertainties of the environment. The higher you go, the greater your freedom to control your destiny but also the higher the degree of stress. The question is not whether you can avoid stress, but how you can control it to maintain your own sense of equilibrium

—George et al. (2007, p. 7).

Although we have known about the positive, long-term effects of social and emotional competence (SEC) (Greenberg et al., 2017; Jones et al., 2015), recently the concept has taken on even greater importance as the world experiences rapid, intense changes that have significantly affected well-being. For many educational leaders, this has led to an increased focus on student social-emotional learning (SEL). Using evidence-based programs that support students' SEL can be essential for improving outcomes, and there are numerous research-based curricula to support the development of these skills (Collaborative for Academic, Social, and Emotional Learning [CASEL], 2013). However, just providing a curriculum is not sufficient. In a recent report, 83% of elementary school principals surveyed identified the need for more professional development to help support students' social-emotional learning and development (Levin et al., 2020). To fully consider SEL needs, a systemic approach should be taken (Mahoney et al., 2020).

One key component for SEL is that students need good role models; seeing what SEC looks like in action is imperative for the development of these skills. Administrators' attendance to their own social and emotional well-being is crucial if they wish to provide a high level of support for teachers, students, families, and communities (Mahfouz & Gordon, 2020). Studies show that administrators are pivotal for supporting teachers' well-being and school climate (Lambersky, 2016; Price, 2012). In fact, administrators with compromised well-being are less able to impact student engagement and whole-school well-being (Maxwell & Riley, 2017). Furthermore, educational leaders are also at risk for burnout and fatigue. When educators burn out, students notice; a recent study by Oberle et al. (2020) found a significant relationship between students' ratings of their teacher's SEC and the teacher's level of self-reported burnout. The lesson is clear: When we do not take care of ourselves, we eventually run out of resources needed to care for others (Mahfouz et al., 2019).

Working in educational leadership is a fulfilling but very challenging job. Robinson and Shakeshaft (2016), using a national survey, found that the most persistent sources of stress reported by superintendents included changing regulations, funding issues, the time commitment of the job, and difficulty managing work-life balance. Multiple studies have found that one of the most significant stressors reported for principals is task overload—that is, not having enough time in the day to get everything done (e.g., Boyland, 2011; Klocko & Wells, 2015). Furthermore, Friedman (2002) found that principals' reported overload was significantly related to burnout. Principals have also noted other stressors, including feeling as if they did not have enough time for adequate attention to instructional leadership, school funding issues, constant interruptions, and the sheer volume of paperwork and emails required on a given workday (Boyland, 2011; Klocko & Wells, 2015).

In addition to challenges experienced with work-life balance, a host of other adverse outcomes can occur if stress management interventions are not employed. A recent survey of 37 administrators in a mid-sized school district in Pennsylvania found that 41% were at risk for anxiety problems and 25% were at risk for depression (Doyle Fosco, Brown, et al., 2023). These administrators reported that work-related stress affected multiple facets of their lives. They reported decreased creativity, focus, and feelings of passion for work; increased anxiety and feelings of being overwhelmed; physical health issues (e.g., headaches, gastrointestinal problems); and exhaustion (Doyle Fosco, Brown, et al., 2023). Troubling effects of stress at home included an obsession about work issues, trouble sleeping, lack of energy, agitation, feeling emotionally drained, and strained family relationships (Boyland, 2011; Doyle Fosco, Brown, et al., 2023). Although educational leaders may have little control over the stressors that occur in academic environments, they can exert some control over their stress level by engaging in healthy stress management behaviors that support their well-being.

Mindfulness-based programs have received attention in the last decade as a way to work more effectively with stress and support wellbeing. Mindfulness is defined by Kabat-Zinn (2003) as "the awareness that emerges through paying attention on purpose, in the present moment, and non-judgmentally to the unfolding of experience moment by moment" (p. 145). Mindfulness practices began being used secularly in the United States in 1979 when Kabat-Zinn founded the Stress Reduction Clinic at the University of Massachusetts Medical School to work with patients who were experiencing chronic pain but had not found relief through the traditional medical routes. Since that time, mindfulness has been incorporated into a variety of settings, including medical, corporate, psychological, juvenile justice, correctional, school, community, and the military (e.g., Himelstein et al., 2012; Jennings et al., 2017; Jha et al., 2017; Kabat-Zinn et al., 1992). Positive outcomes of such programs have included increased resilience and self-regulation and reduced internalizing symptoms and reported stress (Christopher et al., 2016; Himelstein et al., 2012; Jha et al., 2017; Kabat-Zinn et al., 1992).

Several mindfulness-based professional development programs have been designed for the unique challenges of educators. These programs, which include Stress Management and Relaxation Techniques (SMART) in Education (Cullen & Wallace, 2010), Modified Mindfulness-Based Stress Reduction (mMBSR) (Flook et al., 2013), and Cultivating Awareness and Resilience in Education (CARE) (Jennings et al., 2016), have been tested in research studies and shown to support educator SEC and well-being through the use of mindful practices (Klingbeil & Renshaw, 2018; Lomas et al., 2017). Educators who participated in these programs reported reduced personal distress and physical health symptoms and increased self-compassion, mindfulness, and emotion regulation (Flook et al., 2013; Jennings et al., 2013, 2017; Roeser et al., 2013). Furthermore, these programs have shown promise for helping alleviate burnout symptoms through decreased emotional exhaustion and increased feelings of personal accomplishment (Flook et al., 2013; Jennings et al., 2017; Roeser et al., 2013).

Improvements in educator SEC and well-being can have positive downstream effects. Jennings and Greenberg (2009) provided the Prosocial Classroom conceptual model elucidating how teacher characteristics may affect student outcomes; they hypothesized that teachers with greater SEC and well-being would be better able to support healthy student-teacher relationships, effective classroom management, and effective SEL implementation. These positive actions, in turn, could facilitate a healthier classroom climate and improved social, emotional, and academic outcomes for students (Jennings & Greenberg, 2009). A recent report by Mahfouz et al. (2019) presented the Prosocial School Leader model, a parallel model to Jennings and Greenberg (2009) but focused on administrators (see Figure 17.1). This model demonstrates the importance of the cultivation of school leader SEC and well-being to support healthy relationships, strong family and community partnerships, effective leadership, and SEL implementation. Mahfouz and Gordon (2020) further elaborated on this model, concluding that principals' well-being must be prioritized to ensure desired outcomes for students and the school community.

Figure 17.1

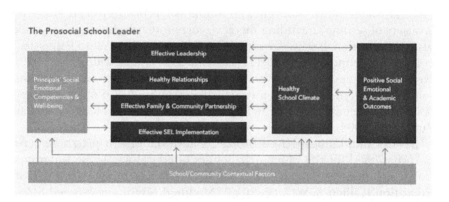

Source: Mahfouz et al. (2019).

Other research has indicated support for the Prosocial School Leader theoretical model. Beatty (2009) discussed the potential negative impacts of principals' inadequate "emotional preparedness to manage their feelings of insecurity" on teachers' well-being and leadership development (p. 194) and discussed the importance of "inner leadership" for authentic collaboration and systemic improvement (p. 197). Grobler and Conley (2014) concluded that intrapersonal emotional competence affected competence in interactions with others and the ability to model effective teaching; it also indirectly affected other instructional leadership components. They found that emotional competence dimensions and instructional leadership components were linked to student achievement as well (Grobler & Conley, 2014). Cherkowski et al. (2020), in their qualitative study examining flourishing for school principals, concluded that "Flourishing in the work of leading seemed to be about creating conditions for teachers, students and others in the school to work together towards shared goals in climates of care, connection, trust, innovation and improvement, fun and laughter" (p. 385).

The rest of this chapter focuses on the Cultivating Awareness and Resilience in Education (CARE) program, which is based on the Prosocial Classroom and Prosocial School Leader models referenced above, and has been researched with teachers and administrators. Information is provided on program components used to promote SEC and well-being, and practical suggestions and resources are offered to illustrate how one can incorporate these practices into work and life.

CARE PRACTICES THAT SUPPORT SEC AND WELL-BEING

CARE is a mindfulness-based professional development program that uses a menu of activities and practices to support and improve SEC and well-being. One of the program goals is to help participants find new ways to handle stressful situations as they arise. We all have ways that we cope with stress. These techniques can be either healthy or unhealthy and effective or ineffective (see Figure 17.2). Consider, for example, working extra hours to cope with job demands. This practice may be effective, in that one may feel a sense of relief when more work is done, but it may not be healthy if done for too long. Extra time spent working can take educational leaders away from their families and other activities they enjoy, leaving them feeling even more depleted. What may be effective in the short term may lead to feelings of burnout if kept up for too long. Take a moment to think about your most frequently used coping skills. Are they effective? Are they healthy? CARE provides additional skills to help cultivate resilience to the stressors inherent in administrative work.

An important caveat about mindfulness practices is that they are not always going to bring feelings of peace and relaxation. While the hope is that, in the long run, our distress tolerance improves and more pleasant feelings arise, during practice, it is about accepting whatever emotions, thoughts, or sensations are happening in the present moment. As the saying goes, "The present isn't always pleasant"; that said, whatever is being experienced is transitory. The longer one practices mindfulness, the more one may notice things change; thoughts, feelings, and bodily sensations all come and go. Acceptance of what is happening doesn't mean giving up hope for improvement; it means being with what is happening right now in an equanimous way. When trying these practices, know that feeling distracted is not uncommon. Each time the mind wanders, it is an opportunity to practice mindfulness and redirect attention, on purpose, in the present

Figure 17.2

Stress Management Techniques

moment, nonjudgmentally. As with any sport or musical instrument, the more we practice, the more skillful we become. The following are a few basic mindfulness practices and activities to consider.

Take Three Deep Breaths

Taking deep breaths [helped] when dealing with an angry grandparent. I stopped talking and started taking breaths as I listened to her speak.

—School administrator.

The most basic of practices that CARE offers is taking three deep breaths, sometimes called a purposeful pause. The basic instruction for this practice is to mindfully attend to the in-breath and the out-breath during three long, slow, deep breaths. One can notice the breath wherever it is felt most strongly; for some people, the breath is felt at the base of the nose, and for others, it is in the rise and fall of the chest. The purpose is just to bring attention to the breath wherever it is felt. This practice helps regulate the autonomic nervous system by activating the vagus nerve (De Couck et al., 2019) and can help increase self-awareness and focus on the present moment. It can also help with self-regulation, giving a moment to pause so that we can respond with care rather than reacting automatically to challenging situations. For example, this type of practice can be done right before entering the school building, or before picking up a phone call from an angry parent.

Deep breathing can also be used in a group setting to encourage attention and focus on what is happening in the present moment. For example, administrators can offer a purposeful pause at the beginning of a meeting to help people settle in. This practice is one of the suggested welcoming inclusion activities in CASEL's Three Signature Practices (CASEL, 2019).

Set Daily Intentions

> *I set intentions in the morning when I first wake up ... I do body scans at night as well.*
>
> —Veteran secondary school teacher.

In CARE, reconnecting with the original values that inspired work in education is essential. Drawing these values intentionally into daily life takes practice. Taking a moment in the morning to set an intention can be vital for alignment with core values. Intentions are often simple—a single word or a phrase that reminds us of how we wish to be today can be enough. Intentions that have been shared in CARE workshops include "Listen more, talk less," "Be kind," and "Focus on one thing at a time." These may sound simple or even a little naïve, but it is surprising how much, if attuned to these intentions, a person can notice—that is, that they are indeed talking too much, letting their temper get the best of them, or trying to multitask in ways that undermine productivity. Intentions are not something to "set and forget"; it is important to check in on them regularly throughout the day. Intentions, unlike goals, cannot be "met"; there is a constant call of recommitment to an intention each time one enters into another conversation or interaction, or when another task needs attention.

Perform a Body Scan

The body scan is a way to practice purposeful, focused attention, becoming aware of what is happening during a time of stillness. It is done by systematically attending to each part of the body and noticing whatever is present, starting either at the head or the feet, and moving attention the entire length of the body. We often notice our bodies when we are in pain, but we do not typically attend to it otherwise. During the practice, you may also notice thoughts and emotions, along with bodily sensations (e.g., tension, tightness, tingling, pulsing), all coming and going. The intention is not to get drawn into these events but rather just allowing them to fade into the background as attention is drawn to the next part of the body. Practicing this equanimity during a body scan can help to strengthen one's ability to engage in a similar way during times of difficulty. CARE program participants often discuss using the full practice before bed or when they wake up in the morning.

This type of somatic practice can also be done at work, although typically in a briefer form. Many people are aware of where they hold stress in the body; common places include the jaw, the shoulders, or the stomach. Taking a moment throughout the day to stop and scan the body, especially the areas prone to holding stress, can help bring awareness to what is happening. It is not uncommon if muscles are left tensed all day to experience pain or discomfort. Bringing this awareness to the body can allow choices to be made on ways to proceed—for example, mindful stretching may be used if tension is found to bring some relief.

Set Healthy Boundaries

Limit work after hours and on the weekends when possible. Attempt to exercise. Spend quality time with friends and family.

—Veteran district leader.

To engage in any sort of self-care, there needs to be time set aside. It is easy, if one is not careful, to allow work to bleed over into even the most basic self-care practices, like eating right or sleeping enough. For example, sleep disturbance is one of the leading consequences of stress (Jackson, 2013). Although it may seem like a good idea to cut into sleep time to get more work done, doing so can have paradoxical effects. Lack of sleep can leave a person exhausted and less effective in performing demanding tasks. Barber et al. (2013) found that those with poorer sleep hygiene had lower self-regulation, higher feelings of depletion, and were less engaged at work.

Allowing enough hours of sleep is essential. Furthermore, stopping work at a reasonable time in the evening to avoid cognitive interference with sleep (e.g., worrying, planning) is vital. There may be a temptation to go ahead and answer a few more emails before bed, but, aside from interfering with sleep, doing so can set expectations that (a) you will regularly answer after-hours emails and (b) others should do the same. Becoming aware of how you spend your time and creating healthy boundaries around work is not only crucial for personal self-care, it also models balance for others.

Make Time for Things You Enjoy

We go camping practically every weekend ... I find that to be relaxing to get away and sit in the woods ... I also enjoy golf because when I am on the course, I am focused only on the moment.

—Veteran district administrator.

Regardless of what it is that you enjoy, it is important to find at least a little time for it as often as possible. While going camping is not something that can be done every day, spending time talking with a loved one, playing with a pet, or getting some exercise is. In a recent study, 43% of administrators surveyed reported working out as a form of self-care they regularly engaged in (Doyle Fosco, Brown, et al., 2023). Aerobic exercise for as little as 20 minutes has been shown to help people feel calmer immediately; in addition, the feelings of calm persisted for several hours afterward (Jackson, 2013). Other forms of exercise, such as yoga and tai chi, have also shown positive benefits when done regularly (Jackson, 2013). Exercise can provide a break from the stressors being experienced, as well as potentially causing changes in neurotransmitters such as dopamine and serotonin (Jackson, 2013).

Consider taking an inventory of the things you enjoy and referring to that list when you are contemplating ways to support your own well-being. Some people have trouble engaging in activities that they enjoy when under stress. There is a tendency to feel guilty, thinking that the time could be better spent on work. It is important to remember that self-care is how we recharge so we have the necessary resources to keep from burning out.

CARE: AN OVERVIEW

The previous section provided a sampling of practices to support well-being; this section provides an overview of the CARE program. CARE was developed by Patricia Jennings, Christa Turksma, and Richard Brown with support from the Garrison Institute and has been offered in a retreat setting during the summer since 2007. In 2015, a revised program was developed specifically for the needs of principals and other administrators.

CARE has shown positive effects through research with teachers (Jennings et al., 2011, 2013, 2017, 2019; Schussler et al., 2016, 2019) and school and district administrators (Doyle Fosco, Schussler et al., 2023; Mahfouz, 2018).

Offerings

CARE includes a menu of mindful awareness practices, emotional awareness skills, caring and compassion topics, and community-building activities. Participants are encouraged to select practices that they can implement in their life and work to help reduce stress and improve well-being. This type of professional development focuses on cultivating skills that educators can use themselves, rather than concentrating on learning skills to teach to others; however, it is not entirely self-focused. CARE also incorporates interpersonal skills such as mindful listening and compassionate responding, which are highly relevant to work-life with students, staff, parents, and others in the school community. Such skills are especially relevant for demonstrating SEC.

Table 17.1

CARE Program Components

Emotion skills instruction	Mindfulness/Stress reduction practices	Compassion practices
Approximately 40%	Approximately 40%	Approximately 20%
1. Introduction to emotions, purpose, universal expressions, relevant brain research 2. How emotions affect teaching and learning 3. Didactic information about "uncomfortable" or negative emotions (anger, fear, sadness) including physiology, cognitive and behavioral responses 4. Didactic information about "comfortable" or positive emotions (joy, appreciation) including physiology, cognitive and behavioral responses 5. Exploring bodily awareness of emotions 6. Exploring individual differences in emotional experiences (emotional profile, triggers & scripts) 8. Practice using mindful awareness and reflection to recognize and manage strong emotions	1. Body awareness reflection 2. Basic breath awareness practice 3. Mindfulness of thoughts and emotion practice 4. Mindful movement practices (standing, walking, stretching, centering) 9. Practice maintaining mindful awareness in front of a group 10. Role plays to practice mindfulness in the context of a strong emotion related to a challenging classroom situation	1. "Caring practice" – A series of guided reflections focused on caring for self, loved one, colleague, challenging person 2. Mindful listening partner practices, one person reads a poem or talks about a problem, partner listens mindfully practicing presence and acceptance

Note: Table from Jennings et al.(2013, p. 379).

Practices are introduced sequentially, starting with brief practices that can be used in the moment (e.g., taking three deep breaths). Longer, more complex practices that can be extrapolated for work or used at home to strengthen awareness (e.g., 10-minute body scans) are introduced later. Emotional awareness skills (e.g., understanding our triggers) are experienced through activities, reflection, and discussion; practices such as "experiencing joy" are also used to help participants identify somatic experiences associated with emotions. Cultivation and recall of these pleasant emotions are encouraged to help in times of stress.

CARE has an explicit recognition of the impact of trauma and how past traumatic and emotional experiences can shape (often without consciousness) current responses to others (e.g., students, teachers, parents). Caring and compassion topics and practices are taught through didactic presentation and discussion on empathy and compassion, and through practices such as "caring practice" (cultivating caring thoughts for self/others) and mindful listening. A workbook is provided for participants and additional resources, including downloadable guided mindfulness practices, blog posts on related topics, and prerecorded webinars, are available through CREATE for Education (see Resources at the end of this chapter).

In addition to the skills and practices taught in CARE, the group format creates a supportive context. Delivered in small groups, the program includes an explicit focus on community-building. Developing a "learning community" has been shown to offer administrators a chance to bond with one another (Mahfouz, 2018), something they don't often have an opportunity to do in their daily work. This can help counter the loneliness inherent with administrative positions, especially for those in smaller school contexts. In addition to being able to discuss issues related to well-being with fellow administrators, there is also a built-in component focused on exploring ways to encourage sustainability by supporting one another outside of the sessions. Furthermore, administrators can also work together to consider ways to support their school communities.

CARE Research

A series of randomized trials, funded by the U.S. Department of Education, have found improvements for teachers who received CARE, including increased mindfulness and adaptive emotion regulation, and decreased personal and physical distress and time urgency (Jennings et al., 2013, 2017); one study also found increased teaching efficacy (Jennings et al., 2013). In qualitative research looking at mechanisms of change related to CARE participation, Schussler et al. (2016) found that teachers reported greater self-awareness and less emotional reactivity; they also gained a greater appreciation of the need for self-care. In later interviews, Schussler et al. (2019) noted that teachers' resilience was supported through improved awareness, nonreactivity, and feelings of self-efficacy, combined with an ability to tolerate feelings of distress. Jennings et al. (2017) reported downstream effects of teachers' participation in CARE, including improvements in classroom organization and emotional support. Brown et al (2023) also found positive results for some teacher-reported student academic outcomes.

More recently, studies have also been conducted with the revised CARE program for administrators. In a qualitative analysis, Mahfouz (2018) found that administrators in a rural Pennsylvania district who took part in a 30-hour CARE program showed improvements in their leadership skills through an increased ability for self-reflection and better relationships with others. As the teachers did, administrators also showed greater attention to their own self-care (Mahfouz, 2018). In a separate study, at the end of a three-day CARE workshop, Doyle et al. (2019) found that 82% of administrators reported improved self-awareness and said that they would be better able to manage behaviors effectively and compassionately.

USING CARE TO CULTIVATE AUTHENTIC LEADERSHIP

In the wise words of Eleanor Brownn (2014), "Self-care is not selfish. You cannot serve from an empty vessel." The skills taught in the CARE program are valuable tools as we consider components that foster authentic leadership. Authentic leadership comes from the cultivation of intrapersonal and interpersonal emotional competence. Walumbwa et al. (2008) define authentic leadership as "a pattern of leader behavior that draws upon and promotes both positive psychological capacities and a positive ethical climate" (p. 94). This style of leadership focuses on understanding our own values and using those values to guide our behavior (Northouse, 2019). Intrapersonal aspects of authentic leadership include self-awareness, values-driven self-regulation, and having a strong understanding of who you are and your place in the educational environment; George and Sims (2007) referred to this as finding your "true north" (p. xxiii). Interpersonal aspects to authentic leadership are important because every day we affect others around us and, in turn, are affected by them (Northouse, 2019). Our Socratic ability to "know thyself" at any given moment—that is, knowing our own emotions, thoughts, feelings, and values—is vitally important to our ability to engage authentically in our relationships with others.

Four Key Components

Walumbwa et al. (2008) postulated four key components of authentic leadership: self-awareness, internalized moral perspective, balanced processing, and relational transparency:

Self-awareness. Developing self-awareness is vital to our well-being and also strengthens leadership. The better we can identify, respect, and value our own inner experiences, the more we are able to offer and model this accepting attitude toward others. Part of the journey of learning about these inner experiences can be simply acknowledging them and sitting with them for a few moments when they occur. Using techniques such as a body scan to notice what is happening in the body, especially when feeling uncomfortable emotions, can help develop this self-awareness. As one CARE administrator participant said, "When I feel myself getting stressed, using the practices helps me to take a mental pause away from things and regroup." This "regrouping" allows time to notice what is occurring in the body and mind, so, as a leader, one can act from a place of awareness based on deeply held values. Knowing one's own strengths, weaknesses, thoughts, feelings, and values helps lay the groundwork for deep understanding of those around us.

Internalized moral perspective. Developing an internalized moral perspective refers to the moral standards and values that serve as a guide for interacting in the world (Northouse, 2019). CARE encourages this process through the identification of the values that support compassionate responding in a leadership role. It can be easy for the values that we once felt so strongly to be set aside in our day-to-day work. In CARE, these values are re-explored and supported through daily intention setting. Rather than being goal-oriented, setting a daily intention has an aspirational focus and can provide a compass that guides us in the work we do.

Balanced processing. Balanced processing is the ability to take in information from all sides and maintain a level of equanimity in the process (Northouse, 2019). As we learn to manage our own emotions, notice potentially triggering situations, become aware of our judgments of others, and cultivate compassion even for those we disagree with, we are more able to maintain this balanced state. CARE practices can help with this processing; one veteran district administrator said they were "much calmer, less judgmental, [and] more focused and attentive" after participating in the program.

Relational transparency. This final component can be challenging because the emotional labor in administrative positions can bend away from authenticity (Gardner et al., 2009). Northouse (2019) noted that relational transparency occurs when "individuals share their core feelings, motives, and inclinations with others in an appropriate manner" (p. 204).

Interpersonal skills such as mindful listening and compassionate responding can be helpful in identifying the best ways to engage in such transparency. One does not have to bear all, but one does need to be genuine, which may mean acknowledging having certain emotions or motivations when it is safe to do so. A leader's willingness to engage in this way can also serve as a model to support staff authenticity.

George (2003) posited that as a person grows in their authentic leadership, they are more purposeful, value-centered, self-disciplined, and relationship-oriented; *they are* willing to share themselves with others andshow genuine interest in the welfare of others. This orientation produces more passionate and compassionate leaders, whose behaviors are more consistent and driven by their values, and who are more connected to their staff (George, 2003). Cultivating these traits through mindful awareness and exploring one's emotional landscape can improve personal SEC and well-being. This personal transformation can also improve staff outcomes. Authentic leadership has been shown to correlate with employee creativity and satisfaction, optimism and trust, and work engagement (Northouse, 2019).

CONCLUSION

In the words of Jon Kabat-Zinn (2005), "While it may be simple to practice mindfulness, it is not necessarily easy" (p. 8). Our minds are wired to go on automatic pilot, to use the same well-worn neural pathways they always have. Mindfulness requires doing something different—that is, continually bringing attention to what is happening in the present moment. Caryn M. Wells (2013), who served as a high school principal for 10 years, talked about the importance of administrators being mindful, saying: "Paradoxically [mindfulness] is not about *striving* to relax, unwind, or do. Instead, [it] is about developing a sense of *being* not *doing*" (p. 344 [emphasis in original]). This act of learning how to *be*, rather than just doing what we always have, can improve self-awareness and self-care (Mahfouz, 2018 [emphasis added]). These improvements can lead to interpersonal changes as well, helping us improve our relationships and our ability to be authentic leaders.

It is not always possible to intervene by reducing the number of actual stressors one is exposed to on the job, so it is imperative that preventive interventions are used to manage the effects of such stressors (Wells, 2013). Mindfulness-based interventions such as the CARE program can offer additional tools to help with the challenges of working in educational environments. This program can be offered to teachers, school staff, and administrators to support social and emotional competence and improve whole-school well-being. Creating a culture of well-being in the school district that supports the SEC of adults through explicit professional development and through leadership modeling of self-care has the potential to alleviate issues of burnout and turnover that plague public education.

Furthermore, as the adults in the school building improve in their own self-awareness and emotion regulation, they are better able to model and use these vital skills with their students. As Dorothy Law Nolte's (1972) famous poem is entitled to convey, "[C]hildren learn what they live"; students' experiences of teacher and administrator SEC, combined with focused SEL curricula that explicitly teach tools and strategies, can ultimately have positive downstream effects on their success. As educators, it behooves us to focus on our own SEC and well-being, if for no other reason than to offer the best education possible for students.

THOUGHT QUESTIONS FOR ADMINISTRATORS

1. How does your well-being affect those around you both in and out of the workplace?
2. How do you set healthy boundaries around your work? What does that look like in your life?
3. Can you think of moments during the workday that you could engage in a mindfulness practice to support your well-being?
4. What would a culture of well-being look like in your school or district? How does taking care of yourself fit in?

THOUGHT QUESTIONS FOR THOSE SUPPORTING ADMINISTRATORS

1. What are the implicit (or explicit) messages given to administrators about work/life balance?
2. How can you support administrators in making healthy choices to prioritize their well-being (e.g., protecting lunch breaks as a time of rest)?
3. What systemic supports can be offered to promote social and emotional competence and well-being for all people in the educational environment?

RESOURCES

- CARE
    - o Learn more about the CARE program and find resources from CREATE for Education: createforeducation.org

- Find guided audio practices from the CARE program at: createforeducation.org/resources/mindfulness-practices/
- Additional information about CARE is available through the Garrison Institute: garrisoninstitute.org/initiatives/programs
- CASEL—A district-wide SEL implementation guide for superintendents: drc.casel.org/superintendent/
- Mindfulness and relaxation
  - Resources are available through the UCLA Mindful Awareness Research Center: uclahealth.org/marc
  - More research and resources related to education are available from the Mindfulness in Education Network: mindfuled.org
  - Wanting to explore different types of relaxation practices? *Insight Timer* has thousands freely available: insighttimer.com
- SEL—Transforming Education offers a school leader a self-reflection tool for the integration of SEL in schools: transformingeducation.org/school-leader-educator-reflection-tools/

ACKNOWLEDGMENTS

I would like to thank Dr. Mark Greenberg and the manuscript reviewers for their willingness to read drafts and provide valuable input on this chapter.

REFERENCES

Barber, L., Grawitch, M. J., & Munz, D. C. (2013). Are better sleepers more engaged workers? A self-regulatory approach to sleep hygiene and work engagement. *Stress and Health*, 29(4), 307–316. https://doi.org/10.1002/smi.2468

Beatty, B. R. (2009). Toward and emotional understanding of school success: Connecting collaborative culture building, principal succession and inner leadership. In L. C. Ehrich & N. Cranston (Eds.), *Australian school leadership today* (pp. 187–216). Australian Academic Press.

Boyland, L. (2011). Job stress and coping strategies of elementary principals: A statewide study. *Current Issues in Education*, 14(3).

Brown, J. L., Jennings, P. A., Rasheed, D. S., Cham, H., Doyle Fosco, S. L., Frank, J. L., Davis, R., Greenberg, M. T. (2023, June 20). Direct and moderating impacts of the CARE Mindfulness-Based Professional Learning Program for Teachers on Children's Academic and Social-Emotional Outcomes. https://doi.org/10.31234/osf.io/2afys

Brownn, E. (2014). *Your whole life is ahead of you* [Blog post]. http://www.eleanorbrownn.com/blog2/self-care-in-not-selfish

Collaboration for Academic, Social, and Emotional Learning (CASEL). (2013). *CASEL Guide: Effective social and emotional learning programs* (Preschool and elementary school ed.). In *Collaborative for academic, social and emotional learning*. http://casel.org/wp-content/uploads/2016/01/2013-casel-guide-1.pdf

Collaboration for Academic, Social, and Emotional Learning (CASEL). (2019). *SEL 3 signature practices playbook*. https://drc.casel.org/uploads/sites/3/2019/02/Summary-The-SEL-3-Signature-Practices.pdf

Cherkowski, S., Kutsyuruba, B., & Walker, K. (2020). Positive leadership: Animating purpose, presence, passion and play for flourishing in schools. *Journal of Educational Administration*, 58(4), 401–415. https://doi.org/10.1108/JEA-04-2019-0076

Christopher, M. S., Goerling, R. J., Rogers, B. S., Hunsinger, M., Baron, G., Bergman, A. L., & Zava, D. T. (2016). A pilot study evaluating the effectiveness of a mindfulness-based intervention on cortisol awakening response and health outcomes among law enforcement officers. *Journal of Police and Criminal Psychology*, 31(1), 15–28. https://doi.org/10.1007/s11896-015-9161-x

Cullen, M., & Wallace, L. (2010). *Stress management and relaxation techniques in education (SMART) training manual*. Impact Foundation.

De Couck, M., Caers, R., Musch, L., Fliegauf, J., Giangreco, A., & Gidron, Y. (2019). How breathing can help you make better decisions: Two studies on the effects of breathing patterns on heart rate variability and decision-making in business cases. *International Journal of Psychophysiology*, 139, 1–9. https://doi.org/10.1016/j.ijpsycho.2019.02.011

Doyle Fosco, S. L., Brown, M. A., & Schussler, D. L. (2023) Factors affecting educational leader wellbeing: Sources of stress and self-care. *Educational Management Administration & Leadership*. https://doi.org/10.1177/17411432231184601

Doyle Fosco, S.L., Schussler, D. L., & Jennings, P.A. (2023) Acceptability of a mindfulness-based professional development program to support educational leader wellbeing. *Mindfulness*. https://doi.org/10.1007/s12671-023-02182-9

Flook, L., Goldberg, S. B., Pinger, L., Bonus, K., & Davidson, R. J. (2013). Mindfulness for teachers: A pilot study to assess effects on stress, burnout, and teaching efficacy. *Mind, Brain, and Education*, 7(3), 182–195. https://doi.org/10.1111/mbe.12026

Friedman, I. A. (2002). Burnout in school principals: Role related antecedents. *Social Psychology of Education*, 5(3), 229–251. https://doi.org/10.1023/A:1016321210858

Gardner, W. L., Fischer, D., & Hunt, J. G. (2009). Emotional labor and leadership: A threat to authenticity? *Leadership Quarterly*, 20(3), 466–482. https://doi.org/10.1016/j.leaqua.2009.03.011

George, B. (2003). *Authentic leadership: Rediscovering the secrets to creating lasting value.* Jossey-Bass.

George, B., & Sims, P. (2007). *True north: Discover your authentic leadership.* Jossey-Bass.

Greenberg, M. T., Domitrovich, C. E., Weissberg, R. P., & Durlak, J. A. (2017). Social and emotional learning as a public health approach to education. *Future of Children, 27*(1), 13–32. https://doi.org/10.1353/foc.2017.0001

Grobler, B., & Conley, L. (2014). The relationship between emotional competence and instructional leadership and their association with learner achievement. *Education as Change, 17*, 201–223. https://doi.org/10.1080/16823206.2013.866003

Himelstein, S., Hastings, A., Shapiro, S., & Heery, M. (2012). Mindfulness training for self-regulation and stress with incarcerated youth: A pilot study. *Probation Journal, 59*(2), 151–165. https://doi.org/10.1177/0264550512438256

Jackson, E. M. (2013). Stress relief: The role of exercise in stress management. *ACSM's Health and Fitness Journal, 17*(3), 14–19.

Jennings, P. A., Brown, J. L., Frank, J. L., Doyle, S. L., Oh, Y., Davis, R., Rasheed, D., DeWeese, A., DeMauro, A. A., Cham, H., & Greenberg, M. T. (2017). Impacts of the CARE for teachers program on teachers' social and emotional competence and classroom interactions. *Journal of Educational Psychology*, 1–19. https://doi.org/10.1037/edu0000187

Jennings, P. A., Doyle, S., Oh, Y., Rasheed, D., Frank, J. L., & Brown, J. L. (2019). Long-term impacts of the CARE program on teachers' self-reported social and emotional competence and well-being. *Journal of School Psychology, 76*, 186–202. https://doi.org/10.1016/j.jsp.2019.07.009

Jennings, P. A., Frank, J. L., Snowberg, K. E., Coccia, M. A., & Greenberg, M. T. (2013). Improving classroom learning environments by Cultivating Awareness and Resilience in Education (CARE): Results of a randomized controlled trial. *School Psychology Quarterly, 28*(4), 374–390. https://doi.org/10.1037/spq0000035

Jennings, P. A., & Greenberg, M. T. (2009). The prosocial classroom: Teacher social and emotional competence in relation to student and classroom outcomes. *Review of Educational Research, 79*(1), 491–525. https://doi.org/10.3102/0034654308325693

Jennings, P. A., Snowberg, K. E., Coccia, M. A., & Greenberg, M. T. (2011). Improving classroom learning environments by cultivating awareness and resilience in education (CARE): Results of two pilot studies. *The Journal of Classroom Interaction, 46*(1), 37–48. http://www.jstor.org/stable/23870550

Jennings, P. A., Turksma, C., & Brown, R. (2016). *Cultivating awareness and resilience in education (CARE) professional development program manual.* Garrison Institute.

Jha, A. P., Morrison, A. B., Parker, S. C., & Stanley, E. A. (2017). Practice is protective: Mindfulness training promotes cognitive resilience in high-stress cohorts. *Mindfulness, 8*(1), 46–58. https://doi.org/10.1007/s12671-015-0465-9

Jones, D. E., Greenberg, M., & Crowley, M. (2015). Early social-emotional functioning and public health: The relationship between kindergarten social competence and future wellness. *American Journal of Public Health, 105*(11), 2283–2290. https://doi.org/10.2105/AJPH.2015.302630

Kabat-Zinn, J. (2003). Mindfulness-based interventions in context: Past, present, and future. *Clinical Psychology: Science and Practice, 10*(2), 144–156. https://doi.org/10.1093/clipsy/bpg016

Kabat-Zinn, J. (2005). *Wherever you go, there you are: Mindfulness meditation in everyday life*. Hatchette Books.

Kabat-Zinn, J., Massion, A. O., Kristeller, J., Peterson, L. G., Fletcher, K. E., Pbert, L., Lenderking, W. R., & Santorelli, S. F. (1992). Effectiveness of a meditation-based stress reduction program in the treatment of anxiety disorders. *American Journal of Psychiatry, 149*(7), 936–943. https://doi.org/10.1037/a0022272

Klingbeil, D. A., & Renshaw, T. L. (2018). Mindfulness-based interventions for teachers: A meta-analysis of the emerging evidence base. *School Psychology Quarterly, 33*(4), 501–511. https://doi.org/10.1037/spq0000291

Klocko, B. A., & Wells, C. M. (2015). Workload pressures of principals: A focus on renewal, support, and mindfulness. *NASSP Bulletin, 99*(4), 332–355. https://doi.org/10.1177/0192636515619727

Lambersky, J. (2016). Understanding the human side of school leadership: principals' impact on teachers' morale, self-efficacy, stress, and commitment. *Leadership and Policy in Schools, 15*(4), 379–405. https://doi.org/10.1080/15700763.2016.1181188

Law Nolte, D. (1972). *Children learn what they live poem*. Workman Publishing.

Levin, S., Leung, M., Edgerton, A. K., & Scott, C. (2020, October). *Elementary school principals' professional learning: Current status and future needs* http://learningpolicyinstitute

Lomas, T., Medina, J. C., Ivtzan, I., Rupprecht, S., & Eiroa-Orosa, F. J. (2017). The impact of mindfulness on the wellbeing and performance of educators: A systematic review of the empirical literature. *Teaching and Teacher Education, 61*, 132–141. https://doi.org/10.1016/j.tate.2016.10.008

Mahfouz, J. (2018). Mindfulness training for school administrators: effects on wellbeing and leadership. *Journal of Educational Administration, 56*(6), 602–619. https://doi.org/10.1108/JEA-12-2017-0171

Mahfouz, J., & Gordon, D. (2020). The case for focusing on school principals' social–emotional competencies. *Management in Education*, 1–5. https://doi.org/10.1177/0892020620932351

Mahfouz, J., Greenberg, M. T., & Rodriguez, A. (2019, October). *Principals' social and emotional competence: A key factor for creating caring schools*. http://prevention.psu.edu/uploads/files/PSU-Principals-Brief-103119.pdf

Mahfouz, J., Greenberg, M. T., Weissberg, R. P., Kim, C., & Turksma, C. (n.d.). *The prosocial school leader: Theory, research, and action*. [Could you provide a publication or a URL for this reference?]

Mahoney, J. L., Weissberg, R. P., Greenberg, M. T., Dusenbury, L., Jagers, R. J., Niemi, K., Schlinger, M., Schlund, J., Shriver, T. P., VanAusdal, K., & Yoder, N. (2020). Systemic social and emotional learning: Promoting educational success for all preschool to high school students. *American Psychologist*. https://doi.org/10.1037/amp0000701

Maxwell, A., & Riley, P. (2017). Emotional demands, emotional labour and occupational outcomes in school principals: Modelling the relationships. *Educational Management Administration and Leadership*, *45*(3), 484–502. https://doi.org/10.1177/1741143215607878

Northouse, P. G. (2019). *Leadership: theory and practice* (8th ed.). SAGE.

Oberle, E., Gist, A., Cooray, M. S., & Pinto, J. B. R. (2020). Do students notice stress in teachers? Associations between classroom teacher burnout and students' perceptions of teacher social-emotional competence. *Psychology in the Schools*, *57*(11), 1741–1756. https://doi.org/10.1002/pits.22432

Price, H. E. (2012). Principal-teacher interactions: How affective relationships shape principal and teacher attitudes. *Educational Administration Quarterly*, *48*(1), 39–85. https://doi.org/10.1177/0013161X11417126

Robinson, K., & Shakeshaft, C. (2016). Superintendent stress and superintendent health: A national study. *Journal of Education and Human Development*, *5*(1). https://doi.org/10.15640/jehd.v5n1a13

Roeser, R. W., Schonert-Reichl, K. A., Jha, A., Cullen, M., Wallace, L., Wilensky, R., Oberle, E., Thomson, K., Taylor, C., & Harrison, J. (2013). Mindfulness training and reductions in teacher stress and burnout: Results from two randomized, waitlist-control field trials. *Journal of Educational Psychology*, *105*(3). https://doi.org/10.1037/a0032093

Schussler, D. L., DeWeese, A., Rasheed, D., DeMauro, A. A., Doyle, S. L., Brown, J. L., Greenberg, M. T., & Jennings, P. A. (2019). The relationship between adopting mindfulness practice and reperceiving: A qualitative investigation of CARE for teachers. *Mindfulness*, *10*(12), 2567–2582. https://doi.org/10.1007/s12671-019-01228-1

Schussler, D. L., Jennings, P. A., Sharp, J. E., & Frank, J. L. (2016). Improving teacher awareness and well-being through CARE: A qualitative analysis of the underlying mechanisms. *Mindfulness*, *7*(1), 130–142. https://doi.org/10.1007/s12671-015-0422-7

Walumbwa, F. O., Avolio, B. J., Gardner, W. L., Wernsing, T. S., & Peterson, S. J. (2008). Authentic leadership: Development and validation of a theory-based measure. *Journal of Management*, *34*(1), 89–126. https://doi.org/10.1177/0149206307308913

Wells, C. M. (2013). Principals responding to constant pressure: Finding a source of stress management. *NASSP Bulletin*, *97*(4), 335–349. https://doi.org/10.1177/0192636513504453

CHAPTER 18

RESPECTING COMMUNICATION SKILLS

The Missing Link for the Well-Being of Educators and Their Schools

Deborah L. Schussler and Jennifer L. Frank

> *It doesn't matter how smart the kid is, if they have problems and you can't deal with them and they can't deal with them, then they're not going to learn anything.*
>
> —Middle school teacher.

The growing realization that students' social-emotional learning (SEL) depends on the social-emotional competence (SEC) of the educators who work with them holds promise for fulfilling the vision of prosocial classrooms (Jennings & Greenberg, 2009) and schools (Mahfouz et al., 2019). Evidence suggests that educator stress provokes student stress (Greenberg et al., 2016; Oberle & Schonert-Reichl, 2016). It is not surprising, then, that recent professional development programs have focused on improving educators' SEC for the multifaceted purposes of mitigating stress and improving well-being for both educators and their students.

Surprisingly, however, these professional development programs that focus on educator SEC do not explicitly teach *communication skills*.[1] Although the features of effective interpersonal communication and conflict management are well known (Becvar & Becvar, 1998; Deetz & Stevenson, 1986; Rosenberg, 2003), communication is not emphasized in educator preservice or in-service professional development programs. Communication is foundational to educator SEC. Without good communication, healthy interpersonal relationships falter, and the likelihood of prosocial schools diminishes.

It is important that effective communication exists at multiple levels, involving teachers and school administrators, to achieve prosocial classrooms and schools. An abundance of research suggests that quality teacher-student interactions enable effectively managed classrooms (see Martin & Dowson, 2009; Pianta et al., 2012). Teachers who engage with students in emotionally supportive ways create positive social contexts for academic learning by developing supportive relationships, designing instruction that capitalizes on students' interests and abilities, implementing behavioral guidelines that promote intrinsic motivation for behavior and academic engagement, and mitigating conflict (Jennings & Greenberg, 2009). There is also research suggesting that administrators enable a positive organizational climate through engaging in what Murphy and Louis (2018) call "positive school leadership," also the title of their book, which includes interpersonal exchanges that build trust and care. Communication is the bedrock of interpersonal relationships, and positive relationships contribute to one's well-being (Cherkowski & Walker, 2018; Seligman, 2011). Therefore, school administrators' ability to communicate effectively and the extent to which their teachers practice effective communication affects all educators' well-being.

Project RESPECT (Responding in Emotionally Supportive and Positive ways in Education Communication skills Training) is a professional development program for secondary educators (i.e., teachers, administrators, and paraprofessionals) that was designed to enhance educators' purposeful communication. It capitalizes on constructs central to educator SEC—constructs such as self-awareness, self-regulation, and empathy-building. In addition, Project RESPECT integrates tenets of effective classroom management, conflict resolution, and academic engagement. It differs from other programs aimed at educator SEC in that it emphasizes the explicit *communication strategies* that help create positive relationships, prosocial classrooms and schools, and motivated learners. When these goals are achieved, classrooms are more productive, and the students and educators who work in those classrooms are more likely to experience less stress and increased well-being. The purpose of this chapter is to show how communication is essential for educator SEC and for developing healthy relationships and student engagement. After a description of Project RESPECT, examples demonstrate how its practices can be used in different settings, along with quotes from educators about their experiences with the program. The chapter concludes with an overview of the research findings.

Respecting Communication Skills 339

BACKGROUND

We use Patterson's Coercive Interaction Cycle as a theoretical framework for conceptualizing how specific educator-student interactions may result in global changes in student and educator behavior, and ultimately student achievement (Patterson et al., 1992). As Figure 18.1 illustrates, the cycle begins when educators respond in a negative, coercive manner to student noncompliance or off-task behavior. Students respond by intensifying their behavior. To avoid conflict, the educator may ignore the student's behavior, resulting in less opportunity for the student to learn (Long et al., 2001; Walker et al., 1995). When a student is not able to engage in the learning tasks of the classroom, they are more likely to engage in off-task behavior, initiating a self-perpetuating cycle. Obviously, this cycle is problematic. By ignoring difficult situations, it reinforces and can intensify students' problematic behaviors; also, by perpetuating the cycle of off-task behaviors, it minimizes students' opportunities to learn. Indeed, studies using this model have found that students in classrooms caught in this coercive interaction cycle experience decreased academic outcomes compared to students in classrooms where educators manage to break this cycle (Granic & Patterson, 2006; Sutherland et al., 2010).

Figure 18.1

Coercive Interaction Cycle

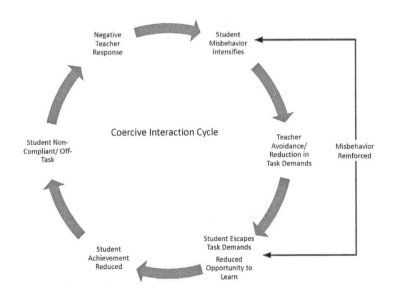

PROJECT RESPECT

Project RESPECT was developed to mitigate the deleterious effects of the Coercive Interaction Cycle, a cycle educators may not even realize exists in their classrooms or schools. The program was designed to: (a) give educators *proactive* skills for building healthy relationships with students, colleagues, and parents so they can engage students academically, and (b) foster productive *responsive* skills for when student-educator conflict occurs. Professional development focusing on SEC generally emphasizes specific domains of educators' *emotional intelligence* (EQ). Goleman (1995) defines EQ as consisting of five domains: self-awareness, emotion regulation, social awareness, relationship skills, and motivation. Educators who are socially emotionally competent are more likely to create emotionally supportive classrooms/schools and less likely to inadvertently engage in the Coercive Interaction Cycle (Brackett et al., 2011; Strati et al., 2017).

Although Project RESPECT was developed primarily for educators who spend most of their day in direct contact with students, such as general education and special education teachers, building principals and district administrators have been a significant part of implementation efforts as it is essential that the program aligns with work school/district goals and philosophies. In addition, because building principals set the tone of the school as an organization, school leaders must model effective communication and emotionally supportive actions as they interact with teachers, students, and parents. Project RESPECT integrates direct instruction, small-group and whole-group discussion, practice, and role play to introduce, explain, and reinforce communication concepts and skills, motivating some administrators to attend Project RESPECT professional development with their teachers.

Project RESPECT explicitly and implicitly teaches skills across all the five EQ domains. It includes modules in self-awareness, empathy, envisioning, growth mindset, conflict management, and nonviolent communication, among others. The knowledge and skills in each module build on each other. Self-awareness, for example, is introduced first because lack of self-awareness of one's values, thoughts, and feelings can lead to misguided interpretations of another's intentions and behaviors (Delpit, 1995; Schussler et al., 2010) as well as to forming unproductive habitual patterns such as that shown in the Coercive Interaction Cycle. Educators are guided through a modified values clarification exercise (see Hayes, 2005) that helps them identify their most important values and beliefs about teaching and the behaviors/actions they take that align with those values and beliefs. Administrators must have skills in self-awareness in order to craft their vision for a prosocial school; educators begin considering how perspective-taking can play a role in their interactions, initially by becoming more aware of how their own values and beliefs affect their perceptions of a situation.

In subsequent modules, educators consider how the values and beliefs of others, especially their students, may result in different perspectives of a particular value or belief. Modules on empathy and active listening emphasize the domains of EQ dealing with social awareness and relationship skills.

Project RESPECT explores empathy as a means of acknowledging students' unmet needs (Klimecki et al., 2014; Miyashiro, 2011); adolescents' problematic behaviors and negative emotions are usually the result of an unmet need. Responding to only the behavior may be a less effective communications strategy, like using medicine to bring down a fever rather than targeting the underlying infection causing the fever. The emphasis on unmet needs is grounded in self-awareness and the self-determination theory (Ryan & Deci, 2017), which emphasizes an individual's need for autonomy (e.g., to be a causal agent in one's life), competence (e.g., to experience mastery), and relatedness (e.g., to connect and experience a sense of caring with others)—needs that manifest in acute ways for adolescents struggling to determine their identity and establish personal agency (La Guardia & Ryan, 2002).

These components of self-awareness and self-determination theory underscore the approach toward academic engagement in Project RESPECT. Through a module on envisioning, educators are encouraged to help their students engage in goal setting and craft their own academic-related identities. A module on growth mindset (Dweck, 2006) helps educators think about ways to build off students' identities and internalize a perspective of continual improvement, even when setbacks occur. Research suggests that a relationship exists between a growth mindset and student motivation, effort, test-score gains, behavior, and confidence (Blackwell et al., 2007; Ehrlinger et al., 2016; West et al., 2016).

Building relationships with students and helping them experience success in the classroom can help prevent off-task and other problematic behaviors. When problems do occur, educators need a way to respond that de-escalates rather than exacerbates the conflict. Conflict management skills include the capacity to advocate for one's position with an open mind, not taking the source of disagreements personally; perspective taking; nonjudgmental information gathering; and flexible problem-solving (Boghossian & Lindsay, 2019; Connor & Killian, 2012). In addition to practicing skills of active listening and emotion self-regulation during confrontational situations, Project RESPECT teaches the specific techniques of nonviolent communication (NVC) (see Rosenberg, 2003), which helps them build empathy by focusing on their own and the other person's unmet needs to reach a mutually acceptable resolution to the conflict.

EXAMPLES

To illustrate how Project RESPECT leverages domains of EQ and principles of effective communication, this section provides examples of how to build self-awareness in administrators and teachers, how to use empathy for conflict resolution, and some helpful ways to begin building a growth mindset in classrooms and schools.

Self-Awareness

> *They [teachers] don't know how to deal with kids that don't live in their circumstances, that's what I see here ... Project RESPECT is a way to maybe make them aware of it. Some of the things they're saying aren't interpreted the way they want them to be interpreted.*
>
> —School superintendent.

Values clarification using InTASC. Self-awareness is essential for establishing the vision of the school and helping the educators within the school perceive situations more accurately so they can best demonstrate their values. To accomplish this, the Project RESPECT program begins with activities and discussion around values and beliefs. We engage educators in a values clarification exercise (see Hayes, 2005), modified specifically for an educational context. Individually, educators are presented with belief statements taken from the 10 critical dispositions of the Interstate New Teacher Assessment and Support Consortium (InTASC) model core teaching standards (Interstate New Teacher Assessment and Support Consortium [InTASC], 2011). These dispositions include such statements as "I respect learners' differing strengths and needs and am committed to using this information to further each learner's development" and "I value planning as a collegial activity that takes into consideration the input of learners, colleagues, families, and the larger community" from the InTASC Standard 1: Learner Development, and InTASC Standard 7: Planning for Instruction, respectively. This exercise is valuable for administrators as well as teachers as it helps each to clarify elemental values for the school as a whole as well as beliefs about what is important in any individual teacher's classroom. Educators complete a 1–5 Likert scale showing strong disagreement to strong agreement on 12 such statements. Anticipating that most educators will show some form of agreement on most of these statements, we then ask them to select the three statements they agree with the most strongly. Educators are then asked to indicate at least two actions for each one that demonstrates their beliefs/values. A discussion should follow, probing which values are most important and why they are important, how educators demonstrate these values, and why there might be areas of misalignment.

This professional development activity could easily occur during a faculty meeting or in grade-level or department team meetings, and a number of modifications or optional extensions can be made. If both teachers and administrators participate in the activity, they can compare their responses to gauge whether school/district values align with teachers' values. Students can complete the assessment for their teachers to give teachers a sense of whether and how their values are perceived by their students. For a more extensive activity, educators can write their own value statements, as they relate to the 10 InTASC standard domains, and then write 2–3 actions they take to demonstrate each value. For example, the broad statement for Standard 1, Learner Development, is "What is important to you in terms of students' cognitive, linguistic, social, emotional, and physical development?" To further extend the activity, educators can be asked to take the InTASC domains and estimate the amount of time spent in activities for each of the 10 domains. They can then participate in a reflective discussion about whether this allotment of time reflects their overall values.

Perceptions. In addition to helping educators articulate and clarify their values and beliefs, the self-awareness module helps educators consider how their values and beliefs influence their perceptions, and how those perceptions influence their actions. For example, during professional development educators are presented with some simple, subjective statements, such as "He is a good student." They have 30 seconds to note what comes to mind when they hear this statement. Responses vary widely, including "He follows directions well," "He is creative," "He completes all his assignments," "He understands the material," "He thinks critically." Educators discuss the differences that could ensue if individuals used the same phrase to refer to a student but held discrepant definitions of that phrase. Facilitators help the educators in the professional development activity to see that language (as well as events) can be ambiguous, but that human beings naturally interpret situations based on their own values and beliefs. Not surprisingly, such interpretations frequently consist of assumptions that could lead to problematic actions.

The starting statements can be modified depending on the purpose of the activity. If the purpose is to unpack assumptions about the school's vision, the facilitator can use a statement such as "It is a quality school." If the purpose is to unpack gender stereotypes, the facilitator can use "She is a good student" and "He is a good student." If the purpose is to consider assumptions around parent involvement, use such statements as "That parent causes problems" or "That parent is helpful." Critical to the discussion is the facilitator guiding the educators to reflect on how different, unstated interpretations of the same phrase could lead to misunderstandings.

If there are teachers experiencing difficulty in classroom management, administrators could use the following activity to help teachers think about how their actions may result from lack of awareness of multiple perspectives. Present the following scenario:

> *Class has started. Students have been given a task. One student is not doing what you have asked. What is your immediate reaction?*

Participants share their responses, which tend to focus on the student and why they are off task. Although many of participant responses demonstrate empathy toward what could be challenging circumstances for the student (e.g., they have a learning disability, they did not have anything to eat that day, they were worried about a family member, they were trying to be the class clown for attention), the responses placed the problem primarily with the student. After sharing their responses, teachers are encouraged to consider the following questions:

- What is my intention here? What is the task that the student is supposed to be doing?
- Is this a reasonable task?
- What can I do differently to support this student?
- What need is not being met for this student at this moment?

Rather than focusing primarily on the student's behavior—which is a natural inclination—teachers are encouraged to consider *alternate explanations* that may emanate from actions within the teacher's control (Kohn, 1995). For example, the student may be bored because the task is too easy; the student may have forgotten to take their medication for ADD; the student may not have understood the directions because they were not stated in a language and tone they *did* understand. Delpit (1995) illustrates how differences in styles of discourse can result in teacher misperceptions, especially when White, middle-class teachers interact with Black students. A simple question—"Would you please put the book back on the shelf?" that was intended as a directive may be mistaken as an option because it was framed as a question. A student unaware of the "language coding" (i.e., that the question was actually a directive) may interpret the teacher in one way—that is, that the student had a choice in putting the book on the shelf. The teacher may subsequently misinterpret the student's behavior as defiant.

The purpose of these perception exercises is to help educators become more aware of possible misguided perceptions and to work toward common understandings. The exercises can be valuable to use with teachers and administrators so that each can dissect how students' actions may be perceived and how both teachers and administrators can take actions consonant with the overall vision and values of the school.

Empathy for Conflict Resolution

> *Students act the way they do because of who they are, what they've experienced. It's not going to be like written on them. It's not going to be something that you're going to know right away but it goes along with that relationship piece of trying to be understanding and compassionate and getting to know a kid without just automatically assuming things or automatically reprimanding for something.*
>
> —Middle school teacher.

A plethora of research on exists empathy (e.g., Luberto et al., 2018; Teding van Berkhout & Malouff, 2016), and programs have been developed that seek to teach empathy in school settings (e.g., Roots of Empathy, Compassionate Schools). In Project RESPECT, the concept of empathy is introduced in a module on social intelligence and revisited in subsequent modules, especially the module on conflict resolution. Empathy is presented as a follow-up to self-awareness, whereby educators are encouraged to develop awareness of and responsiveness to the needs of others, especially their students. During professional development in Project RESPECT, we offer the following definition of empathy to ensure a common understanding: Empathy is a means for understanding another's needs, in which one understands the perspectives and experiences of another while concurrently recognizing a self and other distinction (Miyashiro, 2011). In other words, a person can understand the experience of another whose house is on fire without feeling the need to set their own house on fire to understand that specific experience. In sum, empathy is getting inside of the feelings and needs that the experience evokes for another, and empathic responsiveness or compassion is defined as acting upon this understanding.

Drawing from nonviolent communication, in Project RESPECT we explain that negative feelings are generally a warning signal of unmet need(s) (Rosenberg, 2003). When students express anger, frustration, sadness, or other negative emotions, it indicates a need that is not being fulfilled, as opposed to a direct affront against the teacher or administrator. A basic need (physical or psychological) is an energizing state that, if satisfied, moves toward health and well-being, but if not satisfied contributes to pathology and extreme unease. A number of ways to think about needs are available (see Resources). Maslow's (1954) hierarchy of needs shows a progression whereby it is difficult to support higher level growth needs, like self-actualization, when lower-level needs, like nutrition or safety, are inadequately covered. Self-determination theory (Ryan & Deci, 2017) is a useful way for thinking about needs with adolescents, particularly as it focuses on an individual's needs for competence, relatedness, and autonomy. Self-determination theory relates to motivation because when one's needs in these areas are satisfied, internal motivation increases (Ryan & Deci, 2000). Therefore, rather than controlling student behavior through extrinsic punishment or reward, educators can build empathic connections that help fulfill students' needs for competence, relatedness, and autonomy and bolster their internal motivation.

Recognizing that sometimes educators intend to demonstrate empathy but fall short, participants in the professional development activity discuss a number of common missteps and ways to avoid them. Empathy missteps include advice giving, denying feelings, minimizing the experience, referring to one's own story, casting judgment, and over-analyzing the student's or colleague's motives. Educators instead are encouraged to focus on the person's feelings and needs in the present. During the professional development activity, educators practice with a partner. First, educators must identify two to four potential unmet needs to their choice of a situation with a student. Choices include: a student who speaks disrespectfully to authority figures; a student who turns in a third late assignment; and a student who says, loudly, "I hate school" in the middle of a lesson. These prompts can be adapted to include conflict with a colleague or parent to accommodate participant needs. Then they construct, through writing or role playing, a short dialogue to demonstrate how they would show empathy and avoid empathy missteps. Educators are encouraged to consider potential unmet needs around competence, relatedness, and autonomy, and to acknowledge their own needs as they revise their scenarios.

In a later module on conflict resolution, educators are introduced to even more specific communication strategies to build empathy and work toward resolving conflict in mutually beneficial ways. For example, certain language cues have the effect of putting the educator on the same side as the student (or parent or colleague) in a conflict situation even when conveying the same essential message. These include words/phrases like "and," "as soon as," and "right after." "And" is a powerful word that can replace "but" by maintaining the substance of the message and offering connection instead of division. For example, compare these two statements:

> A: *I hear what you are saying* **and** *I can't do that right now.*

> B: *I hear what you are saying* **but** *I can't do that right now*

These are essentially the same messages. However, unlike the "but," the "and" in Statement A acknowledges the other's viewpoint. "As soon as" operates similarly. Imagine a principal telling a student one of these two possibilities:

> A: *I can give you a pass to go back to class* **as soon as** *I learn more from you about what happened in the lunchroom today.*

> B: *No, you can* not *have a pass. I need to learn more from you about what happened in the lunchroom today.*

Statement A, which places the problem on the situation rather than on the educator, is more likely to strike a tone of cooperation. A simple language shift such as in this example helps put the educator on the same side as the student, while still maintaining the integrity of the message.

The emphasis on empathy and understanding unmet needs is a means of perspective taking that is essential for educators working with students (and colleagues and parents), especially those from sociocultural contexts dissimilar from their own (Warren, 2018). Empathy is introduced as an orientation to establish it as a foundation that guides educators' interactions. The introduction of particular language cues, such as those described in examples A and B above, occurs later in the professional development sequence, once that orientation is established.

Growth Mindset

> *Sometimes, we don't discuss with students about how they're responsible for their own growth and being aware of that. That's been really good [here]. It's something I've actually incorporated a little bit talking to them about the choices that they make … understanding that they have more control over their lives and what they think they do. That's always been nice to maybe reinforce that as well, that you have a choice to learn. You can choose that. You can choose to put forth that effort. Same as explaining to them how they have a choice over their emotions. You can choose to be angry and continue to hold onto that.*
>
> —Middle school teacher

Carol Dweck (2006) popularized the idea of a *growth mindset,* encouraging people to rethink how intelligence and talent are viewed. As the middle school teacher notes above, one can choose how they view their abilities. People with a growth mindset view talent and intelligence very differently from those with a *fixed mindset.* Those with a fixed mindset believe intelligence and talent are fixed. They represent something a person is born with and there isn't much that can be done to change this. It can be general, like believing that a person is either smart or not (and if you're smart, that means you don't have to work very hard!), or it can be specific, like a belief that you are either good at math or you are not. Those with a growth mindset believe that intelligence and talent develop out of hard work and purposeful persistence; no matter what a person is born with, they can always improve, they assert. Leveraging ideas of self-determination theory, whereby students' particular needs for competence and autonomy are fulfilled, educators can motivate students academically by fostering a growth mindset.

There is some research suggesting that a growth mindset is correlated with aspects of academic achievement, like attendance and test-score gains for upper-elementary and middle-school students (West et al., 2016), and persistence in completing challenging work (Blackwell et al., 2007; Ehrlinger et al., 2016). Despite these promising studies, recent meta-analyses (studies combining a large number of studies on a specific topic) suggest that educators should not look to growth mindset as a silver bullet for solving problems of academic engagement and achievement (Sisk et al., 2018). They found that overall, students typically did not experience much academic benefit (in terms of growth on academic achievement). However, economically disadvantaged students and students at high risk of failing benefited the most from a mindset intervention; in addition, the relationship between mindset and academic achievement was stronger for younger students and adolescents than for adults.

Building on concepts of self-awareness and social intelligence and using some of the same language cues from the empathy/social intelligence module, educators are encouraged to think about simple ways to signal to students that persistence, effort, and mistakes are useful for learning. The "and" instead of "but" replacement works well as a way to build off students' strengths while providing a valuable critique. Using "but" overrides the initial compliment with a criticism; using "and" helps the recipient hear both the strength and the critique. For example:

A: *I really like what you did here,* **and** *if you do XYZ I will have an even better understanding of how you figured out that problem.*

B: *I really like what you did here,* **but** *if you do XYZ I will have an even better understanding of how you figured out that problem.*

The "and" in Statement A feels much more encouraging. Students who claim they do not have natural ability or intelligence can be encouraged to use the word "yet" after their defeatist exclamations:

Student: *I'm not good at math.*

Teacher: *You're not good at math* **yet.** *You are working hard on it and making improvements in your understanding every day!*

The teacher can also help students establish an identity for themselves as having particular skills. If students are working through a science lab that seems confusing, the teacher can note, "How would a *scientist* work through this problem?" Students on the school newspaper can answer the question "How would an *ethical journalist* think about this situation?"

In subtle and not so subtle ways, the language that an educator chooses to use can foster or undermine a growth mindset as it can promote or hinder a student's motivation to persist in the face of challenges. Furthermore, if everyone's motivation to learn and develop is central to the values of a school, it is essential that educators communicate this at all levels.

RESEARCH RESULTS

In evaluating the effectiveness of Project RESPECT, we collected qualitative and quantitative data from teachers, students, administrators, and classrooms (manuscripts are in preparation detailing these findings). Compared to a control group that did not receive the Project RESPECT professional development, quantitative teacher self-reports from before the professional development and after they received the professional development showed there were statistically significant improvements in the teaching efficiency of teachers in the Project RESPECT program, their use of positive verbal and nonverbal communication in the classroom, their "withitness" (see Kounin, 1977), and their reported empathy toward students. Student reports of their teachers aligned with what we found in the teacher data. Students noted that after their teachers' participation in Project RESPECT, teachers were more likely to use prosocial interpersonal skills, promote student academic engagement and academic motivation, use positive verbal and nonverbal behaviors ($p = 0.01$, $d = 0.41$), and exhibit teacher withitness.

Qualitative data consisted of feedback educators gave immediately following the professional development (i.e., responses to open-ended questions) and interviews with teachers and school or district administrators after going through Project RESPECT professional development and with administrators who facilitated Project RESPECT in their schools or districts but did not go through the training themselves. The content of Project RESPECT was well received and even viewed as necessary. A high school teacher said, "NVC [nonviolent communication] and conflict management not only deter negative behavior but also maintain rapport, which is why they are the most effective techniques." In feedback we sought immediately after the professional development in rural, urban, and suburban districts alike, conflict resolution and NVC were consistently noted as aspects that were most useful. A special education teacher noted the importance of focusing on the nuance of her language:

> It really helped me to be more cognizant of just like the wording I utilize within my room and how we have positive intentions with our words, but sometimes the way that they're phrased [or] they're utilized aren't conveying that to the kids, so that is helpful. It's more helpful for me to have more tools in my toolkit as far as building relationships with kids and working with different behaviors because not everything works for one kid, or for every kid. To have those backup things to help me continue being better at behavior interventions would be most helpful.

Project RESPECT in some ways reminded teachers of classroom management techniques they learned in their teacher preparation, but it expanded on these by helping educators consider their intentions (or values) and think about ways to communicate their intentions most effectively.

Administrators saw the need for professional development that provided these techniques as well, with most administrators interviewed noting the need for more mental health training in schools and for some kind of interpersonal skills. For example, an assistant principal in a suburban school said, "I think 99% of the problems I see come through my door from a disciplinary standpoint are because of either kids that are not skilled in handling situations, communication or how to deal with life," further noting that "The longer I'm in this job, I see the best thing we can do is to skill the communicators [teachers].... How do you skillfully communicate?... You rarely talk about that at teacher training programs." Given that such a large percentage of the problems administrators manage stem from communication and conflict resolution, everyone stands to benefit when all educators improve their communication skills.

CONCLUSION

The attention being given to educator well-being is encouraging. It represents a realization that student SEL does not exist in a vacuum, that mitigating teacher burnout and administrator turnover are worthwhile endeavors, that improving educator SEC is important for both the educators and the students, and ultimately that prosocial classrooms and prosocial schools are contingent on the well-being of the individuals within them. The domains of emotional intelligence provide a useful guide for working toward the goals of fostering educator SEC and prosocial classrooms. The development of specific communication strategies and language practices can facilitate the enactment of those domains. As few programs have focused on communication, Project RESPECT is designed to fill this gap. It provides compelling evidence that coupling explicit communication strategies with activities to promote emotional intelligence-related domains—like self-awareness, empathy, conflict resolution, and motivation—can help educators be more intentional about their language as well as their values. In doing so, they improve their own well-being, the well-being of the students, and the health of the relationships within their schools and classrooms.

RESOURCES

Reading

Carroll, D., & Carney, J. (2005). Personal perspectives: Using multimedia to express cultural identity. *Contemporary Issues in Technology and Teacher Education, 4*(4), 465–488.

Connor, J. M., & Killian, D. (2012). *Connecting across differences* (2nd ed.). PuddleDancer Press.

Deci, E. L., & Flaste, R. (1996). *Why we do what we do: Understanding self-motivation.* Penguin.

Dweck, C. S. (2006). *Mindset*: The new psychology of success. Random House.

Farrell, T. S. C. (2013). Teacher self-awareness through journal writing. *Reflective Practice, 14*(4), 465–471.

Hayes, S. C. (2005). *Get out of your head and into your life.* New Harbinger Publications.

Johnston, P. H. (2004). *Choice words: How our language affects children's learning.* Stenhouse.

Wilson, T. D. (2002). *Strangers to ourselves: Discovering the adaptive unconscious.* Harvard University Press.

Websites

Empathy at the Cleveland Clinic: https://www.youtube.com/watch?v=cDDWvj_q-o8
Mindset: http://mindsetonline.com/
Mindset: http://www.mindsetworks.com
Self-Determination Theory: http://www.selfdeterminationtheory.org
Self-Knowledge: https://www.frontiersin.org/articles/10.3389/fpsyg.2011.00312/full
Strategies for Teaching Self-Determination Theory: https://www.uaa.alaska.edu/centerforhumandevelopment/selfdetermination/upload/Lesson-Plan-1-13.pdf

TED Talk. Carol Dweck, *The power of believing that you can improve.* http://www.ted.com/talks/carol_dweck_the_power_of_believing_that_you_can_improve?language=en

REFERENCES

Becvar, R. J., & Becvar, D. S. (1998). *Pragmatics of human relationships: A guide to effective communications.* Geist & Russell Companies.

Blackwell, L. S., Trzesniewski, K. H., & Dweck, C. S. (2007). Implicit theories of intelligence predict achievement across an adolescent transition: A longitudinal study and an intervention. *Child Development, 78,* 246–263.

Boghossian, P., & Lindsay, J. (2019). *How to have impossible conversations: A very practical guide.* Da Capo Lifelong Books.

Brackett, M. A., Reyes, M. R., Rivers, S. E., Elbertson, N. A., & Salovey, P. (2011). Classroom emotional climate, teacher affiliation, and student conduct. *Journal of Classroom Interaction, 46*(1), 27–36.

Cherkowski, S., & Walker, K. (2018). *Teacher wellbeing: Noticing, nurturing, sustaining, and flourishing in schools.* Word and Deed Publishing Inc.

Connor, J. M., & Killian, D. (2012). *Connecting across differences* (2nd ed.). PuddleDancer Press.

Deetz, S. A., & Stevenson, S. L. (1986). *Managing interpersonal communication.* Harper Row Publishers.

Delpit, L. (1995). *Other people's children: Cultural conflict in the classroom.* The New Press.

Dweck, C. S. (2006). *Mindset: The new psychology of success.* Ballantine Books.

Ehrlinger, J., Mitchum, A. L., & Dweck, C. S. (2016). Understanding overconfidence: Theories of intelligence, preferential attention, and distorted self-assessment. *Journal of Experimental Social Psychology, 63,* 94–100.

Goleman, D. (1995). *Emotional intelligence.* Bantam Books.

Granic, I., & Patterson, G. R. (2006). Toward a comprehensive model of antisocial development: A dynamic systems approach. *Psychological Review, 113*(1), 101–131. https://doi.org/10.1037/0033-295X.113.1.101

Greenberg, M. T., Brown, J. L., & Abenavoli, R. M. (2016). *Teacher stress and health effects on teachers, students, and schools.* Edna Bennett Pierce Prevention Research Center.

Hayes, S. C. (2005). *Get out of your head and into your life.* New Harbinger Publications.

Interstate New Teacher Assessment and Support Consortium (InTASC). (2013). *Model standards for beginning teacher licensing and development: A resource for state dialogue.* https://ccsso.org/resource-library/intasc-model-core-teaching-standards-and-learning-progressions-teachers-10

Jennings, P. A., & Greenberg, M. T. (2009). The prosocial classroom: Teacher social and emotional competence in relation to student and classroom outcomes. *Review of Educational Research, 79*(1), 491–525.

Klimecki, O. M., Leiberg, S., Ricard, M., & Singer, T. (2014). Differential pattern of functional brain plasticity after compassion and empathy training. *Social Cognitive & Affective Neuroscience, 9*(6), 873–879.

Kohn, A. (1995). Discipline is the problem—not the solution. *Learning Magazine* (October–November).

Kounin, J. (1977). *Discipline and group management in classrooms.* Krieger.

La Guardia, J., & Ryan, R. (2002). What adolescents need. In F. Pajares & T. Urdan (Eds.), *Academic motivation of adolescents* (pp. 193–218). Information Age Publishing.

Long, N. J., Wood, M. M., & Fecser, F. A. (2001). *Life space crisis intervention: Talking with students in conflict* (2nd ed.). PRO-ED.

Luberto, C. M., Shinday, N., Song, R., Philpotts, L. L., Park, E. R., Fricchione, G. L., & Yeh, G. Y. (2018). A systematic review and meta-analysis of the effects of meditation on empathy, compassion, and prosocial behaviors. *Mindfulness, 9*(3), 708–724.

Mahfouz, J., Greenberg, M., & Rodriguez, A. (2019). *Principals' social and emotional competence: A key factor for creating caring schools* [Research brief]. 1–14. EdCan Network.

Martin, A. J., & Dowson, M. (2009). Interpersonal relationships, motivation, engagement, and achievement: Yields for theory, current issues, and educational practice. *Review of Educational Research, 79*(1), 327–365.

Maslow, A. H. (1954). *Motivation and personality.* Harper and Row.

Miyashiro, M. (2011). *The empathy factor.* PuddleDancer Press.

Murphy, J. F., & Louis, K. S. (2018). *Positive school leadership: Building capacity and strengthening relationships.* Teachers College Press.

Oberle, E., & Schonert-Reichl, K. A. (2016). Stress contagion in the classroom? The link between classroom teacher burnout and morning cortisol in elementary school students. *Social Science & Medicine, 159,* 30–37.

Patterson, G., Reid, J., & Dishion, T. (1992). *Antisocial boys.* Castalia.

Pianta, R. C., Hamre, B. K., & Allen, J. P. (2012). Teacher-student relationships and engagement: Conceptualizing, measuring, and improving the capacity of classroom interactions. In S. L. Christenson, A. L. Reschly, & C. Wylie (Eds.), *Handbook of research on student engagement* (pp. 365–386). Springer. https://doi.org/10.1007/978-1-4614-2018-7_17

Rosenberg, M. B. (2003). *Nonviolent communication: A language of life.* PuddleDancer Press.

Ryan, R. M., & Deci, E. L. (2000). Self-determination theory and the facilitation of intrinsic motivation, social development, and well-being. *American Psychologist, 55*(1), 68–78. https://doi.org/10.1037/0003-066X.55.1.68

Ryan, R. M., & Deci, E. L. (2017). *Self-determination theory: Basic psychological needs in motivation, development, and wellness.* Guilford.

Schussler, D. L., Stooksberry, L. M., & Bercaw, L. A. (2010). Understanding teacher candidates' dispositions: Reflecting to build self-awareness. *Journal of Teacher Education, 61*(4), 350–363. https://doi.org/10.1177/0022487110371377

Seligman, M. E. (2011). *Flourish: A visionary new understanding of happiness and well-being.* Free Press.

Sisk, V. F., Burgoyne, A. P., Sun, J., Butler, J. L., & Macnamara, B. N. (2018). To what extent and under which circumstances are growth mind-sets important to academic achievement? Two meta-analyses. *Psychological Science, 29*(4), 549–571. https://doi.org/10.1177/0956797617739704

Strati, A. D., Schmidt, J. A., & Maier, K. S. (2017). Perceived challenge, teacher support, and teacher obstruction as predictors of student engagement. *Journal of Educational Psychology, 109*(1), 131–U152. https://doi.org/10.1037/edu0000108

Sutherland, K. S., Conroy, M., Abrams, L., & Vo, A. (2010). Improving interactions between teachers and young children with problem behavior: A strengths-based approach. *Exceptionality, 18*(2), 70–81. https://doi.org/10.1080/09362831003673101

Teding van Berkhout, E., & Malouff, J. M. (2016). The efficacy of empathy training: A meta-analysis of randomized controlled trials. *Journal of Counseling Psychology, 63*(1), 32.

Walker, H. M., Colvin, G., & Ramsey, E. (1995). *Antisocial behavior in school: Strategies and best practices.* Brooks/Cole.

Warren, C. A. (2018). Empathy, teacher dispositions, and preparation for culturally responsive pedagogy. *Journal of Teacher Education, 69*(2), 169–183. https://doi.org/10.1177/0022487117712487

West, M. R., Kraft, M. A., Finn, A. S., Martin, R. E., Duckworth, A. L., Gabrieli, C. F. O., & Gabrieli, J. D. E. (2016). Promise and paradox: Measuring students' non-cognitive skills and the impact of schooling. *Educational Evaluation and Policy Analysis, 38*(1), 148–170.

NOTE

1. Unless otherwise noted, italic emphasis and quoted expressions throughout are the authors'.

CHAPTER 19

CARING FOR THE CARETAKER

Using Mentoring as Support for School Principals in Self-Care and Mindfulness

Sonya D. Hayes and Jerry Burkett

INTRODUCTION

Being a principal in the 21st century requires complex responsibilities that focus on improving student learning and academic performance and supervising and supporting teachers in effective teaching and learning practices (Lynch, 2012). State and federal policies are increasingly holding principals accountable for student growth, closing performance gaps, decreasing dropout rates, and increasing college and career readiness for all students (Davis & Darling-Hammond, 2012); consequently, the pressure on school principals to improve student outcomes has increased (Lemoine et al., 2018; Markow et al., 2013; Oplatka, 2017). Principals are expected to be professional educators who "operate in multiple dimensions at once, moving from individual capacity to group empowerment to whole school improvement and back again" (Byrne-Jimenez & Orr, 2012, p. 33). Because of the rising pressure in school accountability and the expectation to understand and work well with all stakeholders in varying contexts, principals have reported increased levels of work-related stress and professional burnout (DeMatthews et al., 2019; Oplatka, 2017; Wells, 2016). Many principals have also reported work-related exhaustion from their job demands (Oplatka, 2017), and they often neglect the importance of self-care (Mahfouz, 2020). Beausaert et al. (2016) found that social support, specifically support from colleagues, decreases stress and burnout in school principals. As the only people who understand the stressors of being a principal are other principals, it stands to reason that mentoring may be a way to meet the social-emotional needs of principals.

In the past decade, scholars have developed an ongoing discussion about the need for research into how the role of the principal can be designed to facilitate their work and avoid unwanted stress (DeMatthews et al., 2019; Lindberg, 2012; Mahfouz, 2020). Researchers have established the importance of mentoring in indoctrinating a novice principal into the profession (Daresh, 2004, 2007; Oplatka & Lapidot, 2018) and for the professional development of novice school principals (Clayton et al., 2013; Gumus & Bellibas, 2016; Hayes, 2019). The focus in early studies on mentoring was on skill attainment for novice principals, specifically on how a veteran principal (mentor) supports a novice principal (mentee) in acquiring the needed managerial skills to gain confidence in operating the school (Daresh, 2004). As the role of the principal has evolved in its complexity and responsibility, mentoring school principals should also evolve to include social-emotional support, mindfulness, and self-care practices.

Although few studies have been concerned with how mentoring may be used to support principals in self-care, there are numerous studies on mentoring in the workplace that can be used to conceptualize how mentoring may be used to support principals in attaining self-care skills to support a sustainable work-life balance. Because principals are generally thought to be the caretakers of the school community (i.e., caring for teachers and students), principals must prioritize their own self-care to be able to care for others (Mahfouz, 2020). Drawing on the existing mentoring literature and Nodding's (1984) framework on care, we conceptualize how mentoring can be used to care for the caretaker and support principals in caring for themselves so that they in turn can care for others. We begin this chapter with an overview of principals and work-related stress and then elaborate on the current research on principals and work-life balance. We then discuss Nodding's framework on care and conceptualize how mentoring can be used to care for the caretaker with implications for practice.

PRINCIPALS AND WORK-RELATED STRESS

Crucial changes in the context of a principal's work make the job more challenging than ever (Fullan, 2014). Although all of the responsibilities of the principalship are critical to maximizing the success of a school, the weight of these responsibilities takes a toll on the principals. In this section, we discuss principals and work-related stress caused by school accountability and instructional leadership, social justice, and student advocacy. and public perception of the school.

School Accountability and Instructional Leadership

Work-related stress experienced by campus principals has increased significantly over the past few decades. The 21st century principal is expected to be an instructional leader who carries the burden for school accountability and student achievement, while being a change agent and leader of reform efforts (Mahfouz, 2020). As schools have become more specialized and have evolved to offer far more opportunities for students than in the past, school principals are expected to lead with energy and enthusiasm. Consequently, the workload of principals has continued to increase with new expectations for evaluation and supervision, changing legislative mandates, and mounting pressures for accountability (Wells, 2013; West et al., 2014).

With their numerous responsibilities, school principals often struggle to find the time to focus on instructional leadership. Researchers (Branch et al., 2013; Leithwood et al., 2004; Marzano et al., 2005; Robinson et al., 2008) have established the importance of the principal's role as an instructional leader in improving schools and increasing achievement for all students. Principals have noted, however, that the responsibilities that consume most of their time are managerial in nature, and they desire more time to focus on instructional leadership (Boyland, 2011). Principals have acknowledged that the time needed to deal with disciplinary issues and parental concerns means less time for instructional leadership (Levin & Bradley, 2019); however, the pressures and expectations to increase student achievement and improve instruction still remain.

Social Justice and Student Advocacy

Principals are also stressed due to their commitment to students and advocacy for social justice issues. One of the complex and demanding responsibilities that principals face is leading democratic and socially just schools with a focus on equity and inclusion (DeMatthews et al., 2019; Levin & Bradley, 2019; Rodela et al., 2020; Theoharis, 2010). Social justice leadership expects a principal's commitment to core democratic values and seeks a commitment to fairness and equity in instructional practices, curriculum, and resources (DeMatthews, 2015), as well as advocacy of marginalized students by finding ways to promote diversity and more equitable practices (Theoharis, 2010). School leaders are responsible for building cultural competency among their staff, demonstrating critical consciousness as they advocate for all children and ensuring the academic success of every child they serve. They encounter resistance in their daily work, however (Theoharis, 2010), which causes additional stress and frustration. This resistance emanates from both within the school community and external to the school, including such factors as attitudes and beliefs of staff; a lack of resources, both financial and human; and oppressive mandates that harm students from marginalized groups.

The resistance that principals encounter as social justice leaders can add to their stress as they seek to be advocates for their students. As social justice leaders, principals advocate for the students on their campus and spend time finding resources outside of the school to support students and their families (Burkett & Hayes, 2018; Rodela et al., 2020; Theoharis, 2010). The social-emotional needs of students have grown over the years from societal pressures, and the political and social issues that arise outside of the school seem to work their way into the school (Burkett & Hayes, 2018; Levin & Bradley, 2019). Consequently, principals have faced increased stress in handling political and societal issues such as immigration policies, crises and pandemics, and race-related tensions.

Public Perception of the School

Another work-related stressor that principals experience is the community's perception of schools and the public's dissatisfaction with schools. Mahfouz (2020) explains the stress that principals face in dealing with the community:

> One of the highlighted stressors is the pressure they face from their community ... they are public figures and their behavior is played out in front of all school stakeholders. They are expected to take full responsibility for any conflict, misunderstanding, or mistake that takes place in their building and fulfil all of their duties with considerable urgency. (p. 452)

Parents have high expectations for schools, and when they perceive that schools are not performing well, they begin to question the education their child is receiving and if their tax money is being put to good use (Currie, 2015). In this era of amplified accountability, principals are under immense pressure to improve teaching and learning (Boyland, 2011), but they seldom find the time to devote to the management of instructional issues. Consequently, principals experience work-related stress in finding ways to manage their time and set priorities. Moreover, schools are often portrayed in a negative light by the media. Incidents such as tragic school shootings, teacher strikes, poor test scores, inappropriate teacher-student relationships, budget deficits, and drug/alcohol abuse lead the media's often sensationalized coverage of public schools (Currie, 2015), and principals are bombarded by negative images of schools amplified by the media. As the school's public figure, a principal is responsible for maintaining the school's reputation and communicating its story by all means possible.

The management of stressors that emerge from the public's expectations of being a principal can be a challenge for many principals in the field. Principals often overwhelm themselves with increasing demands from parents and community members. A principal's focus can be constantly heightened, leading to chronic levels of stress that can detract from being successful (Goleman et al., 2002; Mahfouz, 2020; Oplatka, 2017). Principals will work daily in this constant level of heightened stress and anxiety, which create pressures that are often self-inflicted when not managed appropriately (Mahfouz, 2020). The pressures of the job, especially public scrutiny of principals and how well they are handling the job, often lead to a disruption in the principal's work-life balance. This disruption can lead to principal burnout (DeMatthews et al., 2019) and could eventually cause a principal to leave the profession.

PRINCIPALS AND PROFESSIONAL BURNOUT

Burnout

Freudenberger (1974) developed the term *burnout syndrome* and defined it as "a state of mental and physical exhaustion caused by one's professional life" (p. 160). Professional or personal burnout is a process of becoming exhausted due to the excessive demands on the individual's "energy, strength, or resources" (p. 159). Klocko and Wells (2015) researched principal workload stressors that affect principal leadership and identified distinctive aspects of the job that can lead to personal burnout. In the study, principals reported personal workload management, the demands of being an instructional leader on campus, stakeholder accountability, managing professional tasks, and handling conflict as stressors caused by the pressures of the job. Riley et al. (2017) conducted a survey of over 2,800 principals and other school leaders in Australia on principal health and well-being. The study revealed that principals work long hours, with over 77% of participants reporting working over 56 hours per week; among those, 27% of the principals worked up to 65 hours every week. Significant to the study was the finding that school principals report higher levels of burnout when compared to other professions. In the same study, it was also found that principals suffer twice as much with difficulty in sleeping because of professional stress, and they are at a higher risk of being diagnosed with depression. The findings of the Australian study are significant because principals who experience high levels of stress will burn out and show a decline in their leadership performance.

van der Merwe and Parsotam (2012) trace the fate of principals in attempting to manage their own stress: Though the well-being of principals is an essential factor in school improvement, teacher well-being, and student performance, school administrators are expected to manage their own stress and reduce the stress of their faculty and staff. When principals struggle to manage their own stress or lack the coping skills to reduce professional burnout, it becomes difficult for them to lead their schools. As this stress becomes too much for principals to handle, their self-efficacy lessens and they may begin to doubt their ability to do the tasks expected of them (van der Merwe & Parsotam, 2012). Principals need to understand how stress contributes to their burnout and be able to engage in self-care to reduce stress. In this way, self-recognition of principal burnout can help principals identify the early signs of stress and execute plans to manage and reduce the stress that principals experience in the school (DeMatthews et al., 2019; Leiter & Maslach, 2004).

Principal Retention

Clearly, the job demands of the principal have increased and can lead to burnout, depression, and decreased self-efficacy, as noted in the previous section. However, a more significant problem that emerges from the professional burnout of campus principals is retention. Increasing job demands and school accountability have forced principals to leave their positions after only a short amount of time (Catano & Stronge, 2006; Cushing et al., 2003; Howley et al., 2005; Pounder & Merrill, 2001; Rayfield & Diamantes, 2003). In urban school districts, principals typically remain in the position for just three to four years (Fuller, 2012); rural principals remain at their schools for an average of five years (Pendola & Fuller, 2018).

School district leaders need to work to understand the reasons related to the shortage of candidates for school leadership positions (Lemoine et al., 2018; Rayfield & Diamantes, 2003) and should start with professional burnout. Without the proper support in place to help principals manage their work-life balance and the stressors of school leadership, many principals often simply leave the profession. School leaders are noted as being only second to teachers when it comes to improving student outcomes (Leithwood et al., 2004), which means that when the principal leaves the campus, student achievement for the school generally experiences a decline for two years (Miller, 2013). Consequently, supporting and retaining principals in their schools for multiple years is vital to student success (Wells & Klocko, 2018).

Striving for Work-Life Balance

The responsibilities of a school principal include a significant workload increase and long working hours, which lead to both stress and an imbalance between professional time and personal time (Philips et al., 2007; Wells & Klocko, 2018). Since the turn of this century, principals have reported escalating pressure as well as serious concerns regarding time demands (Boyland, 2011; Wells & Klocko, 2018). In a study conducted by the National Association of Secondary School Principals (NASSP) (Levin & Bradley, 2019), principals indicated that their many obligations required a huge time commitment, which often impeded their work-life balance and limited what they can accomplish on the job. The principals in the NASSP study explained that their job responsibilities often required sacrificing time with their spouses and family to meet obligations related to the job of a campus principal (Levin & Bradley, 2019).

Within the past 20 years, there has been a rise in the number of businesses allowing elements of job flexibility for their employees. This dramatic shift in thinking has allowed for a growing movement to improve the work-life balance of employees, allowing people to work part time at home, adjust their working hours, or even work on evenings and weekends to free up portions of the day for meeting family obligations. However, for the school principal, there has been a limited availability of these job flexibility options—and for those principals who have some flexibility in their work hours, these approaches have provided only a small degree of satisfaction for school leaders (Murphy & Sauter, 2011). While many businesses have developed policies on job flexibility with an understanding of the importance of work-life balance and the need to support families, school districts still have a reluctance to change either the job functions of the school leader or their daily routines and expectations (Murphy & Sauter, 2011).

The balance of an individual's personal time with their professional time is a general phrasing of the definition of *work-life balance*. For the school leader, professional time is defined by engagement in work relationships with faculty, staff, students, and the community and the expectations defined by their job description as a principal, all of which can vary. School leaders are often faced with significant time commitments necessary to maintain the functionality of their school (Wells & Klocko, 2018). In contrast, personal time is defined by the roles and expectations taken on by the individual outside of the work or professional environment. These roles can also range widely in scope and vary significantly from person to person. The time commitment that a principal dedicates to the job is still significant enough to often interfere with work-life balance. For example, secondary school principals may be consumed with athletics and fine-arts events while elementary principals may dedicate their time to large PTA meetings, fundraisers, or school plays. Many of these events are held on evenings and weekends, and principals often attend these events as part of their role to connect with the community. These obligations can require a huge time commitment, impeding a principal's work-life balance and limiting what they can accomplish on the job (Levin & Bradley, 2019).

Self-Care

The concept of self-care has emerged to help define the imbalance that can occur in a person's life when professional time is out of balance with personal time. The goal of self-care activities has been to maintain a balance within the individual to prevent the professional time construct from infringing on the individual's personal time and vice versa. Lee and Miller (2013) developed a conceptual model for self-care for social workers that comprises two dimensions of self-care: personal and professional.

There are five primary structures for *personal* self-care:

- Physical, which includes physical activity, adequate sleep, healthy nutritional choices, prevention of illness, intimacy, and general bodily health;
- Psychological and emotional, which includes a positive self-image and a compassionate view of self (recognition of human limits), a recognition of one's strengths, engagement in stress management techniques, mindfulness about triggers that cause stress, and problem solving;
- Social, which includes building and sustaining supportive relationships (participating in the community and maintaining contact with influential and accomplished people);
- Leisure, which includes participation in enjoyable activities (e.g., hobbies, playing sports, spending time with a pet);
- Spiritual, which includes connectedness, faith, and peace (meditation, prayer, reflection, spending time in nature). (p. 99).

There are six primary structures for *professional* self-care:

- Workload and time management, which includes taking breaks, taking vacations, and focusing on work during work hours only;

- Attention to professional role, which includes creating and working toward goals, being mindful of limits;
- Attention to reactions to work, which include personal therapy, mindfulness exercises, limiting discussions of work stressors, journaling, targeted supervision, and debriefing with colleagues;
- Professional social support and self-advocacy, which includes soliciting encouragement and constructive feedback, and guidance from peers through networking;
- Professional development, which includes attending conferences, workshops, or continuing education, reading journals/articles, action research, writing, and mentoring;
- Revitalization and generalization of energy, which includes sustaining energy, encouragement and hopefulness (creating a positive work culture, celebrations of positive outcomes, fostering innovation, and taking part in workplace social events). (pp. 100–101).

Lee and Miller's (2013) conceptual model for self-care in social work can be useful in offering support for school principals through mentoring practices.

SUPPORT FOR PRINCIPALS

We have discussed the myriad of challenges and responsibilities that principals face in their daily role as a campus leader. As previously mentioned, these responsibilities have caused work-related stress and professional burnout that contribute to principals leaving the profession. In addition, we have stated that principals neglect their own self-care and have difficulty with work-life balance. Principals are often reluctant to tend to their own needs or admit when they need support because in doing so, they may subconsciously feel that they would be viewed as a weak leader (Marcus et al., 2019). Principals tend to care for everyone in their community—teachers, students, and parents—and they often create caring cultures with a focus on stakeholders' needs; however, this begs the question: Who takes care of the caretaker? In this section we discuss how mentoring can support principals in their own self-care.

Culture of Care

Noddings (2009) explains that caring relationships consist of two parties—namely, a person who is the caretaker and a person who is being cared for. We contend that principals are the caretakers of the schools that they serve, and *caring* refers to the relationships between principals and school stakeholders. Noddings (1984) further asserts that care exemplifies *engrossment*—where the caretaker provides protection, solicitude for another, and a commitment to the cared-for individual. A core function of school leadership is the idea that principals care for stakeholders by building a sense of community in and with the teachers and students in their schools (Angelle, 2017). Ideally, principals are accessible emotionally as well as physically and intellectually in creating meaningful relationships with teachers, parents, and students; consequently, principals risk being emotionally drained by giving of themselves until they have nothing more to offer. Because principals are tasked with creating caring school cultures through positive relationships, trust, and a sense of belonging (Smit & Scherman, 2016), the supportive nature of interpersonal relationships in a caring school climate is vital for student learning.

Although principals are now looked at as the culture-builder of a campus and the creator of a culture of caring, they have not historically been viewed as caretakers or care givers; moreover, the majority of research on caretaker or care giver well-being centers on medical professionals—mainly doctors, nurses, and counselors—not educators. Caretakers encounter several commonalities in caring for others: high physical and emotional demands (Tamayo et al., 2010), an absence of social support (Dellasega & Haagen, 2004; Hsieh et al., 2008), and increased stress and burnout (Delaney, 2018; Wolf & France, 2017). Moreover, caretakers often experience *compassion fatigue*, which represents an emotional overload that occurs when a caretaker overextends themselves by becoming physically and emotionally overwhelmed with caring for others (Boyatzis et al., 2006). For a principal, compassion fatigue can occur when they encounter an excessive burden of responsibilities in caring for their school community and do not recognize the need for their own self-care. Mahfouz (2020) argues:

> Shifting that notion to help school administrators realize the need for self-care as a crucial element for conserving resources to be able to attend to the needs of others is important. Self-care needs to be part of their professional self-understanding. Social-emotional skills based or mindfulness-based programmes that include self-awareness, self-management could help school leaders address stressors by enabling them to acquire or enhance stress management skills and practices within an experiential learning context. (p. 453)

An intervention for caretakers in practicing self-care includes peer support (Flintham, 2003; Pass, 2009) through mentoring and/or coaching.

Mentoring

Mentoring has become a recognized method of supporting and developing novice principals as they begin their careers; however, there is little research on how mentoring is used as professional support for principals in self-care and well-being (Hayes & Mahfouz, 2020). Traditionally, mentoring is defined as a relationship between an older, more experienced mentor and a younger less experienced protégé for the purpose of supporting and developing the protégé's career (Ragins, 2002). In this capacity, mentors serve their protégés by providing acceptance and support, dispensing advice and guidance, coaching in the ways of the organization, communicating important and sometimes privileged information, offering visibility and exposure, and extending protection (Jacobi, 1991). Some mentoring theorists (Blake-Beard et al., 2007; Ragins, 2002) have asserted that an effective mentoring relationship can mitigate the negative effects of a difficult or stressful work environment. A key element of an effective mentoring relationship is a mutually beneficial relationship between the mentor and mentee that is developmental and supportive (Ragins, 2016). Dutton and Ragins (2007) used the term "high quality mentoring relationships" (p. 388) when discussing positive working relationships and expected that a high-quality mentoring relationship can buffer employees from adverse working conditions. High-quality mentoring relationships "provide safe havens [for individuals to find their] best and authentic selves" (Ragins, 2016, p. 228) and are marked by "mutual experiences of closeness, connection, trust, responsiveness, and vulnerability" (p. 229).

Peer Mentoring

The traditional definition of mentoring assumes a power differential inherent in mentoring relationships, and traditional mentoring is often depicted as a hierarchical relationship, with the mentor in the top/superior position and the protégé in the bottom/inferior position. A nontraditional model of mentorship is peer mentoring (Preston et al., 2014; Rieske & Benjamin, 2015), in which the mentoring relationship is nonhierarchical. Peer mentoring is the pairing of two people in similar contexts that encourage mutual growth and success. It is usually informal and often occurs organically between colleagues; however, school districts can facilitate peer mentoring through peer networks and formalized peer mentoring sessions. Peer mentoring relationships can result in high-quality mentoring relationships where both people benefit from a close relationship that is built on mutual trust and growth (Ragins, 2016). It would be considered a more appropriate form of support to principals in self-care and well-being, as peer mentoring reduces isolation and enhances well-being (Kamrath & Gregg, 2018). In addition, peer mentoring can be effective in helping principals at various stages of their careers and not relegated to supporting only novice principals.

Healthy peer mentoring relationships take time to develop and if school districts decide to implement a peer mentoring program, then district officials should provide time and space for mentoring relationships to form (Hayes, 2019). Principals in peer mentoring relationships in particular need time to develop a mutually beneficial close relationship they can trust in order to practice self-care with confidence.

Reis et al. (2004) explained that peers can develop close relationships through *partner responsiveness*, which includes understanding, respect, care, and support. Through partner responsiveness, peer mentors can provide each other with encouragement, guidance, support, education, and counsel. Principals may need guidance and practice in developing their own active listening and communication skills in order to fully engage in a peer mentoring relationship. Peer mentoring can be transformative, but principals in a peer mentoring relationship should establish a safe space to discuss concerns, hone their skills related to personal growth, and "learn to be authentic and emotionally present in their mentoring relationship" (Ragins, 2016, p. 234). In a study on the U.K. criminal justice system, Buck (2017) outlines the core conditions of peer mentoring as caring, listening, and setting manageable goals. She found that peer mentoring is shown to release stress and anxiety and to explore new ways of handling stress through genuine care, listening, and limited goals. Buck describes the importance of each of these components:

- *Genuine care* is an expression of altruism, based upon understanding . . . peer mentors are motivated by an emotional awareness of what mentees are going through, rather than by personal gain. (p. 6)
- *Listening* is an intervention in itself. It enables people to unburden themselves of problems, to begin to see themselves as capable of self-direction when conditions feel overwhelming and to feel heard. (p. 13).
- *Limited goals* are significant because they seem achievable and motivation is sustained because people see the progress they are making. (p. 16).

A few researchers (e.g., Boyatzis et al., 2006; Steward, 2014) have recommended peer mentoring or peer coaching to support school leaders in self-care and well-being. Boyatzis et al. (2006) hypothesize that the integration of peer coaching would result in principal well-being and assert that school leaders require more relational approaches to their leadership development, including self-care and compassion. Similarly, Steward (2014) found in her study on head teachers and emotional resilience in the U.K. that head teachers—whom we would call lead teachers in the United States—benefit from peer coaching. She recommends, "[C]ontinue to promote coaching for head teachers to provide a professional, nonjudgmental, confidential environment in which they can take time out to reflect and express any feelings of vulnerability" (p. 67). Although these researchers have cited the benefits of peer mentoring for principal well-being, they do not explain what it looks like in practice.

POSSIBLE PRACTICES

We propose that peer mentoring can be a viable option for supporting principals in self-care and well-being. To support practitioners, we offer three recommendations—mentoring, short-term goals, and mindfulness—for practical actions on how peer mentoring may support principals in self-care.

Mentoring

Although mentoring is not the cure for all professional learning needs of school principals, researchers (Clayton et al., 2013; Hayes, 2019; Hayes & Burkett, 2020; Oplatka & Lapidot, 2018) have shown that mentoring reduces principal isolation and builds confidence. Principals need support from a valued peer who understands the complex nature of the principalship. Having a trusted colleague or a network of peers to discuss issues and concerns can be a valuable resource for principals. Through peer mentoring, principals can establish a trusting relationship where they can speak freely about the stress of their job and discuss ways to reduce their stress. Establishing trust takes time, but it can be facilitated through shared norms and expectations (Ragins, 2016). Principals in a peer mentoring relationship should establish shared norms from the onset of the relationship, outlining what each member needs from the relationship and how to ensure confidentiality and open communication. Peers should also conduct frequent check-ins with each other and ask reflective questions about well-being, such as: *What did you do for yourself today? What are you going to do today that is not work related? How will you spend time with your family and loved ones this week? How will you take time off from work or thinking about work this week?* Principals need time to reflect on their own well-being (Mahfouz, 2020), so the focus of mentoring sessions should be on self-care and well-being. Principals can share their work-related and personal stress with one another and discuss how they can work through the stress together. Principals will benefit from having a peer who understands the stressors of being a building leader and serve as a buffer to minimize the effects of that stress.

Short-Term Goals

Establishing short-term goals and holding each other responsible for those goals is important in a peer mentoring relationship (Buck, 2017). Principals in a peer mentoring relationship should create goals together that are focused on self-care and well-being. Principals can choose goals focused on both personal and professional self-care, as outlined in the framework proposed by Lee and Miller (2013). Moreover, exercise and fresh air have been shown to reduce stress and increase well-being (Elmagd, 2016), and peers can create shared goals that include daily exercise or frequent mental breaks outdoors and motivate each other to meet those goals. Mentoring meetings can also occur outdoors, and principals can meet and discuss issues related to well-being while walking outdoors together. Principals should also allow themselves the opportunity to use the mentoring sessions as a break from the daily responsibilities of leading a school; they need support in understanding that prioritizing their own self-care is not selfish, but instead allows the principal to be the best version of themselves (Lee & Miller, 2013; Mahfouz, 2020).

Mindfulness

Mindfulness, which has been found to decrease stress and support well-being, refers to a process that leads to a mental state characterized by nonjudgmental awareness of the present moment experience, including one's sensations, thoughts, bodily states, consciousness, and the environment, while encouraging openness, curiosity, and acceptance (Hoffman et al., 2010). Mindfulness can be beneficial to school leaders in reducing stress and improving overall well-being (Wells & Klocko, 2018); moreover, "professional organizations should offer training in mindfulness for principals through workshops ... training that focuses on dialogue and promotes mindful listening, self-compassion, and mindfulness practice" (p. 168).

In a peer mentoring relationship, principals can attend mindfulness workshops or trainings together and then together practice the slow and deep breathing techniques involved in mindfulness meditation. By engaging in mindfulness meditation in mentoring episodes, principals can strengthen their self-awareness of their stress and anxiety level and be able to alleviate it quickly.

CONCLUSION

The school principal is vital to leading 21st century schools. Supporting and retaining school principals is critical because when principals leave the profession, their expertise, their experience, and their caring leave with them (Fuller, 2012; Wells & Klocko, 2018). Principals are being faced with ongoing pressures of school accountability, standardized testing, student advocacy, and instructional improvement. Moreover, principals are often isolated and lonely, and very few people understand the increasing pressure for principals in leading schools and the stress that arises from that pressure. Mentoring continues to be an effective means for principals' socialization into the profession and for professional learning throughout their career.

Throughout this chapter, (a) we discussed the difficult nature of the principalship and the stressors that accompany the principal's role; (b) we highlighted the principal's role as a caretaker and discussed that while serving in this role, principals neglect their own self-care; (c) we discussed the need for principals to engage in self-care in order to reduce burnout and mediate stress; and (d) we conceptualized that peer mentoring can be useful in supporting principals with self-care and well-being. This entire chapter, in fact, is conceptual in nature, and we recommend that researchers in future studies analyze the relationship between mentoring and self-care and mindfulness. We also suggest that school district officials prioritize the self-care practices of principals by offering professional development opportunities and peer mentoring networks in self-care and mindfulness. Finally, we recommend that school officials give principals the time and space to develop healthy, high-quality mentoring relationships by allowing principals to partner with peers and work together in nontraditional formats (e.g., meeting for walking sessions or lunch meetings during school hours). By helping principals recognize the need for self-care and by giving them the space and tools to do so, school district officials can begin to care for their caretakers.

REFERENCES

Angelle, P. S. (2017). Beliefs and behaviors of two high school principals in developing a sense of school community for students. *NASSP Bulletin, 101*(1), 5–22.

Beausaert, S. A. J., Froehlich, D. E., Devos, C., & Riley, P. (2016). Effects of support on stress and burnout in school principals. *Educational Research, 58*(4), 347–365.

Blake-Beard, S.D., Murrell, A., & Thomas, D. (2007). Unfinished business: the impact of race on understanding mentoring relationships. In B. R. Ragins & K.E. Kram (Eds), *The handbook of mentoring at work: Theory, research, and practice* (pp. 223–247). SAGE.

Boyatzis, R., Smith, R., & Blaize, M. (2006). Developing sustainable leaders through coaching and compassion. *Academy of Management Learning and Education 5*(1), 8–24. https://doi.org/10.5465/amle.2006.20388381

Boyland, L. (2011). Job stress and coping strategies of elementary school principals: A statewide study. *Current Issues in Education, 14*(3), 1–11.

Branch, G., Hanushek, E., & Rivkin, S. (2013). School leaders matter. *Education Next, 13*(1), 62–69. http://educationnext.org/school-leaders-matter/

Buck, G. (2017). The core conditions of peer mentoring. *Criminology & Criminal Justice, 18*(2), 1–23. https://doi.org/10.1177/1748895817699659

Burkett, J. D., & Hayes, S. (2018). Campus administrators' responses to Donald Trump's immigration policy: Leadership during times of uncertainty. *International Journal of Educational Leadership and Management, 6*(2), 98–125.

Byrne-Jimenez, M., & Orr, M.T. (2012). Thinking in three dimensions: Leadership for capacity building, sustainability, and succession. *Journal of Cases in Educational Leadership, 15*(3), 33–46.

Catano, N., & Stronge, J. H. (2006). What are principals expected to do? Congruence between principal evaluation and performance standards. *NASSP Bulletin, 90*(3), 221–237.

Clayton, J. K., Sanzo, K. L., & Myran, S. (2013). Understanding mentoring in leadership development: Perspectives of district administrators and aspiring leaders. *Journal of Research on Leadership Education, 8*(1), 77–96.

Currie, B. (2015). *All hands-on deck*. Corwin.

Cushing, K. S., Kerrins, J. A., & Johnstone, T. (2003). Disappearing principals. *Leadership, 32*(5), 28–29, 37.

Daresh, J. (2004). Mentoring school leaders: Professional promise or predictable problems? *Educational Administration Quarterly, 40*(4), 495–517.

Daresh, J. C. (2007). Mentoring for beginning principals: Revisiting the past or preparing for the future? *Mid-Western Educational Researcher, 20*(4), 21–27.

Davis, S. H., & Darling-Hammond, L. (2012). Innovative principal preparation programs: What works and how we know. *Planning and Changing, 43*(1–2), 25–45.

Delaney, M. C. (2018). Caring for the caregivers: Evaluation of the effect of an eight-week pilot mindful self-compassion (MSC) training program on nurses' compassion fatigue and resilience. *PLoS ONE, 13*(11), 1–20.

Dellasega, C., & Haagen, B. (2004). A different kind of caregiving support group. *Journal of Psychosocial Nursing, 42*(8), 47–55.

DeMatthews, D. E. (2015). Clearing a path for inclusion: Distributing leadership in a high performing elementary school. *Journal of School Leadership, 25*(2), 1000–1038.

DeMatthews, D. E., Carrola, P., Knight, D., & Izquierdo, E. (2019). Principal burnout: How urban school leaders experience secondary trauma on the U.S.-Mexico border. *Leadership and Policy in Schools, 18*(4), 681–700. https://doi.org/10.1080/15700763.2018.1513153

Dutton, J. E., & Ragins, B. R. (2007). Moving forward: Positive relationships at work as a research frontier. In J. E. Dutton & B. R. Ragins (Eds.), *Exploring positive relationships at work: Building a theoretical and research foundation* (pp. 387–400). LEA's organization and management series. Lawrence Erlbaum.

Elmagd, M.A. (2016). Benefits, need, and importance of daily exercise. *International Journal of Physical Education, Sports and Health, 3*(5), 22–27.

Flintham, A. (2003). *Reservoirs of hope*. National College for School Leadership.

Freudenberger, H. J. (1974). Staff burnout. *Journal of Social Issues, 30*(1), 159–164.

Fullan, M. (2014). *The principal: Three keys to maximize impact*. Jossey-Bass

Fuller, E. (2012). *Examining principal turnover*. National Education Policy Center. https://nepc.colorado.edu/blog/examining-principal-turnover

Goleman, D., Boyatzis, R., & McKee, A. (2002). *Primal leadership: Realizing the power of emotional intelligence*. Harvard Business School.

Gumus, E., & Bellibas, M. S. (2016). The effects of professional development activities on principals' perceived instructional leadership practices: Multi-country data analysis using TALIS 2013. *Educational Studies, 42*(3), 287–301.

Hayes, S. D. (2019). Using developmental relationships in mentoring to support novice principals as leaders of learning. *Mentoring & Tutoring: Partnership in Learning, 27*(2), 190–212.

Hayes, S. D., & Burkett, J. R. (2020). Almost a principal: Coaching and training assistant principals for the next level of leadership. *Journal of School Leadership* https://journals.sagepub.com/home/jsl#

Hayes, S. D., & Mahfouz, J. (2020). Principals and mentorship: An international review of empirical research from 1999–2019. *Research in Educational Administration & Leadership, 5*(3), 722–751.

Hoffman, S. G., Sawyer, A. T., Witt, A. A., & Oh, D. (2010). The effect of mindfulness-based therapy on anxiety and depression: A meta-analytic review. *Clinical Psychology, 78*(2), 169–183.

Howley, A., Andrianaivo, S., & Perry, J. (2005). The pain outweighs the gain: Why teachers don't want to become principals. *The Teachers College Record, 107*(4), 757–782.

Hsieh, H., Wang, J., Yen, M., & Liu, T. (2008). Educational support group in changing caregivers' psychological elder abuse behavior toward caring for institutionalized elders. *Advances in Health Science Education, 14*(2), 377–386.

Jacobi, M. (1991). Mentoring and undergraduate academic success: A literature review. *Review of Educational Research, 61*(4), 505–532.

Kamrath, B., & Gregg, J. (2018). Escaping the prison classroom: A case study of correctional teacher turnover and retention. *Journal of Correctional Education, 69*(2), 59–71.

Klocko, B. A., Wells, C. M. (2015). Workload pressures of principals: A focus on renewal, support and mindfulness. *NASSP Bulletin, 99*(2), 332–355. https://doi.org/10.1177/0192636515619727

Lee, J. J., & Miller, S. E. (2013). A self-care framework for social workers: Building a strong foundation for practice. *Families in Society: The Journal of Contemporary Social Services*, *94*(2), 96–103.

Leithwood, K., Seashore Louis, K., Anderson, S., & Wahlstrom, K. (2004). *How leadership influences student learning*. Report commissioned by The Wallace Foundation. https://conservancy.umn.edu/bitstream/handle/11299/2035/?sequence=1

Leiter, M.P., & Maslach, C. (2004). Areas of worklife: A structured approach to organizational predictors of job burnout. In P. L. Perrewe & D. C. Ganster (Eds.), *Research in occupational stress and well-being: Emotional and Physiological processes and positive intervention strategies* (pp. 91–134). JAI Press.

Lemoine, P. A., McCormack, T. J., & Richardson, M. D. (2018). Planning strategies to fill principal vacancies: The issues and some choices. *Educational Planning*, *25*(1), 17–28.

Levin, S., & Bradley, K. (2019). *Understanding and addressing principal turnover: A review of the research*. National Association of Secondary School Principals.

Lindberg, E. (2012). The power of role design: Balancing the principals' financial responsibility with the implications of stress. *Educational Assessment, Evaluation and Accountability*, *24*(2), 151–171.

Lynch, J. M. (2012). Responsibilities of today's principal: Implications for principal preparation programs and principal certification policies. *Rural Special Education Quarterly*, *31*(1), 40–47.

Mahfouz, J. (2020). Principals and stress: Few coping strategies for abundant stressors. *Educational Management Administration & Leadership*, *48*(3), 440–458. https://doi.org/10.1177/1741143218817562

Marcus, L. J., McNulty, E. J., Henderson, J. M., & Dorn. B. C. (2019). *Crisis, change, and how to lead when it matters most: You're it*. Hachette Book Group.

Markow, D., Macia, L., & Lee, H. (2013). *Challenges for school leadership: A survey of teachers and principals*. Harris Interactive for MetLife. https://www.metlife.com/about/corporate-responsibility/metlife-foundation/reports-and research/survey-american-teacher.html

Marzano, R. J., Waters, T., & McNulty, B. A. (2005). *School leadership that works: From research to results*. Association for Supervision and Curriculum Development.

Miller, A. (2013). Principal turnover and student achievement. *Economics of Education Review*, *36*(3), 60–72. https://doi.org/10.1016/j.econedurev.2013.05.004

Murphy, L. R., & Sauter, S. L. (2011). The USA perspective: Current issues and trends in the management of work stress. *Australian Psychologist*, *38*(2), 151–157. https://doi.org/10.1080/00050060310001707157

Noddings, N. (1984). *Caring*. The University of California Press.

Noddings, N. (2009). All our students thinking. In M. Scherer (Ed.), *Engaging the whole child: Reflections on best practices in learning, teaching and leadership* (pp. 91–100). ASCD.

Oplatka, I. (2017). Principal workload: Components, determinants and coping strategies in an era of standardization and accountability. *Journal of Educational Administration*, *55*(5), 552–568.

Oplatka, I., & Lapidot, A. (2018). Novice principals' perceptions of their mentoring process in early career stage: The key role of mentor-protégé relations. *Journal of Educational Administration & History*, *50*(3), 204–222.

Pass, J. (2009). *It's life, but not as we know it*. National Conference of State Legislatures.

Pendola, A., & Fuller, E. J. (2018). Principal stability and the rural divide. *Journal of Research in Rural Education, 34*(1), 1–20.

Philips, A., Sen, D., & McNamee, R. (2007). Prevalence and causes of self-reported work-related stress in head teachers. *Occupational Medicine, 57*(5), 367–376.

Preston, J.P., Ogenchuk, M.J., & Nsiah, J.K. (2014). Peer mentorship and transformational learning: PhD student experiences. *Canadian Journal of Higher Education, 44*(1), 52-68.

Pounder, D. G., & Merrill, R. J. (2001). Job desirability of the high school principalship: A job choice theory perspective. *Educational Administration Quarterly, 37*(1), 27–57.

Ragins, B. R. (2002). Understanding diversified mentoring relationships: Definitions, challenges and strategies. In D. Clutterbuck & B. R. Ragins (Eds.), *Mentoring and diversity: An international perspective* (pp. 23–53). Blackwell.

Ragins, B. R. (2016). From the ordinary to the extraordinary: High quality mentoring relationships at work. *Organizational Dynamics, 45*(1), 228–244. http://dx.doi.org/10.1016/j.orgdyn.2016.07.008

Rayfield, R., & Diamantes, T. (2003). Principal satisfaction and the shortage of educational leaders. *Connections: Journal of Principal Development and Preparation, 5*(1), 38–46.

Rieske, L. J., & Benjamin, M. (2015). Utilizing peer mentor roles in learning communities. *New Directions for Student Services, 2015*(149), 67–77. https://doi.org/10.1002/ss.20118.

Reis, H. T., Clark, M. S., & Holmes, J. G. (2004). Perceived partner responsiveness as an organizing construct in the study of intimacy and closeness. In D. J. Mashek & A. Aron (Eds), *The handbook of closeness and intimacy* (pp. 201–228). Lawrence Erlbaum.

Riley, P., See, S-M., Marsh, H., & Dicke, T. (2017). *The Australian Principal Occupational Health, Safety and Wellbeing Survey (IPPE Report)*. Institute for Positive Psychology and Education, Australian Catholic University.

Robinson, V. M., Lloyd, C. A., & Rowe, K. J. (2008). The impact of leadership on student outcomes: An analysis of the differential effects of leadership types. *Educational Administration Quarterly, 44*(5), 635–674.

Rodela, K., Cochrun, A., Haines, D., & Adelson-Journey, S. (2020). Tiptoeing around the elephant in the room: Discreet activism for social justice in conservative school communities following the 2016 presidential election. *Journal of Education Human Resources, 38*(1), 8–34.

Smit, B., & Scherman, V. (2016). The case for relational leadership and an ethics of care for counteracting bullying at schools. *South Africa Journal of Education, 36*(4), 1–9.

Steward, J. (2014). Sustaining emotional resilience for school leadership. *School Leadership & Management, 34*(1), 52–38. https://doi.org/10.1080/13632434.2013.849686

Tamayo, G., Broxson, A., Munsell, M., & Cohen, M. (2010). Caring for the caregiver. *Oncology Nursing Forum, 37*(1), 50–57.

Theoharis, G. (2010). Disrupting injustice: Principals narrate the strategies they use to improve their schools and advance social justice. *Teachers College Record, 112*(1), 331–373.

van der Merwe, H., & Parsotam, A. (2012). School principal stressors and a stress alleviation strategy based on controlled breathing. *Journal of Asian and African Studies 47*(6), 666–678.

Wells, C. M. (2013). Educational leaders describe a job too big for one: Stress reduction in the midst of leading. *AASA Journal of Scholarship & Practice, 10*(3), 32–45.

Wells, C. M. (2016). *Mindfulness: How school leaders can reduce stress and thrive on the job*. Rowman & Littlefield.

Wells, C. M., & Klocko, B. A. (2018). Principal well-being and resilience: Mindfulness as a means to that end. *NASSP Bulletin, 102*(2), 161–173. https://doi.org/10.1177%2F0192636518777813

West, D. L., Peck, C. M., Reitzug, U. C., & Crane, E. A. (2014). Accountability, autonomy, and stress: Principal responses to superintendent change in a large US urban school district. *School Leadership & Management, 34*(4), 372–391.

Wolf, Z. R., & France, N. E. M. (2017). Caring in nursing theory. *International Journal for Human Caring, 21*(2), 95–108.

CHAPTER 20

SOUL OF LEADERSHIP

Sustaining Principals Through Courage, Presence, and Integrity

Rick Rogers and Mary Watkins

The Toughest Job You'll Ever Love (Rick)

I deeply loved being a principal. Inspired by Roland Barth's book Run School Run *[1980], I decided early in my teaching career that I wanted to be a principal. Roland's later work had a profound impact on my thinking about schools and leadership. I went on to serve as a principal in four districts over 28 years. I enjoyed both the daily interactions and the long-term relationships with children and adults. I was engaged by the challenges of building community and fostering change at the school-level.*

While I worked extremely hard, I was able to sustain the pace because it was a labor of love. As John Dewey wrote, "To find out what one is fitted to do, and to secure an opportunity to do it, is the key to happiness" (Dewey, 1916). Still, when I became eligible to retire, I realized that, despite my happiness, it was indeed time to slow down.

Now that I work to support principals as a coach and facilitator, I am heartened by the talent, dedication, and passion I see among our current crop of leaders. However, I am concerned that our principals are struggling to stay afloat with the emotional and time demands of their work and the impact it has on their personal well-being and their work-life balance. How do we sustain the people who choose to take on what I consider to be, in the words of the Peace Corps slogan, "The toughest job you'll ever love?"

"How Do You Manage It All?" (Mary)

In my education administrative master's program, we discussed stress-management exactly twice. One professor handed out an article for principals (having nothing to do with the course) that advised exercise and healthy eating. Another professor, and mother to teenagers, advised several of us in the Mom crowd: "My house is clean, but not super clean, I can't do drinks on Thursdays with the girls, and family time is at school." The one-page article and the quick chat were helpful, but obviously not enough to capture the social-emotional challenges of the principalship.

I began in my role as high school principal when I was 39 years old, with two children under the age of 7. By the end of year one, I knew that I would need to pay continuous attention to my internal SEL skills in order to sustain myself long term in the role. Being fully present to my family on the weekends presented a real challenge. So, when an email came through from the Massachusetts School Administrators' Association inviting principals to apply for an initiative entitled the Soul of Leadership, I jumped on the opportunity, and was ultimately selected to participate as a member of the first cohort.

The Principal Matters

It is widely understood that principals play a crucial role in cultivating a school culture in which staff, students, and families feel safe, cared for, and valued. Relational trust is critical to a healthy school culture and social and academic outcomes for students (Bryk & Schneider, 2004). Zaretta Hammond's work on culturally responsive teaching challenges educators to "create an environment that the brain perceives as safe and nurturing so it can relax, let go of any stress, and turn its attention to learning" (Hammond, 2015 p. 50).

At the same time, we know that principals experience substantial job-related stress that can compromise their personal well-being as well as their leadership (Mahfouz, 2020; Mahfouz et al., 2019). School shutdowns and the resulting shift to remote learning caused by the pandemic has only underscored these challenges. Anecdotally, principals report working just as hard remotely, while managing increased stress and anxiety as they respond to unprecedented circumstances. School leaders often end up "holding" the feelings of anxiety for those in their communities, contributing to their own overload. Now more than ever, the time is right for school leaders to dig deeper and embrace the relational aspects of their work (Rebora, 2017).

As a former long-time principal now working to support school leaders and as a current high school principal, we share a concern that school leaders will be able to sustain the work. We share a belief that the role of principal needs to be transformed with a renewed emphasis on personal well-being, reflection, and collegial relationships. In this chapter, we introduce a new program that seeks to help school leaders develop the disposition and skills to be fully present, listen mindfully, and reflect, while learning strategies to manage job-related stress and tools to promote a culturally responsive and trusting school community.

SOUL OF LEADERSHIP

Soul of Leadership: Courage, Presence & Integrity offers a unique renewal experience for school leaders. Courage & Renewal Northeast, a regional affiliate of the Center for Courage and Renewal, first created Leading Together: Building Adult Community in Schools (Seigle et al., 2016). Chip Wood, a cofounder of Responsive Classroom, and Pamela Seigle, founder of Open Circle, wrote:

> As prior public school teachers and administrators who helped pioneer professional development programs for classrooms that integrated social, emotional, and academic learning, we became increasingly aware that strategies we were providing to teachers for use with their students were also needed for the adult community of schools and their leaders.

With the support of the Angell Foundation, authors Seigle and Wood collaborated with Rick Rogers and the Massachusetts School Administrators' Association (MSAA) in 2018 to develop Soul of Leadership as a role-alike experience for principals.

Soul of Leadership offers school leaders the time, space, and skilled facilitation to do what Parker J. Palmer (2004) calls "the work before the work" (p. 104). Soul of Leadership enhances participants' capacity as leaders, provides a lived experience of the process of building relational trust, and offers strategies to help leaders strengthen SEL in their adult community. In order to develop their critical capacity for self-awareness and reflection, participants are invited to reflect on their lives and work through contemplative practices drawn from the Center for Courage & Renewal and the fields of mindfulness, social-emotional learning, neuroscience, and poetry, literature, and the arts. The program helps integrate reflective practices into the routine of administrative team meetings and helps teams apply these practices to their daily work.

Program Description

The format includes four single-day retreat sessions, spread quarterly over the course of the school year, combined with three virtual, small-group sessions in between. In-person sessions take place in a circle as a way to create a safe space for shared experience (Open Circle, Responsive Classroom, Circle of Trust). Virtual group sessions began two years prior to virtual meetings, becoming ubiquitous during the pandemic. But unlike administrative meetings to deal with problem-solving and logistical or curricular issues, these virtual sessions have provided needed stress relief by providing time for reflection about personal and professional needs as leaders. The blended format is mutually reinforcing and allows for deepening the relationships of the participants between sessions.

Session are anchored by the "touchstones" (Center for Courage and Renewal, 2022). Many educators have experience in using group norms; however, these touchstones are distinguished by principles and practices that nurture integrity and the courage to act. At the core of the work is the touchstone: "Be present as fully as possible."

Mindful listening is a key skill for leaders and contributes to building authentic relationships. Each of the sessions provide the structure and discipline to allow principals to build their listening "muscle" by practicing mindful listening before responding, and learning to ask open and honest questions (Palmer, 2004) whose purpose is to support the speaker's personal understanding of the issue at hand.

In order to help principals develop the capacity to be more present in their leadership, participants also engage in mindfulness practices, including breathing, meditation, and movement, and consider the three modes of care—receiving care, cultivating self-care, and extending care (Mind and Life Institute, 2020).

Protocols

Soul of Leadership models the use of protocols to provide structures that allow for internal and collective reflection. This section provides a description of some key activities, as well as responses from participants after particularly meaningful sessions. These protocols can be brought back to schools to be used in faculty and team meetings in order to lift every voice.

Poetry. Poetry is a regular feature of the experience. Poems focus on such themes as leadership, courage, gaining perspective, and reconnecting with personal values. Billy Collins (1988) famously wrote that too often we "tie the poem to a chair with rope and torture a confession out of it." Instead, participants reflect on how the poem speaks to them in their life and work.

Reading and responding to poetry in this way creates another opportunity for listening and reflection. Participants take turns reading stanzas of a poem and then are invited to respond to a prompt question or what speaks to them in the poem.

One participant shared the impact of poetry discovered via Soul of Leadership:

> I've referenced poetry when I've needed to "recenter" my focus, and introduced it in several leadership activities with success. In that circumstance, the poem better expressed my hopes for my school at the start of the school year than I could have via a bulleted, digital slide. During the pandemic closure I took a risk and emailed a SoL poem to my high school staff (I was truly worried that it would be laughed off!). Yet, instead of silence, I receive several emails of gratitude. I was also pleased to learn that an English teacher brought it to students so that they could reflect together as a class.

Excellent poetry, recited in community, captures and recreates an emotional wavelength and rhythm that allows for deep connection among participants. Principals may feel poetry is too metaphorical for meetings, but it can be successfully received by staff and students alike.

Steppingstones. In this activity, participants reflect on key events or people in their lives as a means of understanding themselves and who they are as leaders. A volunteer shares with the group what they learned from their reflection. Group members respond by asking open and honest questions as a means of supporting the individual to deeper understanding; they learn to focus on mindful listening rather than on fixing or advising. Repeated sessions allowed all participants to practice these challenging skills. One participant reported on their growth:

> I'm developing a heightened sensibility for whether or not I'm actively listening to people—namely, by noticing and resisting the urge to "add on," shift the narrative back toward myself, or "problem solve." I continue to refine the art of asking open and honest questions.

The art of asking open and honest questions is likely counter intuitive to most solutions-focused principals. However, these skills can be developed if principals are provided with direct instruction and given the space and time to practice.

The Möbius strip. This exercise invited participants to consider whether and to what extent we bring our fullest selves to work (Palmer, 2004). Participants identified the parts of the self they actively present at work and wrote them on one side of a strip of paper; next, they identified the parts of self

they keep hidden during the workday—reserved for life beyond school—
and wrote those on the reverse of the strip. One participant shared:

> Linking the ends of my Möbius strip together into a continuous geometric curve provided me a vision for a more integrated self—a self that is free to flow more fluidly between work and home, a self that is more authentic in interactions and relationships with others at work, and a self that remains in touch with deeply held values while at work.

The exercise pushed participants to consider how the integration (or lack thereof) of self between home and work affects well-being—a critical question for every principal.

CLOSING REFLECTIONS

Conditions in our increasingly complex world challenge us as citizens, and particularly as educators, to help our students develop the pivotal skills of democracy—an understanding that we are all in this together, an appreciation of the value of diversity, an ability to hold tension in life-giving ways, a sense of personal voice and agency, and a capacity to create community.

In order to cultivate this vision, principals must be prosocial leaders (Mahfouz et al., 2019) who ensure that all stakeholders in their school community feel safe, respected, and valued and who develop their own social competencies to handle stress and model caring and culturally responsive behaviors.

In its first five years, Soul of Leadership has reached over 150 principals from diverse communities across Massachusetts. An evaluation conducted by the Center for Creative Leadership found the program to be personally transformative. Principals were much more likely to feel hopeful and experience increased efficacy after the program. Resilience in the face of challenges increased. And principals formed strong collaborative relationships with other principals participating in Soul of Leadership that flourished beyond the program. Ongoing research will look at the impact of the program on improving relational trust between teachers and colleagues and teachers and their principal.

The Who and the Why of Our Vocation (Mary)

The bit of advice offered by my professors in graduate school holds true—sleep and exercise are critical, and you can learn to let go of worries on the weekends. Thanks to Soul of Leadership, I've also learned that developing and maintaining bonds with others who share your calling and who are deeply familiar with the personal challenges of the role is critical.

The consistency of our meetings and frequent return to the "touchstones" of our practice allows me to reflect on my vocational commitment regularly. I feel greater integrity in bringing all of myself to work and back home again. Knowing and reflecting on the "who" and "why" of my vocation has helped to sustain me, especially during the pandemic closures. Furthermore, I have leaned heavily on members of my small group through virtual meetings, and I'm grateful to have had this support system in place prior to the closure.

Finally, my Soul of Leadership experience has reinforced to me that while there is power in speaking, there is substantial power in listening. I would advocate for any new principal to prioritize building a community of support and setting aside ongoing time for reflection.

Presence, Courage, and Integrity (Rick)

During our work together over the past five years, I have been profoundly moved by the depth of caring and reflection that these educators bring to our circle and their role as principal. The positive response is inspiring and gives me hope that today's generation of leaders will be able to sustain their leadership and maintain their equilibrium while facing the inevitable demands and challenges of the work. We must provide our leaders with the time, space, and experiences that will develop their presence as leaders and the courage and integrity to foster strong, equitable, and inclusive school communities in order for them to flourish in "the toughest job you'll ever love."

REFERENCES

Barth, R. S. (1980). *Run school run*. Harvard University Press.
Bryk, A. S., & Schneider, B. (2004). *Trust in schools: A core resource for improvement.* Russell Sage Foundation.
Center for Courage and Renewal. (2022). *Courage and renewal touchstones.* https://couragerenewal.org/library/courage-renewal-touchstones/
Collins, B. (1988). *The apple that astonished Paris.* University of Arkansas Press.
Dewey, J. (1916). *Democracy and education: An introduction to the philosophy of education.* The Free Press.
Hammond, Z. (2015). *Culturally responsive teaching and the brain: Promoting authentic engagement and rigor among culturally and linguistically diverse students.* Corwin Press.
Mahfouz, J. (2020). Principals and stress: Few coping strategies for abundant stressors. *Educational Management Administration & Leadership, 48*(3), 440–458.

Mahfouz, J., Greenberg, M., & Rodriguez, A. (2019). *Principals' social emotional competence: A key factor for creating caring schools* [Issue brief]. Pennsylvania State University.

Mind and Life Institute. (2020). *"Call to Care"* MindandLife.org https://www.mindandlife.org/legacy-programs/care/

Palmer, P. J. (2004). *A hidden wholeness: The journey toward an undivided life.* Jossey-Bass.

Rebora, A. (2017). Perspectives: Whole-school leaders. *Educational Leadership, 74*(8), 7.

Seigle, P., Sankowski, L., & Wood, C. (2016). *Leading together: Building adult communities in schools.* Center for Courage & Renewal.

ABOUT THE AUTHORS

EDITORS

Bradley W. Carpenter, PhD, is a Professor and Chair of the Education Department at Sul Ross State University. A former public-school teacher, assistant principal, and principal Dr. Carpenter has a passion for working with aspiring and current school and district leaders. Specifically, he enjoys his role in helping principals and superintendents realize their identity as transformational and healthy individuals that are best able to serve their communities. Dr. Carpenter's research is focused on three primary areas of scholarship: (a) Leadership Well-Being and Self-Care; (b) Development of Equity-Oriented School Leaders; and (c) How Discourses and Policymaking Shape Federal, State, and Local Policy.

Julia Mahfouz, PhD, is an associate professor and director of the Prosocial Leader Lab at the School of Education and Human Development at the University of Colorado Denver. Her research explores the social, emotional, and cultural dynamics of educational settings placing specific emphasis on mindfulness-based programs and adult social and emotional competencies, specifically that of school administrators and the integration of systemic SEL into principal preparation programs. Her research also examines the relationships among policy, school improvement, Social and emotional learning, and international education.

Kerry Robinson is an associate professor and school administration program coordinator with the Department of Educational Leadership at the University of North Carolina Wilmington. She earned her Ph.D. in Educational Leadership at Virginia Commonwealth University. Previously, she worked in PK–12 schools for 17 years in New Jersey and Virginia as a teacher, building level administrator, and district-level administrator. Her primary research areas include women in leadership, the superintendency, and wellbeing of school leaders. While maintaining a focus on research and teaching, Kerry also commits to supporting the development of aspiring and current leaders through her work with mentoring and building sustainable support networks.

AUTHORS

Chapter 1

Kathleen B. King, PhD, is an associate professor at North Central College in Naperville, IL and former PK–12 school principal. Her research interests center on educational leadership, social emotional learning, marginalized student populations, and school cultures of character.

April Harris is principal at China Spring Intermediate and formerly assistant principal at Midway Middle School. She is a 2022 graduate of Baylor University, earning her Doctor of Education. Her problem of practice focused on assistant principal stress and well-being. April has earned notable recognitions as a public education leader such as, Region 12 Assistant Principal of the Year (2018) and State Assistant Principal of the Year (2019). Additionally, she was recognized for her MMS Community and Beyond project published in *Texas Association of School Administrator's School Business* magazine in 2019–2020, and her MMS Therapy Dog Program published by the National Association of Secondary School Principals in March of 2021. Furthermore, April has presented at the state (TCEA, TASSP) and national level (NAPDS, STW) on the innovative programs and initiatives she and MMS implemented for optimal student success and well-being.

Angel Vales, EdD, is currently an Assistant Superintendent of Information Technology at Austin Independent School District, but has also served as a classroom teacher, school counselor, and central staff administrator for the past 14 years. A significant achievement during his tenure was the design and implementation of the Alcohol and Drug Intervention Program for Dallas Independent School District, which provided free prevention and intervention services, through partnerships with non-profit organizations, for students and families in the District. He also led and improved clinic-based programs for students, which provided a wide array of services, including but not limited to psychotherapy, psychiatry, and medication management. He earned his Doctor of Education in Educational Leadership from Baylor University and currently holds two clinician licenses in Texas, both Licensed Professional Counselor (LPC) and Licensed Chemical Dependency Counselor (LCDC). Aside from his educational journey, Dr. Vales has worked in private practice providing psychotherapy services to children, teens, adolescents, and adults."

Chapter 2

Denver J. Fowler currently serves as an Associate Professor and Department Chair in the Department of Educational Leadership and Policy Studies, within the College of Education, at Southern Connecticut State University. He has over a decade of experience in the higher education setting as an Adjunct/Assistant/Associate Professor, Graduate Program Coordinator, Doctoral Program Coordinator, Department Chair, and Interim Dean. Prior to his tenure in the higher education setting, Dr. Fowler was an award-winning practitioner and served as a Coach, Teacher, Athletic Director, Technology Coordinator, and School Administrator in the PreK–12 educational setting. Dr. Fowler has numerous publications and presentations on the topic of educational leadership. His publications include books, peer-reviewed chapters, and journal articles, as well as articles in top practitioner magazines. Dr. Fowler has presented his research in 20 U.S. states and the District of Columbia, as well as in China, Greece, Italy, Turkey, England, Puerto Rico, Spain, and Africa.

Sarah M. Jouganatos has over 20 years of experience working in education. She has held various roles in the TK–12 system such as teacher, English Language Development (ELD) coordinator, instructional coach, district level administration, and consultant. Currently, Dr. Jouganatos serves as an Associate Professor and Chair of Graduate and Professional Studies in Education Program Coordinator in the Educational Leadership and Policy Studies (TK–12) program, at California State University, Sacramento. Utilizing experience and expertise, Dr. Jouganatos connects practice and theory, in order to equip our future school leaders to challenge the status quo. Dr. Jouganatos's focus is to support and guide her students toward competency using various equity focused leadership styles that can be used in a diverse setting. She has successfully published numerous peer reviewed articles and contributed to various leadership books. Her research areas of interest contribute to areas of leadership practice, equity, instructional best practices, and underserved students.

Chapter 3

Kara Lasater is an assistant professor of Educational Leadership at the University of Arkansas. She has experience working in nonprofit and K–12 public education. Her research interests include the development of family-school partnerships, educators' use of data, and effective preparation of school leaders.

John Pijanowski is a professor and former Fulbright Scholar. He earned a bachelor's degree in psychology from Brown University and a master's and PhD from Cornell University in Social and Philosophical Foundations of Education. His research focuses on how people translate decision-making into action, self-care, and leadership development.

Josh Ray is a practicing public school principal at East Pointe Elementary in Greenwood, Arkansas. He holds an EdD from the University of Arkansas and is an advocate for the well-being of educational leaders and teachers.

Chapter 4

Vicki Bautista is an assistant professor at Creighton University in the department of interdisciplinary studies. She serves as a faculty member and the Assistant Program Director for the online master's in Integrative Health and Wellness. Additionally, she teaches both on campus and online courses in the bachelor's-level Healthy Lifestyle Management program. Bautista has an EdD in Interdisciplinary Leadership and is a Board-Certified Health & Wellness Coach. Prior to working at Creighton, she was employed in a variety of health promotion settings including, nonprofit, government, and research.

Gretchen Oltman is an associate professor at Creighton University. She is an author, attorney, and former high school English teacher. She currently leads the online Organizational Leadership master's degree program and the Sports Leadership graduate certificate program at Creighton. She is the author/coauthor of five books with her work focusing mainly on leadership, education, and the law.

Chapter 5

Benjamin Kutsyuruba is a Professor in Educational Policy and Leadership and School Law in the Faculty of Education, Queen's University at Kingston, Ontario. His teaching and research areas include educational law, policymaking, and leadership; teacher induction and mentorship; trust, ethics, and moral agency; and educational reform and change. Benjamin has worked as a teacher, researcher, manager, and professor in education in Ukraine and Canada.

Terry Kharyati, MEd, is currently a Director General at CEGEP Heritage College in Gatineau, Quebec, Canada. He is a former school principal and a Secretary General/Director of Programs and Evaluation with the Western Quebec District School Board. He is a recipient of 2014 Canada's Outstanding Principals Award. Terry completed his Master's at the Faculty of Education at Queen's University.

Nadia Arghash, MEd, BA, BSc, is a researcher in the field of education at Queen's University, Canada. She is interested in positive psychology as it relates to the conditions that promote well-being for individuals in the educational context. Her research pursuits include positive organizational leadership and thriving for students of higher education.

Chapter 6

Maryann Krikorian serves as a clinical associate professor and academic program director at Loyola Marymount University (LMU) School of Education in the Department of Teaching and Learning. In 2016, she earned a Doctor of Philosophy in Education from Chapman University with an emphasis in Culture and Curricular Studies as a first-generation student. In 2011, she received her Master of Arts in Guidance and Counseling at LMU where she was named Student of the Year for the LMU School of Education and in 2008, earned her Bachelor of Arts in Psychology and Philosophy from California State University, Long Beach. Dr. Krikorian comes from a multi-racial and multi-ethnic background, a multi-ethnic family unit and strives to deepen understandings of diverse perspectives, different forms of knowledge, and holistic approaches to education. Her personal and professional experiences position her well to advocate for learners students as integrated whole beings, emphasizing pedagogical philosophies that facilitate transformative learning and holistic human growth unionize the mind, body, and inner-self. Dr. Krikorian published a book titled, *Higher Education for The People: Critical Methods of Liberatory Practice* (2022), and continues to present at professional conferences, reviews proposals for national and international journals, and has served as an assessor for academic programs and grants. In 2023, she was honored with the LMU Term Faculty Distinguished Teaching Award.

Chapter 7

Irma Eloff is a professor of Educational Psychology at the University of Pretoria. She is a member of the Academy of Science of South Africa (ASSAf) and a founding member of the South African Positive Psychology Association (SAPPA). She is a former dean of Education at the University of Pretoria. She is the founder of the African Deans of Education Forum (ADEF) which is a focal point of the UNESCO International Teacher Task Force, and the current Chair of the Global Network of Deans of Education (GNDE). She has edited the books *Understanding Educational Psychology*, *Keys to Educational Psychology*; and the *Handbook of Quality of Life in African Societies* (Springer).

Ruth "Molly" McGee Hewitt is a veteran educator and leader with over 40 years of experience in public and private education and professional development. Her resume includes serving as a classroom teacher, site, and district administrator as well as an association executive serving educational agencies. She has authored six publications and written over 300 articles for educational publications serving superintendents, elected school board members, and school business officials. She most recently spent 12 years as the CEO/Executive Director of the California Association of School Business Officials. In this capacity she provided professional development and legislative advocacy resources to 34,000 school leaders in California. She is the recipient of over 600 awards and commendations. She currently serves as the principal of McGee Hewitt LLC, serving as an executive and leadership coach to organizations.

Chapter 8

Cameron Hauseman is an Assistant Professor in the Faculty of Education at the University of Manitoba. His research interests are situated in K–12 school leadership and program evaluation, with a specific focus on the work and well-being of school principals. Cameron's work is found in both academic and practitioner-focused publications.

Katina Pollock is Associate Professor of Educational Leadership and Policy in the field of Critical Policy, Equity, and Leadership Studies at the Faculty of Education, Western University. The overall goal of Dr. Pollock's research agenda is to support and improve public education systems; to this effect, her research focuses on supporting school leaders. Specifically, she concentrates on school leaders' work intensification and well-being, policy development and implementation, and knowledge mobilization. Her research with colleagues has been supported by federal granting agencies, provincial governments, and professional associations. Her current SSHRC Insight Grants focus on secondary school principals' work intensification (with Dr. Fei Wang) (2016–2023), and the relationship between policy and principals' work, (with Dr. Laura Pinto and Dr. Sue Winton) (2015–2023). In addition to traditional scholarship, she has also taken on several leadership roles, such as codirector of the UCEA Centre for International Study of School Leadership (2011–2014), Director of the Western Centre for Education Leadership (2014–2018), and codirector of the Knowledge Network for Applied Education Research (KNAER) (2011–2018).

Fei Wang is an associate professor at the Faculty of Education, University of British Columbia, Vancouver, Canada. His research interest focuses on educational leadership and administration, social justice and diversity, cross-cultural and international leadership, The Art of War, school principalship, educational policy studies, and international and comparative education.

Chapter 9

Melinda Lemke, PhD, is an Associate Professor of Educational Policy and an Affiliate Faculty of Global Gender and Sexuality Studies at the University at Buffalo (UB), SUNY. Her research sits at the intersection of neoliberal policy reform, the politics of education, gender-based violence prevention, and public health. Her work can be found in journals such as *Children's Geographies, Journal of Education Policy, Gender and Education,* and *The Urban Review*. Prior to UB, Melinda held a Hillary Rodham Clinton School of Law postdoctoral appointment at Swansea University, Wales, United Kingdom and had a career in U.S. urban public secondary education.

Anthony L. White II is a Social Studies teacher in the Buffalo Public School District, and an adjunct instructor in the Department of Learning and Instruction at the University at Buffalo (UB), SUNY. Currently he is a doctoral candidate in the Curriculum, Instruction, and the Science of Learning program, where his research is focused on African American education, critical race theory, curriculum, and policy.

Chapter 10

Connor M. Moriarty is a Licensed Professional Counselor (LPC) in the state of Pennsylvania and a Gallup Certified Strengths Coach. He earned a dual master's degree from Arcadia University in International Peace and Conflict Resolution and Counseling Psychology with a certification in Trauma and Recovery. While his work is grounded in validated theories and techniques, Connor is also creative, continuously developing his capacity for meeting client needs with innovative strategies. Connor feels most at peace in the great outdoors. He is most drawn to water and trees, particularly places where there are both. Connor is a certified ACA level 1 kayak and stand-up paddle board instructor. Since integrating CliftonStrengths into his work, Connor's approach has become even more unique and effective. With a focus on behavioral and organizational sustainability, the Reset Outdoors Ascent program is the first strengths-and-nature based team conditioning program in the United States.

Kimberly Joy Rushing is a doctoral student and graduate research assistant in Educational Foundations, Leadership, and Technology department at Auburn University. Joy has taught middle school English language arts and gifted education in public and private schools in the southeast for 10 years. She received her Master of Arts in Teaching from Clemson University and her undergraduate degree in English Literature from University of South Florida. Her research projects currently include principal learning and well-being, green leadership and restorative practices, outlier leadership dispositions, and urban/rural school leadership.

Lisa A. W. Kensler is the Emily R. and Gerald S. Leischuck Endowed Professor for Educational Leadership in the College of Education at Auburn University. Lisa's research over the past decade has focused on green schools and the leadership and learning required for transforming schools into more socially just, ecologically healthy, and economically viable communities that also attend to everyone's well-being. In 2017, she and Cynthia Uline coauthored, *Leadership for Green Schools: Sustainability for Our Children, Our Communities, and Our Planet*. Their second book, *A Practical Guide to Leading Green Schools: Partnering with Nature to Create Vibrant, Flourishing, Sustainable Schools*, was published in May 2021.

Chapter 11

Nancy Norman has worked in K–12 and higher education for the past 20 years and has spent much of her career supporting the social-emotional needs of children, youth, and school-based personnel. Dr. Norman is a Professor in Teacher Education at Vancouver Island University, and the Department Chair in the Education Assistant Program at Kwantlen Polytechnic University. She has coauthored several peer-reviewed articles and chapters and presents widely to national and international audiences.

Adrienne Castellon has three decades of experience in K–12 and higher education combined and has worked as a secondary school teacher, elementary principal, education consultant, Director in North and South America in both independent and public schools as well as assistant professor of undergraduate and graduate courses in education and leadership. She is the author of several teacher resources, chapters and articles.

David D. Stinson has worked in higher education for over 35 years and is the Director of the Learning Commons and Accessible Learning at Trinity Western University. He is the creator of the Stinson Wellness and Decision-Making Model and has a passion for integrating theory with practice to create useful, real-world tools for living well. His book, *Aligning Life: The Stinson Wellness Model*, provides an overview and discussion of the model. He has coauthored five peer-reviewed, journal articles discussing how the model might be implemented in the business world.

Chapter 12

Sabre Cherkowski, PhD, is Professor and Director of Graduate Programs in the Okanagan School of Education at the University of British Columbia. She teaches and researches in the areas of leadership, organizational well-being, professional learning, and development, mentoring and coaching, and diversity and education. She recently completed a multiyear research project examining teacher well-being from a positive organizational perspective. She is currently engaged in a research project on well-being, examining positive leadership in schools as a catalyst for sustainable school improvement.

Benjamin Kutsyuruba is a Professor in Educational Policy and Leadership and School Law in the Faculty of Education, Queen's University at Kingston, Ontario. His teaching and research areas include educational law, policymaking, and leadership; teacher induction and mentorship; trust, ethics, and moral agency; and educational reform and change. Benjamin has worked as a teacher, researcher, manager, and professor in education in Ukraine and Canada.

Keith Walker is a Professor of Educational Administration at the University of Saskatchewan in Canada. In large part, Keith's university work consists of research and scholarly writing, teaching with colleagues in the Department of Educational Administration, and service to university and field-based partners. Outside of the University, Keith's work-services primarily consist of: three sector consulting, minister-at-large for the

Christian and Missionary Alliance, ministry across denominations, and executive, leader, and board coaching.

Chapter 13

Kristina N. LaVenia is an Assistant Professor in the School of Educational Foundations, Leadership, and Policy at Bowling Green State University where she teaches courses on leadership for adult development, research methods, and applied statistics. Kristina's research aims to understand how leaders support improved outcomes for marginalized and/or vulnerable groups. Her current projects include: a study of the emotional demands of teaching and leading in schools; a study of interventions and programming to support educators'; well-being; and an evaluation of teacher professional development designed to support culturally responsive practice. Kristina received her PhD in educational leadership and policy as well as a graduate certificate in measurement and statistics from Florida State University. She also completed her doctoral studies as an Institute of Education Sciences (IES) predoctoral fellow and has served as a certified reviewer for the IES What Works Clearinghouse since 2009.

Christy Galletta Horner is an Assistant Professor in the School of Educational Foundations, Leadership and Policy at Bowling Green State University. She received a PhD in applied developmental psychology with a minor in quantitative research methods at the University of Pittsburgh. Her research focuses on the role of emotional culture in the promotion of healthy individual and social functioning. Viewing emotions as sociocultural in nature, she prioritizes participants'; perspectives while also seeking to uncover quantifiable links between emotion-related constructs and developmental outcomes. She uses mixed-methods designs and creative methodological approaches to address the challenges involved in this line of inquiry. Her aim is to find ways emotional transactions can be leveraged in settings such as schools, after school programs, and social media sites to help individuals thrive in their environments.

Judy Jackson May is an Associate Professor of Educational Administration and Leadership Studies in the College of Education and Human Development at Bowling Green State University. She currently teaches in and serves as coordinator for the Leadership Studies Doctoral Program. Dr. May also teaches in the Master of Educational Leadership Program as well serving as coordinator for an undergraduate teacher preparation course for which she wrote a textbook, *Teacher Talk: A 21st Century Guide for Beginning Educators*. Prior to moving to higher education, she served as speech pathologist/audiologist, multiple handicap teacher, school principal in urban and rural districts, and curriculum coordinator. Dr. May has delivered over 60 presentations and workshops at the regional, national, and international level including Honk Kong, Tokyo, Cambodia, and South Africa. She has authored and/coauthored 20 journals articles and book chapters. She also serves as the Northwest Region Manager for the Ohio School Boards Association.

Chapter 14

Delia Estrada, PhD, has served school communities in Los Angeles for over 30 years in Los Angeles. She currently serves as an administrative coordinator for the Induction and Credentialing Unit in LA Unified. In all her work she is committed to studying and applying the tools of Cultural Proficient to build school communities which embrace equitable educational experiences for all children. She also serves as an adjunct professor for California State University, San Marcos. She received her PhD from Claremont Graduate University in 2017.

Marco A. Nava, EdD, has served school communities in diverse educational settings in Los Angeles. In his various roles, he has worked collaboratively with others, fostered partnerships, and leveraged resources that support student learning. Dr. Nava currently oversees the induction and credentialing programs for teachers and administrators in the Human Resources Division of LAUSD. He has provided leadership development seminars to international educators and in 2014 was selected as a Fulbright Principal Exchange participant. Dr. Nava has presented research on school improvement, social-emotional learning, and leadership development at various educational research conferences including the American Educational Research Association (AERA). He received his doctorate in Educational Leadership from the University of Southern California (USC).

Susan Ward Roncalli, PhD, is a veteran teacher with over 30 years of experience as a secondary English Language Arts instructor. She was a National Board- Certified Teacher. She has presented at conferences on service learning and social emotional learning nationally and internationally. Susan served on the California team for the CASEL Collaborating States Initiative and was a member of the Social Emotional Learning National Practitioner's Advisory Group. She currently serves on the California State SEL Policy Workgroup and is a Social Emotional Learning Adviser for the Division of Instruction with the Los Angeles Unified School District. She received her PhD from Claremont Graduate University 2021.

Chapter 15

Jonathan Eckert, EdD, is the Lynda and Robert Copple Professor of Educational Leadership at Baylor University. He taught outside of Chicago and Nashville for 12 years. After completing his doctorate at Vanderbilt University in 2008, he served at the U.S. Department of Education win both the Bush and Obama administrations on teaching quality issues. He is the author of *The Novice Advantage: Fearless Practice for Every Teacher And Leading Together: Teachers and Principals Improving Student Outcomes*, book chapters, and numerous peer-reviewed articles. He has written and presented white papers on Capitol Hill and the National Press Club and has been invited to present all over the U.S. and as far away as Muscat, Oman at a G8-Broader Middle East Summit for education ministers.

Chapter 16

Kent Divoll is an Associate Professor at the University of Houston—Clear Lake. He teaches curriculum and instruction courses at the undergraduate and master's level and works with doctoral students. His research interests include classroom management, middle level education, relational pedagogy, teacher preparation, professional development, and the scholarship of teaching and learning. He has served as the Chair, Vice Chair, and Program Chair for the American Educational Research Association's (AERA) Classroom Management SIG and is the faculty advisor for Kappa Delta Pi at his university.

Angelica Ribeiro is a Curriculum Specialist at Houston Independent School District and the author of *Running into Happiness* and *My Happiness Habit Journal*. She has over 20 years of experience working with language learners and preservice teachers in Brazil and in the United States. Her research interest is second language acquisition. Dr. Ribeiro is passionate about preparing future teachers and spreading positivity.

Chapter 17

Sebrina L. Doyle Fosco's research is focused on methods for the promotion of well-being for caregiving adults and the youth they serve in education and social services. She has been involved for almost a decade in research with mindfulness-based programs in educational settings. Sebrina is also a certified facilitator for Cultivating Awareness and Resilience in Education (CARE), an evidence-based professional development program focused on improving social and emotional competence and well-being for teachers, administrators, and school staff. She also codeveloped the

Mindful Awareness Program (MAP) for Wellness, a brief self-care intervention for staff working in juvenile justice facilities.

Chapter 18

Deborah Schussler is a Professor of Educational Leadership at Pennsylvania State University. Her research examines the development of educators' dispositions and social-emotional competencies and the impact of mindfulness-based interventions on the resilience and well-being of educators and the students they serve.

Jennifer Frank is an Associate Professor of Special Education at Pennsylvania State University. Her research focuses on developing and evaluating school-based prevention practices that modify the social ecology of risk (school-family-peer-individual factors) that gives rise to high-incidence disabilities and preparing the next generation of school-based professionals to implement high-quality prevention practices in school settings.

Chapter 19

Sonya D. Hayes is an Assistant Professor in the Department of Educational Leadership and Policy Studies at the University of Tennessee. Her research interests include leadership development and support for both pre and post service school principals, principal preparation, and leadership for learning. Specifically, she is interested in how principals are prepared and supported for the complex and demanding role of improving teaching and learning.

Jerry R. Burkett is the Assistant Professor of Educational Leadership at the University of North Texas at Dallas. He has more than 21 years of experience as an educator, serving as a teacher, campus and district-level administrator, and professor. Serving as a passionate advocate for public education, Dr. Burkett writes and speaks on a variety of topics, including school finance, instructional technology, brain learning, and the needs of public education in the 21st century. He has spoken at national, state, and regional conferences, various university doctoral cohorts, and community and civic groups.

Chapter 20

Rick Rogers is the program coordinator and a facilitator for Soul of Leadership. He brings over 35 years of experience in public education as a teacher and a principal in urban and suburban settings. He is passionate about the principalship and believes in the power of reflective practice. His current work focuses on supporting principals and leadership teams as a leadership coach and consultant. He has also been a facilitator for the National Institute of School Leadership and an adjunct instructor at UMass Lowell.

Mary Watkins is director, a dual principal and superintendent role, at the William M. Davies, Jr. Career and Technical High School in Lincoln, Rhode Island.

Printed in the USA
CPSIA information can be obtained
at www.ICGtesting.com
CBHW051914300124
3876CB00001B/2